This collection of original essays brings together some of the most prominent figures in Renaissance studies to offer a new focus on the literature and culture of the Early Modern period.

Traditionally Renaissance studies has concentrated on the human subject. The essays collected here bring objects – purses, clothes, tapestries, houses, maps, feathers, communion wafers, tools, pages, skulls – back into view. As a result, the much-vaunted Early Modern subject ceases to look autonomous and sovereign, but is instead caught up in a vast and uneven world of objects. Through critical practices that cross into diverse historical discourses, *Subject and Object in Renaissance Culture* puts things back into relation with persons; in the process, it elicits new critical readings and new cultural configurations.

Cambridge Studies in Renaissance Literature and Culture 8

Subject and Object in Renaissance Culture

Cambridge Studies in Renaissance Literature and Culture

General editor
Stephen Orgel
Jackson Eli Reynolds Professor of Humanities, Stanford University

Editorial board
Anne Barton, *University of Cambridge*
Jonathan Dollimore, *University of Sussex*
Marjorie Garber, *Harvard University*
Jonathan Goldberg,*The Johns Hopkins University*
Nancy Vickers, *University of Southern California*

The last twenty years have seen a broad and vital reinterpretation of the nature of literary texts, a move away from formalism to a sense of literature as an aspect of social, economic, political, and cultural history. While the earliest New Historicist work was criticized for a narrow and anecdotal view of history, it also served as an important stimulus for post-structuralist, feminist, Marxist, and psychoanalytic work, which in turn has increasingly informed and redirected it. Recent writing on the nature of representation, the historical construction of gender and of the concept of identity itself, on theater as a political and economic phenomenon, and on the ideologies of art generally, reveals the breadth of the field. Cambridge Studies in Renaissance Literature and Culture is designed to offer historically oriented studies of Renaissance literature and theater which make use of the insights afforded by theoretical perspectives. The view of history envisioned is above all a view of our own history, a reading of the Renaissance for and from our own time.

Drama and the market in the age of Shakespeare
DOUGLAS BRUSTER, University of Chicago

The Renaissance dialogue: literary dialogue in its social political contexts,
Castiglione to Galileo
VIRGINIA COX, University College London

Spenser's secret career
RICHARD RAMBUSS, Tulane University

Shakespeare and the geography of difference
JOHN GILLIES, La Trobe University

Men in women's clothing: anti-theatricality and effeminization, 1579–1642
LAURA LEVINE, Wellesley College

The Reformation of the subject: Spenser, Milton, and the English Protestant Epic
LINDA GREGERSON, University of Michigan

Voyages in Print: English travel to America, 1576–1624
MARY C. FULLER, Massachusetts Institute of Technology

Subject and object in Renaissance culture
edited by MARGRETA DE GRAZIA, MAUREEN QUILLIGAN, PETER STALLYBRASS, University of Pennsylvania

Subject and object in Renaissance culture

Edited by

Margreta de Grazia, Maureen Quilligan, and Peter Stallybrass

CAMBRIDGE
UNIVERSITY PRESS

Published by the Press Syndicate of the University of Cambridge
The Pitt Building, Trumpington Street, Cambridge CB2 1RP
40 West 20th Street, New York, NY 10011–4211, USA
10 Stamford Road, Oakleigh, Melbourne 3166, Australia

First published 1996

Printed in Great Britain at Redwood Books, Trowbridge, Wiltshire

A catalogue record for this book is available from the British Library

Library of Congress cataloguing in publication data

Subject and object in Renaissance culture / edited by Margreta de
Grazia, Maureen Quilligan, and Peter Stallybrass.
  p.   cm. – (Cambridge Studies in Renaissance Literature and Culture 8)
ISBN 0 521 45471 9 (hardback). ISBN 0 521 45589 8 (paperback).
1. Renaissance. 2. European literature – Renaissance, 1450–1600 –
History and criticism. 3. Material culture – Europe. I. De Grazia,
Margreta. II. Quilligan, Maureen. III. Stallybrass, Peter. IV. Series.
CB361.R34   1996
940.2'–dc20 95–6179 CIP

ISBN 0 521 45471 9 hardback
ISBN 0 521 45589 8 paperback

CE

Contents

viii

Illustrations

ix

Notes on the contributors

Jonathan Dollimore is Professor of English in the School of English and American Studies at the University of Sussex. He is the author of *Radical Tragedy: Religion, Ideology, and Power in the Drama of Shakespeare and his Contemporaries* (1984; second edition, 1989) and *Sexual Dissidence: Augustine to Wilde, Freud to Foucault* (1991), and the co-editor with Alan Sinfield of *Political Shakespeare: New Essays in Cultural Materialism* (1985; second edition, 1994). He has written on the cultural politics of perversion in the nineteenth and twentieth centuries and on sexuality and transgression in the Renaissance. His current work is on a book entitled *Death, Desire, and Mutability*.

Margaret W. Ferguson, Professor of English and Comparative Literature at the University of Colorado, is the author of *Trials of Desire: Renaissance Defenses of Poetry* (1983) and co-editor of *Rewriting the Renaissance: The Discourses of Sexual Difference in Early Modern Europe* (1986), *Re-membering Milton: The Texts and the Traditions* (1987), and *Feminism and Postmodernism* (a special issue of *boundary 2*, 1992). She has recently co-edited Elizabeth Cary's *The Tragedy of Mariam*, and *The Lady Falkland: Her Life* by one of Cary's daughters. She is completing a book entitled *Female Literacies and Emergent Empires: Studies in English and French Cultural History, 1400–1688*.

Marjorie Garber is William R. Kenan, Jr. Professor of English and Director of the Center for Literary and Cultural Studies at Harvard University. She has written extensively on Renaissance theater and on twentieth-century popular culture. She is the author of *Dream in Shakespeare: From Metaphor to Metamorphosis* (1974), *Coming of Age in Shakespeare* (1981), *Shakespeare's Ghost Writers: Literature as Uncanny Causality* (1987), *Vested Interests: Cross-Dressing and Cultural Study* (1991), and *Vice Versa: Bisexuality and the Eroticism of Everyday Life* (1995).

Jonathan Goldberg is Sir William Osler Professor of English Literature at The Johns Hopkins University. He is author of *Sodometries: Renaissance Texts, Modern Sexualities* (1992), *Writing Matter: From the Hands of the English Renaissance* (1990), *Voice Terminal Echo: Postmodernism and English Renaissance Texts* (1986), *James I and the Politics of Literature: Jonson, Shakespeare, Donne, and their Contemporaries* (1983), and *Endlesse Worke: Spenser and the Structures of Discourse* (1981). He has co-edited with Stephen Orgel *John Milton* (1991) for the Oxford Author series, and is the editor of *Reclaiming Sodom* (1994) and of *Queering the Renaissance* (1994).

Margreta de Grazia is Professor of English at the University of Pennsylvania. She has written extensively on the ways in which later semantic and conceptual configurations have given us a partial and skewed view of the English Renaissance. Her book, *Shakespeare Verbatim* (1991), demonstrates how a post-Enlightenment textual apparatus established modern imperatives for editing and reading Shakespeare. She is at present working on *Unmodernizing the Early Modern*, a book concerned with the Early Modern's inveterate obligation to look Modern before its time.

Stephen Greenblatt is Class of 1932 Professor of English at the University of California, Berkeley, and Visiting Professor at Harvard University. His books include *Renaissance Self-Fashioning: From More to Shakespeare* (1980), *Shakespearean Negotiations: The Circulation of Social Energy in Renaissance England* (1988), *Learning to Curse: Essays in Early Modern Culture* (1990), and *Marvelous Possessions: The Wonder of the New World* (1991). He is the General Editor of the forthcoming Norton Shakespeare. His essay in this volume is part of a larger project on art, magic, and sacredness in Early Modern England.

Ann Rosalind Jones is Esther Cloudman Dunn Professor of Comparative Literature at Smith College. Her publications on Early Modern writing include *The Currency of Eros: Women's Love Lyric in Europe, 1540–1620* (1990), a special issue of *Women's Studies* co-edited with Betty Travitsky (1992) *Women in the Renaissance: An Interdisciplinary Forum*, articles on Nashe, Sidney, and Webster, and essays in *Rewriting the Renaissance, The Ideology of Conduct*, and *The Poetics of Gender*. She is currently working with Peter Stallybrass on *Worn Worlds*, a study of clothing in Renaissance England and Europe.

Louis A. Montrose is Professor of English Literature and chair of the Department of Literature at the University of California, San Diego. He has published widely on the poetics and politics of culture, formations of gender, and discourses of discovery in the Renaissance, as well as on theory and method in the historical analysis of literature. He has recently completed *The Purpose of Playing: Shakespeare and the Cultural Politics of Elizabethan Theatre*.

Stephen Orgel is Jackson Eli Reynolds Professor of Humanities at

Stanford University. His books include *The Jonsonian Masque* (1965), *The illusion of Power* (1975), and, with Sir Roy Strong, *Inigo Jones: The Theatre of the Stuart Court* (1973). His edition of *The Tempest* is published in the Oxford Shakespeare series, from which his edition of *The Winter's Tale* is forthcoming; his edition of *John Milton*, co-edited with Jonathan Goldberg, is published in the Oxford Authors series. He is the General Editor of Cambridge Studies in Renaissance Literature and Culture and has just completed *Impersonations: The Performance of Gender in Shakespeare's England.*

Patricia Parker, who has taught at the University of East Africa, the University of Toronto, and as a visitor at Berkeley, is currently Professor of English and Comparative Literature at Stanford University. Author of *Inescapable Romance: Studies in the Poetics of a Mode* (1979) and *Literary Fat Ladies: Rhetoric, Gender, Property* (1986), and co-editor of *Shakespeare and the Question of Theory* (1985), *Literary Theory/Renaissance Texts* (1986), and *Women, "Race," and Writing in the Early Modern Period* (1994), she is currently completing books on Shakespeare and on gender in the Early Modern period.

Maureen Quilligan is Howard and Judith Steinberg Professor of English at the University of Pennsylvania. She is the author of *The Language of Allegory: Defining the Genre* (1979), *Milton's Spenser: The Politics of Reading* (1983), and *The Allegory of Female Authority: Christine de Pizan's "Cité des Dames"* (1991), and the co-editor of *Rewriting the Renaissance: The Discourses of Sexual Difference in Early Modern Europe* (1986). She is presently at work on a collection of essays about incest and authority in the Renaissance.

Peter Stallybrass is Professor of English and a member of the Program in Comparative Literature and Literary Theory at the University of Pennsylvania. He is co-author with Allon White of *The Politics and Poetics of Transgression* (1986), co-editor with David Scott Kastan of *Staging the Renaissance* (1991), and has published on Renaissance and Modern culture and on Marxism. He is at present completing a collection of essays on English Renaissance cultural politics and working with Ann Rosalind Jones on a book about clothes and the formation of identity in Early Modern Europe.

Gary Tomlinson is Professor of Music and teaches Cultural Studies at the University of Pennsylvania. A 1988 MacArthur Fellow, he is the author of *Monteverdi and the End of the Renaissance* (1987) and of *Music in Renaissance Magic: Toward a Historiography of Others* (1993), and has written on music and poetry as interrelated cultural forms in the Renaissance. He is at present completing a book *The Singing of the New World.*

Nancy J. Vickers is Professor of French and Italian and of Comparative Literature at the University of Southern California. She has co-edited *Rewriting the Renaissance: The Discourses of Sexual Difference in Early Modern Europe* (1986) and *Medieval and Renaissance Representation: New Reflections* (1984), and has published widely on Dante, Petrarch, Shakespeare, on canon formation, and on popular culture in the late twentieth century. Her present work addresses the relationship between genre and technology in lyric poetry and music video.

Acknowledgments

The essays in this volume were first written for the conference, Renaissance Subject/Early Modern Object (University of Pennsylvania, 1992). We wish to thank Max Thomas for his invaluable help in organizing the conference and Steve Nichols and Richard Beeman, Associate Deans of the Humanities, University of Pennsylvania, for the grant that made the conference possible.

We would also like to thank Kevin Taylor and Josie Dixon of Cambridge University Press for their early endorsement of the project, David Golumbia for his work in computer-formatting the volume, and Rayna Kalas for her keen attention to the proofs.

Figure 1.1   N. L. Peschier, *Vanitas* (1661)

Introduction

Margreta de Grazia, Maureen Quilligan,
and Peter Stallybrass

There are no subjects in seventeenth-century *vanitas* still-lifes. Only objects. Or more accurately, their subjects are objects: books, pens, hats, purses, coins, jewelry, pipes, bottles. The great novelty of these early still-lifes is that objects have evicted the subject.[1] Only a memory of one remains – the *memento mori* or skull, now an object among objects. And with the subject goes its world. The window space that receded behind the Renaissance subject gives way to the wall or virtual wall that drops behind the object. With such a foreshortening of space comes the standing still of time. While the subject of a painted narrative or history moves through time, objects of a still-life exist in inert stasis. Spatially and temporally secluded, *vanitas* objects appear to have a (still) life of their own. There is no need for a musician to play, a reader to read, a smoker to smoke: flute, book, pipe exist without makers, owners, buyers, users.

Yet the purpose of *vanitas* paintings is to urge the dispensability not of subjects but of objects – the vanity of all the things of this world. By their title (*vanitas vanitatum*, Eccles. 1.2) and by the symbolic encoding of the things represented (signs of transience and mortality), they exhort subjects to renounce objects. But can such a sequestering hold? We have reproduced N. L. Peschier's unusual *vanitas* painting (opposite) precisely because the subject finds its way back into the picture, at the top of the pile of objects, in the upper right-hand corner, head tilted like the skull beneath it. Even in more typical versions, the omnipresent skull itself serves as a reminder of the common materiality of subject and objects.

The viewer too testifies to their attachment. While the skull repels sight, the other objects attract it with their opulent splendor. While bringing to mind the passing of things, the paintings also give those things the permanence of art. In effect, they perform the opposite of what they profess, richly and fully embodying things rather than emptying them out.[2] While their *vanitas* moral would make the objects null and void, the lustre of paint enhances their irresistibility. In addition,

1

reproduction increases their store, so that there are more purses, jewels, books than ever before. Among their number, the *vanitas* paintings themselves must be counted, for they become what they renounce: objects to augment the subject's prestige and wealth, additional earthly things to be coveted, purchased – often at great price – and displayed as ornament. (In later *vanitas* still-lifes, paintings themselves appear among the depicted vanities.)[3]

Renaissance studies have slighted the objects that are the subject of these paintings.[4] It is as if we had listened to their renunciatory moral without seeing their sumptuous allure. For in the main we have proceeded as if it were both possible and desirable for subjects to cut themselves off from objects. The essays collected here aim to address this bias with a basic question: in the period that has from its inception been identified with the emergence of the subject, *where is the object?* This is not to say that the sovereignty of the subject has gone unquestioned in Renaissance studies, especially in recent decades. Indeed the various tautological self-reflexives once thought so characteristic of the Renaissance have lost their transparency as the subject has been seen increasingly to be constructed from the outside.[5] Yet even in recent critiques of Renaissance autonomy, the focus has remained the same: the subject at center and the object beyond the pale. What happens, we wish to ask, once the object is brought into view? What new configurations will emerge when subject and object are kept in relation?

At the outset of this inquiry, it may be useful to turn to an account that, like the *vanitas* still-lifes, questions the viability of separating subject and object. In the "Lordship and Bondage" section of Hegel's *Phenomenology of Spirit*, they are inextricable. The subject passes into the object, the object slides into the subject, in the activity by which each becomes itself. Hegel's dramatization of this complex dialectic goes something like this:

A subject desired verification that he was in truth a subject, more particularly, that he was free of all dependencies on objects. Verification could come only from another subject (in an act of mutual recognition), but how could one subject know the truth of the other any more than of himself? A situation was needed that required the subject to risk all objects – a fight-to-the-death. But a fight-to-the-death could only end in impasse. Though one contestant would be triumphant (unless the struggle resulted in death for both), he would never attain the recognition he desired. For the other contestant, if alive, would be reduced to an enslaved object – disqualified, therefore, as witness to the subject's truth.[6]

Hegel's zero-sum contest seems worth recounting because it so forcibly dramatizes the interrelation of subject and object. It is precisely this interrelation that drops out of the history which has done most to periodize the Renaissance. Jacob Burckhardt's *The Civilization of the Renaissance in Italy* posits an individual as free-standing as the statue of the condottiere Colleoni on the cover of its illustrated English edition.[7] It is only *after* the subject emerges in its individuality that it puts itself in relation to objects. In this respect, the Renaissance subject begins with just that full consciousness of itself that is the ultimate (though hardly assured) end of the Hegelian dialectic of the subject/object or lord/ bondsman. What in Hegel the subject would give up its life to know is in Burckhardt the ready-given of individuality that, when not quelled by a restrictive church or state, will run its fulfilling course.

Self-consciousness for Burckhardt comes about epiphanically rather than agonistically, as the result of revelation rather than struggle. When benighting illusions are stripped away – when the medieval "veil melted into air" – Renaissance consciousness could turn both inward and outward, in both "subjective" consideration of itself and "objective" consideration "of the State and of all things of this world."[8] Burckhardt's "uomo singolare" or "uomo unico" stands before and apart from the object of his attention, confident of his ability to make the object compliant with his political or scientific or artistic will.[9] As Ernst Cassirer maintains in *The Individual and the Cosmos in Renaissance Philosophy* – the philosophical study intended to supplement Burckhardt's cultural history – the subject's relation to the object was that of mastery or would-be mastery: the mind trained and positioned to understand and overcome the object of its interest.[10]

Marx seems to offer a similar narrative of separation in accounting for the rise of capitalism. His recurrent focus on alienation also appears to sever subject and object. The capitalist mode of production estranges the worker from both the product of the worker's labor and the entire material world that is the aggregate of such products. Insofar as the two could be said to conjoin, it seems to be in the unhappy process of commodification: the object comes to overpower the subject, mysteriously incorporating the latter's labor into itself – so that the subject's activity looks like a property of the produced object itself. The mastery of Burckhardt's subject is inverted in this capitalist configuration: commodities come to hold sway over their producers.

The hostility, even violence, of these subject/object relations inflects a whole series of terms which speak to their connection in the negative. To treat a subject like an object is to *reify, objectify*. To treat an object like a subject is to *idolize, to fetishize*. In the modern idiom, the substitution of one term for the other is a theoretical and political problem – a category mistake of the highest order. Might the problem lie in the artificiality of the categories themselves? – that is, in their enforced opposition as binaries? Another look at Marx suggests the interdependency of the two. For it is not only the subject that is lost in commodification: the object too is lost. In the process of converting it to purely quantitative exchange value, commodification depletes the object of its qualities. If 100 paper cups = 5 plastic plates = 30 boxes of matches, the particular qualities of cup, plate, and match evaporate. Commodification is thus not only the vanishing point of the subject into the commodified object but also of the object into pure exchangeability.[11]

Let us return to the lordship and bondage narrative, and continue it by tracing the object, not as Hegel in fact did but as Marx might have.[12] If we situate the bondsman in some imaginary realm outside existing modes of production, we may see her or him in relation not to the lord but to the object she or he is working upon in what Marx terms "a human manner."[13] The object made then takes on inestimable value. For, in working upon it, the bondsman comes to recognize her or his identity as "an objective being" or "objective personality" – that is, a being in need of outside objects and in need of being an outside object to another.[14] The consciousness that comes into formation looks very different from the masterful Renaissance individual. In the experiencing of its double "objectivity," the subject recognizes itself as "a suffering, conditioned and limited creature."[15] Quite unexpectedly, the subject's agency turns out to lie in suffering, in feeling its own corporeal and sensual receptivity as it intently plies its object: "*Passion* is the essential *force* of man energetically bent on its object."[16]

If we allow Hegel's (working) bondsman to stand for the object-as-position and Marx's (uncommodified) product to stand for the object-as-thing, it may be possible to break open what can seem a long and monotonous history of the sovereignty of the subject. In highlighting the subject, Renaissance studies have prodded this history on, for, from its Burckhardtian inception, the period has been identified as "the beginning of the modern era" – what we now term the Early Modern.[17] Once the Modern era is seen to start with the emergence of the subject, the course is set for all of its extensions into the future, from Early Modern through postmodern. We are stuck then with what Foucault has described as "the continuous history [that] is the indispensable correlative of the founding function of the subject." Such a protracted history provides a "citadel" or "privileged shelter for the sovereignty of consciousness" protecting it from displacement and preemption. According to Foucault, this history begins to be written (by Burckhardt, for example) in the nineteenth century, in nervous response to the extensive epistemological mutations (of Marx, for example) that were shaking the subject at its foundations.[18] A long anthropomorphic or humanistic history was then forged to

it is amazing that so many object-oriented studies have been done, from Stny to Smut s.

"shelter" the beleaguered subject from dispersal and hold out the promise of its eventual reinstatement. If Foucault is right, Renaissance studies have been doubly instrumental in sustaining this obsessive teleological history: by keeping the subject out of touch with the object and by staging this exclusion as the beginning of the Modern, an exclusion rehearsed all the way through the Modern and the late Modern and the postmodern.

This collection is not unique in its attempt to reconfigure this history. Indeed, the tendency has increasingly been to reconceptualize the subject in less subjective terms: as a construct responding to changing historical structures, as an effect issuing from the reproduction of an ideological system, as a site caught in the always short-changing play of signifiers. Yet the role of the object here too has been negligible, except to mark and remark the position of the dominated or oppressed term. From the moment of its mid-nineteenth-century inception as subject-oriented, the Renaissance as Early Modern has given short and limited shrift to the object. In the wake of such a tradition, the recent tendency to periodize around the concept of the "Colonial" rather than the "Modern" seems an improvement. The period division "Early Colonial" at least assumes the presence of colonized as well as colonizer, object as well as subject.

The purpose of this collection of essays is not to efface the subject but to offset it by insisting that the object be taken into account. With such a shift, it is hoped that new relations between subject (as position, as person) and object (as position, as thing) may emerge and familiar relations change. If, for example, we do not assume the unidirectional power relationship from top to bottom, then the linkages of subject to object may differ from those of subversion or containment. The proposed shift might also reveal the linkages to be historical; that is, they may change over time, and asymmetrically in relation to each other.

The very ambiguity of the word "ob-ject," that which is *thrown before*, suggests a more dynamic status for the object. Reading "ob" as "before" allows us to assign the object a prior status, suggesting its temporal, spatial, and even causal *coming before*. The word could thus be made to designate the potential priority of the object. So defined, the term renders more apparent the way material things – land, clothes, tools – might constitute subjects who in turn own, use, and transform them. The form/matter relation of Aristotelian metaphysics is thereby provisionally reversed: it is the material object that impresses its texture and contour upon the noumenal subject. And this reversal is curiously upheld by the ambiguity of the word "sub-ject," that which is *thrown under*, in this case – in order to receive an imprint.

We have divided the essays in the present collection into five groups in order to stress their shared focus on some pivotal relationships between subject and object: *Priority of objects, Materializations, Appropriations, Fetishisms, and Objections.* These groupings are somewhat arbitrary, for each essay has ties with other essays in other groups. Yet the rubrics should serve to emphasize the various logics that organize subject/object relations.

The first group takes up the issue of the *Priority of Objects*, each of the three essays demonstrating the consequentiality of objects to subjects. Margreta de Grazia shows the Renaissance to be a mid-nineteenth-century construction based on the mutual exclusivity of subject and object. Arguing against the relevance of this bifurcation in the Early Modern period, she reads *King Lear* as a play that holds both persons and property in place by locking them into one another. The play's various gestures of redistribution end up following the precise course of primogeniture and succession, so that things (estates, clothing, purses) fall back into the hands that stood to inherit them in the first place. In such a tight economy, apocalypse is imagined as superflux – a literal spilling over from the top – a shakedown of superfluous things that calls out for a redefinition of need and excess that the play cannot answer.

Patricia Parker's essay also concerns the way in which material objects impress immaterial subjects. In *A Midsummer Night's Dream*, the crafted objects of the "rude mechanicals" work upon the "airy nothings" of the imagination. Snug's craft as joiner is of particular importance, for the act of joining is basic to theatrical practice: the joining of linguistic parts, the joining of scenes, the joining of costumes, the joint-stool. A dramatist is after all a *playwright*, a craftsman who, like a shipwright or cartwright, fashions his material for practical use. Tracing the play of "joinery" across the corpus of Shakespeare's drama, Parker suggests not only that artifacts precede artifice (the crafting of objects precedes the fashioning of tropes, scenes, and parts), but that "joinery" is part and parcel of other structures – social and political as well as rhetorical and theatrical.

As Parker shows the aesthetic to be informed by the artisanal, Louis Montrose shows the ideal of gentility to depend on material props. He analyzes Edmund Spenser's attempt to make himself a gentleman by seeking not only literary fame, but literal place by real property (house and land). Indeed the two are hardly separable in Spenser's career. *The Faerie Queene*, the great epic eternizing Elizabeth, is lodged between two works concerned with the more personal permanence of land tenure and dynastic continuity: the pastoral *Colin Clouts Come Home Againe* and the lyrical and nuptial *AMORETTI AND Epithalamion*. It is not just England and Elizabeth that are monumentalized in Spenser's verse but also (however precariously) Kilcolman and Spenser. Montrose's introduction of new objective factors forces a reconstrual of certain critical relations: between public and private, monarch and subject, the ideological and the mythopoetic.

Long recognizing the force of the object in technology, scholarship has charted the revolution caused by the printing press during the Early Modern period. When this focus is enlarged to include printed objects, we begin to see how one selfsame text can be two objects: both a full folio on vellum mimicking a codex with hand-tipped illustrations *and* an inexpensive and portable pocketbook. Editors, intent on reproducing the text as a single author's subjectivity, tend to smooth over material differences between volumes, thereby effacing their status as discrete objects. When released from service to sovereign authorship, these objective texts can be seen to have their own surprisingly proliferative semantics, especially when registering the unstable objectifications of gender. Our second group of essays, *Materializations*, traces out the signifying potential of three different sorts of objects: engraved image, (cheaply) printed book, and painted masterpiece.

Stephen Orgel begins this section by insisting upon the power of Renaissance emblems to resist the supposed "fixity of print" by shifting meaning with each context, often with the effect of producing superfluous meanings, particularly in a sexual register. After surveying a series of sexually ambiguous images of royalty ranging from benign nurturance to horrific hermaphroditism, Orgel asks how we are to read a cartouche of Peace and Justice kissing that surmounts a triumphal portrait of Elizabeth I on the title page of an elaborately illuminated atlas. The image regenders a complex series of emblems of male figures in similar gestural contexts; in each instance no certain means can be found for fixing the body within a stable, asexual allegorical meaning. Demonstrating that it is impossible not to see the surface gesture as well as the imperial scheme, Orgel shows how the emblem offers both the excess of tribadism as well as the transcendence of female sovereignty.

Nancy Vickers asks how we can make sense of a more modestly reproduced object: a tiny volume published in 1539 which included the *Hecatomphile* and two separate collections of poems. There is no single author from whose subjectivity the texts proceed; there is no title which can summon a single perspective from which to view the diverse contents. Cheaply produced, it is clearly intended for a popular non-courtly audience; illustrated with the crudest of woodcuts, it is designed to be affordable to a non-elite readership. By displaying the dismembered corpus of feminized love lyric, the volume provided a new juridical class of bureaucratic managers who served the Valois monarchy with a means to consume court culture.

Like Vickers, Ann Jones begins with an object without a certain title and therefore without designated "subject matter." Like Orgel, she encounters the excess of meaning in an image: Velázquez's *Las Hilanderas* (*The Spinners*), a painting of four women spinners before a background in which elegantly dressed women view a tapestry representing Athena's judgment of Arachne's weaving. The painting foregrounds the gendered labor which produces the material precondition of the tapestry – spun thread. Jones traces the literary tradition of weaving contests centered on Arachne from Ovid through the Renaissance, a tradition of contest replayed by the other title given the canvas, *The Fable of Arachne*. The displacement of the first title by the second parallels the absorption of the labor which produced textiles, canvas, and dyes into the self-sufficient work of art.

If the subject (or author or painter) is no longer assumed to be prior to and independent of objects, criticism can attend to a dialectic in which subjects and objects reciprocally take and make each other over. At a time when western Europe had embarked on an extended colonization of the world, such acts of appropriation can be seen as a circulation of objects as well as the oppression of one set of people by another. Objects from the New World circulated in trade networks which placed great value on American artifacts and African slaves as both signs and producers of wealth. Such transvaluations pressure the colonist not only to objectify the other but to entitle himself or herself. The third group of essays, *Appropriations*, concerns specifically colonialist constructions of the object.

As Jones analyzes the appropriation of labor in terms of gender, Maureen Quilligan focuses upon the massive appropriation of labor in the seventeenth-century slave trade. Arguing that the objectifying of the slave is constitutive of the "free subjectivity" of the master, Quilligan points out that the new "liberty" of the Lockean individual is formulated simultaneously with the expansion of slavery. Even more importantly, the notion of property in oneself emerges from the possibility of having property in another. The liberal humanist subject installed by *Paradise Lost* takes shape in part against the African slave, who then becomes the fundamental object. Such a division finds its way into the poem in the guise of problematically gendered discourses about nakedness and labor, distinguishing between free and enslaved labor in terms of the curse on male and female work.

Along with Quilligan, Margaret Ferguson considers gender in relationship to what Arjun Appadurai has called the "social life of things," in this case, feathers as they circulate (or are appropriated) from Guiana to the English stage.[19] At the same time, Ferguson questions an uncritical celebration of Aphra Behn's positioning of herself as a female writing subject. Ferguson argues that while Behn may interrogate the stability of gender categories, she simultaneously reinstates slavery as spectacle. The fetishized feathers come to represent a crucial ambivalence in the staging of the colonized: as naked, pure, innocent *and* as ornamented, luxurious, theatrical. This ambivalence reinstates the dominant categories of femininity which Behn displaces in her representations of European women. Ambivalence here, far from undoing the gaze of the colonizer, proceeds from the production of the colonized as objects: objects of the theatrical spectacle.

Gary Tomlinson turns to a different technique of appropriation: writing. The late sixteenth-century manuscript *Cantares mexicanos* fixes ninety-one Aztec songs in writing – and in the alphabet of the Spanish conqueror. As Tomlinson argues, European writing itself would have been unimaginable to the Mexica for whom language was constitutive of reality rather than representative, participating in a "syntax of things" rather than merely signifying it. Yet Tomlinson insists that the properties of the Aztec words and music can be recovered even from the western document, however foreign its signifying system is to the system it purports to represent. A new semantics is necessary for reading the textual object and for hearing the Mexica voices within it, a reciprocal semantics that would question western perceptual categories at the same time that it would articulate those of the remote Aztec.

The fourth section concerns other forms of reciprocity across time and space – those stimulated by memory. The subject recalls the object and the object recalls the subject. To name such relations *Fetishisms* is not merely to invest objects with the animating properties of subjects, but to underscore the object as a surrogate whose very material stuff can remake the desire for that which it substitutes. Clothes and communion bread are laden with their own materialities; yet they can be made to absorb otherwise evanescent cultural realities especially within the institutionalized contexts of Early Modern theatrical display, symbolic representation, and ritual observance. Such investments suggest that the fetish in Early Modern Europe may be different from that of a later anthropology, different too from its transposition into the marketplace via Marx's fetishism of commodities.[20]

In each of the essays in *Fetishisms*, fixation on a specific object charges it with a life of its own. In analyzing the circulation of clothes in the theater, Peter Stallybrass argues that the modern critique of the fetish depends upon the disowning of the constitutive power of objects. Being clothed (in household or guild livery, for example) was one of the most significant gestures of social organization in the Renaissance. Indeed, salaries were paid in clothing, with its power to incorporate and to transmit memory and status, as frequently as in the more neutral currency of money. Clothing was so valuable that it accounted for the major expense of theatrical companies, exceeding the expense of plays or even of the theaters themselves. Yet while the state unsuccessfully attempted to regulate these crucial markers of distinction, the theater drew upon the massive increase in new and second-hand clothes in the late sixteenth century to stage transferals of clothing in which the subject was constructed and reconstructed by the garments which he or she wore.

Jonathan Goldberg recovers a more personal memory from the Countess of Pembroke's translation of Petrarch's "Triumph of Death," a poem which in the countess's hand memorializes the loss of her brother, Sir Philip Sidney. Modern criticism has failed to recognize the compensatory value of the sister's manuscript, concerned as it has been to establish the secondariness of the female translation to the male original. Discussions of the translation have, therefore, missed the extent to which its complicated switches of gender between speakers (both Petrarch and Mary Sidney) and lost objects (both Laura and Philip Sidney) allow Mary Sidney to compensate for the loss of her corporate identity as sibling, an incestuous identity she preserves too in putting together her brother's posthumous textual corpus, the act by which she consolidates her own position as author.

Stephen Greenblatt looks at another corpus, that present in what is arguably the most problematic sentence in Christianity: *Hoc est corpus meum.* The miracle of transubstantiation was followed by what Greenblatt terms "the problem of the leftover": the status of the Eucharist's material remainder. If Christ was corporeally present in the bread, what happened if the bread made crumbs which mice might eat? It was precisely Christ's material presence that Catholicism insisted upon, as if the Son had been born in a *manger* (as if the Word had been made flesh) in order to himself be *eaten*. And it was precisely the alimentary implications of that insistence that Protestant Reformers fixed upon in demystifying Catholic ritual. As Greenblatt suggests, the material remains of the mystery, the lingering of the scatological after the eschatological, shadows over the literature as well as the theology of the period.

The final two essays by Marjorie Garber and Jonathan Dollimore we have called *Objections,* for objects there are so much in the image of the subject's desire that they seem more like simulacra or sites of loss. Both essays reopen the question of the subject by drawing on psychoanalysis to insist that the object figures as *problem*. In this sense, they could be said to object to the priority of the object as well as its formative effect on the subject. In both essays, the object comes into play conditionally, to be shaped by performance and desire.

Marjorie Garber discusses the chastity test in *The Changeling*, examining the symptoms induced in Diaphanta and Beatrice-Joanna when they drink of glass M. Rather than proving virginity, glass M sets the stage for the simulation of female orgasm. But what can it mean to simulate either chastity or orgasm, to be, as Madonna puts it, "*like* a virgin"? Does not such simulation turn the body itself into a counterfeit object? Counterfeiting always produces a problem of origins and authenticity: in so far as the "fake" can pass, it exposes every "original" as potential fake. Conversely, mimicry may produce the "real"; twentieth-century sex manuals have claimed that to fake orgasm is to learn how to have one. So too in the Renaissance English theater, gender was constructed by feigning. Male and female bodies alike depended upon performance, on the after-effects of simulation.

Jonathan Dollimore's essay also concerns desire, not as mimesis impossible to detect but as lack impossible to fill. Desire is driven less by an object than by intransitive lack. In the Renaissance, it is repeatedly represented as mutability: the "quite chop-fall'n" skull which is all that remains of Yorick; the rose whose "root is ever in its grave." Internalized, this mutability is experienced as sexual desire, and desire, in turn, is driven toward death. Desire, in other words, fixates with anarchic excess less upon a beloved object (for example, the boy of Shakespeare's *Sonnets*) than upon self-dissolution ("Desire is death"). For the beloved object intimates death – always already in a state of decay, even when imagined (in its youth and purity) to withstand mortality. The object, then, comes into being (as fantasy? as death wish?) from the position of loss (remembered or anticipated) and is so cathected to death that desire for it is indistinguishable from desire for death – for suicide, the ultimate collapse of subject into object.

If Garber and Dollimore resist the priority and sway of the object, they nevertheless reintroduce the unstable dialectic of subject and object which, when evaded or bypassed or deconstructed, seems inevitably to lead back to the reinstatement of the sovereign subject. The essays collected here urge an exploration of the intricacies of subject/object relations, so as to undo the narrative we have been telling ourselves over and over again: the rise of subjectivity, the complexity of subjectivity, the instability of subjectivity. What we have to gain from interrelating the object and the subject in the Renaissance is a sense of how objects have a hold on subjects as well as subjects on objects. We need to understand those reciprocal makings and unmakings. We need to understand too why we have traditionally overlooked these reciprocities – particularly in studying that period we have identified with our own point of origin.

Notes

1   For a discussion of the still-life's "assault on the prestige of the human subject," see Norman Bryson, *Looking at the Overlooked: Four Essays on Still Life Painting* (Cambridge, Mass., 1990), p. 61.

2   Bryson discusses the inherently contradictory nature of the *vanitas* still-life, ibid. p. 115.

3   See, for example, David Bailly's "Still Life," which includes reproductions of Bailly's own paintings, as well as a self-portrait and personal memorabilia, discussed by Svetlana Alpers, *The Art of Describing: Dutch Art in the Seventeenth Century* (Chicago, 1983), pp. 106–7, color plate 1.

4   Recent exceptions include: Patricia Fumerton, *Cultural Aesthetics: Renaissance Literature and the Practice of Social Ornament* (Chicago and London, 1991); Douglas Bruster, *Drama and the Market in the Age of Shakespeare* (Cambridge, 1992); and Jeffrey Knapp, *An Empire Nowhere: England, America, and Literature from "Utopia" to "The Tempest"* (Berkeley, 1992).

5   For a wide-ranging list of Renaissance self-reflexives, see William Kerrigan and Gordon Braden, *The Idea of the Renaissance* (Baltimore and London, 1989), pp. 221–2, n.20. For Montaigne's reflexivity, see Terence Cave, *The Cornucopian Text: Problems of Writing in the French Renaissance* (New York, 1979), p. 274.

6   For Hegel's account, see *Phenomenology of Spirit*, trans. A. V. Miller (Oxford, New York, Toronto, Melbourne, 1977), pp. 111–19.

7   2 vols., trans. S. G. C. Middlemore (New York, 1959), vol. I, p. 39.

8   Ibid. vol. I, p. 143.

9   On Burckhardt's emphatically male gendering of this individual, see the Introduction to Margaret W. Ferguson, Maureen Quilligan, and Nancy J. Vickers, eds., *Rewriting the Renaissance: The Discourses of Sexual Difference in Early Modern Europe* (Chicago and London, 1986), p. xv.

10 *The Individual and the Cosmos in Renaissance Philosophy*, trans. Mario Domandi (New York, 1963). See also Kerrigan and Braden, *The Idea of the Renaissance*, pp. 73–81.

11 *Capital*, vol. I, ch. 1, "Commodities," in *The Marx–Engels Reader*, ed. Robert C. Tucker (2nd edn., New York and London, 1978), pp. 302–29.

12 For a Marxist extension of Hegel's dialectic, see Alexandre Kojève, *Introduction to the Reading of Hegel*, ed. Allan Bloom, trans. James H. Nichols, Jr. (Ithaca and London, 1980), ch. 1, pp. 3–30.

13 *On James Mill*, in *Karl Marx: Selected Writings*, ed. David McLellan, (Oxford, 1977), pp. 114–23.

14 "An unobjective being is a *nullity* – an *un-being*," Marx, *Economic and Philosophic Manuscripts of 1844*, in *Reader*, p. 116.

15 Ibid. p. 115.

16 Ibid. p. 116. For another account of the intimate relation between subject

and object, maker and artifact, see Elaine Scarry, "The Interior Structure of the Artifact," in her *The Body in Pain: The Making and Unmaking of the World* (New York and Oxford, 1985), pp. 278–326. For Scarry, however, subjects are necessarily prior to objects, for it is through artifacts that the body extends and projects itself.

17 Felix Gilbert has counted some thirty passages in which Burckhardt identifies the Renaissance with the "modern age," the Renaissance individual with "modern man." *History: Politics or Culture? Reflections on Ranke and Burckhardt* (Princeton, 1990), p. 61.

18 Michael Foucault, *The Archaeology of Knowledge and The Discourse on Language*, trans. A. M. Sheridan (New York, 1972), p. 12.

19 Arjun Appadurai, ed., *The Social Life of Things: Commodities in Cultural Perspective* (Cambridge, 1986).

20 On the migrations of fetishism in and out of commerce, anthropology, philosophy, and other disciplines, see William Pietz, "The Problem of the Fetish," *Res* 9 (1985), 5–17; 13 (1987), 23–45; 16 (1988), 105–23.

God help me — did I really pay for this?

Part I

Priority of objects

1   The ideology of superfluous things:
King Lear as period piece

Margreta de Grazia

> [O]ur basest beggars
> Are in the poorest thing superfluous.

Born in the same year (1818), Jacob Burckhardt and Karl Marx together (though quite independently) gave birth to the Renaissance. Not to the Renaissance as the rebirth of antiquity but to the Renaissance as the birth of the Modern – the Renaissance, that is, as *Early* Modern – the period that anticipated the future rather than recovered the past.[1] In Burckhardt's 1860 *The Civilization of the Renaissance in Italy*, that birth took the form of individualism; in Marx's 1867 *Capital*, it took the form of capitalism. In broad terms (periodization requires them), Burckhardt's cultural history provided Renaissance studies with its working notion of the subject – the individual; Marx's economic theory provided it with its working notion of the object – the commodity.

The differences between Burckhardt and Marx are vast. They wrote two different kinds of history (Burckhardt's cultural history juxtaposed synchronic Nietzschean fragments while Marx's economic history unfolded a diachronic Hegelian continuum) and had two different politics (Burckhardt feared leveling progressive reform while Marx envisioned a revolutionary classless society).[2] There is one thing, however, which Burckhardt's subject and Marx's object have in common: each excludes the other. Burckhardt's individuated subject is cut off from objects; Marx's commodified object is cut off from subjects.

Individuals and commodities

To attain autonomy, Burckhardt's subject must be removed from objects, both those it might own and those it might make. Indeed, the break between the two serves to differentiate the Renaissance from the Middle Ages: "In the Middle Ages both sides of human consciousness – that which was turned within as that which was turned without – lay dreaming or half awake beneath a common veil."[3] Only after the great

Renaissance awakening was the subject able to assume its proper distance from objects: "an *objective* treatment and consideration ... of all the things of this world became . possible." The subjective side also asserted itself: "man became a spiritual individual, and recognized himself as such." It is precisely this distancing of the subject from the object that conferred upon the subject a new power over the external world.[4] Burckhardt's exemplary individuals are often set apart from objects, by low and illegitimate birth like Alberti or by exile like Dante.[5] The same distance, however, can also be cultivated, as it is by the artist who stands apart from his material, the ruler from his state, the humanist from his texts. Like Descartes who begins his *Meditations* by abstracting himself from objects – from the winter cloak he is wearing, from the paper on which he is writing – the subject must remove himself from the world of objects in order to be fully conscious and capable.[6]

Marx's Early Modern object, the commodity, denies its relation to persons by effacing its origin in social production. It is precisely this denial that distinguishes a commodity from any other kind of object: the product of the medieval artisan, for example. The table the artisan makes is a product but no commodity because it retains a relation to him, either through his use or that of his feudal lord. But once that table is exchanged for something outside the maker's domain (money, for example), it enters a system of value in which its relation to social labor is misrepresented as a relation between objects. Objects then give off the false (and fetish-producing) impression that their value is intrinsic to them rather than the result of the social labor that produced them: "The social character of labour appears to us to be an objective character of the products themselves."[7] A wry little allegory in *Capital* has the table taking on airs, standing on its own four feet as if it had come into the world free-standing, and, more pretentiously still, standing on its head, as if to give the Hegelian impression that metaphysical ideas are the basis of material reality rather than the other way around.[8] Footloose and fancy-free, as it were, the table is alienated from its maker – indeed estranged, to the point that it turns on him like a menacing stranger or foreigner: "the object confronts him as something hostile and alien."[9]

Untrammeled by inherited objects, the Burckhardtian individual can flourish on the basis of his own talents. Disengaged from productive subjects, the Marxist commodity can circulate on the basis of its exchange value. In both cases, the Early Modern subject/object schism allows for mobility. Defined by intrinsic merit rather than extrinsic goods ("relying solely on his personal talent"),[10] the bourgeois subject can rise through the social ranks. Valued in its own right ("Could commodities themselves speak, they would say: ... What ... does belong to us as objects, is our value"),[11] the capitalist commodity can circulate freely in the market. Each has to deny the other in order to move freely, the precondition for Modern politics (bourgeois democracy) and Modern economics (capitalism). Indeed it is precisely this movement, this breaking away from an inert feudal period or "Dark Ages," that gives the Renaissance pride of place as the onset of the Modern: the beginning of Modern man for Burckhardt, the beginning of capitalism for Marx.[12] It is at this point that history starts its inexorable progress forward, from Early Modern, through Modern, Late Modern, to Postmodern and perhaps onward beyond that.

The Burckhardtian and Marxian accounts have, without notice, come together in recent discussions of late sixteenth- and early seventeenth-century English theater. Jean-Christophe Agnew has emphasized the importance of the traditional geographical proximity of the theater and the marketplace, the stage and the stalls; the success of both institutions, he argues, depended on fluidity: "the practical liquidity of the commodity form and the imaginative liquidity of the theatrical form."[13] For Douglas Bruster, it is not simply that the theater is *like* a market, it *is* a market ("London's playhouses were, of course, actual markets") based on the same mechanisms of commodification and consumerism:[14] as the market converted money into, say, a slab of bacon, so too the theater converted the price of admission into, say, a fantasy of revenge.[15] The London theater, then, emerges as a locus of double convertibility: where actors change into characters (who often change into other characters) and where money converts into spectacle. The theater thus seems the perfect site for observing the Renaissance as Early Modern: the fluidity of both identities and commodities.

The fluidity that characterizes the Early Modern period is also seen to characterize not only what is arguably its dominant cultural institution, but also the productions of that institution, particularly its most memorable ones – those by Shakespeare. Criticism for the past two generations has tended to situate Shakespeare in history rather than assume his universality. This has generally meant locating him at the start of the ever-receding Modern; what most concerns us here-and-now is seen as having its origins in him there-and-then. Shakespeare thus comes to mark the passage into the modern age, often serving as a transitional figure between Medieval and Modern, his chronology itself often seen to display the break in the historical continuum, his shift from comedy to tragedy coinciding with the break from old to new (coinciding too with the turn of the century), from feudal collectivity to bourgeois indivi-duality, from manor production to market commodification.[16]

In recent years *King Lear* in particular has been read in relation to this historical divide. Numerous readings have removed the play from its indeterminate once-upon-a-time frame (not to mention its wooden Tillyardian frame)[17] to situate it in the historically specific context of its writing (*c*. 1605–10). The play has accordingly been read as dramatizing any number of relations to that momentous transition from one social formation to another (feudal to capitalist) and from one type of individual to another (loyal to self-interested). We thus have readings that, empowered by Lawrence Stone's *Crisis of the Aristocracy*, see *Lear* tottering on the brink between old and new, Hooker and Hobbes, nostalgic for receding social ties and values and wary of emergent selfish drives and impulses.[18] Other readings see *Lear* clearing the way for this break by dramatizing the exhaustion of older structures and beliefs (absolutism, supernaturalism, spiritualism) that cave in from the very weight of their own contradictions in unwitting preparation for their supersession.[19] *Lear* has also been read as venturing a brief sortie into capitalism, only to retreat back to a familiar feudalism – an advisedly "retrograde movement."[20] Still other accounts find the play more impetuous, rushing headlong into the Modern, almost a half-century ahead of its time in anticipating such radical sects as the Levellers and even the Ranters and Diggers, pushing ahead toward the upset of the Civil War, "moving toward something genuinely new" that looks precipitously like the rise of the proletariat – which, it must be said, as portrayed in Lear's invocations and Tom's simulations, look more like the *lumpenproletariat*.[21] Finally, *Lear* has been read so progressively as to extend right into the Modern, specifically that of 1930s sharecroppers and New Deal reform, demonstrating its precocious capacity to engage, especially through the voice of Lear himself, in "an emergent structural analysis of power and class relations."[22] In all these readings, the influence of periodization is at work, predisposing criticism to see the play's issues in terms of the great historical shift from the Medieval to the Modern. Each reading sees the play as more or less intrepidly gesturing toward (or away from) the future, as if it were doing its part to start (or forestall) the rolling historical ball on its teleological course into the Modern.

So what we have is a range of readings positioning *King Lear* in relation to the Early Modern: pre-, proto-, retro-, avant-garde, and ultra/trans-early Modern *King Lear* respectively. As Fredric Jameson concludes, it may be that we have no other way of being historical than by periodizing; some division of the vast historical span is necessary in order to have an object for historical study.[23] The question is, then: in our eagerness to make the Renaissance relevant to the Modern, have we not been precipitous in identifying it as the onset of the Modern? This is not to say that nascent individualism and capitalism cannot be found in England around Shakespeare's time. Yet it is to ask, does it make sense to make the nascent dominant before history does?[24] For that is surely what we do, even by intensely focusing on it as such. There is a way in which seeing the Renaissance as the Early-Now commits itself to the very universalizing tendency that historicizing set out to avoid in the first place. As if *the* relevant history were a prior version of what we already are and live. It is a dynamic universalizing to be sure, rich with gradations and nuances, but a universalization all the same. It is what Foucault following Nietzsche would avoid by replacing a teleologically driven continuum with proliferative genealogies or archaeologies.[25] The reading that follows below makes no pretense of avoiding periodization, however, for it too exists in relation to it. Set resolutely *against* the Modern, it could easily be added to the list compiled above, with a new prefix: *anti*-Early Modern. The essay is about how *King Lear* blocks the mobility identified since the nineteenth century with the Modern – through its locking of persons into things, proper selves into property, subjectivity effects into personal effects – in an attempt to withstand flux or fluidity, superflux or superfluity.

Things and persons

Traditionally it has been Gloucester's experience that has been seen to double Lear's. The title pages of the early quartos, however, suggest that it is Edgar's life rather than his father's that makes up the subplot: "True Chronicle Historie of the life and death of King Lear and his three Daughters. With the unfortunate life of Edgar, sonne and heire to the Earle of Gloster and his sullen and assumed humor of Tom of Bedlam."[26] When character is dominant, Gloucester's plight seems more like Lear's: both are old men suffering at the hands of their children. Once objects are admitted, however, Edgar's story makes the more compelling counterpart: both men are detached from their possessions. Lear and Edgar both comment on their shared experience: Lear imagines that Tom too must have been stripped down by his daughters ("nothing could have subdu'd nature / To such a lowness but his unkind daughters," III.iv.69–70); and behind Edgar's sympathy for Lear is his own experience of being cut off ("that which makes me bend makes the King bow: / He childed as I fathered!" III.vi.109–10). Through the lives of both titular and subtitular characters, the play dramatizes the relation of being and having. As we shall see, removing what a person *has* simultaneously takes away what a person *is*.

If having is tantamount to being, *not* having is tantamount to *non*-being

– to being nothing. Edgar disentitled concludes "Edgar I nothing am" (II.iii.21); Lear divested is, in the Fool's words, an "O without a figure ... nothing" (I.iv.192, 194). And yet both of these descriptions prove too absolute. Though Lear believes that Tom has given away all – "Couldst thou save nothing? Wouldst thou give 'em all?" (III.iv.64) – he misses something; as the Fool points out, Tom "reserv'd a blanket" (65). So too when he claims he himself has given all – "I gave you all" (II.iv.248) – he forgets something, his "reservation of an hundred knights" (I.i.132). Both king and beggar by holding something back (in reserve) hold on to themselves, however fragmentarily. What they cling to (or in Edgar's case, what clings to him) is hardly necessary for subsistence. Lear, as his daughters point out, does not need his train in a household staffed with twice as many to attend him. Nor does Tom's blanket serve his needs; if Regan's gorgeous gown scarcely keeps her warm (because of silk? because décolleté?), it is no wonder "Tom's a-cold" (III.iv.57, 170, and IV.i.52) in his loincloth. As Lear argues in defending his right to keep his retainers, need – subsistence – is not the point:

> O, reason not the need! our basest beggars
> Are in the poorest thing superfluous.

> (II.iv.264–5)

All persons, from highest to lowest, must possess something beyond need – a superfluous thing. Tom's blanket is such a thing, the beggar's equivalent of the king's train, a dispensable item that is all the same constitutive.

Tom's and Lear's superfluous things have more in common than might first appear. Loincloth and retainers encase the body, like clothes generally which at once protect and suit their wearer, like codpieces particularly in their accent on phallic power: Tom's loincloth protects and highlights his generational loins; Lear's entourage "enguards" (I.iv.326) him while exhibiting his chivalric might ("men of choice and rarest parts," I.iv.263).[27] More important than their functional similarity, however, is their material likeness. The retainers would have been liveried in cloth – the cloth that distinguished them as Lear's servants;[28] hence the appropriateness of their being also referred to as the king's "train" that follows him like the trail of a majestic robe (that can, like both tail and garment, be "cut off," II.iv.174). When enlisting Tom as one of his knights – "You, sir, I entertain for one of my hundred" – Lear criticizes his attire, perhaps preferring to see him in livery: "only I do not like the fashion of your garments: you will say they are Persian, but let them be chang'd" (III.vi.78–81). Loincloth would be changed to livery, one superfluous thing becoming the other.

With the addition of Regan's unnecessarily gorgeous robes ("If only to go warm were gorgeous, / Why, nature needs not what thou gorgeous wears't, / Which scarcely keeps thee warm," II.iv.268–70), clothes rank as the play's representative superfluous thing. Practically useless – unable to protect the body from the storm's invasive cold and wet – clothes are expendable and transferable layers to be sloughed off like extra skins ("Off, off, you lendings!" III.iv.108). Like *traps* and *paraphernalia*,[29] clothes refer to property in general as well as cloth articles in particular.[30] The play's unusual use of "accommodations" to refer to clothing rather than lodging reflects its primacy in the play's economy.[31] Valuable in itself, it also represents value, both immobile property like houses (and houselessness)[32] and mobile property like money (or impecuniousness). As the play's two gestural acts of redistributing wealth or shaking the superflux demonstrate, clothes and coins are interchangeable: Lear shakes the superflux by disrobing, Gloucester by disbursing.   *right*

Though property, coins, and jewels belong only to the rich, all persons possess some cloth item, whether sumptuous or scrappy. Cloth then is the universal superfluous thing, the one touch of nature that makes the whole world kin.[33] While for Plato it is the possession of reason that makes a creature human, for Heidegger hands, and for Bergson laughter, for Lear it is the possession of something beyond need. Whether on top or at bottom of the social hierarchy, a person must have some extra thing beyond subsistence in order to be more than an animal: "Allow not nature more than nature needs, / Man's life is cheap as beast's" (II.iv.266–7). Lear's conclusion upon observing Tom that "man is no more than such a poor, bare, fork'd animal as thou art" (III.iv.107–8) is based on a false premise much plainer than the frequently noted metatheatrical one (that Tom's nakedness conceals Edgar which in turn conceals an actor): for Tom is not quite "bare." Wrapped around his salient fork is a blanket, the superfluous thing that by Lear's own reasoning secures man's superiority to beasts.   *like Desd's hanky*

Yet the main function of superfluous things is to mark not ontological distinctions but social ones. Lear pleads for the retention of his unnecessary retainers as if such holdings were a human right, for beggars as much as kings. Yet his defense rests on something less high-minded and anachronistic than natural rights. Sumptuary laws devised to regulate excess were based on the same allowance of excess according to rank. Sumptuary legislation proliferated throughout the sixteenth century, in theory regulating expenditure on attire, partly for economic reasons and partly to avoid what Elizabeth termed "confusion also of degrees."[34] However limited in practice, sumptuary laws were a system for fastening identity onto materiality, persons into cloth, in stratifications ranging from "[loop'd] and window'd raggedness" (III.iv.31) to gorgeous "Robes and furr'd gowns" (IV.vi.164).[35] So too Lear's superfluous things would maintain not simply the difference between man and beast but, more critically, what Goneril terms "the difference of man and man" (IV.i.26). This is the difference made by "blood and breeding" (III.i.40) that manifests itself in "countenance" (I.iv.26–7), though in giving the Bastard the sexual place proper to the Duke, Goneril shows small regard for this "difference," much to Edgar's disgust upon discovering her adulterous relation with the Bastard – "O indistinguish'd space of woman's will!" (IV.vi.271).[36]

Possessions then are the superfluous things, superfluous because unnecessary for subsistence: as Poor Tom's existence proves, at least theoretically, survival is possible with no more than a hovel for shelter, straw for warmth, "the swimming frog, the toad, the todpole, the wall-newt" for food (III.iv.129–30), "the green mantle of the standing pool" for drink (133–4). Yet they are absolutely necessary for upholding social and personal identity. Lear unhinges when his retainers are denied him, as if his retainers held him rather than he them. The disquantitying and abatement of his train diminishes him too, so that his status as both man and king drop dramatically. Like a beggar, he falls to his knees pleading for raiment, bed, and food. Like a woman, he suffers "hysterica passio," unmanned from within by the classic gynecological disorder.[37] He himself admits to losing his shape, vowing to

> ... resume the shape which thou dost think
> I have cast off for ever.
>
> (I.iv.308–9)

His retainers function as containers, so that their removal makes him incontinent: his sides break, his eyes weep, his hysterical heart leaps up. Lear's retainers are, then, anything but dispensable, as is indicated by the many attempts to replace them, both in Lear's mind (through his induction of Poor Tom, his coining to impress soldiers, his commanding that his subjects wildly copulate to provide him with soldiers) and in reality (as "five or six and thirty questrists" race to join him at Dover, III.vii.17; as Cordelia sends out a compensatory "century" or sentry to rescue him, IV.iv.6).[38]

Subjects and objects are so tightly bound in the play's economy that a subject cannot survive the loss of his or her possessions. "To change one's copy" in this period was a common expression for changing one's demeanor, the result of having gained or lost copyhold, the commonest form of land tenure.[39] Kent banished becomes Caius, Cordelia disowned is instantly reinvested by France as Queen of France, and Gloucester disentitled (by Cornwall's charge of treason) attempts to end himself (an act that would have led to the legal confiscation of his property).[40] The opening action of the play puts this principle to test when that paradoxical entity, the sovereign subject, rids himself of his property: the kingdom itself.[41] Lear's "will to publish" is in effect the making public of his will, the dividing of his property among his heirs.[42] One of the sovereign's privileges was, in theory, to will his property as he would, without thought to "the plague of custom" and "curiosity of nations" (I.ii.3, 4) constraining nobles like Gloucester.[43] What is striking about Lear's testation, however, is less *how* he divides his kingdom than *when*. It is a pre-mortem settlement, occurring before rather than after death. In his desire to anticipate the future, Lear is not unlike Edmund. Both cannot wait for nature to take its course, Edmund as eager to inherit as Lear to disinherit. In this respect, *Lear* could be described as a play about a man's attempt to outlast his property – the risks of living testate, as it were. It is not a healthy desire, to be sure – indeed, it could be said that Lear's suicidal desire to undo himself is as unnatural and illegal as Edmund's patricidal desire to undo his father.

Lear's initial attempt to disburden himself of his property might also be reconsidered in light of popular and medical lore on insanity. In Michael MacDonald's discussion of madness in the seventeenth century, numerous symptoms involve forms of self-destruction in which the "self" includes personal property as well as person.[44] Neglect or damage to one's house and clothes were considered as symptomatic of madness as forms of self-affliction. Particularly common was the tearing and the tearing off of clothes, "valuable property," as MacDonald notes.[45] In this context, each of Lear's acts of divestment might signal madness, beginning with his divestment "of rule, / Interest of territory" (I.i.49–50), followed by his abjuration of all roofs, his unbonneting, the removal of his garments and, later, of his boots.[46] Edgar stages the familiar symptoms by stripping down and following the "president/ Of Bedlam beggars" (II.iii.13–14) who stick their arms with "Pins, wooden pricks, nails, sprigs of rosemary" (16).[47] Divestment, disrobing, disaccommodating are all acts of exposure that like self-inflicted wounds betray an unsound mind. According to this criterion, the strongest sign of Lear's sanity is his desire to keep his retainers.

Both plot and subplot dramatize the impossibility of the severance Lear attempts. Persons and things cannot be alienated from one another. Lear's kingdom cannot be given away; Gloucester's estate cannot be taken away. The land seized from Edgar returns to him; so too the kingdom given away by Lear comes back. And the course by which both return is remarkable. The removal of property is dramatized as an act of aberrant (unnatural) will: Lear's premature disposal of his property before death and Edmund's subversive desire to overturn "the plague of custom" and "curiosity of nations" (I.ii.3,4). Yet its return ostensibly happens on its own, in the natural course of things, rather than through any act of human exertion. Lear disposes of the kingdom with great pomp and circumstance and a battle is waged to keep it from him; but it returns to him quietly (almost imperceptibly) through Albany's modest resignation ("we will resign, / During the life of this old majesty, / To him our absolute power," V.iii.299–301). We twice overhear Edmund boldly contrive to dispossess his brother –

> Well then,
> Legitimate Edgar, I must have your land
> (I.ii.15–16)

– and "Let me ... have lands by wit" (II.ii.183) – and witness his success, first with his father (*Glou.* "I'll work the means / To make thee capable," II.i.84–5), and then after his father's disentitlement, with Cornwall (*Corn.* "True or false, it hath made thee Earl of Gloucester," III.v.17–18) so that Goneril, Oswald, and Albany all address him by his appropriated title. But we never hear an antiphonal response from Edgar, "Well then, illegitimate Edmund, I must have back my land." (Indeed his reentitlement gets lost in the pomp and circumstance of the duel that achieves it.) Removal involves disruptive human agency, while return occurs surreptitiously, as if the gods were not so boyishly wanton after all, responsibly returning what was lost, like so many Perditas from another dramatic genre.[48]

As estate clings to person so person clings to estate. That is why, to answer the Fool's pertinent question, "a snail has a house" (II.i.27–8). Disowned (and therefore dispossessed) by his father, "Edgar I nothing am" (II.iii.21); deprived of his 100 knights, "This is not Lear" (I.iv.226). Expropriation fractures identity – with 100 knights gone in a clap, Lear dissolves into tears, breaks into 100,000 flawed pieces. Madness ensues, actual for Lear, feigned by Edgar. Identity dissipates with disentitlement. During the period Edgar is without property, he has no proper name ("my name is lost," V.iii.121), only a generic one – Poor Tom. Edgar's two narratives both involve simultaneous loss of property and identity. His own: dispossessed of his land, he disguises himself. And the one he assumes: dispossessed of his "three suits to his back, six shirts to his body – Horse to ride and weapons to wear" (III.iv.135–7), he drops from courtier/servingman to Bedlam beggar. A series of acquisitions – of clothes and purses – enables Edgar to recover himself in a series of linguistically marked upward gradations from "Madman and beggar too" (IV.i.30), to "A poor unfortunate beggar" (IV.vi.68), to "A most poor man" (221), to "bold peasant" (231), to ceremonious messenger (V.i.38), to chivalric "champion" (V.iii.121) – until he is finally in the position to reclaim his title (his name and land), "My name is Edgar" (V.iii.170), a title which connects him to Lear as well as his father, for, as Regan allows, it was Lear who named him.[49]

It is the identity not only of those born into kingdoms and earldoms that is contingent upon possessions, but also – quite astonishingly – those born into nothing whatsoever. The given names of all the highborn male characters in the play are dropped so that person and property are synonymous: Gloucester, Albany, Cornwall, France, Burgundy, Kent. The nameless poor are christened in Lear's apostrophes after both their lack of clothing, "Poor Naked Wretches," and their lack of estate, "You Houseless Poverty" (III.iv.28, 26, capitals added). The beggar possesses a generic rather than a proper name, "Poor Tom" or "Tom of Bedlam"; the latter form, like a title (compare Earl of Gloucester), affixes person to property (a madhouse for a house) and then collapses the two in just plain "Bedlam" (compare Gloucester). The speech prefixes of the Quarto and Folio distinguish Edmund with no proper name but rather with his legal status – Bastard, short for "unpossessing bastard" (II.i.67), identifying him with his incapacity to inherit land (except by special dispensation).[50] The steward of another's property, having no land of his own (unlike his near namesake Osric who is rich in the possession of much dirt), the hybrid Oswald ("son and heir of a mungril bitch," II.ii.22–3) is called names that associate him with a hodgepodge of movables rather than a stable estate: "three-suited, hundred-pound, filthy worsted-stocking knave" (II.ii.16–17). Servants possess no names at all, even those distinguished by such memorable deeds as the slaying of Cornwall. Regan exclaims "A peasant stand up thus?" (III.vii.79) and Cornwall commands "throw this slave / Upon the dunghill" (96–7) as if to bring him as low as possible for standing up, combining his remains with offal, with filth rather than land. Oswald also calls a peasant (or Edgar's impersonation of one) "dunghill"; this peasant too is uppity, daring to defy the steward's sword with his rustic costard.[51] Oswald – "super-serviceable" (II.ii.18–19) in the Folio or "superfinical" in the Quarto – is himself a social climber, at this very encounter hoping preferment will fall on him for cutting off Gloucester. It is fitting, therefore, that he be put down by the same association with excremental waste in Kent's threat to "daub the wall of a jakes" (II.ii.66–7) with his remains. Those remains, appropriately enough, end up uninterred, just as those of the rising peasant are put upon the dunghill rather than underground, despite Oswald's dying request – "Bury my body" (IV.vi.247).

Superflux

Oswald is associated with lexical excess as well as alimentary waste: "Thou whoreson zed, thou unnecessary letter!" (II.ii.64) referring to the absence of "z" from dictionaries. Both types of superfluity underscore his social dispensability. As Kent's "additions" (24) indicate, Oswald is a supernumerary, the one thing the tight world of *Lear* could do without precisely because he stands for the possibility the play abhors (despite its own generic hybridity) – of hybridization, mongrelization, heterogeneity teeming its way into the hierarchy. Ideally, selfhood from top to bottom would be securely locked into possession, from extravagant to paltry, so that nothing would be left over to throw off the balance – or the imbalance.[52] Yet the balance *is* thrown off, or, in the hydraulic terms invited by the play, the water level spills over – in superflux. The first sign of overspill is the uncontrollable effusion of tears "which break from [Lear] perforce" (I.iv.298), the water drops displaced by the passionate hysterics that threaten to drown or suffocate him in his own fluid. Concurrently another outburst makes itself heard – of cosmic, indeed cataclysmic, proportions: "Storme and Tempest" reads the Folio stage direction. The storm magnifies Lear's lachrymal superflux with a deluvian downpour from above: floodgates and waterspouts, cataracts and hurricanoes, a torrent that raises the water level, as Lear bids the wind "swell the curled waters 'bove the main" (III.i.6). The effect of the overflow is to collapse high into low as the firmament drops to land level, drowning and drenching uppermost steeples and weathercocks, flattening the global sphere into a liquid mass. "Pour on" (III.iv.18), urges Lear, hoping to confound human generation as well as physical creation, bidding that Nature's female receptive molds be cracked, her masculine inseminating germens spilled – so that all distinctions would dissolve in an amorphous muddle.

It is appropriate that Gloucester should appear during the storm, bearing a torch, heralded as "a little fire in a wild field" like "an old lecher's heart" in a cold body (III.iv.111–12), for Gloucester admits (even boasts) himself a spiller of germens: "the whoreson must be acknowledg'd" (I.i.24). While Gloucester may well, as he claims, be reconciled to his past promiscuity, the play certainly is not. Gloucester is "the superfluous and lust-dieted man" (IV.i.67), in that very epithet combining what are not yet two discrete words: luxury and lechery, lavish spending and dissipate fornicating.[53] From the first to the last, the play stigmatizes him as the indiscriminate dispenser of both economic and sexual purses, coin and seed.[54] In the opening scene, he boasts that he is "braz'd" (I.i.11) – hardened like brass – to his illicit deed. His blinding in Act IV, however, makes him (and us) agonizingly sensitive to it. In the play's final scene, Edgar retroactively makes the loss of his father's eyes the price of his adultery (and not, as Cornwall charges, of his treason),[55] explaining to the Bastard:

> The dark and vicious place where thee he got
> Cost him his eyes.
>
> (V.iii.173–4)

Gloucester pays for his whoring with his eyes, forfeiting those "precious stones" (testicles and jewels), leaving "cases" like empty purses. "The dark and vicious place" where the whoreson was begotten was the whore or whorehouse (person and house interchangeable here too);[56] but it was Gloucester who found his way to that "forfended place" (V.i.11), failing to heed Poor Tom's caveat: "Keep thy foot out of brothels, / thy hand out of plackets" (III.iv.96–7).

In a grotesquely displaced recurrence of Gloucester's deed, the foot and hand reappear together, making their way into sexually charged openings. Cornwall uses first his foot (*Corn.* "Upon these eyes of thine I'll set my foot," III.vii.68)[57] and then his hand (*Serv.* "Hold your hand," 73) to put out Gloucester's eyes, called "jelly" (83), a synonym for sperm.[58] The sexual act could be recognized in a gruesome blinding only in a culture steeped in the connection between lust and eyes.[59] Stephen Booth notes the ubiquity of eye for genitalia, male and female.[60] Medical lore attributes loss of eyesight to lechery[61] (and we already know that Gloucester's eyesight is dim – he needs spectacles to read [I.ii.35], and has to squint to see [III.iv.117] or fail to see [IV.vi.136–7]). Iconography makes the same causal connection, as in an image of voluptuous Lechery/Luxury piercing a man's eye with a spear.[62] Gloucester's sexual and optical history follows the same cultural links, as if there were no escaping the sadistic justice Edgar attributes to the gods.[63] Gloucester's punishment subjects him to the violation he committed; it ravishes him so that he is left with "bleeding rings" (V.iii.190), hollow cases as Lear calls them, Gloucester's jewels or stones now gone, as if he were castrated and barren.[64] (The blanket around his legitimate son's loins takes on a new necessity.)[65] Eyesight and lust are again combined when Lear hails Gloucester as "blind Cupid" (the sign of a brothel, IV.vi.137)[66] and hints at the sexual and financial expenditure that has unmanned (emasculated and impoverished) him:

> No eyes in your head, nor no money in your purse.
>
> (IV.vi.145–6)

After his repeated identification with Lechery/Luxury, it is more than likely that it is Gloucester and not Man in the abstract whom Lear tries for adultery in IV.vi. (It is, after all, Gloucester to whom he is speaking both before and after the arraignment.)

> When I do stare, see how the subject quakes.
> I pardon that man's life. What was thy cause?
> Adultery?
>
> (108–10)

Lear's sentence endorses the crime rather than condemning it ("To it, luxury, pell-mell," IV.vi.117), invoking the demise of social order just as he invoked the end of natural order during the storm ("Crack nature's moulds," III.ii.8). He rewards the defendant rather than penalizing him ("There's money for thee," IV.vi.131), as if to replenish his empty purse (with eyes, coin, and seed) and thereby legitimize further promiscuity, to the end of producing a mongrel, bastard population of Oswalds and Edmunds, the result of spilling germens into cracked molds.

In effect, Gloucester is "tried" twice for the same crime, first punished by Cornwall and then acquitted by Lear. Lear extends his forgiveness of Gloucester to all persons ("None does offend," 168) though the flip side of that blanket pardon is his sweeping indictment at Cordelia's death, "murderers, traitors all!" (V.iii.270). Either way, Lear would collapse differences between man and man, so that hierarchy would be engulfed by anarchy – the anarchy of "handy-dandy" and "pell-mell" in which justice and thief, dog and beggar, women and horses, rich and poor, guilty and innocent are indistinguishable.

Tears, rain, sperm – are the play's overflowing liquids, representing the superflux that disorders psyche, cosmos, and polis respectively.[67] The play also entertains economic superflux, the spilling over of possessions from the top that would raise the bottom.[68] Lear disrobes during the storm ("Expose thyself to feel what wretches feel, / That thou mayst shake the superflux to them," III.iv.34–5) in order to redress the gods' unjust distribution, an act he repeats a few moments later ("Off, off, you lendings! Come, unbutton here," 108–9). Gloucester repeats this gesture twice in the next act, giving away first one purse ("Here, take this purse," IV.i.64) and then another ("Here, friend, 's another purse," IV.vi.28). Moreover, he repeats it in the same spirit of evening out inequity:

> So distribution should undo excess,
> And each man have enough.
>
> (IV.i.70–1)

It is no small irony that both his purses should fall right into the very hands which stood to receive the handout in the first place: those of his

legitimate first born. As if charity ended at home and the nature of re-
venue were to come back.

Indeed, since Lear has no male heirs and has disowned his female
heirs, Edgar – Lear's godson – may be the designated beneficiary of
Lear's handouts as well. If Nicholas Rowe had in his 1709 edition
inserted the stage direction "Tossing off his clothes" rather than
"Tearing off his clothes" it would have better corresponded to the act
of shaking the superflux. For Lear is not just taking them off but
flinging them away, to the poor naked wretches who inspire the gesture.
It is in the middle of this shakedown that Poor Tom makes his first
appearance, entering with a reference to the deluvial superflux:
"Fathom and half" (III.iv.37). If he were to snatch up what Lear tossed
off, it would be the second item in an expanding wardrobe (beginning
with his blanket) that will include the best apparel owned by the man
who has served his father for eighty years and the "war-like" garb
(V.iii.143) in which he appears to challenge Edmund. In the right place
at the right time, Edgar might also be the recipient of Lear's donation
when he imagines recruiting soldiers (he did, after all, enlist Tom into
his retinue): "There's your press-money" (IV.vi.86–7). All the superflux
comes Edgar's way as if by fatal attraction – until the end when (Folio)
Edgar, Lear's godson, inherits the kingdom itself. "Who gives anything
to poor Tom?" (III.iv.51) indeed.

There is nothing "handy-dandy" or "pellmell" about the shaking of
superflux, the undoing of excess: it follows the precise course of primogeniture and succession. In the superflux, there is no spilling down from
the top that raises the bottom. Things end up passing from father to son;
and when there is no son (or daughter), from godfather to godson.[69]

What I have called the ideology of superfluous things holds the status
quo in place by locking identity into property, the subject into the object.
What movements there are towards modern fluidity of persons and
things snap back into the same old molds and germens. The Apocalyptic
storm only briefly holds out the millenarian promise that "things might
change or cease" (III.i.7), evoking a long tradition that associates the end
of the world with radical political change.[70] Yet like Lear's and Gloucester's token acts of redistribution, nothing changes or ceases as a result of
what turns out to be, like the (Folio) Fool's utopian prophecy before the
hovel (III.ii.80–94), no more than a chiliastic tease.[71]

Luxury

That the play restrains superfluity at the top – that it can only imagine
"superflux" or overflow in the horrific terms of madness, cataclysm, and

anarchy – returns us to our starting point, this essay's epigraph, Lear's principle of universal excess:

> [O]ur basest beggars
> Are in the poorest thing superfluous.

Far from being self-evident, the axiom contradicts itself: how can the *base*st have something *super*fluous, over-the-top[72] – have extra without having enough? How could those caved in by need – panged by "Necessity's sharp pinch" (II.iv.211) with "houseless heads and unfed sides" (III.iv.30) – have a surplus of anything?[73]

There is a grim illogic to Lear's theory, both semantic and social. For if the poor *did* have more than they needed, they would not still be poor, just as the rich would not be rich if they had less than they needed.[74] The axiom keeps the poor poor and the rich rich by relativizing both need and excess: a man has more or less of both depending on his social position. In *The Needs of Strangers*, Michael Ignatieff refines the axiom by proposing a distinction between *natural need* (food, raiment, clothing) and *social due* (honor, regard): while there may be a universal modicum for the former, the other must be determined by "rank, position and history."[75] The distinction, however, seems applicable only to the rich. It explains why Lear could want more though his needs were met, but not how a beggar could have more than enough when cold and hungry. It would seem that the only excess beggars could know would come from the handouts of the rich, though in their hands gratuitous waste would instantly convert to necessary subsistence. Of course, there is always the possibility that the transferal might be motivated from the bottom rather than the top: that the beggar might enforce the charity of the rich (to paraphrase Poor Tom, II.iii.20) or "take the thing she begs" (to quote Goneril, I.iv.248). Indeed this inversion was threatened annually on St. Stephen's Day, the day after Christmas on which (according to the 1608 Quarto title page) *King Lear* was performed at court.[76] On this day, the poor were entitled to the hospitality and charity of the rich: it was, to borrow Ignatieff's distinction, their due as well as their need. "Stephening" constrained charity, demanded instead of begged it, threatening violence if it were withheld. In this ritualized instance, distribution of the superflux hardly undid excess: it prevented it from becoming undone.[77]

It is not just in *King Lear* that superfluity remains at the top. According to Ferdinand Braudel's extraordinary *Capitalism and Material Life, 1400–1800*, it was not until well into the eighteenth century that luxury ceased to be the exclusive privilege of the rich.[78] For the 400-year span covered by his book, material life at the broad base of society remained essentially the same. Food, drink, houses, clothes, and fashion remained for the masses virtually unchanged for the simple reason that sufficiency made do with what it had.[79] Only at the narrow top where superfluity could afford change was there fluctuation. Sufficiency settled into a static "omnipresent *vis inertiae*," whereas superfluity sought out dynamic variety and change. Once luxury dropped to the lower reaches of society, the *longue durée* of the Ancien Régime ended, and the "fantastic changes" of capitalism were set rapidly afoot. It is Werner Sombart's thesis in *Luxury and Capitalism*, an important work for Braudel, that luxury itself gave rise to capitalism, stimulating production to satisfy desire beyond need.[80] A new ideology of superfluous things then came into being in which surplus (Lear's superflux) was seen to benefit all classes of society, trickling down (instead of spilling over) from the top to raise the standard of living at every level (rather than to level the whole), distribution determined by the mechanistic drives of an "invisible hand" (rather than the charitable handouts of a Lear or Gloucester).

John Sekora provides the long and complex history that leads up to this surprisingly recent tenet in *Luxury: The Concept in Western Thought*.[81] As he shows, until the eighteenth century luxury was condemned as a civic and religious vice rather than commended as an economic stimulus. Until then, it was synonymous with "lechery," both words designating excessive fleshly desire; sometimes it was Lechery, sometimes Luxury, who paraded among the seven deadly sins.[82] Posing a threat to both social hierarchy and the state of the soul, the terms were also interchangeable in sumptuary laws and admonitory sermons. The word decisively split in two during the eighteenth century: while lechery continued to refer to inordinate sexual appetite, luxury, in the context of expanding commercialism, came to designate an excessive appetite for pleasurable goods. It came to designate too the market's commodification of this appetite in the form of pleasurable goods themselves – luxury items. Yet luxury items are hardly Lear's super-fluous things, for the simple reason that they presuppose the very identity that *Lear* makes coextensive with possessions. For individuals (it is now safe to call them that)[83] must *precede* the luxury items through which they project and indulge themselves. If, to return to the opening binaries of this essay, the commodity is an object removed from the subject, then the luxury item is the commodity *par excellence*: both estranged from its producers (who are even less likely to use it than any other product) and expendable to the consumer (who flaunts its expendability by conspicuously consuming it). One might go so far as to say that the luxury item is what the play (as in a dream) fears the superfluous thing will become, without having the historical vantage to know exactly what it is.

What *King Lear* cannot know, however, we know quite well. For we have no trouble conceiving of a self anterior to and independent of objects – constituted in such non-objective realms as biography, language, ideology. What we do not know and what *Lear* knows very well, is how – to deploy a common Renaissance homonym lost to modern pronunciation – what *one* is depends on what one *owns*. How can property be basic – even prior – to personhood?

In several important essays, J. G. A. Pocock has emphasized the long struggle extending well into the eighteenth century to keep the two aligned, to keep what he terms "personality" grounded in changing forms of property.[84] As he points out, in our eagerness to make "liberalism" triumphant, we have allowed Locke's model of autonomy and appropriation too early and too pervasive a sway, largely under the influence of C. B. Macpherson's *The Political Theory of Possessive Individualism*.[85] There is, however, another view of the relation of person to property extending back to Aristotle which Locke far from preempted. According to this classical tradition, "Property was both an extension and a prerequisite of personality."[86] As Pocock points out, this ancient view (a longtime basis for the franchise) was challenged by an increasingly mercantilized society in which stable land was converted to movable and variable money and goods. Yet the real challenge came from the conversion not of immobile to mobile, but of material to immaterial property. From the end of the seventeenth century on, property took on the speculative, even fantastical, form of credit or stock:[87] "Property – the material foundation of both personality and government – had ceased to be real and has become not merely mobile but imaginary."[88] Locke's "possessive individualism" figured as tense alternative to what might be termed "propertied individualism" and the two remained in contest through the eighteenth century.[89]

History has treated what Pocock has demonstrated to have been a strenuous and urgent dialectic as a steady development of only one of its positions. We therefore have lost sight of the long cultural project involved in having to reconceptualize personal identity once its basis in property had begun to shift.[90] Because we live the resolution – understanding ourselves through such dispropertied structures as Freudian childhoods, Lacanian signifiers, Althusserian interpellations – it is hard to imagine both the effort and cost once involved in preparing the way for it. This is precisely what we lose when Renaissance is seen as Early Modern, for – while we are quite sophisticated in our understanding of earlier versions of what we presently are – we have little sense of what the alternatives once might have been.

NOTES

1 On "Burckhardt and the Formation of the Modern Concept," see Wallace
   K. Ferguson, *The Renaissance in Historical Thought: Five Centuries of
   Interpretation* (New York, 1948), ch. 7, pp. 179–94. On Burckhardt's
   frequent substitution of "modern" and "modern man" for "Renaissance"
   and "Renaissance man," see Felix Gilbert, *History: Politics or Culture?
   Reflections on Ranke and Burckhardt* (Princeton, 1990), p. 61. For Marx's
   identification of the sixteenth century with the collapse of feudalism and
   the beginning of modern bourgeois society, see *Manifesto of the Commu-
   nist Party*, in *The Marx–Engels Reader*, ed. Robert C. Tucker (2nd edn.
   New York and London, 1978), pp. 474–5, and *Capital*, pp. 431–5. On the
   relation between Burckhardt and Marx, see William Kerrigan and Gordon
   Braden, *The Idea of the Renaissance* (Baltimore and London, 1989),
   pp. 3–35, and esp. 44–7, and Margaret W. Ferguson, Maureen Quilligan,
   and Nancy J. Vickers, eds., *Rewriting the Renaissance: The Discourses of
   Sexual Difference in Early Modern Europe* (Chicago and London, 1986),
   pp. xvi–xvii.

2 For Burckhardt's antipathy to progressive reform, see Gilbert, *History*,
   pp. 5–6, and David Norbrook, "Life and Death of Renaissance Man,"
   Raritan 8, 4 (1989), 95–7; for Marx's commitment to reform, see Engels's
   "Speech at the Graveside of Karl Marx," in *Reader*, p. 682.

3 Jacob Burckhardt, *The Civilization of the Renaissance in Italy*, trans. Ludwig
   Geiger and Walter Götz (2 vols., New York, 1958), I, p. 143.

4 Kerrigan and Braden discuss Burckhardt's belief that "detachment earns a
   new power over the external world," *Idea*, p. 13.

5 On Alberti's humble origins, see Burckhardt, *Civilization*, I, pp. 148–50; see
   also his praise of the humanist teacher and scholar, Pomponius Laetus,
   pp. 276–8. On the toleration of bastards generally, see pp. 38–40; on the
   benefits of banishment, particularly in relation to Dante, see pp. 145–6.

6 *Meditations on First Philosophy*, in Elizabeth Anscombe and Peter Thomas
   Geach, trans. and eds., *Descartes: Philosophical Writings* (Berkshire, 1986),
   p. 62.

7 Marx, *Capital*, *Reader*, p. 322.

8 Ibid. pp. 319–20.

9 Marx, *Economic and Philosophic Manuscripts of 1844*, *Reader*, p. 72.

10 Burckhardt, *Civilization*, I, p. 229.

11 Marx, *Capital*, *Reader*, p. 328.

12 "We are situated at the close of the cultural movement initiated in the
   Renaissance; the places in which our social and psychological world seem to
   be cracking apart are those structural joints visible when it was first
   constructed," Stephen Greenblatt, *Renaissance Self-Fashioning: from More
   to Shakespeare* (Chicago, 1980), pp. 174–5, quoted by Greenblatt in *Learning
   to Curse: Essays in Early Modern Culture* (New York and London, 1990), p.
   182, n. 4. On how this division marginalizes the Middle Ages, see Lee
   Patterson, "On the Margin: Postmodernism, Ironic History, and Medieval
   Studies," *Speculum: A Journal of Medieval Studies* 65, 1 (1990), 87–108, and
   David Aers, "Rewriting the Middle Ages: Some Suggestions," *The Journal*

of Medieval and Renaissance Studies 18 (1988), 221–40, and *Community, Gender, and Individual Identity: English Writing, 1360–1430* (London, 1988).

13   Jean-Christophe Agnew, *Worlds Apart: The Market and the Theater in Anglo-American Thought, 1550–1750* (Cambridge, 1986), pp. 11–12.

14   *Drama and the Market in the Age of Shakespeare* (Cambridge, 1992), p. 9.

15   Of course, another transaction precedes the audience's payment for a play: the acting company's payment to the playwright(s) for a play, as documented in Henslowe's *Diary*. See Neil Carson, *A Companion to Henslowe's Diary* (Cambridge, 1988), pp. 48, 56–7.

16   On the temptation to make Shakespeare's career correspondent to period divisions, see de Grazia, "Fin de Siècle Renaissance," in Elaine Scarry, ed., *Fins de Siècle: English Poetry in 1590, 1690, 1790, 1890, 1990* (Baltimore and London, 1995), pp. 37–63.

17   For an offsetting of Tillyard's world picture with a cultural materialist dynamic of social process, see Jonathan Dollimore, *Radical Tragedy: Religion, Ideology and Power in the Drama of Shakespeare and his Contemporaries* (Chicago, 1984), pp. 6–8.

18   For two direct applications of Lawrence Stone's *The Crisis of the Aristocracy, 1558–1641* (Oxford, 1965), see Rosalie Colie, "Reason and Need: *King Lear* and the 'Crisis' of the Aristocracy," in R. L. Colie and F. T. Flahiff, eds., *Some Facets of King Lear: Essays in Prismatic Criticism* (Toronto, 1974), pp. 185–219, and Paul Delaney, "King Lear and the Decline of Feudalism," *PMLA* 92 (1977), 429–40. For an earlier treatment of *Lear* as transitional, see John Danby, *Shakespeare's Doctrine of Nature: A Study of "King Lear"* (London, 1951), pp. 18–53, and Marshall McLuhan, *The Gutenberg Galaxy: The Making of Typographic Man* (London, 1962), pp. 11–18.

19   Franco Moretti, "The Great Eclipse: Tragic Form as the Consecration of Sovereignty," in *Signs Taken for Wonders: Essays in the Sociology of Literary Forms*, trans. Susan Fischer, David Forgacs, and David Miller (London, 1983), pp. 42–82, and Stephen Greenblatt, "Shakespeare and the Exorcists," in his *Shakespearean Negotiations: The Circulation of Social Energy in Renaissance England* (Berkeley, 1988), pp. 94–128.

20   Richard Halpern, " 'Historica Passio': *King Lear*'s Fall into Feudalism," in his *The Poetics of Primitive Accumulation: English Renaissance Culture and the Genealogy of Capital* (Ithaca and London, 1991), pp. 215–313, p. 247. Halpern is acutely aware of the problems of reading for a pre-capitalist history and of his own precipitous inclination – "my own book tends to lean forward" – which he counteracts with a genealogical fanning out into "other areas of the social formation – political, cultural, ideological," p. 13. I am much indebted to Halpern's remarkably smart and thoughtful book.

21   Walter Cohen, *Drama of a Nation: Public Theater in Renaissance England and Spain* (Ithaca, 1985), pp. 327–56, p. 345. On Marx's subclass, see Peter Stallybrass, "Marx and Heterogeneity: Thinking the *Lumpenproletariat*," *Representations* 31 (1991), 69–95.

22   Annabel Patterson, " 'What matter who's speaking?' *Hamlet* and *King Lear*," in her *Shakespeare and the Popular Voice* (Cambridge, Mass., 1989), pp. 93–119.

23 "[A]ll isolated or discrete cultural analysis always involves a buried or repressed theory of historical periodization"; Frederic Jameson *Postmodernism, or, The Cultural Logic of Late Capitalism* (Durham, 1991), p. 3. For New Criticism's unvoiced presupposition of history, see Jameson's *Marxism and Form: Twentieth-Century Dialectical Theories of Literature* (Princeton, 1971), pp. 323–4. On the question of dividing history into temporal units, especially the "century," see Daniel S. Milo, *Trahir le temps (Histoire)* (Paris, 1991).

24 See Raymond Williams's important essay, "Dominant, Residual, and Emergent," in his *Marxism and Literature* (Oxford, 1992), pp. 121–7.

25 Foucault, "Nietzsche, Genealogy, History," in *Language, Counter-Memory, Practice*, trans. Donald F. Bouchard and Sherry Simon (Ithaca, 1977), pp. 139–64.

26 Quoted from the facsimile of the 1608 Quarto in *The Complete "King Lear", 1608–1623: Texts and Parallel Texts in Photographic Facsimile*, prepared by Michael Warren (Berkeley, 1989). All subsequent quotes from Shakespeare are from *The Riverside Shakespeare*, gen. ed. G. Blakemore Evans (Boston, 1974).

27 On "train" as "phallus," cut and shortened by his daughters, see Frankie Rubenstein, *A Dictionary of Shakespeare's Sexual Puns and their Significance* (London, 1984).

28 On the maintenance of a liveried retinue by great nobles in the sixteenth century, see Stone, *Crisis*, pp. 201–17. According to Stone, "By the mid-eighteenth century it was generally accepted that 'a livery suit may indeed fitly be called a badge of servility,'" p. 214.

29 For *trappings* and *paraphernalia* as personal belongings, specifically dress, see *OED*.

30 Their symbolic centrality within the play matches their importance outside of it, for the theatrical company itself and for society generally, as Peter Stallybrass argues in "Worn Worlds: Clothes and Identity on the Renaissance Stage," below. Clothes are the basic prop or property of the theatrical company, the attire of the tiring house, its largest investment is vestments.

31 Lear's reference to "unaccommodated man" refers to his nakedness; Edgar's observation upon seeing Lear draped (crowned?) with weeds that a sane man would not so "accommodate" himself also refers to his garb. According to Kenneth Muir, Shakespeare never used the word "in the modern sense," *King Lear*, ed. Kenneth Muir (London, 1985), p. 115, n. III.iv.104–5.

32 For *house*, as "a covering of textile material," see *OED*.

33 For a sharp critique of how Lear posits a need that is both universalized (and therefore egalitarian) and hierarchized (and therefore elitist), see James Kavanagh, "Shakespeare in Ideology," in John Drakakis, ed., *Alternative Shakespeare* (London and New York, 1985), pp. 158–9.

34 "The aims of the attempt to impose state control on dress are more apparent than the effects"; N. B. Harte, "State Control of Dress and Social Change in Pre-Industrial England," in D. C. Coleman and A. H. John, eds., *Trade, Government and Economy in Pre-Industrial England* (London, 1976), p. 143. See also Frank Whigham, *Ambition and Privilege: The Social Tropes of Elizabethan Courtesy Theory* (Berkeley, Los Angeles, London, 1984), pp. 155–69.

35   See the class restrictions on wearing various types of furs in the 1580 Proclamation reproduced by Whigham, that begins with "fur of sables" forbidden to anyone "under the degree of earl." *Ambition*, Fig. 1, pp. 164–5.

36   Her servant Oswald, the issue of cross-breeding (like Edmund), "the son and heir of a mungril bitch" (II.ii.22–3), has the same difficulty recognizing distinctions of blood and breeding, to the outrage of Kent who describes himself as "a gentleman of blood and breeding" (III.i.40). Hence his rebuke to Oswald, "I'll teach thee differences" (I.iv.88–9). For an account of Oswald's status as "a class and sexual *hybrid*," see Halpern, *Accumulation*, pp. 244–5.

37   See Janet Adelman's remarkable reading of Lear's ailment in her book named after it, *Suffocating Mothers: Fantasies of Maternal Origin in Shakespeare's Plays, "Hamlet" to "The Tempest"* (New York and London, 1992), pp. 113–14; pp. 300–1, ns. 27–8.

38   The Quarto reads "century" (a subdivision of a Roman legion) and the Folio "Centery" (often modernized as "sentry"). The two forms work together, suggesting both the number of men (100) dispatched by Cordelia and their function (to guard Lear).

39   I owe the reference to "changing one's copy" and copyhold to Agnew, though he uses it to argue for the capacity of identity to, in effect, forge itself, becoming as ambiguous as falsified copyhold claims. See *Worlds Apart*, p. 58.

40   By saving his father from despair, Edgar also saves his inheritance, for suicide or *felo de se*, like felony of any kind, was punished through the confiscation of property. See Michael MacDonald, *Mystical Bedlam: Madness, Anxiety, and Healing in Seventeenth-Century England* (Cambridge, 1981), pp. 132, 166.

41   Lear's kingdom in this play, like Gloucester's estate, is represented primarily in terms of land, on the model of feudal property law. See Halpern, *Accumulation*, pp. 221–2, 229.

42   For a stunningly informative account of the changes in testamentary practice during Shakespeare's time, their complex dramatization in his plays, and their shocking exploitation in his own will, see Richard Wilson, "A Constant Will to Publish: Shakespeare's Dead Hand," *Will Power: Essays on Shakespearean Authority* (New York, London, Toronto, Sidney, 1993), pp. 184–280. I have also benefited from Katherine Conway's discussion of "dower" and "dowery" as two distinct instruments for transfering property from males to females in her unpublished essay, "Shakespeare's 'Material Girls'."

43   On the fictive nature of this privilege, see Albert Braunmuller's discussion of "Wills and the Crown of England" in his edition of *The Life and Death of King John* (Oxford, 1989), pp. 54–61.

44   *Bedlam*, pp. 128–32.

45   Ibid. p. 130.

46   Halpern also notes Lear's "improvident disposition of his own property" as symptomatic of madness, in *Accumulation*, p. 263.

47   On the histrionics of possessed madmen in Samuel Harsnett's *A Declaration*

of Egregious Impostures and *Lear*, see Greenblatt, "Shakespeare and the Exorcists," *Negotiations*, pp. 94–128.

48 On the elements of pastoral romance in *Lear*, see John Turner, "The Tragic Romances of Feudalism," in Graham Holderness, Nick Potter, and John Turner, eds., *Shakespeare: The Play of History* (Iowa City, 1987), pp. 85–118, and Maynard Mack, *"King Lear" in Our Time* (London, 1966), pp. 63–6.

49 For a characterological reading of Edgar's progression in the role of Poor Tom, see the introduction to Janet Adelman, ed., *Twentieth Century Interpretations of "King Lear"* (Berkeley, 1965), pp. 14–21.

50 On bastards and inheritance, see Alan Macfarlane, "Illegitimacy and Illegitimates in English History," in Peter Laslett, Karla Oosterveen, and Richard M. Smith, eds., *Bastardy and its Comparative History* (London, 1980), pp. 71–85, esp. p. 73.

51 For the class conflict staged by the costard and sword, see Mack, *"Lear" in Our Time*, pp. 53–4. For "the semiotics of execution" that would have been applied to Oswald's death as well as that of Cornwall's servant (stabbed in the back by Regan according to the stage direction in Q1–2, IV.i.80, though simply killed by an anonymous "harmful stroke" in the messenger's report, IV.ii.77), see Stephen Greenblatt, "Murdering Peasants: Status, Genre, and the Representation of Rebellion," in Greenblatt, ed., *Representing the English Renaissance* (Berkeley, 1988), pp. 1–29, p. 11.

52 On fixed land as the paradigm for *Lear's* "Economies of the Zero Sum," see Halpern, *Accumulation*, pp. 251–69.

53 See John Sekora, *Luxury: The Concept in Western Thought, Eden to Smollett* (Baltimore and London, 1977), pp. 46–7.

54 The torch returns in Gloucester's desire for death, a smoldering sexual consummation: "My snuff and loathed part of nature should / Burn itself out" (IV.vi.39–40). On venereal torches and their extinction, see Stephen Booth's prefatory comment to sonnet 153 and his gloss on 153.1, in *Shakespeare's Sonnets* (New Haven, 1977), pp. 533–4.

55 Cornwall's punishment of treason with blinding appears to have no juridical basis. See John H. Langbein's discussion of models of torture in *Torture and the Law of Proof: Europe and England in the Ancien Régime* (Chicago, 1977), p. 67.

56 Adelman identifies the storm with the contaminating dark place of mothers, the rank "sulphurous pit," *Mothers*, pp. 111–14.

57 On the sexual uses of *foot* and *hand*, see Rubenstein, *Dictionary*. See also Gary Taylor's discussion on the Folio's omission of the Quarto's profane and obscene expletive, "Fut," "Monopolies, Show Trials, Disaster, and Invasion: *King Lear* and Censorship," in Gary Taylor and Michael Warren, eds., *The Division of the Kingdoms: Shakespeare's Two Versions of "King Lear"* (Oxford, 1983), pp. 77–8. Compare Katherine's French lesson that involves four repetitions of "Le foot et le count" in *Henry* V, III.iii.51, 52, 56, 59. "Foot" can refer to either female or male genitalia, through its relation to yard (penis) or to "foutre" or fault, a woman's genital crack which is also her moral flaw. See Adelman, *Mothers*, p. 252, n. 26.

58 "A female fishes sandie Roe / With the males jelly newly lev'ned was," Donne, "Progress of the Soul," xxiii, *OED*.

59   Cf. the relation of blindness to castration in psychoanalysis as punishment for Oedipal crime, Sigmund Freud, "The Uncanny," in *The Standard Edition of the Complete Psychological Works of Sigmund Freud*, vol. XVII (London, 1955), p. 231.

60   *Sonnets*, p. 470, n. 2; p. 535, n. 9.

61   On the association of blindness and lechery, see William R. Elton, *"King Lear" and the Gods* (San Marino, Calif., 1966), pp. 111–12, and Adelman, *Mothers*, pp. 295–6, n. 7.

62   On the synonymity of "luxuria," "fornicatio," and "libido" through the Middle Ages, see Morton Bloomfield, *The Seven Deadly Sins* (Michigan, 1952), pp. 64–5, 69, 77. For an image of Lechery spearing a lecher's eye, see Rosemond Tuve, *Allegorical Imagery* (Princeton, 1966), fig. 51.

63   On the difficulty critics have had with Edgar's pronouncement, see Adelman, *Mothers*, pp. 295–6, n. 7.

64   On Gloucester's transformation from man (with stones) to woman (with rings), see Adelman, *Mothers*, p. 107 and p. 297, n. 11.

65   Edgar's generational powers are particularly precious in a play in which dynastic prospects have been blasted through Lear's acts of disowning ("degenerate bastard" [I.iv.254]) and cursing ("Into her womb convey sterility! / Dry up in her the organs of increase," [I.iv.278–9]).

66   See Muir, *Lear*, p. 167, IV.vi.136.

67   Language in this play is similarly inclined to superfluity, matching "the extremity of the sky" (III.iv.102) by pressuring its own extremities: with superlatives and super-superlatives (Tom in an earlier life "out-paramoor'd the Turk" [III.iv.91]), Oswald's offense of superserviceability or superfinicality, Lear's superannuation ("the very verge/Of his confine" [II.v.147–8]) and with pejor-pejoratives ("the basest and most poorest," [II.iii.6–7] "the worst is not / So long as we can say, 'This is the worst'" [IV.i.27–8]). These locutions extend the superflux, pushing beyond the reaches of language, out-topping extremes, beginning with Regan's outdistancing of her eldest sister's superlatives; the base Bastard's resolve to "[top] th'legitimate" (I.ii.21); Edgar's exceeding the account of his father's death – "Twixt two extremes of passion" (V.iii.199) – with another sorrow, which "To amplify too much, would make much more, /And top extremity" (V.iii.207–8); Lear's body stretching out longer than the rack; the play itself finding a way to outlast even "the promis'd end" (V.iii.264). The history of *Lear's* reception indicates that the play itself goes to extremes, pushing beyond the bounds of tragedy, particularly in its superfluous addition of Cordelia's death (not in the sources), an extreme that drove Tate to his uplifting revisions.

68   For the significance of the play's having been first performed (according to the 1608 Quarto title page) at court on St. Stephen's or Boxing Day, a day on which the rich were expected to extend themselves to the poor, see Leah S. Marcus, *Puzzling Shakespeare: Local Reading and its Discontents* (Berkeley, Los Angeles, London, 1988), pp. 148–56.

69   On the substitution of god-relations for blood-relations, see David Sabean, "Aspects of Kinship Behavior and Property in Rural Western Europe before 1800," in Laslett, Oosterveen, and Smith, *Bastardy*, pp. 248–95.

70   On *Lear* and doomsday, see Joseph Wittreich, *"Image of that Horror":*

History, Prophecy, and Apocalypse in "King Lear" (San Marino, Calif., 1984). On the relation between "the desire of the poor to improve the material conditions of their lives" and Apocalypse in Medieval and Reformation Europe, see Norman Cohn, *The Pursuit of the Millennium* (New York, 1961), p. xiii.

71 Cf. Halpern: "The utopian strain, like the lightning that is its counterpoint, flashes briefly in the night of the play and is then swallowed up – along, one assumes, with the concept of need that founded it," *Accumulation*, p. 261.

72 Cf. the *base* Bastard's intention to *top* the legitimate. Cf. too Gloucester's *defects* proving *commodities*.

73 In the face of the impossibility of such computations, Jean Baudrillard has argued that "the 'vital anthropological' minimum does not exist." The level of survival is determined not by any essential human need perceptible at the bottom but rather by surplus expenditure from the top. "In other words, there are only needs because the system needs them." *For a Critique of the Political Economy of the Sign*, trans. Charles Levin (St. Louis, Mo., 1981), pp. 80, 82.

74 I owe my awareness of this fallacious logic to a painting by Peter Golfinopoulos, "The Poor Have Never Lived Well."

75 Michael Ignatieff, *The Needs of Strangers* (New York, 1986), p. 35.

76 I draw here on Leah S. Marcus's account of the play's liturgical context in *Puzzling Shakespeare*, pp. 148–59.

77 For an anthropological account of the complex strategies of giving to retain, see Annette B. Weiner, *Inalienable Possessions: The Paradox of Keeping-While-Giving* (Berkeley, Los Angeles, Oxford, 1992).

78 Trans. Miriam Kochan (New York, Cambridge, 1973). See especially Braudel's two chapters on "Superfluity and Sufficiency," chs. 3 and 4, pp. 121–91. See also Braudel, *The Structures of Everyday Life: The Limits of the Possible*, trans. Sian Reynolds (London, 1981), pp. 183–333.

79 On the tendency of pre-Industrial-Age workmen to work only to relieve want in an economic system that offered no incentives to work for more, see Edgar S. Furniss, *The Position of the Laborer in a System of Nationalism* (Boston, 1920), p. 234, and D. C. Coleman, "Labour in the English Economy of the 17th Century," *Economic History Review* 2nd series, 8 (1956), 289–95.

80 Trans. W. R. Dittmar (Michigan, 1967).

81 Sekora, *Luxury*, cited in n. 53.

82 Ibid. pp. 46–7.

83 On the mid seventeenth-century emergence of this word in its present sense, see Peter Stallybrass, "Shakespeare, the Individual, and the Text," in Larry Grossberg, Cary Nelson, and Paula A. Treichler, eds., *Cultural Studies: Now and in the Future* (New York and London, 1992), pp. 593–612.

84 See especially "Authority and Property: The Question of Liberal Origins" and "The Mobility of Property and the Rise of Eighteenth-century Sociology," in *Virtue, Commerce, and History: Essays on Political Thought and History, Chiefly in the Eighteenth Century* (Cambridge, 1985), pp. 51–71 and pp. 103–23; "Early Modern Capitalism – the Augustan Perception," in Eugene Kamenka and R. S. Neale, eds., *Feudalism, Capitalism, and Beyond*

(London, 1975), pp. 62–83; "Neo-Machiavellian Political Economy; the Augustan Debate over Land, Trade and Credit," in *The Machiavellian Moment: Florentine Political Thought and the Atlantic Republican Tradition* (Princeton, 1975), pp. 423–61.

85   C. B. Macpherson, *The Political Theory of Possessive Individualism: Hobbes to Locke* (Oxford, 1962). For Pocock's critique of Macpherson, see *Virtue*, pp. 60–71.

86   *Virtue*, p. 103.

87   On the relation of fiscal and fictional credit and their unsettling effect on personal identity, see Sandra Sherman, *Finance and Fictionality in the Early Eighteenth Century* (Cambridge, forthcoming).

88   *Virtue*, p. 112.

89   "[T]here is no greater and no commoner mistake in the history of social thought than to suppose the tension [between the two relations of property to personality] ever disappeared," ibid. p. 122.

90   For the insight that "property" gives way to "psyche" after the Renaissance, I owe a long-standing debt to Stephen Greenblatt's "Psychoanalysis and Renaissance Culture," in Patricia Parker and David Quint, eds., *Literary Theory/Renaissance Texts* (Baltimore, 1986), pp. 210–24.

2 "Rude mechanicals"

Patricia Parker

My title is taken from the sneering reference made by Puck in Shakespeare's *A Midsummer Night's Dream* – to the

> crew of patches, rude mechanicals,
> That work for bread upon Athenian stalls,
>
> (III.ii.9–10)

artisans who, as he encounters them in the Athenian woods, are rehearsing the play they are finally chosen to perform before their aristocratic audience in Act V. The reference – as recent critics of the *Dream* remind us – is joltingly topical, inserting "mechanicals" reminiscent of contemporary craftsmen and artisans into the "antique" and aristocratic worlds of Greek mythology and old romance, of Theseus and Oberon.[1] This crew of "patches" includes a carpenter, a weaver, a tinker, a joiner, a bellows-maker, and a tailor (Starveling) whose name evokes the conditions of such "mechanicals" in the decade of the play, introducing hints of the social disruptions associated with weavers and other artisans in the 1590s into what might otherwise appear the timeless "airy nothing" of a "Dream."[2] What I want to do by beginning with these "rude mechanicals" – artisans often either omitted from serious discussion of the play or included with only condescending reference to their bumblings – is to suggest the work they perform, so to speak, within a "dream" that is also traditionally a central Shakespearean "marriage play."[3] To do this, I propose to focus first on the implications of Puck's derogatory epithet and then on the craft of "joinery" represented by one of its player–artisans (the Joiner called "Snug"), as well as more generally by the involvement of all of its "mechanicals" in some form of joining or construction.

"Rude" in its connotations in Early Modern English was already a derogatory term of class distinction, available for contemptuous reference such as the one uttered by Puck, servant to an aristocrat. Within the Shakespeare canon, the term is used with the sense of "ungentle, violent,

43

harsh, rugged" (*OED*), in the "rude uncivill touch" of the "ruffian" in *Two Gentlemen of Verona*, for instance, or the "rough, rude and wildly" of *The Comedy of Errors* (V.i.88). In the sense of "uncivil", it was both opposed and a threat to the civil or civilized, a synonym for the barbarian· or barbaric – the "rude hands" of the "Welshman" in *Henry IV Part I* (I.i.41), the "rude and savage man of Ind" in *Love's Labor's Lost* (IV.iii.218), or the description (and self-description) of Othello as an "erring barbarian" (I.iii.355), "rude" in his "speech" (I.iii.81). Beyond Shakespeare, it is the term for the Irish disciplined by English rule in Hooker's *History of Ireland* ("The rude people he framed to a civilitie & their maners he reformed and brought to the English order").[4] In its sense (from Latin) of "unwrought, unformed, inexperienced," and hence by extension "uneducated, unlearned; ignorant; lacking in knowledge or booklearning,"[5] "rude" also brought with it connotations of something shapeless and needing to be formed – as in King John's

> Set a form upon that indigest
> Which he hath left so shapeless and so rude,
>
> (*King John*, V.vii.27)

lines whose "indigest" (lost in this sense to modern ears) conveys precisely that which needs to be formed, ordered, or "digested" in the sense of submitted to a ruling disposition or ordering. Hence the easy analogy between the "rude" as formless or unshaped material and the political (and class) sense of the "rude" as that which must be governed or ruled – the "rude misgovern'd hands" of *Richard II* (V.ii.5), for example, or the repeated "rude companion," "rude unpolished hinds," and

> ragged multitude
> Of hinds and peasants, rude and merciless
>
> (*2HVI*, IV.iv.32–3)

in the scenes of the rebellion of Jack Cade in Shakespeare's histories.[6]

As a term for the unshaped and unrefined, as well as the ungoverned or ungovernable, "rude" was thus a term linking the unruliness of unshaped *materia* (or "nature") to the lexicon of class distinction. In hierarchical terms, it was the opposite of the aristocratic or gentle as well as of the orderly – as the scenes of the Cade rebellion make clear in their polarities of high and low ("If one so rude and of so mean condition / May pass into the presence of a king," *Henry VI, Part II*), V.i.64–5). In the sense of untutored or unschooled, the term also appears in the "rude multitude" of the "unletter'd" which the social-climbing "bookmen" of *Love's Labor's Lost* are determined to be "singuled" or distinguished from (V.i.81–90), the "unletter'd, rude and shallow" companions of the riotous Hal (*Henry V*, I.i.55), and, beyond Shakespeare, the distinction that Cromwell earlier calls on between "a rude and unlerned person" and a "lerned & experte one."[7] Shakespeare himself, of course – a playwright risen from the ranks of players and artisans – was not just the "upstart crow" but the "rude groom" of Greene's contemptuous description.[8]

"Mechanical" – the second part of Puck's derogatory epithet – was explicitly a term for artisan, one who worked with the material, manual labor, or the work of the "hand" (Shakespeare's "mechanicals" are also described as "Hard-handed men that work in Athens here, / Which never labored in their minds till now"). The "Handie-crafte called Arte *Mechanicall*," in one fifteenth-century definition, was dependent on the "crafte" of the "hand," and hence on the hierarchical division into parts of both body and body politic (in Palsgrave, in the 1530s, "joiner's work" was specifically defined as *menuserie*). Gower's *Confessio Amantis* – a text bodied forth on the Shakespearean stage in *Pericles* – wrote

> Of hem that ben Artificiers,
> Which usen craftes and mestiers,
> Whose Art is cleped *Mechanique*.
>
> (Bk.VII.1691–3)

The "mechanical" – from the earliest English definitions – was connected with the constructed and artifactual in ways that distinguished it as well from the spontaneous or "natural." (It appears, for example, as the labored opposite of both in Antony's refusal of "more mechanic complement" in *Antony and Cleopatra*, IV.iv.32.) In the vertical hierarchy of mind as separated, or "singuled," from matter and the material – a hierarchy inextricably bound up with distinctions of class in Renaissance Neoplatonism – the "mechanical" in Elizabethan culture also designated not only the practical as opposed to the contemplative but more generally an association with the material, the disordered "matter" or *silva* identified in that Neoplatonism with the woods outside Athens, woods that play a signal role in the disordered middle of *A Midsummer Night's Dream*.[9]

As a term of class distinction, the "mechanicall" – like the "rude" already linked with the shapeless and unformed – was thus distinguished from the "gentle," or that proper to "gentles," well into the seventeenth century; Peacham's *Compleat Gentleman* counselled its readers, for example, to avoid "Painting in Oyle" as "mechanique." Donne described "work ... that belongs to the hand, to write, to carve, to play" as belonging to the "mechanique office." Writing itself was distinguished, as a "mechanic" art, from the sphere of the "Gentleman" as late as Etheredge's *Man of Mode* ("Writing, Madam's, a Mechanick part of

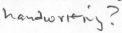
handwriting?

Witt!"). (On the continent, in the period before the *Dream*, it represented for aspiring aristocrats like Montaigne a form of base "mechanics" contrasted with the naturalness and *sprezzatura* of the aristocratic, as described in the influential pages of Castiglione's *Courtier*.)[10]

With "rude," then, the "mechanical" was a familiar term of class distinction in the culture contemporary .with Shakespeare, one used repeatedly as a term of contempt – in Angell Day's reference to "A servant, meanly trained in some Mechanicall Science," in Randle Cotgrave's definition of "Mechanicalized" as "base, vile, ordinarie, meane," or in John Marston's disgust at "each mechanick slave, / Each dunghill pesant."[11] As a term synonymous with the "mean," "vulgar," and unlettered, the "mechanical" – like the "rude" – was associated with the material as something placed at the bottom of a hierarchy, to be governed or ruled.[12] That it was therefore also a term associated with threats to that hierarchy may be readily surmised from references like the one recorded in 1589 to a contemporary topsy-turvydom (or in the current phrase, "preposterous" inversion) in which "mechanicall and men of base condition doo dare to censure the dooings of them, of whose acts they be not worthie to talk," or the fear in another text, from 1606, of the conflation of the "natural" hierarchies of class, that "Princes" themselves will be turned into "mechanistes and artificers."[13]

References to "mechanicals" in Shakespeare are thus most often the embodiment of a distinct class voice, tied to the attempt to "singulate" or distinguish high from low – in York's "Base dunghill villain and mechanical" in *Henry VI, Part II* (I.iii.193); in Falstaff's put-down of the burgher Ford as a "mechanical salt-butter rogue" (*The Merry Wives of Windsor*, II.ii.278); in Coriolanus's

> Do not bid me
> Dismiss my soldiers, or capitulate
> Again with Rome's mechanics;
>
> (*Coriolanus* V.iii.81–3)

in Pistol's reference to a "most mechanical and dirty hand" (*Henry IV, Part II*, V.v.36); or in the rhetoric of degree presented as a "rule in nature" (188) by the Archbishop of Canterbury at the beginning of *Henry V* (I.ii.183–220), in the politically motivated speech that moves from "kings" and "magistrates" to "masons," "civil citizens," and "poor mechanic porters" as part of its urging of the harmonious working of "many" to "one consent" in preparation for the strategic distraction of war in France, a harmony and oneness the next scene's rebellion shows to be far from the actuality of an England rife with rival claims to a "natural" (as distinct from "forged" or constructed) genealogy of descent.

There is also, finally, in Shakespeare the famously anachronistic reference at the beginning of *Julius Caesar* to the Elizabethan laws regulating the movements of artisans and "mechanicals," when Flavius's

> Is this a holiday? What, know you not,
> Being *mechanical*, you ought not walk
> Upon a laboring day without the sign
> Of your profession?
>
> (I.i.2–5)

introduces into that play's antique Roman setting another topical reminder of artisans or "mechanics" and their government.[14] Both players and "mechanics" are linked in Cleopatra's fear that

> Mechanic slaves
> With greasy aprons, rules and hammers shall
> Uplift us to the view. In their thick breaths,
> Rank of gross diet, shall we be enclouded,
> And forc'd to drink their vapor,
>
> (*Antony and Cleopatra*, V.ii.209–13)

as well as in the Egyptian queen's temporally preposterous prophecy that her greatness will be made familiar by "comedians" upon the Elizabethan stage:

> The quick comedians
> Extemporally will stage us, and present
> Our Alexandrian revels: Antony
> Shall be brought drunken forth, and I shall see
> Some squeaking Cleopatra boy my greatness
> I' th'posture of a whore.
>
> (V.ii.216–21)

Theatrical mimicry here is linked with a representation that makes greatness (as Stephen Orgel reminds us) "familiar" – but also with such representation as a form, in every sense, of *mechanical* reproduction.[15]

We need to remember, of course, in approaching both these lines from *Antony and Cleopatra* and the "rude mechanicals" whose play-within-a-play similarly mimics the passions of the aristocrats in *A Midsummer Night's Dream*, that players themselves – culled from the ranks of joiners, weavers, and other artisans – were not only ranged "i' the statute" with vagrants and vagabonds, as the bricklayer's stepson Ben Jonson put it in *Poetaster*, but were also classed among the "mechanicall artes" as distinguished from the ranks of gentlemen in texts such as Ferne's *Blazon of Gentrie* (1586).[16] In contemporary class terms, therefore, the elevation of successful players to the status of "gentlemen born" (as in the hierarchically preposterous case of Shakespeare the "rude groom") involved undermining the professed "naturall" order of lineage and birth through the construction of genealogies that were by contrast crafted or "made" (as Sir Thomas Smith noted in his remarks in *De republica anglorum* on "gentlemen made ... cheape in England"). In the atmosphere of the period described by Lawrence Stone and others, and reflected in contemporary complaints against the elevation of "nobodies" such as that of the herald of York who named "Shakespear ye Player by Garter" among such rude upstarts, the dependence of place and distinction not on the "natural" but on the artificial or "made" introduced the unsettling possibility that degree, hierarchy, and place were themselves less a product of "nature" than forged or fabricated constructions.[17]

The "rude mechanicals" of Shakespeare's *Dream* are associated, then, not just with the artisanal at the bottom (in a dyadic formation) of the social hierarchy (a "Bottom" reflected in the name of its principal player–artisan), but with the material or *materia* as the formless to be both shaped and ruled. In this respect, their inclusion in this play of "shaping fantasies" (V.i.5) – to use the term that furnished the title of the now classic essay by Louis Montrose[18] – begs the question of their relationship to things that might otherwise appear to have nothing to do with this mechanic "crew," with the play's Neoplatonic (and Neoaristotelian) language, for example, or its gendering. But they are also associated explicitly with "joinery" and "joining" in particular, in ways that suggest links between the artisanal, material or artifactual and the joinings in matrimony that form its close.

Let us begin, then, with one of the most telling of Shakespearean evocations of artisanal "joinery." In Act III of *As You Like It*, in a scene charged with resonances for *A Midsummer Night's Dream*, Audrey and Touchstone come together to be joined in what is clearly a suspect matrimony: "This fellow will but join you together as they join wainscot," warns the melancholy Jaques, "then one of you will prove a shrunk panel, and like green timber warp, warp" (III.iii.86–9). "Joining in matrimony" is here identified with "joining" in the strikingly material form of the craft of the joiner, the craft evoked both here and in the character of Snug the Joiner in *A Midsummer Night's Dream*. There is more to be said, however, of "joining" in this scene of marital conjunction from *As You Like It*, apart from the failed phallicism of its "shrinking" rather than (more snugly) "fitting." For the character who is to "couple" – or join in matrimony – Audrey and Touchstone bears the name "Sir Oliver Martext," a name that suggests not only the marrying which in the familiar Shakespearean pun is already marring (as in *Much Ado*), but, more concretely, the marring of a *text*, and hence yet another kind of botching or misjoining.[19] "Joinery," then, in this apparently marginal scene from *As You Like It*, begins to suggest more than the merely minor comic interest of an improper coupling and to forge links between joining (or misjoining) in matrimony, the material constructions of the artisan joiner, and what may seem to modern sensibilities the completely unrelated sphere of the deforming of a text or improper joining of words.

The intersection of such apparently disparate spheres in the wordplay on "joinery" in this scene from *As You Like It* has at its base, then, the artisanal craft of the joiner who fits parts together into a material object. The craft of joinery in the period was a specialized form of fine carpentry – an "Art Manual" (as one Early Modern description put it) "whereby several Pieces of Wood are so fitted and joyned together by straight Lines, Squares, Miters, or any Bevel, that they shall seem one intire Piece"[20] – a "seeming" (as well as seaming or "seam") to which we will return in relation to the botched joinings associated with the "mechanicals" of *A Midsummer Night's Dream*. The joiner, then, was the artisan whose skill it was to construct through "joinery." It is this particular artisan, for example, who crafted joint-stools, the lowly material object used as representative of kingship and justice respectively, in *Henry IV, Part I* and *King Lear*.[21] But the labor of joining, as the *Dream* reminds us through its other "mechanicals," was also the task of an entire range of artisans. (The mason, to cite just one possible instance, was associated with the "jointer," a tool "used for filling with Mortar or for marking the joints between courses of brick or stone.")

"Joinery," however, with other artisanal crafts that consisted in the joining or "fitting" together of parts (into an object, edifice, or other material construction) was also routinely employed in the period as the figure for other kinds of joining, a metaphorical "translation" or extension that made this material craft the basis for a whole range of other conjunctions – from the joining of words into the constructions of reason, logic, and "Syntaxe" (understood as that "part of Grammar, that teacheth the true joyning of words together") to the joining of bodies into the one flesh of marriage and the joining of the body politic into a harmonious whole. In the first context, the syntactical art of "ioyning" was crucial to what Richard Mulcaster's *Elementarie* punningly called "Right Writing." It is this aligning of "writing" and "righting" that Shakespeare exploits, at the end of *Twelfth Night*, and in the wordplay on "their writers do them wrong" (II.ii.350) in *Hamlet*, a play that has to do with a crucial joining (or misjoining) in matrimony, with the "jointress" to a "union," and with the carefully forged joinings of Claudius's succession speech.[22] The proper "ioyning" of words and sentences – in examples too numerous to cite fully here – was thus, in the period contemporary with Shakespeare's *Dream*, the foundation of the construction of order not only in grammar, rhetoric, and logic but also in the social and political hierarchy their ordering reflected. Richard Sherry, for example, counselled in *A Treatise of Schemes and Tropes* (1550), one of the earliest vernacular treatises, that "not only must we chose apte, and mete wordes, but also take heed of placinge, and settinge them in order," since "the myghte and power of eloquucion consisteth in wordes considered by them selves, and when they be ioyned together," a passage that then proceeds to treat of the "naturall order" of discourse that places "men" before "women."[23] His descriptions of words "conveniently coupled" and "ioyned together" have their counterparts in handbooks of writing – or manuals for the hand – which taught (as Jonathan Goldberg, Stephanie Jed, and others remind us) the joining of letters, or cursive script, and in the multitude of textbooks, like John Brinsley's *Ludus Literarius* (1612), that – in an era of incipient literacy and emergent humanist discipline – move from the "dividing" and "ioyning" of syllables to the joining of words and sentences that formed the foundation not only of order in discourse but of "Order" more generally.[24]

Descriptions such as Sherry's of joining in discourse – with their emphasis on what may, and may not, properly be joined – also, however, echo with uncanny closeness the language of joining from the Ceremony of Matrimony in the *Book of Common Prayer* (1549). Similarly, early English humanist texts such as Thomas Wilson's *Rule of Reason* (1551), in their descriptions of the proper "knittyng of woordes," of "partes" properly "coupled," and the rules concerning "what wordes maie be truely ioined together," not only recall the strictures on what may be "lawfully joined" or "knit" from the Ceremony of Matrimony but also resemble the language of union, harmony, and the "knitting" of matrimony summoned, for example, by Theseus in *A Midsummer Night's Dream*.[25] As in Wilson or other such texts, the *Dream* combines proper joining in matrimony and joining in discourse, both subject to laws or rules, with counterinstances of suspect, aberrant or improper joining. And it does so in ways that suggest links between the chronic misplacing and misjoining of words or sentences associated with the so-called "rude mechanicals" and the larger issue of joining in this "marriage" play, including the proper joining of "Jack" and "Jill" that produces its culminating (and consummating) close.

The material craft of joinery also stands in this period, finally, as a figure for unions of other kinds, including the mystical "Copula" of

Christ as the basis of both matrimonial conjoining and Christian *communitas*. (A *Homily* of 1547 – employing precisely this artisanal figure – counsels that "We cannot be *ioynted* to Christ our Head, except we be glued with concord and charitie one to another.").[26] In all of the senses of "joinery" in this contemporary semantic network, the figure of the artisan joiner brings together the joining of pieces of wood into an object, the union of marriage and body politic, and the "right writing" of order in discourse, a joining which texts such as Sherry's or Wilson's instructed their readers can also be botched or marred by improper couplings, just as the generational "right writing" of sanctioned matrimony was shadowed by unlawful joinings (including same-sex couplings) which influential works such as Alain de Lille's *Complaint of Nature* excoriated as both "unnatural" and "ungrammatical."[27]

Such metaphorical extension or "translation" of the material craft of joining was also, it needs to be emphasized, part of the appropriation of the crafts of "mechanicals" in contexts that treat of artisans themselves as in need of governance. Sir Thomas Smith's already-cited *De republica anglorum*, for example (a text that presents itself to the "gentle Reader" as the "honorable ... travaile" of "an expert workemaister"), begins its discussion of "Governement" with elaboration on what it means to rule – not initially in the sense of domination or political governance (a sense that appears in this text only later and secondarily), but rather by reference to the artisan's or carpenter's "rule," the tool that "is alway to be understoode to be straight," the instrument "to which all workes be to be conformed."[28] It then moves from the "right rule whereby the Artificer and Architect doe judge the straightnesse of everyie workemans worke" to the ruler of a commonwealth, or its "governement," as that "part or member ... which doth controwle, correct [the 1583 edition also has "and direct"] all other members of the commonwealth." When, therefore, Smith comes to the section of his text that has to do with those who use such instruments, they themselves are classed under "The Fourth Sort of Men Which *Doe Not Rule*" – "day labourers, poore husbandmen, yea marchantes or retailers which have no free lande, copiholders, all artificers, as Taylers, Shoomakers, Carpenters, Brickmakers, Bricklayers, Masons, & c.," who "have no voice nor authoritie in our common wealth, and no account is made of them but *onelie to be ruled, not to rule ...*"

Puttenham, similarly, in *The Arte of English Poesie*, is concerned not only to employ the artisanal metaphor but also to insist on critical differences between its artisanal base and its translative extensions, to compare the poet with, but also to distinguish him from, the artificer. In Book III ("Of Ornament") he insists that

> it is not altogether with him as with the crafts man, nor altogether otherwise then with the crafts man, for in that he useth his metricall proportions by appointed and harmonicall measures and distaunces, he is like the Carpenter or Ioyner, for borrowing their tymber and stuffe of nature, they appoint and order it by art otherwise then nature would doe, and worke effects in apparance contrary to hers. ... But for that in our maker or Poet, which restes onely in devise and issues from an excellent sharpe and quick invention, holpen by a cleare and bright phantasie and imagination, he is not as the painter to counterfaite the naturall by the like effects and not the same, nor as the gardiner aiding nature to worke both the same and the like, nor as the Carpenter to worke effectes utterly unlike, but even as nature her selfe working by her owne peculiar vertue and proper instinct and not by example or meditation or exercise as all other artificers do, is then *most admired when he is most naturall and least artificiall.*[29]

Thomas Wilson's *Rule of Reason* – the first introduction into English of Greek or Athenian "Logicke" and the text from which Quince's mispunctuated Prologue derives in Act V of *A Midsummer Night's Dream* – exploits in its very title the doubled meanings of "rule" in the artisanal as well as political sense. Elsewhere, Wilson draws on another influential early text on the crafts of various "mechanicals" in "order" to describe the necessary order of both cosmos and realm:

> By an order Realmes stande, and lawes take force. Yea by an order the whole worke of nature and the perfite state of all the elementes have their appointed course. By an order we devise, we learne, and frame our dooynges to good purpose. By an order the Carpenter hath his Squyre, his Rule, and his Plummet. The Tailour his mette Yarde, & his measure: the Mason his Forme, and his Plaine, and every one accordyng to his callyng frameth thynges thereafter. For though matter be had, and that in greate plentie: yet al is to no purpose, if an order be not used. As for example: What availeth Stoone, if Masons doe not worke it: What good dothe clothe, if Tailours take no measure, or do not cutte it out: Though Tymber be had for makying a Shippe, and al other thynges necessarie, yet the shippe shal never be perfite, till worke men begynne to set to their handes, and ioyne it together. In what a comenly order hath God made man, whose shape is not thought perfite, if any parte be altered: yea al folke would take hym for a monster, whose feete should occupie the place of his handes. An army never getteth victorie, that is not in araie and sette in good order of battail. So an Oration hath litle force with it, and doth smally profite, which is utterde without all order. And needes must he wander, that knowes not howe to goe, neither can he otherwyse chouse, but stumble: that gropyng in the darke, can not tel where he is ... [30]

All in this description of the necessity of "order" – by the author of a text on the "rule" of "Reason" – has to do with a shaping of "matter" or the material, the forming of the formless or "rude." Once again, the entire passage is striking in its resonances for *A Midsummer Night's Dream*, where "rude mechanicals" misjoin body parts ("I see a voice! . . . / To spy and I can hear my Thisby's face," V.i.192–3), where Bottom's body is monstrously joined to the head of an ass, and where lovers disjoined in the interlude in the woods outside Athens finally wander, grope, and stumble in the dark, unable to find their way before the play, returning to Athens and Theseus, makes its "Ende."

We have already seen "mechanics" and a straightening "rule" linked in the corpus of Shakespeare, in Cleopatra's scorn of "Mechanic slaves / With greasy aprons, rules and hammers" or in the topical reference to "mechanicals" at the beginning of *Julius Caesar*, a group that includes a "carpenter" and his "rule" (I.i.6–7). There may even be a punning reference to the carpenter's *gnomon* ("a rule, a square or squire to know any thing by," as Florio defined it) in the resonances of *nomen* and "no man" in lines that characterize the Joiner of *A Midsummer Night's Dream*. The "gnomon" in the metaphorical sense of "canon" or "rule" was repeatedly used for "ruling" in the political sense, just as in texts like Smith's *De republica anglorum* or Wilson's *Rule*, artisanal metaphors permeate discussions of the governance of a realm.[31] We might recall Spenser's recourse to the metaphorics of building or construction in the "goodly Frame" of Temperance, in the first book (II) to treat explicitly of governance in *The Faerie Queene*; the contemporary sense of "framing" or fashioning that depends on education understood as "edification"; or, in Renaissance Neoplatonism, the figure of the artifex or laboring *Demiourgos* who fashions the cosmos itself. Yet in class terms, this labor is appropriated as a series of metaphors "translated" to a higher purpose, leaving the artisanal behind, firmly subordinated at the bottom of a hierarchy.

Let us return, then, from the metaphorics of joinery in the period contemporary with the play – and the associations of an artisanal "rule" with the forming, shaping, or ruling of the *materia* – to the joinings and misjoinings associated with "rude mechanicals" in *A Midsummer Night's Dream*, traditionally both a Shakespearean "marriage" play and a celebration of civil order and cosmic harmony by its end. The Ceremony of Holy Matrimony from *The Book of Common Prayer* repeatedly emphasizes not only conjunctive union or joining – with the prohibition "Those whom God hath joined together let no man put asunder" – but also, as earlier remarked, what may and may not "lawfully be joined." And, as has long been recognized, its language is echoed repeatedly throughout the *Dream*, from the opening anticipation of Theseus' "nuptial hour" to the joinings in matrimony that produce its conventionally hierarchical close. When, however, the language of this Ceremony is most explicitly recalled within the play, in Helena's reproach to Hermia in Act III ("And will you rent our ancient love asunder / To join with men in scorning your poor friend?," III.ii.215–16), the echo is sounded not for a sanctioned joining but rather for a couple that cannot lawfully be joined – female to female (or in the theatrical context it shares with *As You Like It*, transvestite boy to transvestite boy), a misjoining that would contravene what, in authorities such as Alain de Lille, are not only the laws of God and nature but the "right writing" of grammar and discourse.

The echo, then, is itself curiously disjunctive, simultaneously recalling the foundational text of matrimony on what may be "lawfully" joined but shifting it to the context of an unlawful coupling – the "unnatural" counterpart of the misjoinings of words that Sherry, Wilson, and the rest inveigh against in their formulation of rules for the correction of the "rude." Botchings or misjoinings of words, however (with other kinds of misjoining), are precisely what the "rude mechanicals" enact repeatedly throughout *A Midsummer Night's Dream*, just as their attempt to "disfigure or present" (III.i.60–1) the "lamentable tragedy" of Pyramus and Thisbe before their aristocratic audience disjoins or dismantles the elements of otherwise naturalized theatrical illusion. What I want to suggest in what follows is that there is an intimate relation between their laying bare of the joints and seams of theatrical spectacle (their determined materializing of it, for example, into the actual production on stage of Moonshine or Wall) and their repeated disfiguring or deforming of what Theseus, the play's representative ruler, calls the ordered "chain" of discourse (V.i.125–6), an order explicitly linked with "government" (124). I then want to suggest links between their suspect "joinery" and the ending of this "marriage" play, with its conventional joinings in matrimony of "Jack" to "Jill," an "Ende" (to use Wilson's term) that re-rights the unlawful joinings and misjoinings of the play's disordered middle in the woods, beyond the walls of the civic and civil.

All of the *Dream*'s "rude mechanicals" are, first of all, not only connected with forms of material joining or construction but furnished with names that suggest their erotic counterparts. Snug the Joiner, the artisan who (paradoxically) plays the sundering or rending Lion, who "deflowers" Thisbe and who insists (in the passage that plays on gnomon, *nomen*, and no man) that he is "a man as other men are" (III.i.43–6), evokes that "fit" or snug joinery which (as in *As You Like It*) links sexual fitting or joining with joining in carpentry. Bottom the Weaver – homophonically "Wiver" – recalls in his name the phallic shape of the "bottom" or core on which a weaver's yarn was wound, as well as the weaving of generation in which the couples of this marriage play are finally "knit" (IV.i.181). Francis Flute the Bellows-mender combines the "Flute" that is slang for the male member, the "belly" linked etymologically with "bellow," and the suggestions of the sexually liberal or promiscuous in "Francis" or "frank." Snout the Tinker (the artisan who plays both Wall and "Wall's hole," V.i.121) evokes bawdy jests about the tinker who serves maids to "stop up their holes"; and a similar phallic suggestiveness surrounds the carpenter "Peter" Quince, whose last name also recalls the wedge-shaped "quines" or "quoins" used for building "houses." Starveling the Tailor, whose craft evokes "tails," is linked to the joke about the gossip who falls on her back and cries "tailor" (II.i.51–7), and his thinness, it is suggested, explains why, within this predominantly phallic mode of naming, he takes only female parts.[32] *well, that was certainly a stretch.*

All of the so-called "rude mechanicals," then, are associated by their names and trades with erotic counterparts to joining and fitting. As Thomas Clayton and others have pointed out, moreover, the double- (or multiple-) meaning sexual references associated both with these players and with the "chink" and "hole" of their play-within-a-play also ambiguously evades the homo/hetero divide, suggesting (ungrammatically) neither an exclusively heterosexual reference nor any single bodily orifice. It is therefore appropriate that when Peter Quince assigns the roles for the play or "show" they are to perform before their superiors, he instructs the artisan–players as follows – "masters, here are your parts, and I am to entreat you, request you, and desire you to con them by tomorrow night" (I.ii.99–101) – lines whose ambiguous "parts," in proximity to "con," suggest the conning of "parts" both dramatic *and* sexual, a link repeated in the description of this show as "conn'd with cruel pain" (V.i.80) and the sexual (and class) overtones of "to do you service" (81).[33]

Appropriately for a tale which in the Ovidian source of their play-within-a-play is told by weavers, the mechanicals' production of Pyramus and Thisbe comes to its end with references to the Weaver Fates, who extend but finally terminate the "thread" of life (V.i.336–41). The name of the weaver "Bottom" in particular links him directly with this translated sense of weaving, since the "bottoms of thread" long acknowledged to be behind his name also served in the period as the familiar material figure for precisely such an extending or spinning out of discourse, "skeins or bottoms of thread, to be unwinded at large," as Francis Bacon, for example, put it in his description of the dilation or amplification of discourse, with its attendant danger of tedious prolixity.[34] The mechanicals' own tediously amplified play (V.i.56, 251) –

which has repeated attention called to its extension – comes to its end
both with reference to the Weaver Fates and with the promise (recalling
the departure of its artisanal "Wall") that "the wall is down that parted
their fathers" (337–8), in ways that link the amplification of the entire
play before its final punctuating end or "point" (and the phallicism of
the "nuptial hour" impatiently anticipated by Theseus, whose wooing
was accomplished by his "sword," I.i.16),[35] with the artisanal craft of
weaving.

The "rude mechanicals" of the *Dream*, then, bear names and trades
simultaneously suggestive of the artisanal and of the bodily, as well as of
the weaving and joining of words. But they also, in their botchings and
misjoinings, provide continual parodic mimicry of the mechanics of what
Theseus (echoing the language of the textbooks) terms the ordered
"chain" of words (V.i.125). In the scene of the artisans' play-within-a-
play, where (out of fear that they will be hanged, "every mother's son,"
I.ii.78) they expose the machinery of theatrical "show," explicit attention
is called to their links with the construction of discourse when Demetrius
the aristocrat remarks, of the Wall played by the tinker Snout, that it is
the "wittiest partition" he has ever "heard discourse" (V.i.166–7), a term
that links this "sensible" (182) artisan "Wall" to the tradition of verbal
"partition."[36]

Demetrius's remark, then, links this bodily *and* material Wall (with
its double-meaning "stones" and "chink") to the tradition of discursive
"partition" as the ordered division of a discourse. But each of the
scenes of the *Dream* in which these "rude mechanicals" appear calls
attention, by contrast, to their deforming or scrambling of proper
"partition" as well as their disruption of proper "ioynyng" and
division into "parts." The first scene in which they appear is shot
through with parodic evocation of the familiar contemporary prescrip-
tions for ordering and disposition. When Quince the Carpenter asks
"Is *all* our company here?" (I.ii.1), Bottom the Weaver advises "You
were best to call them generally [apparent malapropism for "severally"
or "individually"], according to the scrip" (2–3), and proceeds to
lecture his artisan–director on the proper ordering of his address
("*First*, good Peter Quince, say what the play treats on; *then* read the
names of the actors; and *so grow to a point*," 8–10). The individual
players then "spread" themselves (15) and the company is divided into
"parts." In the casting scene in Act I, Bottom wants to play all the
parts at once, and has to be ruled by his carpenter–director. In the
rehearsal scene in Act III, Thisbe/Flute speaks "all his part at once,
cues and all" (94–5), as if it were one continuous unpunctuated line or

sentence, joining what should be kept apart. And finally, in the scene of
their performance in Act V, Quince delivers the disjointed Prologue
based on the example of misjoining from Wilson's *Rule* and, by missing
the proper punctuation or "pointing" (118), severs what should be
joined and joins what he should not, in the process disfiguring an
ostensible compliment to the aristocrats into its opposite.[37]

The "rude mechanicals" of this play, then, join what should not be
joined and partition or sever what might otherwise be united. But, in
addition to the ways in which their performance of the play of
Pyramus and Thisbe provides a distanced (and distancing) mimicry of
what transpires in the larger aristocratic plot, their repeated botching
of proper joining and construction has even broader implications for
this "marriage" play, viewed, so to speak, from the "bottom" up.
There is much in the play itself that encourages looking at both
Theseus' order and the end over which he presides from the "bottom"
or underneath, as from the perspective of the misjoinings of these
"rude mechanicals." The radical scriptural echoes that surround the
dream of Bottom himself already provide a subversive perspective on
the civic order associated with Theseus, Athenian ruler of the play, by
echoing (as well as marring) a text that contrasts the wisdom of the
"low" to the more limited comprehension, and "reason," of Athens
and the "rulers of this world." The echo ironizes, before the fact,
Theseus' own speech on "cool reason" and what it "comprehends"
(V.i.6) – when Bottom, awakening from his dream, echoes a text that
calls into question the temporal hierarchies of rule, and abandons the
attempt at an orderly or comprehending discourse ("No more words.
Away!" IV.i.42):

Man is but an ass if he go about to expound this dream. Methought I was – there
is no man can tell what. Methought I was – and methought I had – but man is
but a patched fool if he will offer to say what methought I had. The eye of man
hath not heard, the ear of man hath not seen, man's hand is not able to taste, his
tongue to conceive, nor his heart to report, what my dream was. I will get Peter
Quince to write a ballad of this dream: it shall be called 'Bottom's Dream,'
because it hath no bottom; and I will sing it in the latter end of a play, before the
Duke. Peradventure, to make it more gracious, I shall sing it at her death.
(IV.i.205–17)

Critics of the *Dream* have long recognized that Bottom's words on
awakening from his dream are a scrambling of 1 Corinthians 2 on a
"mystery" beyond the "wisdom" of the "rulers" of this world and that
"Bottom" the "ass" sees more of the bottomless "bottom of Goddes
secretes" (Geneva 1557 version) than the play's Athenian ruler who seeks
to establish a bottom to things, to "comprehend" and control what is

beyond his wisdom.[38] In fact, the subversive scriptural echoing in
Bottom's awakening goes much further here, to echo as well the Athens
that fails to credit what it takes as "strange things" (Acts 17) and the
Bottom-like *raptus* and vision of 2 Corinthians 12. The latter evokes
another "translation" ("Bless thee, Bottom ... thou art translated,"
III.i.118–19) into a realm of "unspeakable words, which it is not lawful
for a man to utter" (2 Cor. 12.4), together with a similarly stammering
inability to put this vision into any kind of orderly discourse. If the
"mechanical" in the period was distinguished from the contemplative, it
is – in this play's "preposterous" unsettling of this hierarchy – the
"mechanical" Bottom (not the "ruler" Theseus) whose vision recalls the
scriptural instance *par excellence* of visionary experience, the rapture or
raptus of St. Paul that no word is adequate to describe. Theseus' order,
like his "wisdom," is revealed in its limitation, then, by the juxtaposition
of the scene of Bottom's awakening with this Greek ruler's signature
speech on "cool reason" and rejection of "visions" (V.i.2–22). But this
juxtaposition also imports into the play the possibility of a broader
ironizing of Theseus' order within *A Midsummer Night's Dream*, and of
his "comprehension" in the sense of containment and control.

   The mispointed Prologue of Quince the Carpenter in Act V transforms
an ostensible compliment to the artisans' aristocratic audience into its
opposite – echoing the famous instance from Udall's *Merrygreek* disseminated through Wilson's *Rule of Reason* as an example of misjoining.
It does so in the context of a play set in Athens (source of the "Reason"
or logic that Wilson and other upwardly mobile English humanists
sought to import into England, but also site of the "wisdom" undercut
by a lowlier "folly" in the passage from Corinthians) and through an
apparently unintentional botching by another merry Greek. It also,
however, echoes the "points" or "periods in the midst of sentences" from
an earlier passage in the play, the appropriation or "comprehension" by
Theseus, one of the "rulers of this world," of the similarly apparently
bumbling inarticulateness of his subjects as certain sign of their service to
him:

> Where I have come, great clerks have purposed
> To greet me with premeditated welcomes;
> Where I have seen them shiver and look pale,
> *Make periods in the midst of sentences*,
> Throttle their practis'd accent in their fears,
> And, in conclusion, dumbly have broke off,
> Not paying me a welcome. Trust me, sweet,
> Out of this silence yet I pick'd a welcome,
> And in the modesty of fearful duty

I read as much as from the rattling tongue
Of saucy and audacious eloquence.
Love, therefore, and tongue-tied simplicity
In least speak most, to my capacity.

(V.i.93–105)

The lines convey, as Louis Montrose points out, more than this Athenian ruler, or an earlier generation of Theseus-centered critics of the play, comprehend, with implications for the artisan–players' bumbling "interlude" this same ruler claims to be able to "amend" (V.i.209).[39] Punctuation or "pointing" is itself a matter of proper severing and joining: as famous contemporary instances attested, it could radically transform a message by altering what was joined with what. By its misplacing of "periods" or endpoints, the mispointed Prologue of the carpenter Quince (recalling the negative example in Wilson's *Rule*) manages to deform or mangle an ostensible compliment to *his* ruler, and aristocratic audience, by such misjoining. It does so, moreover, in ways that link the disruption by these "rude mechanicals" of the ordered "chain" of discourse to the ironizing of the play's own culminating "period," "point," or end.

Let us turn, then, from this subversive mispointing to the relation between the misjoinings repeatedly associated with the play's "mechanicals" and the "righting" of the improper joinings of its disordered middle by the orthodox couplings that enable its ending as an apparently conventional "marriage" play. We have already noted that the treatment of the abuses of proper joining in *The Rule of Reason* – as in other such texts – involves terms highly evocative when placed beside the play on "joining" and "partition" in *A Midsummer Night's Dream*. The first of the disorderings treated by Wilson – "the iognyng of woordes that should be parted" – involves the kind of misjoining that the artisans' garbled language constantly commits. The second – the "dividing of thinges, whiche should be ioigned together ... or elles a dissevering of twoo partes, which should be but one" (p.169) recalls the severing "Wall" that, in their play of Pyramus and Thisbe, enacts a separation or sundering of what might otherwise be joined. But beyond this, the mechanicals' aberrant "iogning" of what cannot be "ioigned together" (as in the strictures of texts like Wilson's that recall the Ceremony of Matrimony) also has implications for the aberrant joinings associated with the play's disordered middle (where, as Puck puts it, things turn out "preposterously," III.ii.121), before that final closural "ende" or "point" – from the temporary sundering and misjoining of lovers to the misjoining of Bottom's body to the head of an ass, and this "ass's" erotic as well as hierarchically preposterous union with a Queen.

Puck's term for this interim of disorder ("preposterously") makes
explicit the links between the scrambling of the ordered "chain" of
discourse to which the scenes of the "mechanicals" call sustained attention, the "unnatural" reversals of hierarchy in this middle, and the forms
of "righting" exercised by the return to Athens and the conventional
class and marital joinings of its end. For "preposterous" itself was the
familiar term not just for disorders in discourse but also for "arsy-versy"
reversals of hierarchy like that which in the play's "midsummer" interval
elevates or translates Bottom the "ass," as indeed for all inversions
understood in the period as "unnaturall."[40] Contemporary discussions of
the "naturall and seemely order" of discourse routinely described as
"preposterous" (or by the disorderly figure of *hysteron proteron*) what
they called "Faults opposed to natural & necessary order" and hence
"consisting in disorder and confusion" – confusions involving, in class
and gender terms, placing "Mistresse" before "Master," lower before
higher, or "Counsell" before "King."[41] "Preposterous" verbal and social
disordering is joined, in such discussions of proper joining and "meete
placing of words," by figures like the one Puttenham translated as "the
Changeling" or the figure of "Exchange" (from Greek *Hypallage*).[42] And
both have their counterparts in the *Dream*'s interim of disorder in the
woods where things turn out "preposterously" (III.ii.121) – where maids
pursue men as if the story of Apollo and Daphne were reversed (II.i.231),
where Bottom the artisan is consort to a Queen, and where a rebellious
Titania temporarily overrules her husband and lord. The figure of
"exchange" is embodied in the play's literal "changeling" boy who forms
the hinge of the plot of Titania's preposterous rebellion against Oberon's
rule, a link with verbal exchanges made even more explicit by Puttenham's direct invocation of the changeling of English faery lore in his
description of the rhetorical figure which "using a wrong construction
for a right, and an absurd for a sensible, by manner of exchange"
similarly changes the proper places of words. Hypallage – or the figure of
"exchange" – is the kind of verbal scrambling the "rude mechanicals" of
the *Dream* routinely commit, changes of place "whereby the sense is
quite perverted and made very absurd." Yet – like the "changeling" boy
– it also might stand for all of what is exchanged or changes place in the
play's disordered middle,[43] where Helena gets unwelcome fulfillment of
her wish to be "translated" to Hermia (I.i.191), where the "translated"
(III.i.114) Bottom becomes a substitute for that changeling, and where
(in ways that subvert the sovereignty of individuality and agency) the
aristocratic lovers themselves are both transported and exchanged, as if
they were less independent characters than movable, substitutable units
or terms.

The telos or end of marriage itself as the orthodox form of "coupling" is also opposed in this play's disordered middle by the possibility of the "misjoining" (or, in Wilson's terms, "ioigning together of those things which should be dissevered") of Helena and Hermia. Lysander's plea to be allowed to share "one bed" with Hermia in the wood ("One heart, one bed, two bosoms, and one troth," II.ii.42) echoes the Ceremony of Matrimony in its "two" made "one." Yet the language of the marriage ceremony is even more clearly echoed, as we have said, in Helena's complaint against Hermia's desertion of *their* former oneness:

> Injurious Hermia! Most ungrateful maid!
> Have you conspir'd, have you with these contriv'd,
> To bait me with this foul derision?
> Is all the counsel that we two have shar'd,
> The sisters' vows, the hours that we have spent
> When we have chid the hasty-footed time
> For parting us – Or, is all forgot?
> All school-days' friendship, childhood innocence?
> We, Hermia, like two artificial gods,
> Have with our needles created both one flower,
> Both on one sampler, sitting on one cushion,
> Both warbling of one song, both in one key,
> As if our hands, our sides, voices and minds,
> Had been incorporate. So we grew together,
> Like to a double cherry, seeming parted,
> But yet an union in partition,
> Two lovely berries moulded on one stem;
> So, with two seeming bodies, but one heart;
> Two of the first, like coats in heraldry,
> Due but to one, and crowned with one crest.
> And will you rent our ancient love asunder
> To join with men in scorning your poor friend?
>
> (III.ii.195–216)

The language of "joining" pervades this evocation of the "union in partition" of female and female – in Helena's "but you must join in souls to mock me too?" (III.ii.150), "now I perceive they have conjoin'd all three" (III.ii.193), and repeated "two" made "one." But Helena's "Will you rent our ancient love asunder, / To join with *men* in scorning your poor friend?" (III.ii.215–16) – echoing "Those whome God hath joyned together: let no man put asunder" from the Ceremony of Matrimony – shifts that Ceremony's generic "man" to specific "men" in a way that alters the authoritative text itself, applying it to a female "union" disrupted by "men" (216). Helena's speech unmistakably recalls the instance of such female coupling from Lyly's *Gallathea* (one of the *Dream*'s long-acknowledged sources), and behind it a different Ovidian subtext, not the male–female love of Pyramus and Thisbe but the story of Iphis and Ianthe widely disseminated in the Renaissance as an emblem of such forbidden love before its own heterosexual "righting" or correction (a story repeated, however, as titillating narrative, in such influential texts as the epics of Boiardo and Ariosto or the Bradamante-Malecasta episode of Spenser's *Faerie Queene*, and available in the period, as John Boswell has demonstrated, as the familiar classical instance of a forbidden "lesbian" coupling).[44]

This female–female coupling has, at least until recently, been given shorter shrift in criticism than other (including erotic) aspects of the play.[45] Yet Helena's speech – as passionate, Valerie Traub has rightly maintained, as anything in this erotically charged play – introduces into its disordered middle a reminder of an unorthodox gynoerotic or same-sex joining (or mis-joining) that not only manages to evoke, even as it appropriates, the dominant language of *male* friendship but also forges links with the Amazonian past (and exclusively female community) already represented by the history of Hippolyta as the play begins.[46] Both are represented in the play as something superseded, already in the past and overcome. Yet both stand nevertheless (along with the *sotto voce* witness of the theater's own transvestite context) as examples of potential joinings divergent from (and "sundered" by) the orthodox joinings sanctioned by the "point" of this comedy's conventionally consummating end, with its coupling only of that which can "lawfully" be "ioyned," the properly heterosexual joining of "Jack" and "Jill" crudely formulated by the servant Puck who acts as its instrumental agent ("Jack shall have Jill; / Nought shall go ill; / The man shall have his mare again, and all shall be well," III.ii.453ff).

The impassioned speech of Helena in the woods also invokes the work of artificers ("like two artificial gods") and the crafting of a material object ("Have with our needles created both one flower, / Both on one sampler, sitting on one cushion"), this time (like the Weaver Fates or weavers who tell the story the artisan–players perform) a product of *female* craft, though in class terms different from the handicraft of the artisanal.[47] And it summons explicitly – in its

> coats in heraldry,
> Due but to one, and crowned with one crest
>
> (III.ii.213–14)

– the very patriarchal emblem of the joining of houses in which women themselves normatively functioned as objects of exchange, a reminder in the middle of the apparent "airy nothing" of this ostensibly insubstantial *Dream*, of the reality of the heterosexual joinings in matrimony that were also, primarily, transfers of property, here translated to a different, and unsanctioned, union.

We have remarked the sense of "rude" as formless or unshaped and of the artisan or "mechanical" as a craftsman associated with the shaping, forming, and "ruling" of the material, though not with other forms of "rule" (in the sense, for example, that the figures of Carpenter, Mason, and other artisans appear in the text of the social-climbing Wilson, author of *The Rule of Reason*). Yet the *materia* or material to be formed and shaped has also (in the Neoplatonic and Neoaristotelian traditions so influential for the language of the *Dream*) a long-standing association with the "matter" of the female as something to be shaped, formed, and ruled. What needs, then, to be underscored in a reading attentive to the complex intersections and subordinations of class *and* gender within this play (a "rude" or shapeless *materia* associated with "mechanics" unable to "rule" and the ruling of the unruly "matter" of woman within it) is that this language of shaping and governing pervaded both contemporary discussions of hierarchy or rank and treatments of the "naturall" subordination of female to male. The use in the *Dream* of an explicitly Neoplatonic language – and its shaping *Demiourgos* – is introduced early on in the evocation of the patriarchal power of the father Egeus to "dispose" of his daughter Hermia ("As she is mine, I may dispose of her," I.i.142) and its confirmation by the "ruler" Theseus:

> One that composd your beauties, yea, and one
> To whom you are but as a form in wax
> By him imprinted, and within his power
> To leave the figure or disfigure it.
>
> (I.i.48–51)

The Neoplatonic language of the "figure in wax," as of printing or imprinting shades, here, in Theseus' restatement, into the language of male parthenogenesis, of reproduction without the detour, or error, of the feminine. Montrose and others point to the exclusion of mothers from this opening scene, dominated by Theseus and by paternal concerns.[48] Yet the language of Theseus' speech and its counsel on the figuring and disfiguring of daughters is joined in the play by the Neoaristotelian language surrounding the play's one extended description of the matter of a mother. This is the pregnant votaress of Titania whose "issue" is the changeling Indian boy, who becomes the issue in the contest between Oberon's rule and the rebellion of Titania, the play's principal unruly female:

His mother was a vot'ress of my order;
And in the spiced Indian air, by night,
Full often hath she gossip'd by my side;
And sat with me on Neptune's yellow sands,
Marking th'embarked traders on the flood:
When we have laugh'd to see the sails conceive
And grow big-bellied with the wanton wind;
Which she, with pretty and with swimming gait,
Following (her womb then rich with my young squire)
Would imitate, and sail upon the land
To fetch me trifles, and return again
As from a voyage rich with merchandise.
But she, being mortal, of that boy did die;
And for her sake do I rear up her boy;
And for her sake I will not part with him.

(II.i.123–37)

The passage presents (once again, in retrospect) a female-centered world reminiscent of the Amazons, a world, in C. L. Barber's words, of "women who gossip alone, apart from men and feeling now no need of them."[49] It also, as Margo Hendricks has recently demonstrated (eliciting the dimension of empire and race generally missing from discussions of the *Dream*), does so in the context of a passage that elides "female *and* geographic fecundity," a feminine eroticism with an exotic India, a conflation facilitated more broadly within the play by the traditional association of such orientalism with the Athens already linked with the conquest of Amazons and of a feminized East.[50] In relation to Oberon's dominion, it evokes as well, however, a more contemporary empire, topically adumbrated by Oberon's reference in this same scene to an "imperial" (Western and English) rather than Eastern or Indian "vot'ress" (II.i.163) and the hints in this earlier passage of the voyages, trade, and "trifles" of English mercantile exchange. The two forms of ruling or dominion are linked in the description of female fertility here as the dominant Aristotelian one in which the pregnant mother herself is a vessel "rich with merchandise," the father the formal or efficient cause, the mother or matrix simply the "material," just as its implicit patriarchal and imperial counterpart is the eventual appropriation of this commodiousness by the passing of the "changeling" Indian boy into Oberon's control.[51]

The passage materializes, into the language of "vessels" associated both with a passive female bearing and with this expanding dominion, the familiar Aristotelian language of the female as formless "matter" or material, as well as object of exchange. What is important again, however, for the links forged within the play between such shaping, ruling, and dominion and the presence within it (not literally, as in *Love's Labor's Lost*, of a "rude and savage man of Inde" but) of "rude mechanicals" associated with both the material and the formless is that the Aristotelian tradition of generation itself employed, for this male shaping and ruling, the artisanal metaphorics of the "builder" of a "house": "The seede [of the male] is the efficient beginning of the childe, as the builder is the efficient cause of the house ... the seede of the man doth *dispose* and prepare the seede of the woman to receive the forme, perfection, or soule."[52] It is even more important, moreover, for the joinings and eventual "rightings" that bring closural form to the disordered middle of *A Midsummer Night's Dream*, that the informing male is here described as "disposing" this female matter or material, the patriarchal counterpart of the tradition of discursive ordering or "righting" in which (as in the passage from Wilson) a plentiful material or "matter" must submit to the "work man," and the proper "disposition and apte orderyng of thynges." "Disposition," as I have argued extensively elsewhere, connects the patriarchal control of a formless, shapeless, and potentially unruly female "matter" to the ruling (and proper joining) of words in discourse, their ordering and shaping so as to "grow to a point" or (in Wilson's words) to reach a *telos* or "Ende." It is the term as well for the taming of unruly wives, for the obedient wife "*framed* after the special *disposition* of her husband."[53] The "issue" of the pregnant Indian votaress – vessel "rich with merchandise" – is finally (in a "frame" not unlike Spenser's) surrendered to Oberon's dominion in a progression both patriarchal and imperial, part of the "shaping fantasy" of rule.

The disposing or disposition of a passive or unruly female "matter," then, like the ruling of the "rude" or the extending of "governement" and dominion, is the counterpart in the period contemporary with Shakespeare's *Dream* of the disposing and ordered joining of words in discourse, what Spenser (in the book that erects this "frame" of governance) called "Words, well dispost" (*The Faerie Queene*), II.viii.26). Hierarchy or class becomes the dominant division of the play's final act and "Wall," as the formerly unruly young women are silenced as wives and the aristocratic audience speaks with condescension or contempt of the unrefined artisans' production. But the "rude mechanicals" of Shakespeare's play – by their constant disruption of proper joining and disposition and by their inverse association, as artisans, with the appropriated metaphors of "rule" – also provide a perspective within the play from which to view this closural disposition and its "righting" as a frame that is itself constructed rather than cosmic or "naturall," a shaping or "figuring" that claims the prerogative to amend, or correct, both errant

oh
sentence!

females and the artisans' apparently innocently "disfigured" production,
just as their insistence on laying bare the mechanics of theatrical illusion
(on exposing the means of its construction rather than producing the
seamless or naturalized) calls attention, both within and beyond the play,
to the production of other illusions and spectacles, including the theatrics
of power itself.

To focus, then, on the emphasis on the mechanical and constructed, as
on misplaced "points," introduced into the play – and its apparent
concluding civil and cosmic harmony – by so-called "rude mechanicals"
is to give these artisanal figures a central role in the ironizing of the *telos*,
end or final "point" of the play, itself an ending in which it is also
virtually impossible to know where to place the final or definitive
consummating "period."[54] The harmonious ending of Shakespeare's
Dream – as much of more recent criticism of it has demonstrated – is
already ironized by its more negative reminders of Theseus' own more
varied history and of the sequel to this particular joining in matrimony
that haunt Oberon's final blessing of its "issue," as well as by the rustic
"bergomask" performed there by these artisan–players, in contrast to the
cosmic harmony figured by the newly fashionable dances of the court
elites.[55] The ironic perspective on conventional closure already demonstrated by the unconventional "Jack hath not Jill" of *Love's Labour's
Lost* (V.ii) or Sly's unconsummated desire for the transvestite page of
The Taming of the Shrew, shadows the structures of "growing to a point"
through which *A Midsummer Night's Dream* accomplishes its own
apparent period. "Joining" itself was one of the contemporary terms for
closure or ending.[56] But the disjunctions and parodic deformations
committed by characters dismissed by their superiors as "rude mechanicals" opens this play's own ending to the seaming (as well as seeming) of
the

> parted eye
> When everything seems double,
>
> (IV.i.189–90)

exposing its more conventional joinings to be the *exercise* of closure, the
mechanical production whose "rule" brings about its sanctioned matrimonial end.

Instead, then, of what certain strains of early New Historicism
represented as Shakespearean identification with the strategies and
closural procedures of containment, the mis-joinings and botched constructions of the so-called "rude mechanicals" throughout the *Dream*
make possible a double (and more detached) perspective on the profes-
sedly "natural" order of this ending, an estrangement that allows such

closure to be viewed as the naturalized "righting" that enables the very conjunctions on which "rule" and "governance" depend.[57] The proclaimed order and harmony of this *Dream*'s end involves, I would argue, something like Frank Whigham's sense of the contradictions inherent in the representation of aristocratic *sprezzatura* as spontaneous and "natural" when, like the professed "natural" order of discourse, it was offered as a product for reproduction, mastery of whose rudiments (cognate of "rude") was part of the construction of new elites whose power depended not just on this edification but on concealing its joints and seams.[58] To focus on such "mechanics" in a play as apparently insubstantial as *A Midsummer Night's Dream* might itself seem to constitute a form of rudeness, mechanical in the extreme. (Who, among contemporary audiences or readers, for example, even notices that the scene in Act I that introduces Bottom and the other artisans involves an extended parody of the very Athenian legacy of reason, logic, and ordering that its Athenian ruler later evokes through the image of the ordered "chain"?) There may seem as well to be an incommensurability between "mechanics" and "dream" – though not for a generation brought up on Freudian dreamwork and its linguistic counterparts, on the graphism of the mystic writing pad, or on Lacanian notions of the unconscious as structured like a language. To underline the sense of "mechanical reproduction" – in every sense – that the artisan–players introduce into the play is to produce a very different view of Shakespeare's *Dream* from the insubstantial "airy nothing" of Romantic readings (the legacy, say, of Hazlitt and Lamb), or the anachronistic assumptions of subjectivity and agency belied by the transportability, and translatability, of its characters and terms.[59]

To place such an emphasis on "mechanical reproduction" in the *Dream* is to see in it too something of what is conveyed, elsewhere in Shakespeare, in the mechanical iterations of the Henriad or in the burgherly context of *The Merry Wives of Windsor*, a play whose own "green world" (with its evocations of more antique custom) is overlaid with multiple reminders of replication and iteration, of the mechanics of printing, books, and other forms of reproduction. The Copula itself, we might remark, is strikingly materialized in *Merry Wives*, where the traditional conjoining or "atonement" associated with the "Host" is displaced into verbal and corporeal fragments that confuse "sentences" and "senses" or make "fritters of English." The "translation" of Bottom – his transporting to another realm – is there echoed in the material grounding of such transports in the more burgherly play's reminders that the activity of "construing" or translating was itself a form of "construction." Its own explicit scene of humanist edification – tutoring in the prescribed pedagogical form of the translation of words (IV.i) – has its counterpart in Falstaff's project to "construe" and "translate" the "familiar style" of the wife he intends to draw into a profitable adultery, in scenes that link adultery with another kind of edification ("a fair house built on another man's ground"), as with a mistaken erection, an evocation of the material senses of "translation" or bearing away that not only involves simultaneously words, goods, and burgher wives but raises in each the problem of "reproduction."[60]

To focus on the work done within and beyond the *Dream* by the joining and sundering performed by "rude mechanicals" is to be able, finally, to move beyond this single Shakespearean play to the exploitation more generally in Shakespeare of a pervasive semantic network of joints and seams, as well as the issue of a "seeming" dependent on disguising as "natural" that which is constructed or forged. *Hamlet* foregrounds this naturalized forgery most tellingly, perhaps, in the "forged process" (in early modern English, "narrative") that enables the joinings and sequiturs of Claudius's succession (I.v.37), a narrative "forged" in the sense of both constructed and falsified, one related both to other "forgeries" (II.i.20) within the play and to the Polonian rhetoric of a succession as natural as that "night" follows "day" (I.iii.79). Yet even the earliest Shakespearean histories – read by an earlier generation of historicists as a dramatic endorsement of Tudor apologetics – repeatedly expose the language of "lineal" or "natural" succession as the product not of nature but of the joinings and genealogies forged by the workings of "smooth discourse" (*3H6*, III.iii.88).

Preoccupation with "joining" is everywhere in Shakespeare, from the "twain" made "one" of *The Phoenix and the Turtle* (a "union" by which both "Reason" and "Property" are "appalled") to the explorations of the implications of "one flesh" in the contortions of Adriana's complaint in *The Comedy of Errors* that her husband, as her "flesh," communicates his "harlotries" to her, or the syllogistic logic through which Hamlet concludes Claudius, his incestuous uncle, to be his "mother." The foregrounding of the copula in its rhetorical as well as sexual and material sense extends in Shakespeare to the materializing of verbal joins that produces the stage habitation of *Twelfth Night* out of the single performative "This *is* Illyria." Exploitation of the dramatic implications of what may not be "joined" in the orthodox (or "natural") sense informs the inconsummate conclusion of Sly's overtures to the transvestite page of *Shrew*, the ending of *Merry Wives* where characters anticipating a heterosexually consummating end find themselves mated instead with boys, or the closural ambiguities of *Twelfth Night*, which ends not

[margin handwritten note: Sure, drag Hamlet in.]

only with "mutual joinder of your hands" (V.i.156–61) but with a count betrothed to a still cross-dressed boy. Fascination with unorthodox or unlawful joinings informs the language of the go-between in Iago's urging of Cassio to entreat Desdemona (herself a transvestite boy) to "splinter" the "broken *joint* between you and her husband" (*Othello*, I.ii.328) or the simultaneous repulsion and obsession with "monstrous" couplings that feed the fantasies of the offstage union of human and bestial, white and black, Venetian virgin and "thick-lips" Moor. In *As You Like It*, the suspect joinery of Audrey and Touchstone leads as well to the set of conditionals by which Rosalind/Ganymede prepares for the joining of the "country copulatives" and the notorious Folio text where "Hymen" pronounces not "thou mighst join *her* hand with his" but "thou mightest ioyne *his* hand with his."[61]

Harping on "joints" and "joins" also appears elsewhere in Shakespeare in contexts linked explicitly to the constitution of the "frame" of government, as well as of body politic and degree, in ways that call attention to the simultaneously material and bodily junctures of such constructions. Where the language of order and degree (or the harmony of the "joint and several") is most manifestly a rhetorical production – in *Troilus and Cressida*, for example, in the speech of Ulysses that appeals to the "unity and *married calm* of states" (I.iii.100) – the language of joining is replayed on both sides of the scene as the *reductio ad absurdum* of discursive or logical division, in Achilles' butchers' assessment of his Trojan counterpart ("thee, Hector, quoted joint by joint"), the division of Troilus that renders him a "minced man," or the description of Ajax as having "joints of everything but every thing out of joint" (I.ii.28), bloated bodily emblem of the bloated "matter" of the war as of a disjointed body politic, in a play that (like *Hamlet*) issues from a period rife with controversies over union and succession.

The changes rung on "joinery" in the Martext scene of *As You Like It*, or in the deformations of the "rude mechanicals" of *A Midsummer Night's Dream*, also beg to be set beside the encomiastic language of "conjunction" in Shakespeare's two tetralogies of histories. The rhetoric of Hall's *Union of the Two Noble Families of Lancaster and York*, for example, is of movement from division to unity, from the sundering and civil discord of the Wars of the Roses to the Tudor peace effected by the joining in matrimony of Richmond and Elizabeth, presented as each family's "indubitate heir." And it calls on the entire contemporary hierarchy of such conjunctions, from the Copula by which "man was joined to God" to the "union of man and woman in the holy sacrament of matrimony," the "conjunction of matrimony, celebrate and consummate" between the two houses that replaces the history of "discord" by

the "concord" and "harmony" of Tudor succession.[62] Such providenti-
alist language – presenting Richmond's victory over Richard III as the
apocalyptic "point" or period of this history – was of course commonplace in Tudor writing. But Shakespeare's staging of this rhetoric in the
context of dramatic histories that preposterously rearrange the order of
the Tudor chronicles undoes the sense of culminating conjunction and
hence the *telos* or "end" on which the structure of a providential line
itself depends. Richmond's speech at the end of *Richard III* transcribes
out of Hall the "fair conjunction" (V.v.20) and the simultaneously
marital and political joining of "divided York and Lancaster" (*R3*,
V.v.27) that underwrites both this apocalyptic rhetoric and the presentation of Richmond and Elizabeth (whom "God's fair ordinance" does
"conjoin together," 31) as the "true succeeders of each royal house" (30).
But in the hinge between the two preposterously ordered tetralogies, in
which *Richard III* leads directly (and achronologically) into the beginning
of the history of discord in *Richard II*, the speech not only looks forward
to this renewed sundering but backward within *Richard III* itself to the
cobbled rhetoric of "lineal true-derived course" (III.vii.130–6, 197–200)
in Buckingham's oratorical urging of Richard's shaky claim to England's
throne and its implications for the fragilely constructed claim of the
Tudors themselves to be lineally and hence "naturally" derived, rather
than successors of a line patently forged by political expediency.[63]

The rhetoric of Tudor power itself, then, is a rhetoric that depends
crucially on "joining" but one whose joints have already been exposed by
the forgings of "smooth discourse" in Buckingham's oratory and by
Richard's farcical exploitation of the expedient basis of genealogical
succession. Reading the Tudor rhetoric of divine "joining" and "conjunction" through the "joinery" of *As You Like It* or *A Midsummer
Night's Dream* suggests, then, the possibility not just of a radically
different reading of the rhetoric of cosmic, political, and marital union
delivered by the "mechanic" player who plays the future Henry VII, but
a perspective on the rhetoric of "natural" succession within the histories
as a whole, including the "joining" and "joints" to come in the second
series – the "fester'd joint" (V.iii.85) and "weary joints" (V.iii.105) of
Richard II or the concern over whether "all our joints are whole" (*1H4*,
IV.i.83) and the "fever-weaken'd joints" (*2H4* I.i.140) of both body and
body politic in the plays of the usurper Bolingbroke. The mispunctuating
or mispointing committed by the "rude mechanicals" of *A Midsummer
Night's Dream* also suggests implications for the problem of governing
historical punctuation or ends in the finale to the entire series of
Shakespearean histories, the attempt by Henry V to establish a frame of
definitive beginning and end around his rule, an attempt at closure and

"point" undone by the links that join his reign and exemplary humanist history with its more unsettling after and before, as by the temporally "preposterous" reminder at its close of the son whose succeeding failures had already preceded his father's triumphs on the stage. Instead, then, of the apocalyptic "point" celebrated in the Lancastrian or Tudor chronicles of this Henry, the undoing of the triumphant closure of *Henry V* by its joining with an Epilogue that extends beyond his history also subverts this ruler's "shaping fantasies," shifting the syntax and Aristotelian closure of what might otherwise appear a dramatic version of Hall's *Victorious Acts of Henry V* into a very different punctuation or pointing, one that imports subversive reminders (or "edification" of a different kind) from its excluded margins.[64]

We have already remarked that preoccupation with joints and seams – and with joinery in its most material form – extends in Shakespeare to the joint-stool that serves as a stand-in for Goneril in *King Lear*, the play that begins with an epochal act of partition involving the division of a kingdom and with a retrospectively disastrous joint investiture of power ("I do invest you jointly with my power, / Pre-eminence ... ," I.i.132). It has often been remarked that the dramatization of this divisive "partition" in *Lear* comes at a moment of contemporary Jacobean history preoccupied with "union."[65] But it also needs to be noted that the lowly material object evoked in this "joint-stool" is the same one that stands as the theatrical representative of king and throne in *Henry IV Part I* (II.iv.380), and that this material surrogate (not just the most common of artisanal objects but also associated with the "close-stool" as a different kind of "throne") also links bodily and societal high and low, a conjunction that would soon be disjoined by the success of the "civilizing" process of singulation or distinction chronicled by Elias and Bourdieu.[66]

The harping on joinings and joints in Shakespeare also includes jointures and "jointresses," in contexts that call attention to the exchange of women as part of the construction of a "house," as well as to the dependence on the material – or transfers of property – that underlies such matrimonial "joins." Gertrude the "imperial jointress" of *Hamlet* (I.ii.9) – described by Claudius as

> so *conjunctive* to my life and soul,
> That, as the star moves not but in his sphere
> I could not but by her

– is the most striking instance here of the hinge or join (if Saxo and Belleforest are to be credited) on which the sequiturs of Claudius's own succession may depend, in the play that harps incessantly on a poisoned joining before this "jointress" intercepts a poisoned "union" (V.ii.272) at its end. Capulet's reference to his daughter's "jointure" at the end of *Romeo and Juliet* (V.iii.296) evokes ironically the Ovidian tale of Pyramus and Thisbe and its sundering replayed in an apparent comic context in *A Midsummer Night's Dream*. And references to jointures and jointresses appear in the response of Rosalind (disguised as Ganymede) to the prospects of Orlando as a younger son ("a snail ... carries his house on his head; a better jointure I think than you can make a woman," IV.i.54–6) in *As You Like It*, the comedy that features not only the marred "joinery" of Audrey and Touchstone but also the residue of more unconventional joinings "as you like it" not entirely dispelled by the more orthodox hymeneal joinings of its end. References to jointresses and jointures in Shakespeare underscore the material bases of apparently romantic couplings, the "hundred and fifty pounds jointure" offered for Anne in *The Merry Wives of Windsor* (III.iv.48) or the "jointure" Tranio promises her father will be Bianca's in *The Taming of the Shrew* ("Besides two thousand ducats by the year,/ Of fruitful land, all which shall be her jointer," II.i.369–70). In the latter, such reminders evoke as well the material context in which chivalric "titles" and "deeds" have been replaced by the "titles" and "deeds" of bourgeois property, and where, in the patriarchal context of such negotiating, Bianca and Anne are part of an exchange in which women themselves are "moveables."[67] (They also recall the intrusion of matters of property into the "wooing" scene of *Henry V*, a scene whose romantic union is explicitly contingent on the patently material negotiation happening simultaneously off-stage, the transfer of territory that by Henry's demand must accompany the joining in matrimony that transfers a French Kate to the dominion of her English lord.)

In texts ranging from early English treatises of logic like Wilson's *The Rule of Reason* to descriptions of the "order of an householde called *Oiconomia*" (as Dudley Fenner put it) or treatments of "government," concern with what can lawfully be joined (and what should be distinguished or separated) emerges in this period as a crucial aspect not just of the construction of order in marriage and the body politic but also of that very "civilizing process" (to reinvoke Elias's phrase) that would in its later phases in England involve the "righting" (including the corrective editing) of Shakespeare's plays themselves as "deformed" and "rude." In order to suggest how wordplay on "joining" and "misjoining" relates the language of these plays to this emerging Neoclassicism, we need to read plays like *A Midsummer Night's Dream* in ways that connect its disfiguring of the rules of the new humanist discipline by "rude mechanicals" to the broader issue of the joinings, and orders, its end appears to underwrite. Apprehension of the play's famous metadramatic aspect would lead in this regard not to the purely formalist or self-reflexive, but rather to its linkages with the partitions and joins of other Early Modern structures, social and political as well as rhetorical, logical, and grammatical. In evoking the language and implications of proper joining in matrimony as in discourse, of sequential disposition, and of the forming and controlling of a potentially unruly *materia*, the play so frequently read (by a hostile as well as by an admiring criticism) as a Shakespearean embodiment and endorsement of the "Elizabethan World Picture" enables, by its inclusion of these "mechanicals," a contrary awareness of the work that is done by the forging of these orders and "chains." It suggests, therefore, not just the formal possibilities of such disjunctive wordplay but the play's replaying, or holding up to "show," of the naturalized terms of an emergent ideology.

Humanist discourse was frequently also an elitist discourse, tied to the emergence of these new elites. It is repeatedly parodied in Shakespeare – from the grammar scene involving a schoolboy "Will" in *Merry Wives* (critically marginalized, at least until recently, in Shakespeare studies) to the deformations that produce, in *Much Ado*, not only the scramblings of Dogberry, counterpart to the "rude mechanicals" of the *Dream*, but a character actually named "Deformed." Part of the larger critical enterprise involved here is the learning (or relearning) of a language and semantic resonance contemporary with Shakespeare that might allow us to approach such apparently marginal matters as the parodies by artisan "mechanicals" of the language of governance or order in discourse, and to begin to perceive the links between this form of governance and a context in which the joining of words and sentences and the order of marriage and the body politic were related forms of "joinery."

Players themselves, as earlier remarked, traced their origins to joiners, weavers, and other "mechanicals." C. L. Barber remarks on the fact that "when the clowns think that Bottom's transformation has deprived them of their chief actor, their lament seems pointedly allusive to Shakespeare's company and their play."[68] What difference, we might then ask, does it make for *Hamlet*, for example (the play that harps so incessantly on joining and mis-joining, on "unions" and jointresses, and on the time itself as "out of joint"), that Richard Burbage, the actor who first played the Prince born to "set it right," the figure whose "*antic* disposition" threatens Claudius's *ruling* disposition, was the son of a joiner, one of the artisans featured in *A Midsummer Night's Dream*? Actor–playwrights like Shakespeare – as Theodor Leinwand has recently reminded us – were already (in a system increasingly more triadic than dyadic) counted among the "middling sort," distinct from both aristocratic "high" and artisanal "low."[69] Yet the perspective in Shakespeare's case seems to have encouraged a distance or detachment from the naturalized language of joints and joins – in ways that enable a perspective on it as, in every sense, a form of craft – in contrast, say, to the case of the Wilson of *The Rule of Reason*, who, in disclaiming his own provincial background, took such frequent pains to illustrate linguistic solecisms and improper join-ings through the disparagement of anonymous "country fellows," blun-dering awkwardly before their social betters.[70]

One of the methodological presuppositions here is that Shakespearean wordplay is not the ornamental quibble that the subsequent triumph of such Neoclassicism eventually succeeded in reducing it to, but involves instead a network whose linkages (across scenes and across the bound-aries of individual plays) expose (even as the plays themselves may appear simply to iterate) the orthodoxies and ideologies of the texts they evoke. To become aware of the multiple implications of "joining" in apparently marginal scenes, such as the one from *As You Like It* or those involving the "mechanicals" of *A Midsummer Night's Dream*, is to begin to discover a whole range of material wordplay in Shakespeare, including the materiality of "translation" itself as a transporting of words, like cloth or goods, from place to place. Far from being wordplay conceived from the perspective of that later Neoclassicism, as either "fatal Cleo-patra" or decorative "quibble," the exploitation of joinery throughout the canon of Shakespeare enables a critique of the multiple forms of joining in the plays, including those associated with the orthodoxies that would condemn Shakespeare himself as uncouth and "rude." To read the mystical, marital or apocalyptic language of union or "joining," as of the "joint" and "several" in the plays, is to return to the "seem" (or "seam") of the definition of "Joynery" itself as an "Art Manual" through which "several Pieces of Wood are so fitted and joyned together ... that they shall *seem* one intire Piece," and through it to the joining and seeming of "smooth discourse," the hierarchies it forges and the orders it constructs.

NOTES

1 See, for example, Michael D. Bristol, *Carnival and Theater: Plebian Culture and the Stucture of Authority in Renaissance England* (New York, 1985), p. 174; Theodore B. Leinwand, "'I believe we must leave the killing out': Deference and Accommodation in *A Midsummer Night's Dream*," *Renais-sance Papers* (1986), 11–30; Annabel Patterson, *Shakespeare and the Popular Voice* (Oxford, 1989), ch. 3. I am grateful for the readings this study received from David Bevington and Margreta de Grazia, and the responses from Theodore Leinwand, Louis Montrose, and Paul Yachnin that sharpened my

thinking about the implications of the play's own strikingly dyadic language of "high" and "low." Unless otherwise noted, italicization here and throughout is mine and the text used for quotations from Shakespeare is *The Riverside Shakespeare*, ed. G. Blakemore Evans (Boston, 1974).

2　See Patterson, *Popular Voice*, on the continuing conception of the play as "airy nothing" which, at least until Jan Kott's emphasis on "Bottom" and Peter Brooks's 1970 production, held center-stage.

3　Sylvan Barnet's Signet edition, for example, might be seen as representative of an entire critical tradition in this regard.

4　*OED* cites Holinshed II.141/2.

5　See John Gower's *Confessio Amantis* (1390) in *The English Works of John Gower*, ed. G. C. Macauley (London, 1900–1), Bk. IV, 11. 946–7.

6　See *Henry VI Part II*, IV.x.31; III.ii.271; IV.iv.32–3.

7　See Roger B. Merriman, *Life and Letters of Thomas Cromwell* (2 vols.; Oxford, 1902), II, p. 27, for the 1536 Cromwell text.

8　We might also cite here Nashe's attack on "mechanical mate[s]" who "think to outbrave better pens with the swelling bombast of a bragging blank verse." See Alexander B. Grosart, ed., *The Life and Complete Works of Robert Greene* (15 vols., 1881–3; rpt. New York, 1964), XII, p. 144; and Ronald B. McKerrow and F. P. Wilson, eds., *The Works of Thomas Nashe* (5 vols., Oxford, 1958), III, p. 311.

9　This sense of the practical or material as distinct from the rational and contemplative also stands behind such references as the mathematician John Dee's to a "*mechanicall* mathematician" and to "A Mechanicien, or a *Mechanicall workman*" as he "whose skill is ... [to] finish any *sensible* work." See John Dee, "A Praeface specifying the chiefe sciences," *The Elements of Geometrie of Euclid* (London, 1570), aiijb. With reference to the woods outside Athens, Margreta de Grazia suggested in response to this essay that the sense of "wode" in "wood" adds a dimension of disorder/madness to the semantic network of the "rude." Hugh of St. Victor early on described the mechanical arts as a debased, artificial, "adulterate" art, deriving *mechanicus* from Latin *moechus* (adulterer). See Jerome Taylor, ed., *The "Didascalion" of Hugh of St. Victor* (New York, 1961), p. 191 n. 64. In "Explicit Ink," forthcoming in Louise Fradenburg and Carla Freccero, eds., *The Pleasures of History: Reading Sexualities in Premodern Europe* (New York, 1995), Elizabeth Pittinger comments on Latin forms such as *moechocinaedus*, which extend the meaning to lewd and debauched behavior (including sodomy).

10　See respectively Henry Peacham, *Compleat Gentleman* (London, 1634), p. 129; John Donne, *Sermons* (London, 1640), p. 364; George Etherege, ed. H. F. B. Brett-Smith (2 vols., Oxford, 1927), II, p. 251. John Donne, *Sermons*, 37 (1640 edn.), p. 364; George Etherege, *Man of Mode* (1678), IV.i.

11　See respectively, Angell Day, *The English Secretary* (1625), II.106; Randle Cotgrave, *A Dictionarie of the French and English Tongues* (1611; rpt.) (Menston, UK, 1968); and Marston's *Scourge of Villanie* (1599), in *The Poems of John Marston*, ed. Arnold Davenport (Liverpool, 1961), p. 96.

12　The *OED* gives the following range under "mechanic": "Having a manual occupation; working at a trade"; "Belonging to or characteristic of the 'lower orders'; vulgar, low, base"; and, under "mechanician": "One who practises or is skilled in a mechanical art; a mechanic, artisan." The meanings it cites under "mechanical" include "Concerned with or involving material objects or physical conditions" and the "mechanical" as contrasted with the spontaneous.

13 For the range of "preposterous" inversions, see Patricia Parker "Preposterous Events," *Shakespeare Quarterly* 43, 2 (Summer 1992), 186–213; and for the two cited texts, see respectively *True Coppie of a Discourse ... in the Late Voyage of Spaine and Portingale* (1598) in Alexander B. Grosart, ed., *The Huth Library* (London, 1881), p. 102; and John King, *Sermons* (1606), cited in *OED* as the first use of "mechanist."

14 See Edward J. White, *Commentaries on the Law in Shakespeare* (St. Louis, Mo., 1913), p. 415.

15 See Stephen Orgel, "Making Greatness Familiar," in Stephen Greenblatt, ed., *The Power of Forms in the English Renaissance* (Norman, Okla., 1982); on the temporal anachronism here, see Marjorie Garber, "'What's Past is Prologue': Temporality and Prophecy in Shakespeare's History Plays," in Barbara Lewalski, ed., *Renaissance Genres* (Cambridge, Mass., 1986). As with Hippolyta at similar moments in the *Dream*, it is Cleopatra's class rather than gender position that is foregrounded here.

16 See David Riggs, *Ben Jonson: A Life* (Cambridge, Mass., 1989), pp. 9–10, 17, 53–4; and John Ferne, *Blazon of Gentrie* (1586, rpt. NY., 1973), sig.A6s, quoted in Frank Whighan, *Ambition and Privilege: The Social Tropes of Elizabethan Courtesy Literature* (Berkeley, 1984), p. 19.

17 See Sir Thomas Smith, *De republica anglorum* (1583), ed. Mary Dewar (Cambridge, 1982), pp. 71–2, a passage that also appears in Harrison's *Description of England* in the 1587 editions of Holinshed's *Chronicles*; Sam Schoenbaum, *William Shakespeare: A Documentary Life* (Oxford: Clarendon Press, 1975), pp. 166–73.

18 Louis A. Montrose, "*A Midsummer Night's Dream* and the Shaping Fantasies of Elizabethan Culture: Gender, Power, Form," in Margaret W. Ferguson, Maureen Quilligan, and Nancy J. Vickers, eds., *Rewriting the Renaissance: The Discourses of Sexual Difference in Early Modern Europe* (Chicago and London, 1986), pp. 65–87.

19 "Martext" here also possibly evokes suggestions of the Puritan exegetical torturing of texts. Interestingly also, "mar" appears in Bishop Cooper's 1589 invective against the anti-episcopal Martin Marprelate (whom he calls "Martin Marprince, Marstate, Marlaw, Marmagistrate"), in a passage that gives a fuller sense of the "marring" threatened by disorder. See Richard Helgerson, *Forms of Nationhood: The Elizabethan Writing of England* (Chicago and London, 1992), pp. 250–1.

20 *OED* gives, under joiner, "A craftsman whose occupation it is to construct things by joining pieces of wood; a worker in wood who does lighter and more ornamental work than that of a carpenter, as the construction of the furniture and fittings of a house, ship, etc." For the quotation, see Joseph Moxon, *Mechanick Exercises* (1683), ed. T. L. De Vinne (2 vols., New York, 1896), I.59.

21 For the joint-stool, see John Palsgrave, *L'esclarcissement de la langue francoyse* (1530): "Joyned as a stole or any other thynge is by the joyners craft."

22 For a fuller reading of the importance of "joining" in *Hamlet*, see Patricia Parker, *Literary Fat Ladies: Rhetoric, Gender, Property* (London, 1987), pp. 119–20.

23 See Richard Sherry, *A Treatise of Schemes and Tropes* (London 1550), p. 22.

24 See, among others, Jonathan Goldberg, *Writing Matter: From the Hands of the English Renaissance* (Stanford, 1990), and Stephanie H. Jed, *Chaste Thinking: The Rape of Lucretia and the Birth of Humanism* (Bloomington, 1989), with John Brinsley's *Ludus Literarius* (London, 1627), p. 18.

25 See Thomas Wilson, *The Rule of Reason Conteinying the Arte of Logique*, ed. Richard S. Sprague (Northridge, Calif., 1972), eg. pp. 9, 12, 20, 22, 42.

26 See *Homilies* (1547), 1. Contention, p. 2.

27 See Alain de Lille, *The Complaint of Nature*, trans. Douglas M. Moffatt (Hamden, Conn., 1972), with, *inter alia*, R. Howard Bloch, *Etymologies and Genealogies: A Literary Anthology of the French Middle Ages* (Chicago, 1983), pp. 133ff.

28 See Sir Thomas Smith, "To the Reader," *De Republica Anglorum*, p. 45.

29 See George Puttenham, *The Arte of English Poesie*, ed. Baxter Hathaway (Kent, Ohio, 1970), pp. 312–13.

30 Thomas Wilson, *The Arte of Rhetorique* (1553; rpt. Amsterdam and New York, 1969), fols. 83–4.

31 See Frankie Rubinstein, *A Dictionary of Shakespeare's Sexual Puns and Their Significance* (London: Macmillan, 1984), p. 196, and Snug the Joiner's "I am a man as other men are" and "let him name his name" (III.i.147); John Florio's *Queen Anna's New World of Words* (1611; rpt. Menston, UK, 1968), "a rule, a square or squire to know any thing by." The *OED* also cites the metaphorical use of "gnomon" as "A rule, canon of belief or action," as in W. Sclater, "Making Scripture my gnomon and canon" (1626). John Barret's *Alvearie or Quadruple Dictionary* includes the following under "Ruling and government": "A precept, a forme, a determinate rule, or fashion..."; "To be lord and maister ... to have sovereigntie, to beare rule"; "To rule and governe his children"; "A rule or squire. *Norma, Regula, ae ...* A carpenters rule, or line"; "To rule paper"; "To frame, or rule according to reason"; "The tooth whereby the age of an horse is known, that which sheweth the houres in a diall, a rule to knowe any thing by. *Gnomon, is.*"

32 On the names of the "mechanicals," see Wolfgang Franke, "The Logic of Double Entendre in *A Midsummer Night's Dream*," *Philological Quarterly* 58 (1979), 282–97.

33 On "show," see Parker, *Literary Fat Ladies*, pp. 103–7, 129–30, and "*Othello* and *Hamlet*: Dilation, Spying and the 'Secret Place' of Woman," *Representations* 44 (Fall 1993), 60–95. On the anal, homosexual, as well as heterosexual, suggestiveness of such images (including the *rima* or "chink" of the play of Pyramus and Thisbe), see Thomas Clayton "'Fie what a Question's That if thou Wert Near a Lewd Interpreter': The Wall Scene in *A Midsummer Night's Dream*," *Shakespeare Studies* 7 (1974) pp. 101–13; and James L. Calderwood, *A Midsummer Night's Dream* (London, 1992), pp. 117–45.

34 See Bacon, *The Advancement of Learning*, ed. G. W. Kirchin (London, 1915), p. 149 (Book II.xviii.8); and the description of Armado in *Love's Labor's Lost* ("He draweth out the *thread of his verbosity* finer than the staple of his

argument" V.i.16). See also John Grange's *The Golden Aphroditis* (London, 1577), whose lines ("A bottome for your silke it seemes / My letters are become, / Which oft with winding off and on / Are wasted whole and some") are cited in the Arden editor's note (p. 77n.) on a sexually suggestive line in *Two Gentlemen of Verona* ("you must provide to bottom it on me"). See also *The Taming of the Shrew*, IV.iii.138 ("a bottom of brown thread"), and *Henry IV Part I*, III.i.104–5. Barret's *Alvearie* also gives under "Round" the expression "To divide, or winde thred in bottomes." Barret's further listing of "Bottome of thread" under "Clew" and the reference in John Minsheu's *Ductor in Linguas* (London, 1617) to a "Bottome, or clue of thread or yarne" (p. 48) suggests interesting affinities with the "clue" to the labyrinth or maze from the story of Theseus and Ariadne, particularly given the period of "amaze" in the woods in *A Midsummer Night's Dream*.

35   See Madelon Gohlke, " 'I wooed thee with my sword': Shakespeare's Tragic Paradigms," in Murray M. Schwartz and Coppélia Kahn, eds., *Representing Shakespeare: New Psychoanalytic Essays* (Baltimore, Md., 1980).

36   On rhetorical "partition," see the Arden gloss on these lines (*A Midsummer Night's Dream*, ed. Harold F. Brooks, The Arden Shakespeare [London, 1979]), and Patricia Parker "Dilation and Delay: Renaissance Matrices," *Poetics Today* 5, 3 (1984), 519–29.

37   See also Homer Swander, "Editor vs. Text: The Scripted Geography of *A Midsummer Night's Dream*," *Studies in Philology* 87, 1 (1990), 83–108, on the period (not there in Folio or Quarto) introduced by editors which shifts the sense of the line "My mistress with a monster is in love near to her close and consecrated bower" and hence, in his opinion, creates a mistaken critical identification of the woods with faeryland.

38   See 1 Corinthians 2: 6–10. On the Geneva Bible "Bottom of Goddes Secretes," see Thomas B. Stroup, "Bottom's Name and His Ephiphany," *Shakespeare Quarterly* 29 (1978), 79–82.

39   In Theseus' proclamation that "The lunatic, the lover, and the poet / Are of imagination all compact," that "Lovers and madmen have such seething brains, / Such shaping fantasies, that apprehend / More than cool reason ever comprehends," the social order of his rule depends, as Louis Montrose suggests, on his ability "to *comprehend* – to understand and to encompass – the energies and motives, the diverse, unstable, and potentially subversive *apprehensions of the ruled*." See Louis A. Montrose, "*A Midsummer Night's Dream* and the Shaping Fantasies of Elizabethan Culture: Gender, Power, Form," in Margaret W. Ferguson, et al., *Rewriting the Renaissance*, pp. 65–87.

40   See Parker, "Preposterous Events," pp. 186–94.

41   See Henry Peacham, *Garden of Eloquence* (1577; rpt. London, 1593), pp. 118–19; with Richard Sherry's "There is also a *naturall order*, as to say: men & women, daye and night, eastè, and weste, rather than backwardes," in his *A Treatise of Schemes and Tropes*, p. 22.

42   See Puttenham, *The Arte of English Poesie* (London, 1589), p. 184. Miriam Joseph, in *Shakespeare's Use of the Arts of Language* (New York and London, 1966), p. 55, cites Hypallage or Puttenham's "Changeling" – a form of *hyperbaton* or departure from ordinary order – as the kind of

"misplacing of words" which Bottom seems addicted to, from his "I see a voice" or "hear my Thisby's face" to his scrambling of the order of 1 Corinthians 2, beginning with "The eye of man hath not heard."

43 See David Marshall, "Exchanging Visions: Reading *A Midsummer Night's Dream*," *ELH* 49 (1982), 543–71, esp. 568ff.

44 See John Boswell, *Christianity, Social Tolerance, and Homosexuality* (Chicago, 1980), pp. 83, 237.

45 Joseph Porter, in *Shakespeare's Mercutio* (Chapel Hill and London, 1988), p. 150, rightly notes the heterosexual bias in Shakespeare criticism whose "vantage is more exclusively orthodox than is Shakespeare's" own, but, in his own emphasis on male friendship and homoeroticism in Shakespeare, slights female–female pairings and eroticism in the plays, though his remarks on the ways in which "received ideas" are "subjected to various sorts of question and subversion" in the plays would readily extend to the case of Helena and Hermia in the *Dream*.

46 See Valerie Traub's discussion of the "gynoerotic" in this passage, in *Desire and Anxiety: Circulations of Sexuality in Shakespearean Drama* (London and New York, 1992), p. 107, and, on male friendship, Alan Bray, "Homosexuality and the Signs of Male Friendship in Elizabethan England," *History Workshop Journal* 29 (Spring 1990), 1–19.

47 We need to remember here, as throughout, the differences as well as complex interrelations between the class and gender hierarchies of the play, especially pronounced in the role of the aristocratic women in the final scene.

48 See Montrose, "Shaping Fantasies," and Janet Adelman's discussion of parthenogenesis in *Suffocating Mothers: Fantasies of Maternal Origin in Shakespeare's Plays, "Hamlet" to "The Tempest"* (New York, 1992) pp. 201–19. Though Shakespeare's representations of biological reproduction are more various than the male-centered model Montrose adduces here, Montrose is certainly right in linking Theseus' figure of imprinting with the resonances within the play of the Aristotelian model of active (male) and passive (female), a figure which also has other, more Neoplatonic, resonances.

49 C. L. Barber, *Shakespeare's Festive Comedy* (Princeton, 1959), p. 137. Titania's account of the Indian votaress's pregnancy also evokes different models from the figure of imprinting on wax (including impregnation by the wind), in ways that suggest contesting views of biological reproduction, though Oberon eventually wins the contest over this "issue."

50 See Margo Hendricks, "Obscured by Dreams: Race, Empire and Shakespeare's *A Midsummer Night's Dream*," forthcoming. This aspect of the *Dream* would benefit from juxtaposition with Richard Eden's *Treatyse of the Newe India* (London, 1553) and with *Huon of Bordeaux* from which its Oberon is taken. In *Huon*, Oberon and Faeryland are linked geographically with the "Inde" that is the Middle East as well as with Babylon (also the site of the Pyramus and Thisbe story and associated with Semiramis). Oberon – far from being a romance character unconnected with empire – is there the offspring of Julius Caesar. In the other mythology central to the play, Theseus' defeat of the Amazons is invoked in the final play of Aeschylus's Oresteian trilogy, where father right is judged to be superior to mother right. On the association between Theseus' defeat of the Amazons and the

transition from matriarchy to patriarchy, as well as the triumph of Athenian logos and "reason," see Froma Zeitlin, "The Dynamics of Misogyny: Myth and Mythmaking in the *Oresteia*," *Arethusa* 11 (1978), 149–84. The feminizing of the East in opposition to Athens included the construction of the Persians as feminine.

51   On the relation of the language of copia or commodiousness to commodities, see Parker, *Literary Fat Ladies*, pp. 140–51. On the relation of "light" and "dark" and references to cultural otherness in the *Dream* and other Early Modern instances, see Kim F. Hall, " 'I rather would wish to be a blackmoor': Beauty, Race, and Rank in Lady Mary Wroth's *Urania*," in Margo Hendricks and Patricia Parker, eds., *Women, "Race," and Writing in the Early Modern Period* (London and New York, 1994).

52   See *The Problemes of Aristotle* (London, 1597), with Montrose, "Shaping Fantasies," p. 73, and Parker, *Literary Fat Ladies*, pp. 116–17. For Aristotle's use of the image of the "carpenter," see Aristotle, *De Generatione Animalum* (12 vols., Oxford, 1912–50), V, 730b.

53   See Parker, *Literary Fat Ladies*, p. 117.

54   When the Wall or discoursing "partition" of the mechanicals' play finally departs, there is an echo of Apocalypse, with its definitively punctuating "point" or "period" (*"Thisbe:* 'Tide life, 'tide death, I come without delay," V.i.201). But the larger play ends with a "night" looking forward once again to a dawning which is temporally still to come and Puck's speech as the lovers go to bed includes yet another "hungry lion" (V.i.357), this time an allusion to the New Testament text (2 Peter) on the trials *before* the apocalyptic dawning.

55   In contrast to the less ambiguous Theseus of *Two Noble Kinsmen*, the *Dream* famously includes reminders of Theseus' trials with women: "The battle with the Centaurs" (V.i.44), the story of a wedding (at which Theseus himself was present) which ended in violence and attempted rape; "The riot of the tipsy Bacchanals, / Tearing the Thracian singer in their rage," a reminder of the power of female violence; the subsequent disastrous history of Hippolytus, the "issue" of Theseus and Hippolyta (ironically, given Oberon's prayer that "the issue there create / Ever shall be fortunate," V.i.391–2), including echoes of Seneca's *Hippolytus*, cited in the Arden Appendix I, pp. 140–4. On the implications of the bergomask, see Skiles Howard, "Hands, Feet, and Bottoms: Decentering the Cosmic Dance in *A Midsummer Night's Dream*," *Shakespeare Quarterly* 44, 3 (Fall 1993), 325–42.

56   For "jointe" as "closure" as well as "ioyning" or "seame," see Cotgrave, *A Dictionarie*, under "Iointe" and "Ioinct." For the Shakespearean association of dramatic closure with final "joining," see, for example, the "mutual joinder of your hands" at the end of *Twelfth Night* (V.i.156–61).

57   For critiques of early New Historicist notions of containment, see, among others, Patterson, *Popular Voice*, and Bristol, *Carnival and Theater*. See also the discussions of theatrical subversion in David Scott Kastan, "Proud Majesty Made a Subject: Shakespeare and the Spectacle of Rule," *Shakespeare Quarterly* 37 (1986), 459–75; Franco Moretti, " 'A Huge Eclipse': Tragic Form and the Deconsecration of Sovereignty" and Stephen Orgel, "Making Greatness Familiar," the latter both in *Genre* 15 (1982), 7–48. My

own critique of the model of subversion and ultimate containment – as well as of traditional, as well as more recent, views of the *Dream* that identify the subordinations of its ending (either positively or negatively) with endorsement by its playwright – comes out of a sense that what the play itself presents as (on the one hand) the often separate spheres of its artisans and aristocrats also intersect in ways that introduce the possibility of a double perspective on Theseus' "governance" as well as on the orthodox joinings and subordinations of its end. These points of intersection (and *sotto voce* commentary) include, as I have tried to argue, Bottom's "So grow to a point" (or end) in the parody of the new textbook forms of discursive ordering in the casting scene; the echoes of Theseus' "periods in the midst of sentences" in Quince's mispointed Prologue and other scramblings by these "rude mechanicals" of what Theseus terms the ordered "chain" of discourse and Hippolyta the Amazonian Queen calls "sound in government"; the disjunction between the "sensible" (bodily and material) Wall of the artisan's play and the aristocrat Demetrius's disparaging comparison of it to a discursive or logical "partition"; the gap between the aristocrats' courtly aesthetic (and the concluding rhetoric of cosmic harmony) and the intrusion of the artisans' bergomask into this ending presided over by Athenian Theseus; and the echo of the 1 Corinthians text on the wisdom of the "fool" and the limited comprehension of "rulers of this world," with its own application to Greek logos or reason, just before Theseus' signature speech on "cool reason" and what it comprehends, along with the links between the artisans' mis-joinings and the end of the play where more orthodox joining is so important. For the argument that the artisans and aristocrats of the play inhabit separate spheres, see Paul Yachnin, "The Politics of Theatrical Mirth: *A Midsummer Night's Dream, A Mad World, My Masters*, and *Measure for Measure*," *Shakespeare Quarterly* 43, 1 (Spring 1992), 51–66.

58 See Frank Whigham, *Ambition and Privilege*, 93–5.

59 See David Marshall, "Exchanging Visions," and Harry Berger, Jr., "What Did the King Know and When Did He Know It? Shakespearean Discourses and Psychoanalysis," *South Atlantic Quarterly* 88 (1989), 811–62.

60 For emphasis on "mechanical reproduction" in the Henriad as well as *Merry Wives*, see Parker, *Literary Fat Ladies*, pp. 27–31, 69–77, and on the comedy in particular Parker, "*The Merry Wives of Windsor* and Shakespearean Translation," *Modern Language Quarterly* 51, 3 (1991), 225–61, and Elizabeth Pittinger, "Dispatch Quickly: The Mechanical Reproduction of Pages," *Shakespeare Quarterly* 42 (1991), 389–409.

61 See, for example, the choice of "join her hand with his" in the Arden Shakespeare text of *As You Like It,* ed. Agnes Latham (London, 1975) and the note (p. 127) explaining the choice: "The F reading *his*, in the first line of the couplet, is pretty clearly a misreading of *hir* . . ." On this "misreading," see Jeffrey Masten, "Textual Deviance: Ganymede's Hand in *As You Like It*," in *Field Work: Sites in Literary and Cultural Studies*, eds. Marjorie Garber, Rebecca Walkowitz, and Paul B. Franklin (forthcoming).

62 See Edward Hall, *The Union of the Two Noble Families of Lancaster and York* (1548).

63 On the shakiness of the Tudor claim, see for example Peter Saccio,

Shakespeare's English Kings: History, Chronicle, and Drama (New York, 1977), pp. 179ff, and the Arden edition of *Richard III*, ed. Antony Hammond (London and New York, 1981), p. 331n.

64   On the links between the territorial "marches" or borderlands (associated with the rival earls of March) and the temporal "margins" that threaten Henry's self-enclosed history, see Parker "Preposterous Events," p. 204, which cites David Scott Kastan's *Shakespeare and the Shapes of Time* (Hanover, N.H., 1982) on the undoing of Henry's boundaries.

65   See, for example, Leah S. Marcus, *Puzzling Shakespeare: Local Reading and its Discontents* (Berkeley, Los Angeles and London, 1988), pp. 148–59, and Richard Halpern, *The Poetics of Primitive Accumulation: English Renaissance Culture and the Genealogy of Capital* (Ithaca and London, 1991), ch. 6.

66   See Norbert Elias, *The Civilizing Process*, vol. I, *The History of Manners*, trans. Edmund Jephcott (New York, 1978), and Pierre Bourdieu, *Distinction: A Social Critique of the Judgment of Taste*, trans. Richard Nice (Cambridge, Mass., 1984).

67   See Parker's analysis of the figure of inventory in relation to women as "moveables" in *Literary Fat Ladies*, ch. 7. In *Shrew*, interestingly, it is the unruled Kate who calls Petruchio a "join'd stool" (II.i.197–9) and "moveable," and the only apparently submissive Bianca refuses to yield as a "breeching scholar" to her "masters' construction" (III.i). On the latter, see Parker, "Preposterous Events," pp. 198–9.

68   See Barber, *Shakespeare's Festive Comedy*, p. 149; Alfred Harbage, *Shakespeare and the Rival Traditions* (1952; rpt. New York, 1968), pp. 4ff.; and Walter Cohen, *Drama of a Nation* (Ithaca and London, 1985), pp. 136–85, on the "artisanal" character of the contemporary English theater.

69   See the argument in Theodor Leinwand, "Shakespeare and the Middling Sort," *Shakespeare Quarterly* 44, 3 (Fall 1993), 284–303. Paul Yachnin also argues in "Theatrical Mirth" for the importance of a context for the artisans of the *Dream* that is more triadic than the dyadic opposition of "high" and "low." It is undeniably true that figures like Burbage or Shakespeare need to be seen as part of the rise of the "middling sort" in the period. The play itself, however, continually evokes this more dyadic language, both in its reference to the "rude mechanicals" as "Hard-handed men" that "never labored in their minds till now" and in its polarization of low and high involved in the aristocratic view of the "mechanicals" as "asses" and "fools" (associated with the "bottom" of the social hierarchy or body politic, but also part of the "high brought low" tradition of the text from 1 Corinthians echoed in Bottom's awakening from his dream, which includes a reference to a "latter end" that may suggest implications for the conclusion or latter end of the play itself).

70   See John D. Cox, *Shakespeare and the Dramaturgy of Power* (Princeton, 1989), p. 52.

3 Spenser's domestic domain: poetry, property, and the Early Modern subject

Louis A. Montrose

The first Folio of the collected *Works of England's Arch-Poet, Edm. Spenser* was published posthumously in London in 1611, five years before publication of the Folio of Ben Jonson's *Workes*. The precedence accorded to the latter publication acknowledges its socio-literary significance as an act of textual self-monumentalization. In Jonson's *Workes*, a living writer fully exploits the resources of the printed book in order to assert his proprietary relationship to his own writings, and to claim the central place in his culture to which the merit of his works entitles him.[1] Thus, long before the establishment of a legal concept of author's copyright, the notion of intellectual and literary property was beginning to emerge in self-consciously authorial printed books. Spenser himself did not fully accomplish a project like Jonson's. Nevertheless, we may understand Spenser's own publication process, unfolded over the last two decades of the sixteenth century, to have been as calculated as Jonson's in its appropriation of the resources of the printed book to shape a distinctive and culturally authoritative authorial persona, even though the resulting corpus had different contours and a different articulation of parts. Indeed, it is arguable that Spenser provided Jonson's most immediate and most significant native precedent and model for such a project – an argument that finds some corroboration in the recently rediscovered copy of the 1617 Folio of Spenser's *Works* that was owned and copiously annotated by Jonson.[2]

Spenser's ambition for an exalted literary status, like Jonson's, was inextricably bound up with his relatively humble social origins and limited social expectations. This Poet who boldly claimed for himself so central a role in literary history and in his own society may have been the son of the John Spenser who, in 1566, was designated "a free jorneyman" in "the arte or mysterie of cloth-makynge" by the City Company of Merchant Taylors.[3] In any event, Spenser attended the Merchant Taylors School, where he was entered as a "poor scholar." He continued his Protestant–humanist education at Pembroke Hall, Cambridge, in the status of a "sizar." In return for board, lodging, and instruction, this status obliged him to discharge the duties of a household servant in the college, such as waiting table upon his better-born fellow students.[4] The foundation for Spenser's modest ascent from his obscure and impoverished origins into the lower echelons of gentility was his profession of letters. This he employed not only as a poet but also as a secretary; in both capacities, he was a client of his betters – the episcopacy, the aristocracy, and the crown.[5] This social ascent by humanist means was finally secured through a series of positions as a minor official in the colonial administration of Ireland, and by the acquisitions of real property facilitated by those positions. It was by virtue of his MA that Spenser could begin to think of himself as Master Spenser; however, it was only after he had begun to acquire land and offices in Ireland that he could fully consider himself, and be formally acknowledged as, a gentleman.[6] In no less than five of his poems printed between 1591 and 1596, Spenser claimed or implied his kinship with the rich, powerful, and ennobled Spencers of Althorp. Aristocratic and royal patronage, state employment, and expropriated Irish property gave some substance to such aspirations and pretensions. In his own lifetime, Spenser was acclaimed as a poet; and, given his apparently urban and artisanal origins, he was relatively successful in his bid for advancement. Nevertheless, he always remained on the social and economic, as well as on the geographic, margins of that community of privilege whom he addressed and presumed to fashion in his poetry.

Spenser's authorial self-fashioning proceeds by aggrandizing the socially subordinate writer as a subject of and in his own text, and by constituting that text as a printed book which can function as the vehicle of the writer's social, material, and literary advancement. Unlike some of his better-born fellow poets, Spenser sought print, and sought to construct and to sustain an authorial persona in a corpus of generically varied printed poetry books. In the process of linking Spenser to such fellow poets of his generation as Sidney and Ralegh, literary historians tend to minimize the profound differences in their socio-economic and political circumstances, and to sentimentalize the patronage-based terms of their "friendship." A literary vocation of the sort followed by Spenser, or later by Jonson, would have been wholly incompatible with the status and prospects of Sidney or Ralegh; those courtier–soldier–scholars aspired to perform such deeds as would make matter for others' songs. In "A Letter of the Authors, expounding his whole intention in the course of this worke," addressed to Sir Walter Ralegh and printed in the first edition of *The Faerie Queene* in 1590, Spenser declares that "the generall end ... of all the booke is to fashion a gentleman or noble person in vertuous and gentle discipline." Spenser claims both a moral duty and a rhetorical power to inform and reform the subjectivities of his socially superior readers as they read. It is precisely by sustaining these claims in his writing that the writer fashions himself into what his text so resonantly titles "the Author." In Spenser's case, the discursive authority of authorship was being appropriated by a subject whose social origins and achieved status limited his access to other and perhaps more tangible modes of authority and honor. "The Author" is fashioned by means of discursive forms that are realized in the printed book, a material object that through reproduction and circulation generates cultural capital.

Spenser synthesized a distinctive Elizabethan authorial identity out of a variety of cultural materials – residual as well as emergent, dominant as well as subordinate.[7] Let me briefly suggest something of this variety. The ostentatious apparatus of *The Shepheardes Calender* (1579) presents "our new Poete" in an edition befitting Virgil's eclogues. The prefatory epistle by E. K. also announces Theocritus, Mantuan, Petrarch, Boccaccio, Marot, and Sannazzaro as poetic models – to which may be added the native makers, Chaucer, Skelton, and Gascoigne. A highly self-conscious and self-promoting correspondence between Spenser and his friend Gabriel Harvey quickly followed the *Calender* into print. With their Latin poetry and witty and familiar Latin conversation, their disquisitions on meter and other learned topics, and their eclectic and cosmopolitan reading lists, these two letter books printed in 1580 take on the appearance of advertisements for the talents of ambitious young Elizabethan humanists. Spenser and Harvey present themselves as participants in the collective consciousness of publishing intellectuals, that international "Republic of Letters" that had begun to flourish among the humanists of the early sixteenth century.[8] In the first edition of *The Faerie Queene* (1590), Spenser exploits and extends the semiotic resources of late medieval allegory; and simultaneously, in the very conceit of Faeryland, he gives a local habitation and a name to an emergent notion of literary fiction as an imagined world under the circumscribed authority of its creator.[9] By various rhetorical means – by invocation and apostrophe, and by simile and allusion – Spenser's authorial persona claims a residual link to the classical and biblical traditions of inspired and prophetic speech. At the same time, his allegorical constructs and narrative techniques manifest a strong affinity with the contemporary ethos of Reformation Protestantism. Here I am thinking not only of the poem's occasional anti-Catholic polemics and Apocalyptic imagery but also of its frequent focus upon monitoring the ethical conduct of its characters and the ethical responses of its readers. This increasingly consequential Protestant insistence upon the moral agency of each believer had profound socio-political implications, which were already beginning to produce new and potentially dissident forms of subjectivity in the monarch's subjects.

That writing poetry might be a means to make his fortune and raise his rank was a possibility that Spenser took seriously enough to have it proclaimed in print – and subjected to comic irony – at the beginning of his career. In *Three Proper, and wittie, familiar Letters* (1580), Harvey addresses Spenser as "M. Immerito," the self-effacing authorial persona used in the envoy to *The Shepheardes Calender*. In the same letter, Harvey also identifies Spenser with Colin Clout, the inspired and aspiring poetic persona of the *Calender*:

> Master *Collin Cloute* is not every body, and albeit his olde Companions, *Master Cuddy* and *Master Hobbinoll* be as little beholding to their *Mistresse Poetrie*, as ever you wilt: yet he peradventure, by the meanes of hir special favour, and some personall priviledge, may happely live by *dying Pellicanes*, and purchase great landes, and Lordshippes, with the money, which his *Calendar* and *Dreames* have, and will affourde him.[10]

Harvey's irony notwithstanding, on 25 February 1591, Spenser's royal Mistress granted him "hir special favour" – namely, a royal pension of fifty pounds *per annum*, which seems to have been paid regularly thereafter.[11] This was a substantial sum, and material evidence that the dedication of the 1590 *Faerie Queene* to Queen Elizabeth did not go unacknowledged. True, the royal pension was not large enough to enable Spenser to purchase great lands and lordships; nevertheless, the rhetorical skills that he had put at the service of the state during the prior decade had already helped him to rise to the status of a landed English gentleman in Ireland.

Richard Helgerson has emphasized Spenser's projection in his poetry of a serious authorial self and an ethically normative authority – features identified by Helgerson as hallmarks of a poet "laureate."[12] However, Spenser's emulation of the Virgilian progression was idiosyncratic. While following classical and continental precedent in making the writing of a heroic poem the culmination of the poet's vocation, Spenser surrounded and punctuated the installments of *The Faerie Queene* with lyric and narrative poems and poetry collections in a variety of subordinate kinds – complaint, satiric beast fable, eclogue, sonnet, epithalamium. Most of these shorter Spenserian poems symbolically inhabit – and were literally printed within – the textual interstices between the first edition of *The Faerie Queene* of 1590, which included Books I through III, and the second edition of 1596, which added Books IV through VI. These highly varied shorter poems are characterized in part by allusion to and commentary upon Spenser's ongoing heroic poem, and by the expression of values and sentiments that are shaped against the projects of royal adulation and courtly service – projects which ostensibly define the heroic task of England's Arch-Poet. These collections of short poems constitute what might be thought of as a set of counter-generic reflections upon the heroic poem and upon the personification of the Elizabethan state who is figured within it as its muse, patroness, subject, and audience.[13]

The relations of power between ruler and subject are graphically manifested on the dedication page of *The Faerie Queene*. The Queen's proper name is inscribed in upper-case letters, in both the 1590 and 1596 editions. In the 1590 edition (fig. 3.1), the name of "Her most humble servant" appears in the lower right-hand corner of the page, in much smaller and italicized type, with only the initial letters capitalized and his given name abbreviated to "Ed." The layout of the dedication page in the 1596 edition (fig. 3.2) suggests a considerable aggrandizement of the Spenserian authorial persona vis-à-vis the monarch: now the name of Elizabeth's superlatively abjected subject, her "most humble servant," appears in full, is capitalized throughout, and is printed in the same size and style of type as is the name of the ruler – in other words, "ELIZABETH" and "EDMUND SPENSER" have been christened in the same font. Although still positioned below "ELIZABETH," "EDMUND SPENSER" is horizontally centered upon the page, occupies a full line, and becomes the subject of a sentence almost equal in length to the preceding invocation of the queen. Most significantly, in dedicating, presenting, and consecrating "THESE HIS LABOURS TO LIVE WITH THE ETERNITIE OF HER FAME," the poet suggests a reciprocal relationship between his powers and those of the monarch: if his labors are to live with the eternity of her fame, it is precisely because her fame is made eternal in and by his living labors. There is an extraordinary shift in the *relative* importance of the Queen and her subject – in the relative importance of the Poet and *his* subject – between the 1590 and 1596 title pages. And this shift is itself an implicit consequence of the publication of the first edition of *The Faerie Queene*: by this I mean that it is a consequence not only of the poem's royal reception but also of its circulation in print. For Spenser, the material process of reproducing and distributing his poetry in printed books was culturally empowering.

The encomiastic strategy deployed in the 1596 dedication is not unlike that which is foregrounded by the shepherds in *Colin Clouts Come Home Againe*. This extended eclogue was written and published between the 1590 and 1596 editions of *The Faerie Queene* – its dedicatory epistle is dated 1591, its title page, 1595. Its narrative provides a fictionalized

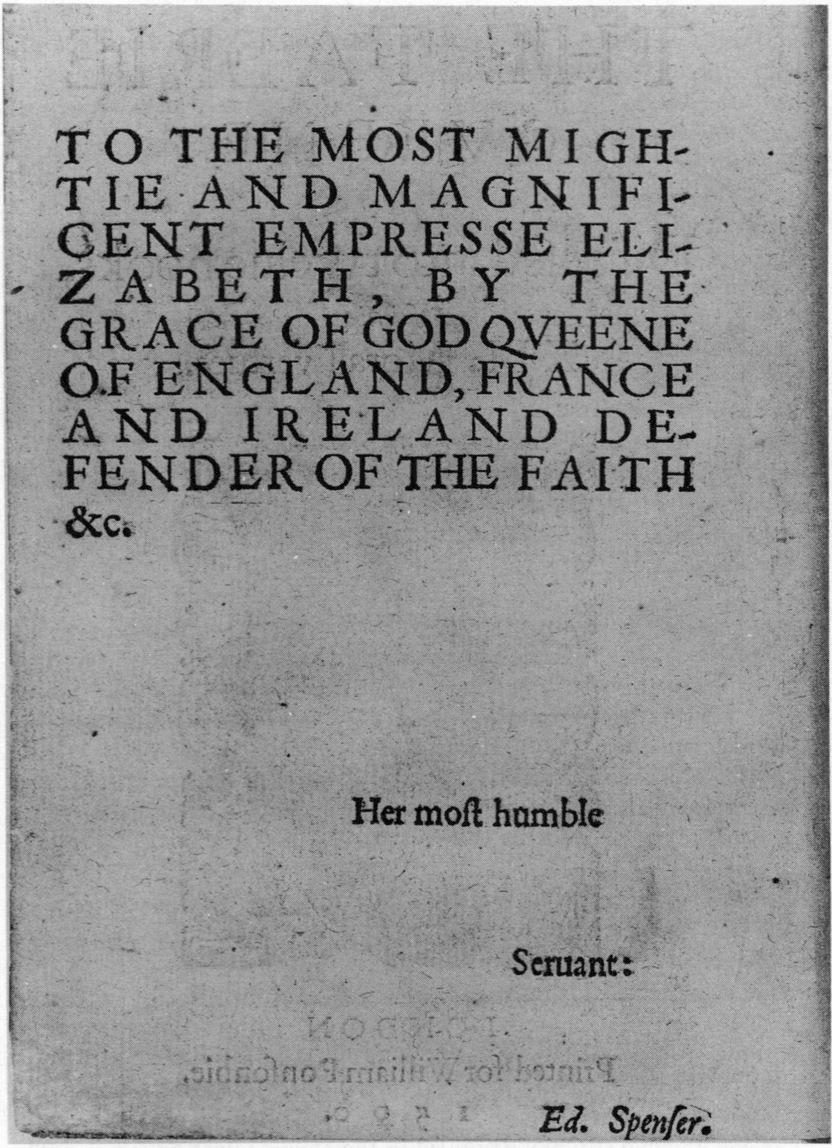

TO THE MOST MIGH-
TIE AND MAGNIFI-
CENT EMPRESSE ELI-
ZABETH, BY THE
GRACE OF GOD QVEENE
OF ENGLAND, FRANCE
AND IRELAND DE-
FENDER OF THE FAITH
&c.

Her most humble

Seruant:

Ed. Spenser.

Figure 3.1 Dedication page to the 1590 edition of *The Faerie Queene*.

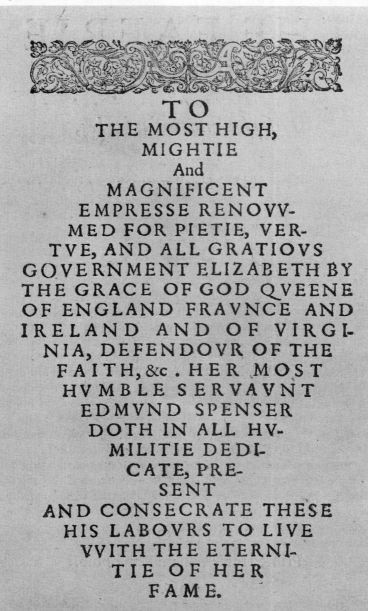

TO
THE MOST HIGH,
MIGHTIE
And
MAGNIFICENT
EMPRESSE RENOVV-
MED FOR PIETIE, VER-
TVE, AND ALL GRATIOVS
GOVERNMENT ELIZABETH BY
THE GRACE OF GOD QVEENE
OF ENGLAND FRAVNCE AND
IRELAND AND OF VIRGI-
NIA, DEFENDOVR OF THE
FAITH, &c. HER MOST
HVMBLE SERVAVNT
EDMVND SPENSER
DOTH IN ALL HV-
MILITIE DEDI-
CATE, PRE-
SENT
AND CONSECRATE THESE
HIS LABOVRS TO LIVE
VVITH THE ETERNI-
TIE OF HER
FAME.

Figure 3.2   Dedication page to the 1596 edition of *The Faerie Queene*.

account of the Queen's reception and reward of Spenser's work –
presumably, the 1590 *Faerie Queene* – as facilitated by the good offices of
Sir Walter Ralegh:

> The shepheard of the Ocean (quoth he)
> Unto that Goddesse grace me first enhanced,
> And to mine oaten pipe enclin'd her eare,
> That she thenceforth therein gan take delight,
> And it desir'd at timely houres to heare.
>
> (*CCCHA*, 358–62)

In the naive response of the shepherds to Colin's account of his royal
reception, the poet foregrounds his own self-serving encomiastic strategies:

> By wondering at thy *Cynthiaes* praise,
> *Colin*, thy selfe thou mak'st us more to wonder,
> And her upraising, doest thy selfe upraise.
>
> (353–5)

The circulation of the printed book may well have served to augment the
praise of the monarch but its capacity to aggrandize the social identity of
the writing subject was, proportionally, far greater. By 1596, in the first
edition of Book VI of *The Faerie Queene*, the poet could pose in print the
coy rhetorical question, "Who knowes not *Colin Clout*?" (*FQ*, 6.10.16).

Although the Queen's name is ostentatiously inscribed upon the
dedication page of *The Faerie Queene*, it does not appear in the text of
the poem itself. Elizabeth Bellamy has recently sought to explain this
conspicuous exclusion by means of the discourse of deconstruction.
Bellamy construes the production of *The Faerie Queene* as impelled by a
never-accomplished desire to name Queen Elizabeth, which naming
would secure the ontological ground for the poet's epic enterprise: "The
drive toward Elizabeth as unmediated Pure Name stalls in the succession
of aberrant references that delay the coincidence of meaning and being,
and the unreadability of her Proper Name is narrated through a chain of
merely figural substitutions indefinitely deferred from an ultimate convergence with pure signification."[14] At the risk of appearing unsophisti-
cated, I must say that it seems to me quite obvious that Spenser has no
difficulty in invoking the name of Elizabeth when he so chooses: the
appearance of "ELIZABETH" on the dedication page of *The Faerie
Queene* is a case in point. Another, equally striking, occurs in *Amoretti*
74, a sonnet built upon the conceit that the poet's mother, sovereign, and
mistress all bear the name Elizabeth. The critical task is not to explain
why Spenser cannot invoke Queen Elizabeth but rather to propose why
and where he may choose not to do so. In this instance, it may be that
the Early Modern writing subject is not confronting an ontological

aporia but rather is exercising his limited agency by an act of discursive resistance.

The fact that "ELIZABETH" is inscribed upon Spenser's book but not invoked within Faeryland may be due in part to the special status and properties of the dedication page among the rhetorical and typographical subgenres of the Early Modern printed book-text. The dedication page is a liminal discursive space, one that (in Robert Weimann's phrase) lies between the text in the world and the world in the text: not unlike the urban margin where civic and state jurisdictions met and royal entries were symbolically staged, the initial pages of a book are the threshold to the fiction, where the relationship of power between writing subject and royal patron may be fully acknowledged and negotiated by means of a prefatory apparatus. If Elizabeth is not actually named in the body of *The Faerie Queene*, it may be because, by suspending or deferring royal nomination, the poet is also in some sense suspending or deferring the full acknowledgment of his subjection to an authority outside the poem, to the sovereign who exists beyond the boundaries of the fictional space within which he represents and recreates her by other names, names of his own selection or invention. Elizabethan rhetorical and juridical canons strongly censured duplicitous and amphibological discourse. Officially, linguistic indeterminacy was viewed as a symptom of what the Homily "concernyng Good Ordre and Obedience to Rulers and Magistrates" excoriated as "all abuse, carnall libertie, enormitie, syn and babilonicall confusion."[15] Nevertheless, for the writing subject of the Early Modern state, the perpetual play of signification could also be construed as something other than a source of epistemological and ontological anxiety or despair. To at least some later Elizabethan writers, including Spenser, it suggested the possibility of achieving a measure of discursive autonomy from the official system of meanings by which they and their texts were authorized.

When Michel Foucault asks, "What is an Author?" his own answer is that "the author is an ideological product." Foucault poses his question in order to disrupt our habitual construal of the Author as an individual creator who is the originating source of a text. This disruption opens the way to Foucault's analysis of the very concept of Author "as a variable and complex function of discourse." When he suggests that "the coming into being of the notion of 'Author' constitutes the privileged moment of *individualization* in the history of ideas, knowledge, literature," Foucault's paradoxical point – a point central to his later work on discursive disciplines – is that such individualization is itself a socially produced technique for delimiting and controlling the interpretive activity of the state's subjects.[16] Accordingly, the self-monitoring interiority of the individual subject becomes the very medium of ideological containment and social reproduction. Foucault's own anti-humanist project is to anatomize the subject's subjection to the disciplinary discourses of power. I find this aspect of Foucault's social vision – his apparent occlusion of a space for human agency – to be extreme. In other words, my intellectual response is that his argument is unconvincing, and my visceral response is that it is intolerable. However, in responding to Foucault's provocation, I do not seek to restore to the individual the illusory power of self-creation; nor do I wish to remystify the social production of the text, to reassert its status as an expression of the autonomous author's singular creative genius. Even when considered as an ideological mystification, rather than as an actual material practice, such an assertion of creative autonomy is properly the manifestation of a later phase of European culture, the hallmark of Romanticism; it is barely discernible in Elizabethan England, despite anachronistic efforts to find it there. Any meaningful response to Foucault's provocative concept of the "author-function" will commence, not by rejecting it, but rather by expanding and refining it, by giving greater historical and cultural specificity and variability both to the notion of Author and to the possible functions it may serve. Thus, I find myself in sympathy with Robert Weimann's proposal that Foucault's polemical move necessitates a complementary analysis of discourse as a function of the subjects whose labor is objectified in its production. Weimann writes of the later sixteenth century as providing new scope for a writer's "own choice of productive strategies vis-à-vis the increasing availability of those means, modes, and materials which, practically and imaginatively (though not necessarily juridically), he can make his own." He concludes that "the study of discourses as '*objects* of appropriation' must be complemented by their study as ... agencies of knowledge, pleasure, energy, and power."[17] In the later sixteenth century in England, those agencies were articulated through the culturally innovative commercial media of the public theater and the book trade.

It may be reductive to treat the modern notion of Authorship, as Foucault does, merely as an ideological *product*, the sole function of which is to exert the state's hegemonic control over the "proliferation of meaning" in discourse. In particular, it may be anachronistic to reduce "the Author" to such a function during the sixteenth and early seventeenth centuries, when both the modern state and the modern author were emergent phenomena. Like the princes of other Early Modern states, Queen Elizabeth seems to have aspired to be the absolute ruler of the signifying process. Meaning was a matter of state; the interpretive activities of subjects were always regarded with a fundamental suspicion,

Well now.

and were subjected to whatever means of surveillance and coercion the government could muster.[18] Those means were relatively limited and unreliable, however, and the complexity and diversity of actual social and discursive practice in no way conformed to a theoretical absolutism or to ideological closure. Within the delimited discursive space of their own printed texts, writing subjects of the Early Modern state might contest, appropriate, or merely evade its semiotic prerogatives. In such circumstances, the author-function may have helped to *disseminate* discursive authority more than it worked to contain it. This does not mean, however, that the discursive authority thus released began to accrue exclusively to writers – as if the life of writing were wholly confined within a textual universe, in which the Author had displaced the Monarch as the absolute ruler of the signifying process. The technological, socio-economic, and ideological conjunction of printing, literacy, Protestantism, and market capitalism meant that printers and book-sellers, as well as editors, translators, redactors, commentators – and readers, too – also shared in this proliferating process by which cultural meanings were formulated, glossed, disputed, subverted, and displaced. Thus, as far as the writing culture of Early Modern England is concerned, what Foucault calls "the coming into being of the notion of 'Author'" ("What is an Author?" 141) may be construed as evidence of the ideological ferment that was beginning to stir in the later years of Elizabeth's reign – a ferment that would lead within half a century to an extraordinary heteroglossia in printed books, and to armed struggle that was both rooted in and framed as ideological struggle.[19]

Addressing a reading public as well as a royal patroness, "the Author" shapes and authenticates, through the medium of the printed book, the subjectivity of a writer whose social position might otherwise have rendered him little more than a functionary of his patron. The writer fashions his book as a gift and as a commodity; he inserts it into the economies of patronage and publishing, the court and the market. If Spenser frequently exalts himself as an Author, he also frequently represents himself as an obsequious and rueful client, bound to the still-dominant patronage mode of literary production. He is empowered to protest and resist this subjected position from a contrary position that the intellectual egalitarianism of humanist scholarship, the growth of the book trade, and the emergent culture of bourgeois Protestantism had now begun to make possible. A critical articulation of the relationship between the Spenserian text and its Elizabethan matrix cannot merely refer the latter term to some synthetic historical context or cultural ambience, against which we are to interpret "Spenser." Instead, such an articulation should point us toward the heterogeneous and sometimes contradictory inscriptions of Elizabethan ideology in the Spenserian text itself, toward those discursive means by which Spenser's writing bears witness to the historical conditions of its own possibility.

In an essay on *The Shepheardes Calender*, the poem in which Spenser's ambition for an exalted literary status was ostentatiously inaugurated, Paul Alpers has proposed that Spenser created a "domain of lyric" which, through the medium of print, could reach a knowledgeable and heterogeneous readership beyond the Queen and the court, and might thus confer upon its author "a qualified but nonetheless genuine independence" in the form of "literary authority." Alpers writes that his metaphor of a poetic *domain* is meant to answer the call that I had earlier made in my work on Elizabethan pastoral, a call for a critical articulation of Elizabethan literary forms and conventions with Elizabethan ideologies and social practices. He suggests that the metaphor of poetic domain answers that call by conceiving "of 'aesthetic space' in terms of rule and authority."[20] Although "rule and authority" express lordship in explicitly political terms, a domain – as Alpers goes on to suggest – is at root a legal and socio-economic metaphor:

> The concept of *demesne* refers to land tenure. In this context, it is applied either to the absolute ownership of the king, or to the tenure of the person who held the land to his own use, mediately or immediately, from the king ... In every case, the ultimate (free) holder, the person who seems most like an owner of the land, and who has a general right of doing what he pleases with it, is said to hold the land in demesne.[21]

Its etymological origin in concepts of real property points the metaphor of poetic domain toward an analysis of the ideological and material conditions of emergence of Spenser's literary corpus and of his authorial identity.

     From this perspective, I find the metaphor of poetic domain to be especially relevant to the two small poetry books printed in 1595, each of which is dominated by the elaboration of an autobiographical fiction: one, pastoral in mode and dedicated to Sir Walter Ralegh, containing *Colin Clouts Come Home Againe*, as well as *Astrophel* and other elegies for Sidney; the other, amatory, comprised of *AMORETTI AND Epithalamion*. Pastoral and amatory poems occupy humble and middling positions, respectively, in the Elizabethan hierarchy of literary genres; the symbolic spaces that they inhabit – the former, rustic; the latter, domestic – are peripheral to that of the heroic poem, which occupies an aristocratic and courtly space that is at once stylistically elevated and socially central.[22] Although minor in scope and status, relative to *The*

Faerie Queene, the small lyric and narrative forms of *Colin Clouts Come Home Againe* and *AMORETTI AND Epithalamion* nevertheless command a pivotal place in the corpus of Spenser's works. They do so, I believe, precisely by foregrounding the publicly inconsequential subjects of the poet's autobiographical fictions and investing them with the rhetorical energies hitherto reserved for his encomia of the monarch; and, furthermore, by calling attention to this very process of displacement.[23] In their strategies for generating meaning, these poetry books constitute generically and materially distinct but mutually articulated parts of a printed literary corpus. From this perspective, my present concern is with the ideology of form – or, more precisely, with the ideologically motivated and ideologically consequential inter-relationship of forms. In *Colin Clouts Come Home Againe* and in *Epithalamion*, the metaphor of a poetic domain reaches its most materially specific Spenserian form, because in these poems a rhetoric that affirms the poet's literary authority coincides with a thematics of property, marriage, and lineage that enhances his social authority. In short, the construction of a *poetic* domain here coincides with the foundation of a *domestic* domain. In what follows, these two poems will be the focus of my analysis, although I shall also be concerned to suggest that the same nexus of topics informs the *Mutabilitie* cantos and *A View of the Present State of Ireland*.

What I mean by a "domestic domain" is something more specific than, and in some ways rather different from, the set of meanings that have come to be associated, in Spenser studies, with the term "privacy." It is now customary to describe the trajectory of Spenser's poetry, following the publication of the first three books of *The Faerie Queene* in 1590, in terms of a growing alienation of the authorial voice from its heroic and encomiastic project, as an increasingly conspicuous split between the public and private spheres of poetic and poetically represented experience. The core texts for this view have been the later cantos of Book Six of *The Faerie Queene*, The Legend of Courtesy, and the apparently fragmentary and posthumously printed *Mutabilitie* cantos (1609), as well as the predominantly amorous and pastoral poetry collections printed in 1595–6. In these poems, conditions of cosmic mutability, political turmoil, or cultural corruption may call forth in the narrator or in one of the narrative's characters an impulse to withdraw into poetry, meditation, or love. The binary formulation of public/private that is frequently employed to characterize these poems tends to privilege privacy as the source of meaning, value, solace. To the private or personal are attached versions of authenticity that may be grounded in an aesthetics of imaginative autonomy, a metaphysics of spiritual transcendence, or a psychology of erotic and familial attachments.

Richard Helgerson has put this critical perspective concisely and well:

In his last works, in Book VI of *The Faerie Queene*, in the *Amoretti* and the *Epithalamion*, in the hymns of Divine Beauty and Love, and, to an extent, in the two Mutability Cantos ... Spenser does come home, as he did in the last section of *Colin Clout*. He comes home to the pastoral, the personal, and the amorous ... Whatever the laureate's obligation to the public world, it is in this private realm that he finds the source of his inspiration. (*Self-Crowned Laureates*, 97)

"Private realm" is a suggestive phrase, suggestive of privacy as a symbolic space providing the conditions for intellectual and aesthetic or spiritual autonomy. "Private realm" suggests, then, something akin to the circumscribed, imaginative autonomy that is described in an Elizabethan courtly maker's memorable phrase, "my mind to me a kingdom is," or in Sir Philip Sidney's ringing description of "the Poet, freely ranging within zodiac of his own wit."[24] Yet such analogues, from the writing of ambitious and well-placed Elizabethan courtier poets, also suggest that public life is the defining condition of privacy, and that political subjection is the defining condition of imaginative autonomy. Indeed, the very emergence of a concept of "privacy" may be construed as an effect of the state's increasing concern to regulate the lives of its subjects.[25] Implicit in the concept of the domestic is the institution of the household. This is not a place apart from the public sphere so much as it is the nucleus of the social order, the primary site of subjectification. Thus, I have chosen to emphasize the domestic, rather than the private, precisely because I wish to suggest that privacy is a social and material condition, grounded in the historical and cultural specificities of time and place, rank and gender.

Critics who celebrate Spenser's celebration of privacy neglect to take into account that Spenser actively constructs the dialectical tension, and occasional opposition, between the public and the private in poetry that is written for print. Whatever autobiographical circumstances we may specify or surmise as sources or originating conditions for this poetry, they have been conspicuously and elaborately shaped into an autobiographical fiction in the Spenserian text. The paradox of this apparently inward-turning autobiographical fiction is that it valorizes the private precisely by publishing it. Indeed, I would suggest that the significance of this development in Spenser's writings is that it articulates in courtly literary genres, and disseminates through the commerce of print, an ideology of privacy and domesticity that had already been embraced by elements of the new Tudor aristocracy and gentry, and was beginning to emerge in what would eventually become its dominant modern form. Although he has sometimes been characterized as one of the more backward-looking of Elizabethan writers, our sage and serious Poet exploited the resources of an emergent commercial mode of cultural production so as to enhance his symbolic capital in ways that princely or aristocratic favor alone could not, and this enhancement led in turn to further possibilities for material advantage through the still dominant system of patron–client relations. Spenser's motives were undoubtedly to affirm his status as a gentleman rather than to assert his place in the vanguard of the bourgeoisie. Nevertheless, we may see in some of the thematic preoccupations of his later poetry, adumbrations of those values and aspirations that came increasingly to characterize the lives of the middling sort and the culture of mercantile capitalism.[26]

Colin Clouts Come Home Againe is a curious and, I think, a pivotal work in Spenser's poetic corpus. Nevertheless, it is also a text that has been relatively neglected by Spenser's critics – perhaps because its title strikes them as undignified and its autobiographical allegory as naive. Yet I think there is something important – and, for an Elizabethan poem, something unusually resonant – even in the title of *Colin Clouts Come Home Againe*, precisely because here Spenser announces the foreconceit of his poem as being grounded in notions of home and homecoming. In his important study of Jonson's "To Penshurst," Don Wayne emphasizes that poem's place in the "creation of a new kind of space occupied by the family and called the *home*," which was in turn a corollary of an emergent proprietary (though still patriarchal) concept of the individual. In Jonson's poem, as Wayne points out, "the house is still an aristocratic house, and the family still bears traces of the feudal extended household."[27] As an instantiation of the emergent ideology of home, Spenser's poem may claim primacy over Jonson's not merely on the basis of chronology but also because the home that the poet celebrates and memorializes is not his patron's but his own. There is an element of equivocation regarding the locus of the poet's homecoming, an equivocation between England and Ireland, that points forcefully toward the paradoxical social identity of the colonist, for whom a departure from his native place has become a return home. The place to which Colin comes home is the pastoral world but the place to which Spenser comes home is now Ireland. Although Spenser's eclogue of return was not actually printed until 1595, he subscribes his dedicatory epistle to Sir Walter Ralegh, "From my house of Kilcolman, the 27. of December. 1591." The poet finds his home where he founds his house – not in England but in the Munster plantation.

The ironic nuances of the pastoral mask, its ways of simultaneously concealing and revealing meanings, can best be savored when *Colin Clouts Come Home Againe* is read as a mixed-genre intertext that encompasses in a dialogical relationship both Spenser's dedicatory epistle to Ralegh and the eclogue itself. At the beginning of the poem's narrative, Colin Clout and the Shepheard of the Ocean meet in the pastoral world of Ireland. Here they sing, but not in the agonistic form conventional in the eclogue. They do not sing in competition for a prize but rather for their mutual pleasure; they perform in perfect, homoerotic reciprocity:

> He pip'd, I sung; and when he sung, I piped,
> By chaunge of turnes, each making other mery,
> Neither envying other, nor envied.
>
> (76–8)

The courtly deceit and backbiting attacked later in the poem – as well as its debasements of both love and poetry – find their antithesis here. The songs sung by the shepherds strongly contrast two modes of courtship, the one leading to complaint and the other to content. At the same time, their very performance is itself a source of mutual pleasure, which seems to be more readily available to English gentlemen when they are rusticated in Ireland than it is when they are resident at the English court.

The Shepheard of the Ocean is a transparent pastoral mask for Sir Walter Ralegh, himself a seaman and from a West Country family of mariners. Ralegh was nicknamed "Water" by Queen Elizabeth; he reciprocated by fashioning his personal cult of devotion to his royal mistress as the attraction of the Ocean to Cynthia, the Moon goddess. Spenser and his patron were now neighbors and fellow undertakers in the Munster plantation – although Inchiquin, Ralegh's estate, was some fourteen times larger than Spenser's.[28] A disappointed courtier, the Shepherd of the Ocean sings of his cruel mistress:

> His song was all a lamentable lay,
>   Of great unkindnesse, and of usage hard,
> Of *Cynthia* the Ladie of the sea,
> Which from her presence faultlesse him debard.

When this Petrarchan lover cries

> Ah my loves queene, and goddesse of my life,
> Who shall me pittie, when thou doest me wrong?

his amatory anguish has political point. Like his prototype in Ralegh's own complaint of *The Ocean to Scinthia*, the courtier represents himself as a victim of injustice.[29] The poem's inaugural representation of Cynthia is as a cruel mistress indeed.

In contrast to the plaintive lyric produced by the Shepherd of the Ocean, Colin produces a narrative of conflict between filial obedience and romantic desire, between the dictates of a father bent upon preferring his daughter to a socially advantageous match and the resourcefulness of young lovers bent on union. The first shepherd's song articulates the frustrated desire characteristic of Elizabethan sonnet sequences, and of the poems and pageants in which Petrarchan topoi were adapted to the courtship of the royal mistress. In contrast, the second shepherd's song shares with *AMORETTI AND Epithalamion* the mythos of courtship's trials leading to a joyful union. However, as always in Spenser, erotic fulfillment is fragile, and achieved at considerable cost: the fluvial lovers' secret is discovered, Bregog's channel is filled with rocks, his waters are scattered, and he loses his identity. The ethos of the subjected Ocean's attraction to the unattainable Moon is courtly and politic; that of the match between Mulla and Bregog, the two Irish rivers of which Colin sings, is rustic and domestic. The songs of the two shepherd–poets exemplify two fundamental and distinct modes of courtship. These paradigms underlie much of the rest of the poem, their variations being presented in alternation and in a latent tension or contradiction that the poem does not finally resolve.

Its Virgilian heritage rendered Renaissance pastoral a kind hospitable to meditations upon the poet's progress – and one in which the indissolubility of poetic and social motives clearly manifested itself. Elizabethan pastorals could be worked so as to celebrate, anatomize, or instruct courtly society; and they could be made to articulate alienation from courtly corruption and the degradation of clientage in such a way as to reaffirm the writer's own virtue and gentility. In such terms, *Colin Clouts Come Home Againe* is a paradigmatic text of Elizabethan pastoralism; it is, by turns, a record, an anatomy, and a model of Elizabethan courtship. It indicts courtly corruption and decadence; portrays the ideal courtier; catalogs and appraises Spenser's fellow poets in a benevolently patronizing way, while obliquely criticizing their lack of courtly patronage; and praises the Queen and aristocratic patronesses with manifestly self-interested extravagance. The satiric, plaintive, and recreative modes kept relatively distinct in the individual eclogues of *The Shepheardes Calender* here conjoin and alternate within a single, extended, and episodic eclogue. Extremes of courtly compliment and anti-courtly censure clash within what the author coyly refers to in his dedicatory epistle as "this simple pastorall"; encomiastic and ironic strategies call attention to themselves, as if the poem were written to exemplify the duplicitousness that Puttenham ascribes to the eclogue.[30]

When Colin has told them about the wonders of his journey to Cynthia's court, his rustic companions respond with a naively pointed question:

> Why, *Colin*, since thou foundst such grace
> With *Cynthia* and all her noble crew:
> Why didst thou ever leave that happie place,
> In which such wealth might unto thee accrew?
>
> (652–5)

The question marks the poem's precipitous shift from the extremity of praise for the person of the monarch to the extremity of criticism for her court (660–730, 749–94). Court life

> is no sort of life
> For shepheard fit to lead in that same place,
> Where each one seeks with malice and with strife,
> To thrust downe other into foule disgrace,
> Himselfe to raise: and he doth soonest rise
> That best can handle his deceitfull wit,
> In subtil shifts, and finest sleights devise,
> Either by slaundering his well deemed name,
> Through leasings lewd, and fained forgerie:
> Or else by breeding him some blot of blame,
> By creeping close into his secrecie;
> To which him needs, a guilefull hollow hart,
> Masked with faire dissembling curtesie,
> A filed toung furnisht with tearmes of art,
> No art of schoole, but Courtiers schoolery.
>
> (688–702)

Spenser criticism has sometimes taken his indictment of courtly corruption and his praise of the monarch as non-contradictory; it has taken at face value his conjoining of satire and sycophancy. However, Queen Elizabeth is scarcely separable from her court, which was not merely a collection of individuals but the central cultural institution and an essential ideological apparatus of the state. The Queen was the embodiment of the state, and she maintained and supervised her court in order to serve her own purposes and to reflect her glory. An attack on the degeneracy of the court is always an implicit indictment of the monarchical regime – a necessarily oblique indictment, of course, and usually combined with an overcompensatory encomium of the sovereign.

Colin's extended catalog of contemporary English poets (376–455) includes numerous suggestions that service to Cynthia may be unrewarding: Harpalus is

> woxen aged,
> In faithfull service of faire *Cynthia*;

> (380–1)

Corydon is "meanly waged" (382); Palamon "sung so long untill he quite hoarse grew" (399); Alabaster is not "knowne to Cynthia as he ought" (402); the Shepheard of the Ocean "spends his wit in loves consuming smart" (429); and, of course, "Astrofell is dead and gone" (449). Here Colin flagrantly contradicts his initial assertion that, in England,

> learned arts do florish in great honor,
> And Poets wits are had in peerelesse price

> (320–1)

Moreover, the contradiction is presented, scathingly, in precisely the terms Puttenham uses to characterize and commend the "profession of a very Courtier, which is in plaine termes, cunningly to be able to dissemble" (*Arte of English Poesie*, p. 299). Spenser writes in the bitter final stanza of The Legend of Courtesie that the poet who seeks a courtly audience must "seeke to please, that now is counted wisemens threasure" (*FQ*, 6.12.41). In the rhetorical strategies of his own courtly encomia, of course, Spenser himself is what Puttenham calls "a cunning Princepleaser" (17), one whose sycophancy serves his literary and material self-advancement. The compromises and contradictions of Spenser's own position are marked in the tonal extremities and disjunctions of his text.

Colin indicts the lovers of Cynthia's court for profaning Love's "mightie mysteries" into "a complement for courting vaine", and this indictment leads him into his culminating role as a mystagogue of Neoplatonic Eros (791–894):

> Of that God the Priest thou shouldest bee:
> So well thou wot'st the mysterie of his might,

quoth Cuddy.[31] Renaissance Neoplatonism's syncretic, poetic theology of love provides the rusticated writer with a position of spiritual and aesthetic authority, from which he may address and judge his social betters. Colin's Cupid is a "dread Lord, that doest liege hearts possesse":

> So we him worship, so we him adore
> With humble hearts to heaven uplifted hie,
> That to true loves he may us evermore
> Preferre, and of their grace us dignifie.

> (815–18)

The worship, love, and preferment associated with Cynthia and her court have now been displaced. Indeed, the poet's pastoral persona goes so far as to invent an aristocracy of virtue from whose ranks Elizabethan courtly lovers are explicitly excluded,

> For their desire is base, and doth not merit,
> The name of love, but of disloyall lust:
> Ne mongst true lovers they shall place inherit,
> But as Exuls out of his court be thrust.
>
> (891–4)

Colin/Spenser has now reversed the terms of courtly inclusion and exclusion: his position of rustication in Ireland allows him to enjoy a central place at a court where Cupid reigns in place of Cynthia.

Another version of the alternative or counter-court provides the frame for the whole eclogue. At the very opening of the poem, Colin is discovered,

> Charming his oaten pipe unto his peres,
> The shepheard swaines that did about him play:
> Who all the while with greedie listfull eares,
> Did stand astonisht at his curious skill.
>
> (5–8)

In *Colin Clouts Come Home Againe*, the tension within Spenser's sense of his vocation – and, more broadly, within his relationship to the cultural and political center of Elizabethan society – is figured in two distinct and potentially opposed settings: the royal court, where the queen is the cynosure, and the pastoral world, where the shepherd–poet is the cynosure. The striking shifts of topic and tone that characterize this poem are resonances of its contradictory representations of the writer as a Poet of Orphic powers and as a humble client to his social superiors. Throughout Spenser's poetic corpus, the poet's voice is characterized by an oscillation between self-aggrandizement and self-abasement, between vaunting and wailing. This oscillation is inadequately explained by recourse either to literary convention or to personal psychology; it is the literary inscription of a lived contradiction that is indissolubly social and subjective. In more senses than one, then, *Colin Clouts Come Home Againe* is a poem of place.

In his catalogue of court ladies, Colin devotes considerable space to Phyllis, Charillis, and Amaryllis. These are, he tells us,

> the sisters three,
> The honor of the noble familie,
> Of which I meanest boast my selfe to be.
> And most that unto them I am so nie.
>
> (536–9)

This and the succeeding allusions establish that these three "Nymphs" from Cynthia's "retinew" are the well-married daughters of Sir John and Lady Katherine Spencer of Althorp. As noted earlier, Spenser claims or implies his kinship with the rich, powerful, and ennobled Spencers of Althorp in no less than five of his poems printed between 1591 and 1596.[32] Here, in the not-so-humble shepherdly persona of "Colin Clout," Edmund Spenser reaffirms his consanguinity with the fairest "of all the shepheards daughters which there be" (556).

The pastoral mode of Spenser's courtly compliment is by no means merely decorative, for the Spencers of Althorp had risen to enormous wealth, property, and prestige under the Tudor dynasty precisely by means of careful and aggressive *pastoralism*. The father of these "shepheards daughters," Sir John Spencer, was widely acknowledged to be the master shepherd of the day. Over the course of a century, the Spencers had risen from being humble graziers on rented pastures to become the greatest sheep farmers and perhaps the wealthiest subjects in the land.[33] Their spectacular socio-economic ascent by means of pastoral farming appears to have been unique in the Tudor period. One social historian has observed that the Spencers "had built up their wealth by the same methods which enabled yeomen to become gentlemen – the practice of agriculture, coupled with restraint in expenditure, though carried on higher up the social scale, and supplemented by gains from favourable marriages. The corner-stone of the Spencer edifice had been sheepfarming, conducted under ideal conditions" (Finch, *Wealth of Five Northamptonshire Families*, p. 65).

The social ambitions of the recently gentrified pastoral poet may well have gained sustenance from the spectacular success of his putative kindred. Certainly, the strongly and explicitly autobiographical element in *Colin Clouts Come Home Againe* marks an uncommon and especially resonant conjunction of pastoral as môde of poetic production with pastoral as mode of agrarian production. In a poetic kind ostensibly dedicated to the rejection of worldly ambition, the poet pursues his claim to kinship with a family that had risen to great estate by capitalizing upon the material practices from which the conventions of pastoral poetry are derived.

In subject and style, the homely love tale that Spenser gives to Colin in *Colin Clouts Come Home Againe* is utterly unlike his lavish encomia of the Queen as Eliza, Cynthia, and Gloriana. Yet the tale is nevertheless an oblique celebration of the material fruits of Spenser's assiduous courtship of the monarch, and of his colonial service to her regime. In the text of the poem, the writer's pastoral persona creates an allegorical narrative of curious topographical specificity. An etiological myth explaining the confluence of two personified rivers – Bregog and Mulla – endows with tutelary spirits two streams – the Bregog and the Awbeg – that respectively flow through and bound the 3,028-acre estate granted on 26 October 1590 to "Edmund Spenser, gentleman." The property had formerly belonged to Sir John Fitzgerald of Desmond, who had been executed for treason; it was now Edmund Spenser's, "To hold forever, in fee farm, by the name of 'Hap Hazard'."[34] This grant resulted from a royal confiscation of vast tracts of land in Munster that had been the property of the rebellious English Irish Earl of Desmond and his followers; these lands were redistributed by the Crown to English gentlemen, who were to undertake to settle English families as their tenant farmers. As deputy clerk to the Council of Munster, Spenser would have been intimately familiar with this project, which had been in process for several years. Massive legal complications were involved in the project of redistributing to Englishmen more than half a million acres of escheated lands and adjudicating Irish claims to them. Between 1584 and 1589, several successive royal commissions were established to survey and inventory the attainted and forfeited lands, to divide them into seignories and assign them to undertakers, and to try the titles of claimants against the new grants. Lord Roche subsequently wrote that English Irish claimants like himself had had "great expectations of justice, with favour and expedition at the hands of the commissioners," but that those expectations were disappointed, and the claimants "were left entangled and subject to the suppressions and heavy hand of the undertakers without redress as before and every one discontented." Even one of the English undertakers had to concur: Sir William Herbert wrote to Lord Burghley that "our pretence in the enterprise of plantation was to establish in these parts piety, justice, inhabitation and civility with comfort and good example to the parts adjacent. Our drift now is, being here possessed of land, to extort, make the state of things turbulent, and live by prey and by pay."[35] Herbert's remarkably candid critique turns the language of Spenser's *A View* upside down; the English undertakers, the erstwhile agents of the civilizing process, have themselves become the very predators whom they are bent to reduce to order.

A notable instance of the prolonged and bitter conflict between English undertakers and Irish claimants to the escheated Munster lands pitted Edmund Spenser, gentleman, against Maurice, Lord Roche. Much of the estate granted to Spenser was claimed by Lord Roche, his neighbor and a member of the old English Irish aristocracy. As early as 1589, before Spenser had officially received his patent, he and Roche were exchanging formal charges. On 12 October 1589, Roche wrote to Secretary Walsingham, accusing Spenser of taking possession of lands to which he falsely pretended title, of threatening and beating Roche's tenants and servants, and stealing their cattle. On the same day, in his administrative capacity, Spenser endorsed a bill against Lord Roche, charging him with speeches and actions in contempt of the Queen's sovereignty, as well as with acts of intimidation and violence against Spenser himself, his fellow undertakers, and their tenants.[36] In the office of deputy to the Clerk of the Council of Munster, Spenser wrote, as Roche himself had put it, with the "heavy hand of the undertakers."

In Spenser's poem, the shepherd–poet creates a scenario in which the fluvial lovers deceive Mulla's

> Old father *Mole*, (*Mole* hight that mountain gray
> That walls the Northside of *Armulla* dale),
>
> (104–5)

and the powerful suitor whom he favors, "Which *Allo* hight, Broad water called farre" (123). The poet identifies himself with the masculine river/ lover, whose erotic devotion is triumphant over adversity:

> But of my river *Bregogs* love I soong,
> Which to the shiny *Mulla* he did beare.
> And yet doth beare, and ever will, so long
> As water doth within his bancks appeare.

"My house of Kilcolman," writes Spenser in his epistle; "my river Bregog," sings Colin in his lay. Similarly, in *The Faerie Queene*, the poet invokes "Mulla mine" at the marriage of the Thames and the Medway (*FQ*, 4.11.41), and "my old father *Mole*" in the *Mutabilitie* cantos (*MC*, 6.36); in *Epithalamion*, he summons "Ye Nymphes of Mulla" to deck his bride on his own wedding day (56). In these instances, we hear, through the poet's rustic mask, the gentleman's claim to legitimate possession, at once assertive and uncertain: "To hold forever, in fee farm, by the name of 'Hap Hazard'."

The "TWO CANTOS OF *MUTABILITIE*: Which, both for Forme and Matter, appeare to be parcell of some following Booke of the *FAERIE QUEENE*," were first printed in the posthumous 1609 edition of the poem. They contain what is perhaps Spenser's most remarkable conjunction of the universal and the particular, the cosmic and the personal, for here his conceit is that "great dame *Nature*" (*MC*, 7.5) holds court in his own neighborhood:

> Eftsoones the time and place appointed were,
> Where all, both heavenly Powers, and earthly wights,
> Before great Natures presence should appeare,
> For triall of their Titles and best Rights:
> That was, to weet, upon the highest hights
>   Of *Arlo-hill* (Who knowes not *Arlo-hill*?)

> That is the highest head (in all mens sights)
> Of my old father *Mole*, whom Shepheards quill
> Renowmed hath with hymnes fit for a rurall skill.
>
> (*MC*, 6.36)

Spenser's autobiographical mythopoeia is continued in a digression that reworks the myth of Diana and Actaeon in order to provide an etiology for the present fallen and desperate state of Ireland. Munster has been ravaged by wolves which the colonialist poet identifies with the island's indigenous inhabitants. The nymph of Diana who precipitates the event is directly linked to Spenser's locale and to the mythos of *Colin Clouts Come Home Againe*:

> Amongst the which, there was a Nymph that hight
>   *Molanna*; daughter of old father *Mole*,
> And sister unto *Mulla*, faire and bright:
> Unto whose bed false *Bregog* whylome stole,
> That Shepheard *Colin* dearely did condole,
> And made her lucklesse loves well knowne to be.
> But this *Molanna*, were she not so shole,
> Were no lesse faire and beautifull then shee:
> Yet as she is, a fairer flood may no man see.
>
> (6.40)

The parenthetical negative interrogative locution in stanza 36 resonates with that in *FQ*, 6.10.16 ("who knowes not *Colin Clout*?"), functioning to mark the narrative as autobiographical allegory. In the reference to "my old father *Mole*" (36), the telling possessive pronoun is proprietary (as in "*Mulla* mine") and also suggestive of filiation: having identified himself with "my river *Bregog*" in *Colin Clouts Come Home Againe*, the poet here construes Mulla's "old father *Mole*" also to be his own father by marriage.

Spenser's familiar displacement of property claims into topographical myth is now given a cosmological setting within the context of Nature's judgment of the relationship between the universal principles of constancy and change. It is upon Arlo hill – within Spenser's immediate geographical locality, and wholly within his imaginative domain – that *Natura naturans* will definitively try all rights and titles. In other words, the cosmological allegory of the *Mutabilitie* cantos may be read, from a materialist perspective, as an exorbitant transposition of Spenser's ambitious and anxious concern regarding the security of his property and rank – the legitimacy of his title – as an English settler in the Munster plantation. It would be reductive to read such a materialist reading as being reductive; on the contrary, it provides a salutary example of the mutual implication of the universal and the particular, the material and the spiritual, that is an essential element of Spenser's allegory. The Irish locus is increasingly conspicuous in Spenser's later poetry – including Books V and VI of *The Faerie Queene*, as well as the posthumously printed *Mutabilitie* cantos – and in each instance, the universal human condition of mutability is being exemplified in terms of the particular conditions of existence of the writing subject, an English gentleman undertaker in the Munster plantation in the later 1590s.

In 1595, the year in which Edmund Spenser advertised his own new status as a landed gentleman in *Colin Clouts Come Home Againe*, the Clarenceux King of Arms concocted for Sir John Spencer a new pedigree – putatively "collected out of divers records, registers, evidences, ancient seales of Armes, sundry willes and Testamentes" – that now derived the Spencers of Althorp from "the auncient family" of Le Despencer and related them to the earls of Winchester and Gloucester.[37] Colin's tale of Bregog and Mulla is a way of endowing Spenser's newly acquired socio-economic status with what the poet claims is "auncient truth confirm'd with credence old" (103). Thus, for the writer himself, the publication of the pastoral poet's topographical mythopoeia serves a function not entirely unlike that of the fabulous genealogies devised by obliging Elizabethan heralds for Tudor arrivistes like the Spencers of Althorp. Sir John Spencer and Master Edmund Spenser – the shepherd and his apparent kinsman, the poet – were simultaneously engaged in analogous strategies of social self-legitimation at very different strata of the social hierarchy, each being impelled by an appropriately graded combination of ambition and insecurity. The river marriage in *Colin Clouts Come Home Againe* figures the founding of the writer's own house, of Spenser's own local and modest dynasty. At the same time, the poem's extended catalog of court ladies advertises his connection to the already well-established but still ascendant house of Spencer, thus making visible the dynamics of kinship and patronage, status and property, that enabled, and were reproduced in, Spenser's own limited and precarious upward mobility.

Spenser's mythopoeia is a symbolic means of legitimating his claim to the rank of gentleman in the English political nation; and it is also a symbolic means of making his newly adopted and hostile homeland – his freshly expropriated, hotly disputed, and always imperiled Irish property – more fully his own by the transformative and perpetuating powers of his art. This is myth-making in the explicitly ideological sense of the word: it is an instance of mystification, a sanctioning naturalization of contingent social relations and disputed property rights. The grant of the 3,028-acre seignory of Kilcolman to Spenser included the old castle and manor; it authorized him to empark 151 acres for deer, and to procure as his tenants 2 dozen English families of varying status and property rights. He had now achieved a dominion – and a demesne – of the sort that his friend Harvey had jocularly imagined a decade earlier, when he wrote that "Master *Collin Cloute* ... may ... purchase great landes, and Lordshippes, with the money, which his *Calender* and *Dreames* have, and will affourde him." Having thus arrived triumphantly "at home," Spenser now chose to name his domain "Hap hazard," thus resonantly – and prophetically – suggesting that his good fortune remained under the aegis of Mutability. For beyond the particularities of Spenser's property disputes with his English-Irish neighbor, the whole of the Munster plantation was vulnerable to attacks by the "wild" Irish. Indeed, only three years after the printing of the poem, Kilcolman was sacked and burned during the course of Tyrone's rebellion.[38] It was with a certain ironic justice that Spenser came home again to London for the last time as a refugee, a dis-placed person.

The publisher's Epistle Dedicatory to *AMORETTI AND Epithalamion* strongly implies a special relationship between that volume and *Colin Clouts Come Home Againe*. Ponsonby, who also published the first edition of *The Faerie Queene*, elaborates in his epistle a version of the sea passage between Ireland and England that figures in *Colin Clouts Come Home Againe*: Spenser is absent in Ireland, and his Muse has been "long wished for in Englande." The poems themselves have crossed the seas from Ireland, where they were written, to England, where they will be printed. The volume's two commendatory sonnets pick up the theme of Spenser's absent Anglo-Irish Muse, one of them actually addressing him as Colin. The multiple authorship characteristic of the prefatory genres of Early Modern books demonstrates that print is a collective medium, and publication a collective enterprise. Such prefatory genres are here being used collaboratively by the poet and his associates so as to shape an authorial identity, confer authority upon it, and prepare its readership.

The poetry book entitled *AMORETTI AND Epithalamion* constitutes a sonnet sequence and an epithalamium as a composite text – a text that is mixed in form, genre, and occasion, but unified by joint publication, narrative sequentiality, and the parallel formatting of one sonnet and one stanza per page. Construed as a sequence, *Amoretti* sketches the narrative of a courtship that culminates in betrothal (*Amo*, 67–9), and eventuates in the marriage celebrated in the epithalamium that completes the volume; as such, it is a sonnet sequence remarkable and perhaps unique not only among Elizabethan sequences but among Renaissance sonnet sequences generally. And although the use of autobiographical material was by no means unusual in sonnets, the fusion of bridegroom with poet in an epithalamium seems to have been unprecedented.[39] The Irish allusions in the dedicatory epistle and commendatory sonnets of *AMORETTI AND Epithalamion* give a material specificity to the poet's erotic autobiography. Within the poetic texts, the localization of Spenser's autobiographical fiction in Ireland is present not only in such explicit details as the *Epithalamion*'s invocation of "Ye nymphes of Mulla" but also in the remarkably elaborate and oblique calendrical symbolism that structures the whole poem: analysis of the number of stanzas and numbers and lengths of lines appears to fix the date (St. Barnabas's Day, 11 June) and chart the hours of the poet's wedding day, and to locate the blessed event in southern Ireland.[40] Thus, Spenser's Irish home – and the poetic celebration of the nuptial that founds his domestic domain there – becomes the personal and material reference point for a cosmic vision. The theme of this vision – which *Epithalamion* shares with the Garden of Adonis episode in Book III of *The Faerie Queene*, the Legend of Chastity, and with the *Mutabilitie* cantos – is that, through marriage and procreation, the apparently haphazard existence of mortal human subjects becomes

> eterne in mutabilitie
> And by succession made perpetuall.
>
> (*FQ*, 3.6.47)

As is the case in *Colin Clouts Come Home Againe*, the Irish allusions in *Epithalamion* help to create a locus of meaning and value that is defined in part by its otherness from London, the court, and the Queen. This latter suggestion is also taken up explicitly in *Amoretti* 33 and 80, although here the contrast is made in generic rather than geo-political terms: the poet sets forth an opposition between the project of celebrating his own beloved in sonnets and that of celebrating his royal mistress in *The Faerie Queene*. In *Amoretti* 33, the poet confesses that the perturbations of love make him neglect his "taedious toyle," his duty to

> that most sacred Empresse my dear dred,
> not finishing her Queene of faery.

In *Amoretti* 80, he contrasts the paradoxical recreative confinement characteristic of both the love sonnet and the domestic domain to the anxious labor of heroic poetry and royal service:

> After so long a race as I have run
>   Through Faery land, which those six books compile,
>   give leave to rest me being halfe fordonne,
>   and gather to my selfe new breath awhile.
> Then as a steed refreshed after toyle,

> out of my prison I will breake anew:
> and stoutly will that second worke assoyle,
> with strong endeavour and attention dew.
> Till then give leave to me in pleasant mew,
> to sport my muse and sing my loves sweet praise:
> the contemplation of whose heavenly hew,
> my spirit to an higher pitch will rayse.
> But let her prayses yet be low and meane,
> fit for the handmayd of the Faery Queene.

The juxtaposition and implied opposition of erotic and imperial encomia is also a rhetorical feature of *Colin Clouts Come Home Againe*. The encomium of Cynthia (*CCCHA*, 332–51) elicits a response from the rustic auditors that I have noted above in discussing the dedication of *The Faerie Queene* – namely, a spontaneous encomium for the encomiast:

> By wondering at thy *Cynthiaes* praise,
> *Colin*, thy selfe thou mak'st us more to wonder,
> And her upraising, doest thy selfe upraise.

(353–5)

Having been invited by a shepherdess to give equal time to the nymphs of Cynthia's court, Colin begins his next catalog (464–583) with a paean to an unnamed maid that culminates in the poem's numerically central lines:

> And I hers ever onely, ever one:
> One ever I all vowed hers to bee,
> One ever I, and others never none.

(477–9)

Whether or not Spenser intended an identification of this figure with a particular woman, the rhetorical/ideological relevance of the encomium and of its strategic placement in the middest is that the object of the poet's devotion is explicitly *not* Cynthia but rather one of her nymphs. As if in compensation, the catalog of court ladies is followed by the poem's longest and most resplendent encomium to Cynthia (590–647), separated into two parts by Cuddy's interjection calling attention to Colin's transgression of pastoral decorum. The first part focuses upon Cynthia's excellences; the second, upon the aggrandizing and perpetuating powers of Colin's own art: "Her name recorded I will leave for ever" (631); "My layes made of her shall not be forgotten" (642). The encomium links the excellences of the Queen to the excellences of her poet, and renders the former dependent upon the latter for their articulation and perpetuation. Thus, this passage is an extended illustration of the formula that, in upraising the Queen, the poet upraises himself – as, indeed, is the dedication of the 1596 edition of *The Faerie Queene*, "TO LIVE WITH THE ETERNITIE OF HER FAME."

The final appearance of Colin Clout and the anonymous object of his love, in Book VI of *The Faerie Queene*, the Legend of Courtesy, has the air of an apotheosis. This celebrated digression from a larger pastoral episode isolates Colin and his poetic entourage from the poem's mere rustics: upon Mount Acidale, the "gentle Shepheard" (6.10.29) is free from contamination by "the ruder clown"; the latter's ascent is barred by "a gentle flud" (6.10.7). The figure at the center of the concentric circles of nymphs and Graces to whom Colin pipes upon the summit of Mount Acidale is neither a queen nor a goddess but a lass unparalleled. The Graces themselves have advanced her "to be another Grace":

> Another Grace she well deserves to be,
>   In whom so many Graces gathered are,
>   Excelling much the meane of her degree;
>   Divine resemblaunce, beauty soveraine rare,
>   Firme Chastity, that spight ne blemish dare;
>   All which she with such courtesie doth grace,
>   That all her peres cannot with her compare,
>   But quite are dimmed, when she is in place.
> She made me often pipe and now to pipe apace.
>
> Sunne of the world, great glory of the sky,
>   That all the earth doest lighten with thy rayes,
>   Great *Gloriana*, greatest Majesty,
>   Pardon thy shepheard, mongst so many layes,
>   As he hath sung of thee in all his dayes,
>   To make one minime of thy poore handmayd,
>   And underneath thy feete to place her prayse,
>   That when thy glory shall be farre displayd
> To future age of her this mention may be made.
>
> (FQ, 6.10.27–8)

Spenser's Colin alludes to his earlier vision of Eliza, Gloriana's pastoral counterpart, in the "Aprill" eclogue of *The Shepheardes Calender*; and this conspicuous allusion draws attention to his process of re-vision:

> Lo how finely the graces can it foote
>   to the Instrument:
> They dauncen deffly, and singen soote,
>   in their meriment.
> Wants not a fourth grace, to make the daunce even?
> Let that rowme to my Lady be yeven.
>
> (SC, "Aprill," 109–14)

Whereas the various female figures celebrated by Colin in the *Calender* are transformations of each other, the fourth Grace on Mount Acidale is explicitly distinguished from and opposed to the idealized imperial type of the Queen.[41] In virtue and beauty, and in the grace and courtesy with which she reciprocates his devotion, Colin's transfigured country lass transcends her place in the social hierarchy. The humble shepherd–poet must beg the forgiveness of his sovereign for his violation of both poetic and social decorum. The praise of Colin's beloved is to endure as a manifestation of Gloriana's enduring glory. Yet Gloriana's name will endure – so the poet implies – because she has been raised in his poem. And, as the whole episode has so resoundingly asserted, the source of Colin's inspiration is not the imperial vision of Gloriana but rather the intimate vision of his beloved. Ultimately, then, Gloriana owes her enduring glory to the poor handmaid whose praise is placed beneath her feet.[42]

The "countrey lasse" (*FQ*, 6.10.25) celebrated by Colin upon Mount Acidale recalls not only the Eliza of "Aprill" but also the beloved and loving mistress and spouse who is the subject of the poet's encomia throughout *AMORETTI AND Epithalamion*:

> that little that I am, shall all be spent,
> in setting your immortal prayses forth.
> Whose lofty argument uplifting me,
> shall lift you up unto an high degree.
>
> (*Amo*, 82)

Whatever her virtues, this paragon must nevertheless be merely "fit for the handmayd of the Faery Queene" (*Amo*, 80). Colin's juxtaposition of his beloved and his sovereign upon Mount Acidale transposes into the pastoral mode an audacious encomiastic strategy that Spenser had already explored in his persona as the poet–lover of *Amoretti*. This complex audaciousness may perhaps best be illustrated by a reading of *Amoretti* 74:

> Most happy letters fram'd by skillful trade,
>   with which that happy name was first desynd:
>   the which three times thrise happy hath me made,
>   with guifts of body, fortune and of mind.
> The first my being to me gave by kind,
>   from mothers womb deriv'd by dew descent,
>   the second is my sovereigne Queene most kind,
>   that honour and large richesse to me lent.
> The third my love, my lives last ornament,
>   by whom my spirit out of dust was raysed:
>   to speake her prayse and glory excellent,
>   of all alive most worthy to be praysed.
> Ye three Elizabeths for ever live,
>   that three such graces did unto me give.

The first quatrain of the sonnet is an address to and invocation of a name, rather than a personage; the second and third quatrains perform a triadic unfolding of the name's referent; and the couplet celebrates the re-creative process of textualization itself, the process enacted in the preceding lines. If the subject of the sonnet is the gifts that the poet has received from his Three Graces, then its object is to become that gift with which he can requite them.

That Queen Elizabeth should be the subject of such a slight and familiar form as the sonnet was hardly unusual. The royal cult was fashioned so as to turn Petrarchan, Marian, and other related cultural forms to the negotiation of the complex and delicate relationship between the feminine ruler and her masculine subjects, whose collective interests she embodied and upon whose loyalty her regime was wholly dependent. Thus, the political anomaly of the woman prince generated a paradox in the decorum of poetic kinds: because, as Spenser put it in the Letter to Ralegh, the Queen bore "two persons, the one of a most royall Queene or Empresse, the other of a most vertuous and beautifull Lady," the mean style and witty familiarity of amorous poetry were as appro-priate to her praise as were the high style and grave formality of heroic poetry. And, of course, the representation of the sovereign and of the subject's relation to her varied with the formal norms and constraints of the mode in which they were being constructed.

That the poet's sovereign should occupy the two central lines of his sonnet is an expected gesture of homage that is nevertheless belied by a more basic displacement: for the subject of the sonneteer's praise is not his royal mistress – who was, indeed, every Englishman's mistress and no one's – but rather his own beloved. For the purposes of this discussion, the particular interest of *Amoretti* 74 is precisely in its simultaneous inclusion of the princely subject and its conspicuous refusal to make her the principal subject of its praise. The Queen shares the second quatrain with the poet's mother; his "love" has the third quatrain to herself. In the cramped quarters of the sonnet, Elizabeth Tudor must yield place and space to Elizabeth Boyle.[43] The first and second Elizabeths – the poet's natural and political mothers – are linked and distinguished by the play on "kind," but also by the parallel between the maternal *gift* of life and the royal *loan* of status and livelihood: the former is free and irrevocable; the latter, conditional and subject to withdrawal, both a reward and a means of control. In the difference between "gave" and "lent" is implied the condition of the subject's subjection. Thus, the quatrain reveals a binary structure based not only upon analogy but also upon opposition, an opposition represented in explicitly social metaphors – that is, in the contrast between status or identity as derived by birth and blood (in this instance, "dew descent" from the mother) and that acquired in royal service.

The hierarchical norms of Spenser's culture clearly imply that the spiritual gift conferred by the third Elizabeth transcends those of nature and state: she is the divine artificer, "by whom my spirit out of dust was raysed." She is the source and the end of his writing; it is she who authorizes him to write, and to write of her. Now, all of this would be an unremarkable Petrarchan hyperbole were it not that the hyperbole does its work at the expense of the Queen, whose very inclusion makes more tangible, and raises the stakes of, the poet's encomium. This is what gives it what I have called its complex audaciousness. Such an effect is especially striking in the poet's reference, in line 11, to his love's "glory excellent." In *Amoretti* 13, the poet describes his beloved's "most goodly temperature" in an attenuated Petrarchan oxymoron, as "Myld humblesse mixt with awfull majesty." (This was itself a trope used of Queen Elizabeth, as in Sir John Hayward's description of her as "coupling mildnesse with majesty."[44]) But the impact of such appropriations of royal attributes and epithets is both more effective and more audacious, as in *Amoretti* 74, when royalty itself is close by. To attribute the imperial virtue of "glory excellent" to a mere private woman in the textual presence of Spenser's own Gloriana seems not only hyperbolic but provocative.

The poem's basic conceit – that of the poet's own feminine trinity all meeting in one name – works counter to the cultic claim for the Queen's unique and inclusive womanhood. One of the fundamental aspects of the royal cult was its appropriation of the characteristic stages of the domestic life-cycle of Tudor Woman, its representation of the Queen as simultaneously the fertile and selfless mother, the virtuous and beautiful mistress, and the careful and devoted wife of her people.[45] In *Amoretti* 74, however, the very inclusion of the Queen between the poet's mother and his mistress resists and restricts her totalizing claim upon the affective powers of the Elizabethan feminine. At the same time that he fully acknowledges his sovereign, the masculine subject implicitly repudiates her maternal and erotic claims upon him. The sonnet's homage to royal power and grace is presumably sincere; nevertheless, its text bears an antithetical relationship to the royal cult that has generated the conventions within which it is written. In reshaping the gender-specific cultural terms that have been shaped by the sovereign herself, the writing subject seeks to appropriate and confine the monarch to his own uses.

In *Epithalamion*, Spenser draws attention to his appropriation for a personal and bourgeois occasion of a celebratory genre normally reserved for the politically and dynastically significant marriages of members of

royalty and the aristocracy.[46] Thus, the poet–bridegroom's proprietary
first stanza:

> Ye learned sisters which have oftentimes
> Beene to me ayding, others to adorne:
> Whom ye thought worthy of your gracefull rymes,
> That even the greatest did not greatly scorne
> To heare theyr names sung in your simple layes,
> But joyed in theyr prayse:
> . . .
> Helpe me mine owne loves prayses to resound,
> Ne let the same of any be envide,
> So Orpheus did for his owne bride,
> So I unto my selfe alone will sing.
>
>   (1–6, 14–17)

The opposition is foregrounded again in the remarkable passage in
stanza 21, in which the moon as Cinthia peeps through the window to
interrupt the pleasures of the poet's wedding night:

> Who is the same, which at my window peepes?
> Or whose is that faire face, that shines so bright,
> Is it not Cinthia, she that never sleepes,
> But walkes about high heaven al the night?
> O fayrest goddesse, do thou not envy
> My love with me to spy.
> . . .
> And sith of wemens labours thou hast charge,
> And generation goodly dost enlarge,
> Encline thy will t'effect our wishfull vow,
> And the chast wombe informe with timely seed,
> That may our comfort breed.
>
>   (372–7, 383–7)

As in the recurrent episodes of interrupted intimacy in Book VI of *The
Faerie Queene* – which include the disruption of Colin's piping to his lass
– so here the private is not merely defined by its juxtaposition to the
public; it becomes apprehensible precisely in the moment of its violation.
In this instance, by evoking that aspect of Cynthia–Diana which connects
her to childbirth, the poet–bridegroom rhetorically assimilates the mili-
tantly virginal Queen/goddess to his epithalamium; he seeks to put her
into domestic service.

The trajectory of *Epithalamion* moves from privacy to domesticity.
The initial condition of the poet–bridegroom is solitary: "I unto my selfe
alone will sing"; here privacy bears the etymological burden of *privation*.
The unfolding nuptial narrative moves the poet–bridegroom into the
companionate condition of marriage. In the final stanza, it moves him

toward a vision of the family as a dynastic unit, a lineage enduring and prospering through time –

> eterne in mutabilitie
> And by succession made perpetuall
>
> (*FQ*, 3.6.47)

– and beyond time to a final "Sabaoths sight":

> That we may raise a large posterity,
> Which from the earth, which they may long possesse,
> With lasting happinesse,
> Up to your haughty pallaces may mount,
> And for the guerdon of theyr glorious merit
> May heavenly tabernacles there inherit,
> Of blessed Saints for to increase the count.
>
> (417–23)

This passage is an example of what Kenneth Burke calls the socio-anagogic mode, in which such terms of social status as merit and inheritance, achievement and ascription, are transcoded into the order of grace.[47] The vaulting ambition of the meanly placed subject who hopes to see his progeny mount up to haughty palaces is legitimated as the metaphorical vehicle of a spiritual aspiration. The upward sweep of Spenser's wedding song encompasses courtship, marriage, and family formation, leading to the temporal perpetuation of a lineage, and the ultimate sanctification of its members. *Epithalamion* renders with remarkable concision an ideology of the Protestant, propertied, and patriarchal family of Early Modern England. The process of courting, wedding, and establishing a family is the overall generic/narrative schema of *AMORETTI AND Epithalamion*, and this Elizabethan social process articulates with those adumbrated in the narrative and descriptive schemata of *Colin Clouts Come Home Againe*. These occasional poems construct the authorial persona as both a public and a domestic subject by means of profession, property, and marriage, and they celebrate the founding of his house in Ireland. In the autobiographical fictions of these two printed poetry books, Spenser discursively records and amplifies the establishment of his social identity, the aggrandizement of his authority and honor, by means of clientage and kinship, state service and artistic excellence, marriage and lineage, the acquisition of land and the publication of *The Faerie Queene*. In the year 1597, *The Shepheardes Calender* was reprinted in a fifth edition, and Spenser purchased the castle and lands of Renny in County Cork as a provision for his son, Peregrine.[48] I hope to have suggested by the foregoing argument that these two events are not unrelated.

For Spenser and for his poetic personae, the shepherd and the bridegroom, the identity, authority, and honor deriving from the establishment of a domestic domain are achieved – and are, perhaps, for someone of Spenser's relatively humble social origins, only fully achievable – on the Elizabethan periphery, in the colonized space of Ireland or "the New World."[49] In such marginal places, Englishmen construed their expropriation of land occupied by the indigenous inhabitants to be synonymous with the civilizing process. The New English administrators and planters in Ireland felt that they could – indeed, felt that they had a duty to – deny the right of natural possession to the "wild" Irish because they lived in a near-savage condition of superstition and disorder, and because they were foragers who neither cultivated the land nor conceptualized it as real property according to English customs of tenure and inheritance. Moreover, these Elizabethan Protestant gentlemen viewed with possibly greater abhorrence the old English-Irish population, whom they judged to have degenerated into the rudeness, superstition, and violence characteristic of the natives. An essential part of the civilizing process undertaken by the Elizabethan administration was the surveying, mapping, and subdividing of the land – a project of discovery and appropriation that had an analogue in the genre, method, and content of Spenser's *A View of the Present State of Ireland*.[50] Spenser's affinity for pastoral poetic conventions notwithstanding, the social and ecological policy that he sought to put into practice in Ireland was unremittingly anti-pastoral:

Look into all the countries that live in such sort by keeping of cattle, and you shall find that they are both very barbarous and uncivil and also greatly given to war ... Since now we purpose to draw the Irish from desire of wars and tumults to the love of peace and civility, it is expedient to abridge their great custom of herding and augment their more trade of tilling and husbandry. (*VPSI*, 158)

Central to the civilizing process proposed in *A View* were the breaking up of extended bonds of kinship and service among the Gaelic Irish, outlawing of the custom of elective land tenure known as tanistry, and suppression of the practice of transhumance (*VPSI*, 6–7, 49–50, 149–50, 155–8). Migratory and marauding pastoralists were to be ordered into households and settled as farmers.

In *A View of the Present State of Ireland*, Eudoxius enumerates the benefits that will accrue to tenants from the provision of longer and more secure leases:

By the handsomeness of his house, he shall take great comfort of his life, more safe dwelling, and a delight to keep his said house neat and cleanly, which now, being as they commonly are rather swinesteads than houses, is the chiefest cause of his so beastly manner of life and savage condition ... and to all these other commodities he shall in short time find ... his own wealth and riches increased and wonderfully enlarged by keeping his cattle in enclosures. (82–3)

Although still denied the full participation of ownership, the tenant will have a stake in the socio-economic regime to which he is subjected; and he will internalize it in his cleanliness and tidiness, and in the pride and pleasure that he derives from the material comforts that it affords. Irenius and Eudoxius, the interlocutors in Spenser's dialogue, concur that this domestication of the tenant ultimately serves the interests of the landlord and the state by improving the property and thus the long-term profits of the former and enhancing the order and security of the latter (81–3). As a property owner and landlord, Spenser stood to benefit financially from the civilizing process.[51]

It was as an English "undertaker" living and writing in the Munster plantation, and writing about the means by which Englishmen like himself might civilize Ireland, that Spenser made in passing his most explicit and resounding statement of an Early Modern English and Protestant form of individualism. In *A View of the Present State of Ireland*, in the course of an argument against the traditional obligations of service that keep the willful, obstinate, and rebellious Irish "lords and captains" well supplied with followers, he declares that: "Here in England ... the noblemen, however they should happen to be evil disposed, have no command at all over the commonalty, though dwelling under them, because every man standeth upon himself, and buildeth his fortunes upon his own faith and firm assurance" (*VPSI*, 147). The quoted passage begins by characterizing the socio-political relationship between the commons and the lords of Spenser's England, in which feudal relations have disappeared and obligations of retaining have become attenuated. This discourse on the political relationship of free-holders to the aristocracy and the state then modulates into an assertion of the individual conscience, will, and responsibility of all godly subjects, regardless of their ascribed status in the social order – although not necessarily regardless of their gender. Thus, an emergent Protestant and entrepreneurial mode of subjectivity runs athwart traditional hierarchies of authority and deference, patronage and clientage. Spenser contains his articulation of such a relatively advanced political position by contextua-lizing it within a loyal Elizabethan subject's discourse on the unruly and ungodly practices of Irish "lords and gentlemen" – practices punished by massive expropriations of the very sort that gave Spenser his Irish estate. The freeborn and godly English masculine subject who is celebrated in this passage from the *View* is ideologically at one with the bridegroom whose temporal ambitions and eternal aspirations are espoused in the final stanza of *Epithalamion*.

If I suggest that part of the work to be performed by *Colin Clouts Come Home Againe* and *Epithalamion* was to make their author feel at home in Ireland, I do so unsentimentally, with an awareness that for Spenser to have felt "at home" in Ireland would have taken the successful implementation of the project of total subjugation and appropriation set forth in his *View of the Present State of Ireland*. It is not my intention to efface the obvious and significant matters of genre, style, and rhetorical strategy that differentiate *Colin Clouts Come Home Againe*, *Epithalamion*, or the *Mutabilitie* cantos from *A View of the Present State of Ireland*; I do wish to suggest, however, that the material and ideological concerns that are the explicit subject of the prose dialogue also exert a strong pressure upon the poems, and undergo a range of literary displacements and sublimations within them. The *View* manifests the darker side of Spenser's investment of his whole personal and family future in Ireland. In it, Spenser employs the conventions of dialogue toward a sweeping and systematic program for the eradication of traditional Irish culture and society, and the violent imposition, from the ground up, of a society and culture conformable with the dominant institutions, beliefs, and practices of Elizabethan England – one which would be controlled by transplanted Englishmen such as Spenser himself. The employment of dialogue is only partially successful in providing a formal containment of the potential contradiction in Spenser's program, between the humanist ideals of civility that are its ostensible goal and the acts of violence and expediency that must be its means.[52]

The humanist end of Spenser's *A View* was to fashion Ireland in virtuous and gentle discipline; its Machiavellian means were shaped and impelled by the material circumstances of Spenser's own position there. He was part of an isolated and embattled minority of recently arrived English-born and Protestant administrators and settlers, who saw themselves not only in a hostile relationship to both of the indigenous populations – the Gaelic Irish and English-Irish – but also in an unsympathetic relationship to the conservative monarch, court, and government in England, who tended to favor the old English-Irish nobility rather than the new English colonists, and who resisted the potentially revolutionary measures advocated by Spenser and his colleagues.[53] From Spenser's perspective, the attitude of the Elizabethan regime was putting at risk the security and success of the New English plantation in Munster, and was thus jeopardizing his personal and family future. I believe that the complex and vexed ideological positioning of Spenser's new Anglo-Irish identity is felt as a shaping (or deforming)

force throughout his later poetry, and that it is registered not only as a struggle to impose English civility upon Irish savagery but also as a resistance to, or alienation from, the metropolitan center and from the symbolic personage of the Queen, who had at the beginning of Spenser's career provided a focus and ground for his poetic vocation. These material and ideological circumstances, I suggest, provide an extra-literary referent for the alternative centers of authority and the alternative feminine subjects of celebration that are so conspicuously represented in Spenser's poetry subsequent to the first edition of *The Faerie Queene* in 1590.

The poems in both of the poetry books I have been discussing do their work of masculine subject-formation – their fashioning of the humble poet as a virtuous and prosperous gentleman – by foregrounding their Irish locus and defining themselves in contradistinction to the Eliza-bethan courtly center and to the task of celebrating the Faerie Queene. In the generically marginal texts of *Colin Clouts Come Home Againe* and *AMORETTI AND Epithalamion*, Spenser calls attention to his position on the social and geo-political margins of Elizabethan courtly and aristocratic culture; and the Poet's persona – variously shepherd, lover, and bridegroom – reinvents this margin as an emergent and alternative center. In the later cantos of the last completed book of *The Faerie Queene* and in the posthumously printed and apparently fragmentary cantos of *Mutabilitie*, the pastoral and lyric modes and the Irish locus have come to dominate the heroic poem itself; the margin now seems to have become the center. The observation of this significant shift in Spenser's poetic corpus should not obscure the fact that he was deeply complicit in the creation and service of that system from which he seems to have been increasingly alienated; and that, throughout his career, he looked to his prince and her court for recognition and reward.

The foregoing analysis of Spenser's positioning as an Elizabethan subject qualifies Stephen Greenblatt's reading of Spenser's "self-fashioning." In *Renaissance Self-Fashioning*, Greenblatt produced a salutary analysis of the interrelationship between Spenser's *View* and his poetry.[54] He represents the process of identity-formation in the Spenserian text as accomplished through symbolic and physical acts of regenerative vio-lence, enacted against those objectified agents of disorder who threaten a civilization that is centered upon Spenser's sovereign: "Spenser sees human identity as conferred by loving service to legitimate authority, to the yoked power of God and the state" (222). Greenblatt's characteriza-tion of the ideology of Spenser's writings is based upon an analysis of Book II, canto 12 of *The Faerie Queene*, the episode of Guyon's destruction of The Bower of Bliss and his binding of its proprietress, the enchantress Acrasia. His analysis of Elizabethan cultural homologies assimilates the exotic and demonic Acrasia to various forms of ethnic otherness, Amerindian and Irish, and it assimilates Guyon's enactment of regenerative violence to Reformation iconoclasm, as well as to initiatives for the extirpation of the indigenous cultures of Ireland and the New World. By constructing, projecting, and mastering such radical forms of otherness, a collective, civilized Englishness sought to define itself. Greenblatt demystifies Elizabethan ideals of civility, revealing them to be anxious, repressive, and rapacious modes of domination. In the process, he construes the politics of the Spenserian text in terms of the poet's enthusiastic identification with an ideology of royal absolutism: "*The Faerie Queene* is ... wholly wedded to the autocratic ruler of the English state" (174). "In the face of a deep anxiety about the impure claims of art" (190), Spenser wholly submits his imaginative powers to those official fictions which enhance the power of the state by celebrating the person of the sovereign. In other words, although Greenblatt undermines idealized notions of an inclusive and harmonious Elizabethan World Picture, the final result of his subtle analysis is, nevertheless, to reaffirm the traditional representation of Spenser as an unequivocal celebrant of Elizabethan political and social orthodoxies – the Spenser most unsubtly referred to by Marx as "Elizabeth's arse-kissing poet."[55]

During the 1960s, Spenser scholars began to pay increasing attention to his later poetry – a reflex, so it seems to me, of the increasing sympathy that some of these academics felt toward the Spenserian mythopoeia of a circumscribed and imperiled pursuit of the contemplative life. Book VI, canto 10 of *The Faerie Queene* – the episode in which Colin Clout's communion with the Graces is disrupted by the intrusion of Sir Calidore, and the pastoral world itself is destroyed by the incursion of the brigands – has had a special resonance and poignancy for the older generation of contemporary Spenserians. This may be so, in part, because the episode came to evoke the undermining of aesthetic – and thus, by association, of critical – purity that commenced in the tumultuous 1960s. When, in 1980, Greenblatt linked Spenser's poetic creation to his active engagement in the systematic destruction of Hiberno-Norman civilization, he was breaching the prevailing decorum of Spenser studies and challenging the containment policy by which academic literary criticism preserved the aesthetic space of *The Faerie Queene* against the material and ideological pressures of history. Greenblatt's concern was neither to celebrate nor to vilify the Spenserian self that he had delineated but rather to explore the wider ideological struggles within which it was fashioned, and the human costs of that fashioning.

The cultural politics that are currently ascendant within the academic

122   *Louis A. Montrose*

discipline of literary studies call forth condemnations of Spenser for his racist/misogynist/elitist/imperialist biases. Today, "our new Poete" presents himself to students of English literature as a charter member of The Dead White Male Poets' Society. I have no investment in rehabilitating Spenser's character; nor do I have a wish to recuperate "the poets' poet" who, according to Coleridge, achieved in *The Faerie Queene*, "the marvellous independence and true imaginative absence of all particular space or time."[56] On the other hand, I am concerned that in their eagerness to present their political credentials or merely to make an academic fashion statement, some contemporary workers in the field have lost interest in trying to hear the ideologically alien voices that are intrinsic to the historicist dialogue. Our new historicisms have pointedly insisted that we are implicated in the histories that we (re)construct, and that our present understandings of the past are necessarily limited and partial. It does not follow, however, that our final object is to assign praise or blame on the basis of how closely the actors and texts of the past accord with our own values and beliefs, or that we should merely abandon any effort to understand the past in its own terms. Although I feel neither a need nor a desire to apologize for Spenser's conduct and beliefs concerning Ireland, I am concerned to understand them in the context of his complex positioning as a gendered and classed Elizabethan subject, to comprehend the linkages between subjectivity and ideology that impelled and rationalized such conduct and beliefs. Throughout this essay, I have been arguing against an understanding of Spenser's relationship to royal authority as either wholly assenting or wholly oppositional, and in support of one that allows for the multiplicity, discontinuity, and inconsistency of Spenserian attitudes toward the monarch, the courtly establishment, and the state, without assuming that he was either merely hypocritical or merely muddled.[57] In the complexities and contradictions of his values, motives, and conduct – if not in the achievements of his art – Spenser was a representative Elizabethan.

he certainly produced more text than most...

NOTES

Earlier versions of this essay were presented to audiences at the 1991 Convention of The Modern Language Association in San Francisco and the 1992 conference on Renaissance Subject/Early Modern Object at The University of Pennsylvania.

1   See the excellent studies by Richard C. Newton: "Jonson and the (Re-)-Invention of the Book," in Claude J. Summers and Ted-Larry Pebworth, eds., *Classic and Cavalier: Essays on Jonson and the Sons of Ben* (Pittsburgh, 1982), pp. 31–55; and "Making Books from Leaves: Poets Become Editors," in Gerald P. Tyson and Sylvia S. Wagonheim, eds., *Print and Culture in the Renaissance: Essays on the Advent of Printing in Europe* (Newark, Del.,

1986), pp. 246–64. Also see Richard Helgerson, *Self-Crowned Laureates: Spenser, Jonson, Milton and the Literary System* (Berkeley, 1983), esp. pp. 21–54; Joseph Loewenstein, "The Script in the Marketplace," *Representations* 12 (Fall 1985), 101–14.

2 See James A. Riddell and Stanley Stewart, "Jonson Reads 'The Ruines of Time'," *Studies in Philology* 87 (1990), 427–55, esp. 429–33.

3 See Ray Heffner, "Edmund Spenser's Family," *Huntington Library Quarterly* 2 (1938–9), 79–84.

4 See Alexander C. Judson, *The Life of Edmund Spenser* (Baltimore, 1945), pp. 30–1.

5 Spenser's secretarial career, and the modality of secrecy that it imparts to his poetic vocation, is the subject of a study that appeared after this essay was drafted: see Richard Rambuss, *Spenser's Secret Career* (Cambridge, 1993). Although this stimulating monograph rides its secretarial thesis rather hard, its claim that "Spenser's vocational aspirations and agendas as a poet are never cordoned off from his professional pursuit as a secretary of office, status, and political influence" (p. 9) fully accords with my own perspective.

For an early discussion of Spenser's pursuit of office, status, and political influence, see Louis A. Montrose, "'The perfecte paterne of a Poete': The Poetics of Courtship in *The Shepheardes Calender*," *Texas Studies in Literature and Language* 21 (1979), 34–67; rpt. in Mihoko Suzuki, ed., *Critical Essays on Spenser* (New York, forthcoming). The present essay builds upon that earlier one, as well as upon Montrose's subsequent study, "The Elizabethan Subject and the Spenserian Text," in Patricia Parker and David Quint, eds., *Literary Theory/Renaissance Texts* (Baltimore, 1986), pp. 303–40.

6 For an enumeration of these acquisitions of land and offices between 1580 and 1598, see Frederic Ives Carpenter, *A Reference Guide to Edmund Spenser* (1923; rpt. New York, 1950), pp. 15–22.

7 For an articulation of the dynamic model of culture and ideology from which these terms derive, see Raymond Williams, *Marxism and Literature* (Oxford, 1977).

8 See Elizabeth L. Eisenstein, *The Printing Press as an Agent of Change: Communications and Cultural Transformations in Early-modern Europe* (2 vols., 1979; rpt. in one vol., Cambridge, 1980), esp. pp. 136–40.

9 See the seminal essays of Harry Berger, Jr., now collected in two volumes: *Second World and Green World: Studies in Renaissance Fiction-Making* and *Revisionary Play: Studies in the Spenserian Dynamics* (Berkeley, 1988).

10 The Spenser–Harvey correspondence is quoted from *Spenser: Poetical Works*, ed. J. C. Smith and E. de Selincourt (1912; rpt. London, 1965). Quotation from p. 628. *The Faerie Queene* (*FQ*) is quoted by book, canto, and stanza from the edition of A. C. Hamilton (London, 1977); *Colin Clouts Come Home Againe* (*CCCHA*), *Amoretti* (*Amo*), and *Epithalamion* (*Epi*) are quoted from *The Yale Edition of the Shorter Poems of Edmund Spenser*, ed. William A. Oram, Einar Bjorvand, Ronald Bond, Thomas H. Cain, Alexander Dunlop, and Richard Schell (New Haven, 1989). *A View of the Present State of Ireland* (*VPSI*) is quoted from the modern-spelling edition by W. L. Renwick (Oxford, 1970).

11   See Herbert Berry and E. K. Timings, "Spenser's Pension," *Review of English Studies*, new series, 11 (1960), 254–9.
12   See Helgerson, *Self-Crowned Laureates*, pp. 55–100.
13   Montrose has discussed Spenser's figurations of his sovereign in "The Elizabethan Subject and the Spenserian Text."
14   Elizabeth J. Bellamy, "The Vocative and the Vocational: The Unreadability of Elizabeth in the *Faerie Queene*," *ELH* 54 (1987), 1–30.
15   *Certain Sermons or Homilies (1547) and A Homily against Disobedience and Wilful Rebellion (1570): A Critical Edition*, ed. Ronald B. Bond (Toronto, 1987), p. 161. For a stimulating discussion of Elizabethan rhetoric and political ideology, see Patricia Parker, *Literary Fat Ladies: Rhetoric, Gender, Property* (London, 1987), pp. 97–125.
16   See Michel Foucault, "What is an Author?" (1969), in Josué V. Harari, ed., *Textual Strategies: Perspectives in Post-Structuralist Criticism* (Ithaca, 1979), pp. 141–60; quotations from pp. 159, 158, 141, respectively.
17   Robert Weimann, "'Appropriation' and Modern History in Renaissance Prose Narrative," *New Literary History* 14 (1983), 459–95; quotation from 468–9. Also see his "Text and History: Epilogue, 1984," in Robert Weimann, *Structure and Society in Literary History*, expanded edn. (Baltimore, 1984), pp. 267–323, esp. pp. 293–302. I am indebted to Weimann's materialist critique of Foucault.
18   See, for example, D. M. Loades, "The Theory and Practice of Censorship in Sixteenth-Century England," *Transactions of the Royal Historical Society*, series 5, 24 (1974), 141–57; Annabel Patterson, *Censorship and Interpretation: The Conditions of Reading and Writing in Early Modern England* (1984; rpt., with a new introduction, Madison, Wis., 1990); Janet Clare, *"Art made tongue-tied by authority": Elizabethan and Jacobean Dramatic Censorship* (Manchester, 1990); Richard Dutton, *Mastering the Revels: The Regulation and Censorship of English Renaissance Drama* (Iowa City, 1991).
19   See, for example, the following works by Christopher Hill: *Intellectual Origins of the English Revolution* (Oxford, 1965); *The World Turned Upside Down: Radical Ideas During the English Revolution* (New York, 1972); *The Collected Essays of Christopher Hill, Volume One: Writing and Revolution in 17th Century England* (Amherst, Mass., 1985), esp. pp. 3–95.
20   Paul Alpers, "Pastoral and the Domain of Lyric in Spenser's *Shepheardes Calender*," *Representations* 12 (Fall 1985), 83–100; quotations from 94–5. Alpers's reference is to Montrose's essay, "Of Gentlemen and Shepherds: The Politics of Elizabethan Pastoral Form," *ELH* 50 (1983), 415–59.
21   F. W. Maitland, in *Oxford English Dictionary*, under "demesne," sense I.1 (also cited in Alpers, "Pastoral and the Domain of Lyric," 95). Also see *OED*, under "domain," etymology and sense 1.
22   See, for example, the comments on the decorum of social and generic hierarchies in George Puttenham, *The Arte of English Poesie* (1589), ed. Gladys Doidge Willcock and Alice Walker (Cambridge, 1936):

In every of the sayd three degrees, not the selfe same vertues be egally to be praysed nor the same vices, egally to be dispraised, nor their loves, mariages, quarels, contracts and other behaviours, be like high nor do require to be set fourth with the like stile: but every one in his degree and decencie, which made that all *hymnes* and histories, and Tragedies, were written in the high stile: all Comedies and Enterludes and other common Poesies of loves, and such like in the meane stile, all *Eglogues* and pastorall poemes in the low and base stile, otherwise they had bene utterly disproporcioned. (152–3)

23 For another perspective on "the autobiographical fiction that becomes so conspicuous a part of [Spenser's] poetry after 1590," see Donald Cheney, "Spenser's Fortieth Birthday and Related Fictions," *Spenser Studies* 4 (1984), 3–31. Cheney suggests that "the poetry written or at least published between the two installments of *The Faerie Queene* traces a pattern of related fictions which bear on the new directions given to the major poem in 1596," and that this later poetry instances "a poetics dominated by a sense of time's urgency, of darkening shadows in private and public sectors alike" (3).

24 I quote the opening line of "In praise of a contented minde," from the manuscript text printed in Steven W. May, *The Elizabethan Courtier Poets: The Poems and Their Contexts* (Columbia, Mo., 1991), pp. 283–4. The poem has usually been attributed to Sir Edward Dyer but May contends that the Earl of Oxford's claim is "slightly stronger" (312). I have used the text of Sidney's *Defence of Poetry* in *Miscellaneous Prose of Sir Philip Sidney*, ed. Katherine Duncan-Jones and Jan van Dorsten (Oxford, 1973); quotation from 78.

25 See, for example, Norbert Elias, *The Civilizing Process*, trans. Edmund Jephcott (2 vols., 1939; New York, 1978); Roger Chartier, ed., *Passions of the Renaissance* (1986) vol. III, *A History of Private Life*, trans. Arthur Goldhammer (Cambridge, Mass, 1989).

26 In *Penshurst: The Semiotics of Place and the Poetics of History* (Madison, 1984), Don E. Wayne makes the point that, "by the end of the sixteenth century and long before the consolidation and triumph of a 'bourgeois ideology' in England, images and values we tend to identify as middle class had already begun to appear in the transformation of the aristocracy's self-image" (p. 25).

27 See Wayne, *Penshurst*, pp. 23–8; quotations from pp. 24, 26. Wayne's intertextual reading of Jonson's poem and the Sidneys' estate elucidates "the equation of power and of personal identity with private property, the image of house and land as the visible domain of property and of identity, the notion of home and family as the legitimating spiritual nucleus of that material domain, and a corresponding view of history" that occluded the social and material bases of historical change (pp. 26–7). Wayne's compelling analysis of "To Penshurst" has enabled my understanding of *CCCHA*.

28 Ralegh's 42,000-acre estate was ordered reduced to 12,000 acres in 1589, but it does not appear that the Queen's order was executed. See Edward Edwards, *The Life of Sir Walter Ralegh ... Together with His Letters* (2 vols., London, 1898), I, p. 96.

29 Typical of Ralegh's complaint is the following: "No other poure effecting wo, or bliss / Shee gave, shee tooke, shee wounded, shee apeased" ("The 11th: and last booke of the Ocean to Scinthia," printed from the undated holograph in *The Poems of Sir Walter Ralegh*, ed. Agnes M. C. Latham [1951; rpt. Cambridge, Mass., 1962], p. 27, lines 55–6). On Ralegh's personal cult of royal devotion, see Walter Oakeshott, *The Queen and the Poet* (New York, 1961).

30   See Puttenham, *Arte of English Poesie*, p. 38: "The Poet devised the *Eglogue* long after other *drammatick* poems, not of purpose to counterfait or represent the rusticall manner of loves and communication: but under the vaile of homely persons, and in rude speeches to insinuate and glaunce at greater matters, and such as perchance had not bene safe to have disclosed in any other sort." For an extended analysis of the politics of Elizabethan pastoral, see Montrose, "Of Gentlemen and Shepherds."

31   For a judicious analysis of Spenser's relationship to Renaissance Neoplatonism, see Robert Ellrodt, *Neoplatonism in the Poetry of Spenser* (Geneva, 1960); and, for a brilliant contextualization of Spenser's imagery in terms of Italian Neoplatonic philosophy and iconography, see Edgar Wind, *Pagan Mysteries in the Renaissance* (enlarged and rev. edn., Harmondsworth, 1967).

32   Spenser dedicates one of the poems in his volume of *Complaints* (1591) to each of the three "nymphs": in offering *The Teares of the Muses* to Alice, Lady Strange, Spenser writes that "the cause for which ye have thus deserved of me to be honoured (if honour it be at all) are, both your particular bounties, and also some private bands of affinitie, which it has pleased your Ladiship to acknowledge"; he presents *Mother Hubberds Tale* to Anne, successively Lady Compton, Mountegle, and Buckhurst, "having often sought opportunitie by some good meanes to make knowen to your Ladiship, the humble affection and faithfull dutie, which I have alwaies professed, and am bound to beare to that House, from whence yee spring"; he dedicates *Muiopotmos* to Elizabeth, Lady Carey, as an act of service, "not so much for your great bounty to my self, which yet may not be unminded; nor for name or kindreds sake by you vouchsafed, being also regardable; as for that honorable name, which yee have by your brave deserts purchast to your self." In addition to these poems and *CCCHA*, see *Prothalamion* (1596): "Though from another place I take my name, / An house of auncient fame" (130–1).

33   See Mary E. Finch, *The Wealth of Five Northamptonshire Families 1540–1640*, Publications of the Northamptonshire Record Society, 19 (1956), pp. 38–65.

34   See Carpenter, *A Reference Guide to Edmund Spenser*, p. 39. For a more detailed discussion of Spenser's property and the Munster plantation project, see Pauline Henley, *Spenser in Ireland* (Cork, 1928), pp. 51–63; and the recent and thorough study by Michael MacCarthy-Morrogh, *The Munster Plantation: English Migration to Southern Ireland 1583–1641* (Oxford, 1986), pp. 1–135. For a sometimes fanciful narrative of Spenser's life at Kilcolman, see Judson, *Life of Edmund Spenser*, pp. 125–35.

35   The comments by Roche and Herbert are quoted in R. Dunlop, "The Plantation of Munster 1584–1589," *English Historical Review* 3 (1888), 250–69; quotations from 265–6. I have benefited from Dunlop's detailed study of the establishment of the plantation.

36   See *Calendar of the State Papers, relating to Ireland, of the Reign of Elizabeth, 1588, August–1592, September, preserved in Her Majesty's Public Record Office* (1885; rpt. Nendeln, Liechtenstein, 1974), p. 247.

37   See Horace J. Round, *Studies in Peerage and Family History* (Westminster, 1901), pp. 279–329; the 1595 pedigree is quoted from Round, pp. 294–5.

38 For a narrative and analysis of the events, see Anthony J. Sheehan, "The Overthrow of the Plantation of Munster in October 1598," *Irish Sword* 15 (1982–3), 11–22; also, MacCarthy-Morrough, *Munster Plantation*, pp. 130–5. "A breife note of Ireland," addressed to the Queen "Out of the ashes of disolacon and wastnes of this your wretched Realme of Ireland," is a contemporaneous account attributed to Spenser; it is printed from manuscript in *The Works of Edmund Spenser, A Variorum Edition*, vol. IX, *Spenser's Prose Works*, ed. Rudolf Gottfried (Baltimore, 1949), pp. 233–45; quotation from p. 236. The famous if unreliable source for the disastrous personal impact of the rebellion upon Spenser is Jonson's *Conversations with Drummond*: "That the Irish having Robd Spensers goods & burnt his house & a litle child new born, he and his wyfe escaped, & after he died for lake of bread in King street and refused 20 pieces sent to him by my Lord of Essex & said he was sorie he had no time to spend them" (*Ben Jonson*, ed. C. H. Herford and Percy Simpson [11 vols., Oxford, 1925–52], I, p. 137).

39 On the relationship of *Amoretti* to the Petrarchan tradition and to the patterning of other Renaissance sonnet sequences, see O. B. Hardison, Jr., "*Amoretti* and the *Dolce stil novo*," *English Literary Renaissance* 2 (1972), 208–16; Carol Thomas Neely, "The Structure of English Renaissance Sonnet Sequences," *ELH* 45 (1978), 359–89; Reed Way Dasenbrock, "The Petrarchan Context of Spenser's *Amoretti*," *PMLA* 100 (1985), 38–50. On the relationship of *Epithalamion* to the history and conventions of the epithalamium, see Thomas M. Greene, "Spenser and the Epithalamic Tradition," *Comparative Literature* 9 (1957), 215–28. On *AMORETTI AND Epithalamion* as a unified poetry book, see Carol V. Kaske, "Spenser's *Amoretti and Epithalamion* of 1595: Structure, Genre, and Numerology," *English Literary Renaissance* 8 (1978), 271–95.

40 See A. Kent Hieatt, *Short Time's Endless Monument* (New York, 1960); Hieatt, "The Daughters of Horus: Order in the Stanzas of *Epithalamion*," in William Nelson, ed., *Form and Convention in the Poetry of Edmund Spenser* (New York, 1961), pp. 103–21.

41 For an extended discussion of Colin's relationship to Rosalind, Eliza, and Dido in *SC*, see Montrose's study, " 'The perfecte paterne of a Poete': The Poetics of Courtship in *The Shepheardes Calender*."

42 Here Spenser momentarily touches the radical socio-spiritual strain in the pastoral tradition: "He hath put down the mighty from their seat, and hath exalted the humble." On the appropriation of this element into the "Aprill" eclogue of *SC* and other Elizabethan royal pastorals, see Louis A. Montrose, " 'Eliza, Queene of shepheardes' and the Pastoral of Power," *English Literary Renaissance* 10 (1980), 153–82; rpt. in H. Aram Veeser, ed., *The New Historicism Reader* (New York, 1994), pp. 88–115.

43 Spenser was married to Elizabeth Boyle, a kinswoman of Sir Richard Boyle, later the first Earl of Cork, during the mid 1590s. Scholars invariably assign the marriage date to 11 June 1594, solely on the "evidence" of *AMORETTI AND Epithalamion*. She is presumably the third "Elizabeth" praised in *Amo* 74. For further information and speculation, see Douglas Hamer, "Spenser's Marriage," *Review of English Studies* 7 (1931), 271–90. Hamer presents

evidence that this was Spenser's second marriage; for Elizabeth Boyle, it was
the first of three.

44   Sir John Hayward, *Annals of the First Four Years of the Reign of Queen
     Elizabeth* [*c.* 1612], ed. John Bruce, Camden Society, ser. 1, vol. VII (1840;
     rpt. New York, 1968), p. 6.

45   I have discussed this appropriation in a number of essays. See, in particular,
     Louis A. Montrose, " 'Shaping Fantasies': Figurations of Gender and Power
     in Elizabethan Culture," *Representations* 2 (Spring 1983), 61–94; rpt. in
     Stephen Greenblatt, ed., *Representing the English Renaissance* (Berkeley,
     1988), pp . 31–64.

46   Mixing with the biblical, classical, and cosmological allusions that fill
     Epithalamion are details that not only localize the setting in Ireland but also
     mark it as urban and of the middling ranks. Thus, in stanza 8, "Minstrels"
     make music with pipe, tabor, and croud, "The whyles the boyes run up and
     downe the street" (137); in stanza 10, the poet–bridegroom asks, rhetorically,
     concerning his bride: "Tell me ye merchants daughters did ye see / So fayre a
     creature in your towne before" (167–8); and in stanza 15, after the marriage
     ceremony, he commands, "Ring ye the bels, ye yong men of the towne, /
     And leave your wonted labors for this day" (261–2).

47   See Kenneth Burke, *A Rhetoric of Motives* (1950; rpt. Berkeley, 1969),
     212–21. My reference to a "Sabaoths sight" alludes to the prayer for
     redemption, sanctification, and rest with which the final stanza of the
     Mutabilitie cantos concludes:

> For, all that moveth, doth in *Change* delight:
> But thence-forth all shall rest eternally
> With Him that is the God of Sabbaoth hight:
> O that great Sabbaoth God, graunt me that Sabaoths sight.

(MC, 8.2)

48   See Carpenter, *A Reference Guide to Edmund Spenser*, p. 21.

49   On the practical and ideological links between the Elizabethan colonizing
     projects in Ireland and North America, see Nicholas Canny, *Kingdom and
     Colony: Ireland in the Atlantic World, 1560–1800* (Baltimore, 1988). For
     further discussion of Elizabethan masculine subject formation in the "New
     World," see Louis A. Montrose, "The Work of Gender in the Discourse of
     Discovery," *Representations* 33 (Winter 1991), 1–41; rpt. in Stephen Green-
     blatt, ed., *New World Encounters* (Berkeley, 1993), pp. 177–217.

50   See R. Dunlop, "Sixteenth-Century Maps of Ireland," *English Historical
     Review* 20 (1905), 309–37; J. H. Andrews, "Geography and Government in
     Elizabethan Ireland," in Nicholas Stephens and Robin E. Glasscock, eds.,
     Irish Geographical Studies in Honour of E. Estyn Evans (Belfast, 1970),
     pp. 178–91; Bruce Avery, "Mapping the Irish Other: Spenser's *A View of
     the Present State of Ireland*," *ELH* 57 (1990), 263–79. In *VPSI*, Spenser's
     Irenius recommends that the English in Ireland emulate Romulus and King
     Alfred by subdividing the country into smaller and smaller units for
     purposes of administration and surveillance (pp. 143–4). Andrews, "Geo-
     graphy and Government in Elizabethan Ireland," p. 187, reproduces a
     "Proposed lay-out of a Munster seignory of 12,000 acres," drafted in 1586.
     The plan is remarkable for its highly symmetrical organization of space: a

square with a church at its center, divided into quadrants, each of which is subdivided into about two dozen quadrangular and triangular individual holdings.

51 When the "plot of her majesty's offers for the peopling of Munster," originally drawn up in December 1585, was amended in June 1586, its effect was to aggrandize the economic position of the undertakers. Comparing, for a 12,000-acre seignory, the differences in terms between the original and amended plans, Dunlop points out that "while the number of families to be planted ... has increased from eighty-six to ninety-one, and while the demesne land of the undertakers has grown from 1,600 acres to 2,100, the number of freeholders has decreased from fourteen to six. This alteration must have been intended for the benefit of the undertakers" ("The Plantation of Munster," 257–8).

52 See Ciaran Brady, "Spenser's Irish Crisis: Humanism and Experience in the 1590s," *Past & Present* 111 (May 1986), 17–49; and the ensuing debate between Brady and Nicholas Canny, in *Past & Present* 120 (August 1988), 201–15. Also see Brady, "The Road to the *View*: On the Decline of Reform Thought in Tudor Ireland," in Patricia Coughlan, ed., *Spenser and Ireland: An Interdisciplinary Perspective* (Cork, 1989), pp. 25–45.

53 See Nicholas Canny, "Edmund Spenser and the Development of an Anglo-Irish Identity," *Yearbook of English Studies* 13 (1983), 1–19; and Canny, "Identity Formation in Ireland: The Emergence of the Anglo-Irish," in Nicholas Canny and Anthony Pagden, eds., *Colonial Identity in the Atlantic World, 1500–1800* (Princeton, 1987), pp. 159–212, esp. pp. 159–77. Also see Canny, "Introduction: Spenser and the Reform of Ireland," in Coughlan, *Spenser and Ireland*, pp. 9–24. Ciaran Brady cautions against the position that Spenser's *A View* is representative of a unified New English perspective: "There was not in the 1590s, as indeed there never had been among the Elizabethans, an agreed way of comprehending or of dealing with Ireland and the Irish. Thus Spenser's opinions, while being acceptable to many among the New English, would have been quite unpalatable to many more" ("Spenser's Irish Crisis," 22).

54 Stephen Greenblatt, *Renaissance Self-Fashioning: More to Shakespeare* (Chicago, 1980), pp. 157–92. Important subsequent studies from which I have benefited include Julia Reinhard Lupton, "Home-Making in Ireland: Virgil's Eclogue I and Book VI of *The Faerie Queene*," *Spenser Studies* 8 (1987), 119–45; Patricia Coughlan, " 'Some secret scourge which shall by her come unto England': Ireland and Incivility in Spenser," in Coughlan, *Spenser and Ireland*, pp. 46–74; Anne Fogarty, "The Colonization of Language: Narrative Strategies in *A View of the Present State of Ireland* and *The Faerie Queene*, Book VI," in *Spenser and Ireland*, pp. 75–108.

55 See *The Ethnological Notebooks of Karl Marx (Studies of Morgan, Phear, Maine, Lubbock)*, transcribed and ed. Lawrence Krader (Assen, 1972), p. 305. Marx refers to Spenser as "Elizabeths Arschkissende Poet" in the course of a commentary on discussions of land tenure in *A View of the Present State of Ireland*.

56 See Coleridge's "notes for lectures and marginal notes in a copy of *The Faerie Queene* (1818)," excerpted in Paul J. Alpers, ed., *Edmund Spenser: A*

Critical Anthology (Harmondsworth, 1969), pp. 138–47; quotation from
p. 144.
57   I discuss such a model of ideology and agency in "New Historicisms," in
Stephen Greenblatt and Giles Gunn, eds., *Redrawing the Boundaries: The
Transformation of English and American Literary Studies* (New York, 1992),
pp. 392–418.

Part II

Materializations

4   Gendering the Crown

Stephen Orgel

I am concerned here with the interpretation of Renaissance symbolic imagery in relation to certain issues of gender construction, particularly in the representation of royalty, but I want to begin with the question of interpretation itself. How do we know how to read a Renaissance image? In the simplest cases, we have Renaissance guides to interpretation, in the form of iconologies and handbooks of symbolism. Yet such cases immediately become less simple when we observe that reading imagery through them depends on reading texts, and therefore shares in all the interpretive ambiguity of that process: the reading of texts is a dialectical, and sometimes even an adversarial, procedure. Interpretation depends, moreover, on what texts we select as relevant, and even on what we are willing to treat as a text.

I begin with the well-known emblem of the pelican (fig. 4.1), which Renaissance iconologies declare to be *typus Christi*. Here, in Valeriano's *Hieroglyphica*, she resembles the phoenix, rising in flame from the top of the cross. Most often she is the model of *caritas*, selflessly nourishing her young with her heart's blood. Cesare Ripa's *Bontà* (*Kindness*) (fig. 4.2), holds the pelican feeding her offspring. The image is gendered, but the female is an attribute of the male: the maternal *caritas* is a type of Christ.

The image's applicability, however, is more profligate than this. The pelican topos is invoked by Laertes, vowing to avenge his father's death:

> To his good friends thus wide I'll ope my arms,
> And, like the kind life-rend'ring pelican,
> Repast them with my blood.
>
> (4.5.145–7)

The pelican's gift of life has become a metaphor for killing, and the image of maternal love and familial piety is also an image of vengeance. John of Gaunt, berating Richard II, says

Figure 4.1   The pelican as symbol of Christ, from G. P. Valeriano Bolzani, *Hieroglyphica* (1610).

> O, spare me not, my brother Edward's son; ...
> That blood already, like the pelican,
> Hast thou tapped out and drunkenly caroused.
>
> (2.1.124–6)

The attention here has shifted from the altruistic mother pelican to her brood callously accepting her bounty. King Lear uses the topos for a similarly vitriolic indictment of his "pelican daughters" (III.iv.77), who have taken the all he gave them. In these cases, even Laertes' family piety is gone; the pelican is a type not of the *caritas* typified in the relation of parent and child, but of its precise opposite, filial ingratitude – reading is an adversarial procedure. The contradiction, however, is both eminently logical and a function of interpretation, and all these readings remain strictly within the terms set by the emblem itself: if the mother pelican is a type of the endlessly self-sacrificing Christ, the next generation of pelicans are, it follows, a race of cannibals – the only way to have the topos is to have it both ways. The *caritas* emblem in *Lear* is therefore of a piece with the play's invocation of the barbarous Scythian

Figure 4.2   *Bontà (Kindness)* holding a pelican feeding her young with her own blood, from Cesare Ripa, *Iconologia* (1611).

Or he that makes his generation messes.

(I.i.116–17)

There is to my knowledge no Renaissance handbook in which the pelican is revealed as a type of inhumanity, but this is obviously no impediment to its interpretation as such: the Shakespearean examples are not at all unusual, and the interpretive technique in which anything can also be its opposite (as well as any number of other things) is so common as to constitute a critical topos in the age. Thus, the story of Apollo and Daphne was for Bernini about lust, and the laurel tree meant that if we give in to our passion, we will end with only bitter leaves and berries;[1] but for George Sandys the fable was about chastity, and the laurel tree meant that if we adhere to our virtue we will be preserved.[2] The Pygmalion story told Arthur Golding that the man who reserves his love exclusively for virtuous women will be rewarded with an ideal wife,[3] but it told Sandys that there is no woman so chaste that she cannot be brought to yield by sufficient entreaty,[4] and it told William Caxton that a servant may, with sufficient effort on the part of her master, be turned into a lady.[5] Even within individual handbooks, the breadth of interpretive possibility often seems both endless and, for modern readers looking for a key to Renaissance symbolism, distressingly arbitrary. Renaissance iconographies and mythographies are in this respect the most postmodern of texts, in which no meaning is conceived to be inherent, all signification is constructed or applied; the fluidity and ambivalence of the image are of the essence.

With the polysemous pelican in mind, let us now turn to an image that looks to modern eyes particularly disconcerting. Figure 4.3 is a transvestite portrait of François I done by the Fontainebleau artist Niccolò Bellin da Modena around 1545. The poem appended to it explains that though the king is a Mars in war, in peace he is a Minerva or Diana – as with the pelican, the feminine has become an attribute of masculinity. To attempt to account for this extraordinary image by claiming that it cannot mean what it appears to mean is, in a sense, to miss the point; the poem is there precisely to redirect the obvious response: therein lies its wit – it is genuinely outrageous. It descends from those moralizations of the story of Hercules and Omphale that invert the charge of effeminacy, and praise the transvestite hero for embodying the virtues of women as well as of men. The topos, in a less extreme form, also served to celebrate François' son, Henri II, this time as a specifically military hero (fig. 4.4).[6] The imagery by this time has been almost naturalized, and the wit

Figure 4.3   Transvestite portrait of François I, engraving by P. Chenu
(*c*. 1545) after Niccolò Bellin da Modena.

Figure 4.4   Medal of Henri II.

particularly has disappeared. Just as the maternal pelican was an emanation of Christ the king, so this image says that gender is subordinate to the purposes of royalty. Analogously, the English government was shortly to declare that for legal purposes, Queen Mary Tudor was a man.

The imagery of transvestism is positive, even heroic here. It has quite different implications, however, when applied to François' grandson Henri III.[7] In figure 4.5, the effeminate king is a monstrous harpy; the breasts, says the accompanying commentary, indicate how profoundly he has violated nature – to be a moral hermaphrodite is now no longer a virtue. He holds in his right hand, in a case that is half reliquary, half

PORTRAIT· MONSTRÜEUX· ET· ALLEGORIⒺUE· D'HENRI· iii·

Figure 4.5   Henri III as a harpy, anonymous drawing.

looking-glass, a portrait of the perfidious Machiavelli – effeminacy has become an aspect of unprincipled politics. In figure 4.6, another satiric attack on the king, the noble effeminacy of his father and grandfather is inverted: the royal hermaphrodite is elaborately coiffed, beardless, with a suggestion of breasts, and without a codpiece – beneath his clothes, says this image, the king is really a woman. The accompanying verse says "I am neither male nor female; why should I choose? I enjoy the pleasures of both." The figure in the poem has it both ways, but in fact, in the image, the unstable gender has been stabilized: the king's effeminacy is not a heroic role, but a revelation of his true nature.

Attacks on Henri and his *mignons*, including accusations of sodomy, were part of the repertory of political satire throughout his reign, and even after, providing cautionary emblems of the moral obligations of kingship. The attacks come from conservative Catholic sources, and have to do with Henri's accommodations with the Huguenots – sodomy here

Figure 4.6   Henri III as hermaphrodite; the hermaphrodite as a cross-dressed woman. Frontispiece to Thomas Artus, Sieur d'Embry, *Les hermaphrodites* (1605).

Figure 4.7   The effeminate man as bearded lady, from Sebastián de Covarrubias Orozco, *Emblemas morales* (1610), II, no. 164.

is a code word for Protestantism. Representing the effeminate king as a woman in drag, however, was unquestionably less inflammatory than representing him as a womanish man would have been, on the model of his heroic father and grandfather – the iconography of his dangerously subversive sexuality is precisely what is being avoided. The imagery was, nevertheless, no doubt understood: in figure 4.7, a Spanish emblem of 1610, it is inverted once more. The commentary says that this is a bearded lady, not a transvestite man, but it is offered as a warning against male effeminacy; the accompanying poem presents the 'afeminado' as a monster, combining the polymorphism of the verses on Henri the transvestite with the moral outrage of the commentary on Henri the harpy.[8]

Perhaps we can bridge the gap between the image that cannot mean what it says and the image that cannot say what it means with a mythological drawing by Giulio Romano (fig. 4.8). Art historians have identified the subject as Apollo, his viol discarded, making love to a youth, Hyacinthus or Cyparissus, as a woman observes the scene.[9] Commentators call the woman a voyeur, and note that such a figure is

Figure 4.8 Orpheus, a youth, a maenad, wash drawing by Giulio Romano.

Figure 4.9 Personifications of silence, Harpocrates on the right, from Cesare Cartari, *Les Images des Dieux* (1623).

Figure 4.10   Emblem of Silence, from Andrea Alciato, *Emblemata* (1531).

commonly found in Giulio's licentious images, but this ignores the woman's curious gesture. If the god is really Apollo, the gesture would seem to be the gesture of silence, the index finger on the lips, indicating the requisite discretion at divine indecency. The gesture was originally that of the god Harpocrates, shown in figure 4.9 on the right, patron of hermetic, hence silent, knowledge. In the earliest editions of Alciato's emblems, it becomes the gesture of the wise man, who knows to keep his counsel (fig. 4.10). By the mid-century, the gesture of wisdom becomes a topos for the scholar, poring over his book (fig. 4.11), indicating now not only that wisdom keeps its counsel, but also that study requires silence and, more specifically, that the mark of the scholar is his ability to read silently. And the quintessentially male emblem of the philosopher and scholar, like the pelican in reverse, was quickly transferred to women: figure 4.12 is the goddess Agenoria, so called, according to Charles Estienne, from *agendum*, "what must be done," hence the goddess of deeds-not-words.[10] Figure 4.13 shows the bottom line, Geoffrey Whitney's virtuous wife: "Her finger stays her tongue to run at large."[11] Like Giulio Romano's discreet voyeur, the good woman is the silent woman.

This is as far as art history will take us; but as a reading of the mythological drawing, the account fails to satisfy me. Giulio Romano's woman looks more distressed than discreet; moreover, her finger appears

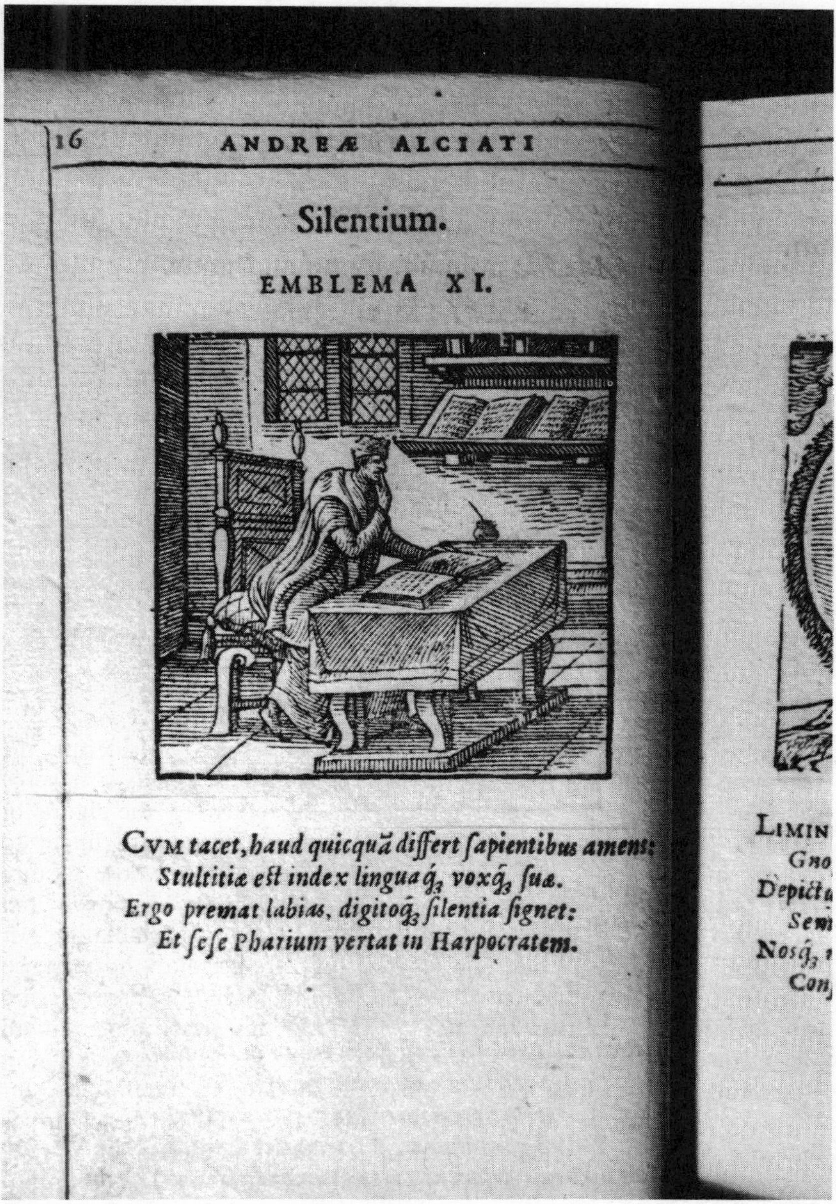
16 ANDREÆ ALCIATI
Silentium.
EMBLEMA XI.
Cvm tacet, haud quicquã differt ſapientibus amens:
Stultitiæ eſt index linguaq́; voxq́; ſuæ.
Ergo premat labias, digitoq́; ſilentia ſignet:
Et ſeſe Pharium vertat in Harpocratem.

Figure 4.11 Silence; the form used for the emblem from the mid sixteenth century on, from Andrea Alciato, *Emblemata* (1621).

Figure 4.12 The silent goddess Agenoria, from Pierre Cousteau, *Pegma* (1555).

to be in her mouth, not on her lips. In any case, considering the notorious profligacy of Renaissance symbolism, it is usually a mistake to stop with a single interpretation. Let us return to the figure of Silence: Pierio Valeriano describes the personification, with finger to mouth; but he also includes the image in figure 4.14, whose gesture appears the same but is in fact intended to be *biting* his finger, and represents, Valeriano says, *Meditatio vel Ultio* – Meditation or Revenge. If these seem odd alternatives, they are certainly no more so than the pelican's eminently logical combination of charity and cannibalism. Giulio used the gesture at least one other time, for an angry Mars with an armed Venus (fig. 4.15), a sketch for a painting in which they are expelling a fury from a garden of putti. Giulio's voyeur certainly looks more vengeful than meditative, and if the figure is indeed a vengeful woman rather than a salacious observer or a silent accomplice, then the pederastic musician is surely not Apollo but Orpheus, who turned to boys after the death of Eurydice and was credited with the introduction of pederasty into Greece, an insult to

Vxoriæ virtutes.

To my Siſter, M. D. COLLEY.

T H I S repreſentes the vertues of a wife,
    Her finger, ſtaies her tonge to runne at large.
The modeſt lookes, doe ſhewe her honeſt life.
The keys, declare ſhee hathe a·care, and chardge,
    Of huſbandes goodes: let him goe where he pleaſe,
    The Tortoyſe warnes, at home to ſpend her daies.

M 3

Figure 4.13 Wifely Virtue, from Geoffrey Whitney, *Choice of Emblemes* (1586).

Figure 4.14   Meditation or Revenge biting his finger, from G. P. Valeriano Bolzani, *Hieroglyphica* (1610).

womanhood that was ultimately avenged by the murderous bacchantes, of whom the observer – if this analysis is correct – is now clearly one.

This brings us to a larger issue: how far is this (or any) image limited, or defined, by such an explanation? Naturally I believe that my interpretation of this drawing is right and that all the art historians have been wrong; but the drawing was not, therefore, up to this moment meaningless, or even misinterpreted. Images are not limited by their inventors' intentions; moreover, they always say more than they mean – like Hamlet's players, they cannot keep counsel. The controlling, limiting, explanatory word represents only the secrets the wise man or the good woman keep to themselves, the secrets of meaning, which are, paradoxically, public knowledge; but the image represents far more – beyond the silent woman lies the vengeful fury, beyond *Caritas* lies inhumanity,

Figure 4.15   Venus and Mars as avengers, drawing by Giulio Romano.

behind all of these lies the unspoken. The image, unlike the word, that is, also represents what does not signify, the unexplained, the unspeakable – all those meanings we reject because we believe nobody in the Renaissance could have conceived them. With this by way of introduction, let me turn now to the royal impresa that is the real subject of my paper. Figure 4.16 is the title page to Saxton's *Atlas of England and Wales*, published in 1579, the first national atlas ever undertaken, patronized and largely paid for by the Crown. It is unsigned, but has been ascribed to Remigius Hogenberg on stylistic

Figure 4.16   Christopher Saxton, *Atlas of England and Wales* (1579),
title page.

Figure 4.17   Peace and Justice embracing (detail of fig. 4.16).

Figure 4.18   Peace and Justice embracing. Detail of the title page of
G. Braun and F. Hogenberg, *Civitates Orbis Terrarum* (1598), Part 5.

grounds. I begin with a quick survey of the iconography. In a large central niche, Queen Elizabeth is enthroned between two heroic male figures, Astronomy, left, holding a celestial sphere, Geography, right, with a terrestrial globe and compass. On the plinths below them are the female figures of Fortitude with her column on the left, and Prudence with a serpent and looking-glass on the right. Tudor roses adorn the outer sides of the molding. On the throne itself, lions sit at the front bearing shields with the initials E/R, and atop the chair-back two male figures in classical armor stand guard. On the frieze are two small classical heads, that on the right clearly male, and crowned, that on the left ambiguous, but possibly female, and two grotesque masks. In a cartouche in the middle, Peace, naked, with an olive branch, embraces Justice, clothed, with a breastplate and carrying a sword; behind Justice, Cupid or a putto carries a set of scales. Above these, two putti carry wreaths, and the royal arms appear in the center, supported by a crowned lion and a griffin. Below the whole composition, within a double cartouche, is a Latin poem in praise of Elizabeth, and on either side of this are two more personifications of geography and astronomy: on the left, a cartographer draws a map of England; on the right, an astronomer observes the heavens with a cruciform sighting instrument, and, beyond them, observes the Queen.

My concern here is with the central impresa (fig. 4.17), certainly the most intriguing part of the iconography. Above the Queen, in an oval at the center of the frieze, is a group of three figures. A naked woman bearing an olive branch and an armed woman bearing a sword embrace; behind the armed woman, a putto holds a set of scales. The loving union of Justice and Peace is predicted by Psalm 85, "iustitia et pax deosculatae sunt," and Roy Strong therefore calls the impresa an allusion to that biblical verse.[12] Now it is certainly true that the iconography of peace and justice were to become, in the 1580s, an essential element in the re-creation of the royal image: Strong calls attention to the proliferation of such imagery, epitomized in a portrait of 1585 attributed to Marcus Gheeraerts in which Elizabeth holds an olive branch while the sword of justice lies at her feet.[13] The problem, however, with viewing the embracing women as an allusion to the psalm is that Justice and Peace kiss only in the Vulgate.[14] The Geneva Bible and the Bishops' Bible – that is, the Elizabethan Protestant bible – say that "*righteousnes* and peace shall kisse one another," a reading followed by the Authorized Version, which is in fact a more accurate rendering of the Hebrew than the Vulgate's "justice." Is Elizabeth's impresa, then, really alluding to the Catholic scripture?

The question (as is usual with such questions) begs a number of others and conceals a set of very complex relationships. The simple answer is

Figure 4.19   Queen Elizabeth I between columns, engraving by Crispin de Passe (1596).

Figure 4.20   Impresa of Emperor Charles V.

yes, in the sense that the emblem does not originate with Elizabeth, and in its original form it certainly depends on the Vulgate text. It was the impresa devised for Pope Julius III, much commented upon and appears on a stucco relief in the Villa Giulia. This is too badly eroded to be clearly photographed, but the image by the end of the century was widely circulated, and is visible, for example, on one of the title pages to another atlas, Georg Braun and Franz Hogenberg's compendious and magnificent *Civitates Orbis Terrarum* (fig. 4.18). For Elizabeth's iconography to retain an allusion to the Vulgate is probably not surprising; Milton, even in his most radically Protestant years, always uses the Vulgate form of biblical names. But the source of the emblem is certainly ironic: Julius III was vilified in England as a persecutor of Protestants, and was even called Antichrist.[15]

In one sense, all this reveals is, once again, the notorious profligacy of Renaissance symbolic imagery, its endless adaptability to conflicting, and often diametrically opposed, ideologies. But at the same time, the adaptation of Roman Catholic imperial iconography was an increasingly visible element in the creation of a British royal self. In Crispin de Passe's 1596 engraving of the Queen (fig. 4.19) Elizabeth stands between the pillars of Hercules, originally devised as an impresa of the Emperor Charles V (fig. 4.20), and signifying his determination to sail "Plus

Figure 4.21   Memorial portrait of Queen Elizabeth I, engraving by Crispin de Passe (1603).

Figure 4.22 *Queen Elizabeth I*, The Sieve Portrait (*c.* 1580) by Cornelius Kettel (?).

Ultra," to retake the Holy Land and expand his empire beyond the boundaries of Europe; it subsequently became the impresa of his son Philip II of Spain, the husband of Elizabeth's Catholic half-sister Mary Tudor. The Queen's image, with its naval background, not only celebrates the maritime victory over her brother-in-law in 1588, and the more recent naval triumph at Cadiz, but, at a time when the exploration and colonization of the New World were starting to be a critical element in English political life, asserts Elizabeth's own imperial claims, to Wales, to Ireland, and to the lands beyond the sea. The Herculean columns of the Most Catholic King are hung with trophies of her triumph, the arms of England on the left, of the Tudors on the right. Atop the columns are, on the left, the pelican feeding her young with her own blood, the emblem of *Caritas* applied here to Elizabeth's care for her people; on the right, a phoenix rises in flame, asserting at once the Queen's uniqueness, her virginity, and, so many years after the scandal of her mother, the immaculateness of her birth.[16] An open book beside her, alluding (once again in the Vulgate's rendering) to the 88th Psalm, declares that she has made God her help. The imagery here was public and familiar; its deployment, however, was political and intensely personal.

There may, therefore, have been something quite self-conscious about the appropriation of a papal emblem for Saxton's frontispiece. But there is a significant difference between the papal and the Elizabethan impresas. The Pope's version consists only of the two women, both clothed; to create the Queen's emblem, Peace has been undressed, and the putto bearing scales has been added. The revision both simplifies and complicates the image. To begin with, it serves to clarify the identity of the armed goddess: she is not the warlike Bellona or the militant Pallas, but Justice, a figure who may logically unite with Peace. In fact, though the sword was a more common attribute identifying Justice than the scales familiar to us (Othello fears lest Desdemona's balmy breath "persuade / Justice to break her sword," not to drop her scales), its warlike implications were sometimes felt to be troublesome. Thus Crispin de Passe's memorial engraving of the Queen (fig. 4.21) takes no chances, clearly labeling not only the sword but the word of God that supports it; and God's word, once again for this English Protestant, is Latin.

Yet the scales could easily have been introduced without the putto. The cherub in company with a naked Peace brings into the emblem a set of implications that are quite different from those of Pope Julius's impresa. If the erotic force of the original image is subsumed in the psalmist's allegory, with the women clothed and their identity controlled

Figure 4.23   *Dido* (*c.* 1500–5) by Andrea Mantegna.

by their attributes of olive branch and sword, the English version makes the issue of female sexuality insistently manifest. A naked woman accompanied by a putto inescapably suggests Venus and Cupid; and indeed, one's first impression of the impresa is that it represents the more commonplace coupling of Venus and Mars – in the topos, the armed woman, Pallas or Bellona, has replaced the god of war. Nor is the association of Venus with Elizabeth necessarily unintended: Saxton's Atlas was published in 1579, in the midst of the negotiations over the Alençon match, the last time the Queen was to represent herself as a marriageable woman. The allusion to Venus, moreover, makes a genealogical claim: Elizabeth is descended from Venus, the mother of Aeneas and the great-grandmother of Brutus, legendary founder of Britain and Elizabeth's ancestor. The goddess of love is the source of the British royal line.

The erotic is clearly the main issue in the iconography of the series of Sieve portraits from the same period. In figure 4.22, the most elaborate of the paintings, Elizabeth stands beside a column, a type of Fortitude. The Queen holds a sieve, emblem of her chastity, an allusion to the story of the Roman vestal Tuccia, who, when accused of unchastity, proved her virginity by carrying water from the Tiber to the Temple of Vesta in a sieve. But what is represented in the ovals on the column are scenes from the story of Dido and Aeneas. Dido often served as a type of Elizabeth; the analogy was an easy one, since the Carthaginian queen's given name was Elissa – by the end of the century, the name is being recorded in mythological and historical dictionaries as Eliza. The multiple allusion sets two traditions about Dido against each other: one, considered historical, in which Dido, the chaste widow of Sychaeus, commits suicide to prevent her enforced marriage to a neighboring king, and Virgil's poetic one, considered fictitious, in which she succumbs to the charms of Aeneas and is destroyed by her passion. The double allusion ingeniously provides Elizabeth with both genealogical and typological ancestors, Aeneas and Dido; the sieve assures us that she will be an embodiment of the chaste Dido, not the fallen one. When the monarch was a woman, such assurances were always necessary. Mantegna depicted the chaste Dido (fig. 4.23), standing before her own funeral pyre holding the urn containing her husband's ashes. Elizabeth is invoked as both Venus and Vesta by John Lyly in *Euphues and his England*: "having the beauty that might allure all … , she hath the chastity to refuse all, accounting it no less praise to be called a virgin, than to be esteemed a Venus"; and he goes on to compare her to the notable vestals Aemilia and Tuccia.[17]

The vestal here is obviously privileged over the goddess of love. But the scene in Saxton's impresa is unquestionably erotic, and it shows Venus, moreover, paired with another woman – the biblical reference, indeed, has had to be toned down: "deosculari" is a good deal stronger than embracing, a demotic word for a deep kiss, the word for the kind of kissing people do in the comedies of Terence. Lesbian sexuality is all but invisible in surviving sixteenth-century English sources (in contrast, for example, to French texts of the period, both literary and legal) and it is tempting to assume that for the Renaissance, whatever English women might do with each other, it did not constitute sex. This is very largely the case with sex between men: despite the legal and theological fulminations against sodomy, with very few exceptions, it was a vice conceived to be practiced only by foreigners. It is also true that in much (though by no means all) of the standard gynecological literature, female sexuality exists primarily to evoke, and satisfy, male sexuality; and in this context, the notion of two women making love would be literally inconceivable.

This is the version of Renaissance gynecology that modern commentators have tended to concentrate on. Nevertheless, I do not think it settles the matter; the nature of women is no more stable than the nature of images, and the Renaissance is full of alternative gynecologies. By the 1590s, Thomas Nashe could write an obscene poem, *A Choice of Valentines*, in which a dildo figures significantly; it is evidently not a novelty, but a familiar instrument, and though it is used in the context of sex with a man, it constitutes a powerful testimony to the English Renaissance's conviction that, whatever gynecology says, women do indeed have an independent sexuality, which needs to be satisfied. By the 1590s, a word for lesbian sex has entered the language: tribadry. It is deployed, in the earliest example I have found, in a way that is neither uncomprehending nor hostile. John Donne's correspondent T. W. writes in a verse letter,

> Have mercy on me and my sinful muse,
> Which, rubbed and tickled with thine, could not choose
> But spend some of her pith, and yield to be
> One in that chaste and mystic tribadry.[18]

In Ben Jonson's usage a decade later (the earliest citation in the *OED* – not a good guide in this sort of investigation), the word becomes a term of contempt for women who have declared their independence of men. Pallas Athena, the "mankind [mannish] maid," is sent off to join the muses, "thy tribade trine," a lesbian trio, to

> invent new sports;
> Thou nor thy looseness with my making sorts[19]

– the "making" being, I would think, both his poetry and his own kind of sex, that "doing" which, he says, following Petronius,

> a filthy pleasure is, and short
> And done, we straight repent us of the sport.[20]

These two examples suffice to show that sex between women was both conceivable and conceived, and to suggest the breadth of the English Renaissance response to it. "Chaste and mystic tribadry" therefore may well be an element in the impresa that hangs above Elizabeth's head, and its point would be, like the substitution of Pallas/Bellona for Mars, to preserve at once Elizabeth's sexuality and her virginity. The same strategy is evident in the extraordinary passage in Sir Philip Sidney's *Arcadia* describing Pamela and Philoclea in bed together:

> They impoverished their clothes to enrich their bed, which for that night might well scorn the shrine of Venus; and there cherishing one another with dear, though chaste, embracements, with sweet, though cold, kisses, it might seem that Love was come to play him there without dart, or that weary of his own fires, he was there to refresh himself between their sweet-breathing lips.[21]

I do not think it can be argued that such a scene would not have been considered overtly sexual in 1590: Sidney's insistence that the embracements were chaste, the kisses cold, are surely there to contradict the inevitable assumption that they were, respectively, libidinous and hot. The usual way of dealing with this sort of thing is to declare it masculine titillation because the author was a man. But *Arcadia* was written for the Countess of Pembroke and her circle, and the readership of romances was overwhelmingly female. If the relation between texts and their readers means anything, then the passage is feminine titillation as well. Elizabeth's impresa too was, no doubt, devised by a man; but it insists on the absolute authority of the feminine: beauty and love, wisdom and military valor, and justice, are presented as functions of female sexuality, militant chastity and innocence under maternal control (in that order, reading from left to right). The iconography is, so far as I know, unprecedented, but it is characteristically Elizabethan in its determination both to include and to disarm the realities of lust and conquest within the concept of imperial power.

The image of Elizabeth as patron of geography makes an imperial claim: the arms of England at the top are crowned specifically with an imperial crown; and virginity was an increasingly critical element in that claim. The essential relation between the imperial and the virginal is clearly implicit, for example, in Ralegh's selection of the name Virginia for his new colony: this was devised as a compliment to Elizabeth, but the name was not, say, Elizia or Tudoria. The epithet acknowledges the extent to which virginity had become, by the last years of Elizabeth's reign, a crucial attribute of royal power.

However, virginity is a double-edged sword, and power is constituted, paradoxically, in the ability, and authority, to deflower it. We have only to recall Ralegh's famous passage on Guiana: "To conclude, Guiana is a country that hath yet her maidenhead, never sacked, turned, nor wrought. ... It hath never been entered by any army of strength, and never conquered or possessed by any Christian prince."[22] In the potential of virginity lay not only civilization but the promise of infinite bounty within a hegemonic order. Needless to say, however, in Ralegh's construction it is only Elizabeth's chastity that must be preserved intact; impenetrable herself, she is the Christian prince who is to enter and possess the virgin land. Ralegh's plans for Guiana – which are Elizabeth's plans: he acts in her name and on her authority – are amply indicated by his servant Lawrence Keymis's description of the country as a potential prostitute soliciting trade: "whole shires of fruitful rich grounds lying now waste for want of people do prostitute themselves unto us, like a fair and beautiful woman in the pride and flower of desired years."[23] Elizabeth is constructed here as a type of Pallas, a "mankind maid" in Jonson's hostile epithet; it is to her imperial virginity that the new land is being prostituted. Whether the persona implied in such assertions was one that she constructed for herself or one that was constructed for her is beside the point; the foreign policy was hers, and when divine and mystic tribadry becomes a principle of foreign policy, there is no reason to expect it to be less predatory than any other imperial ideology.

I have been, I confess, quite surprised at how far I was able to pursue this reading of Elizabeth's impresa without feeling that I had lost the sense of its historical context. I am always wary of historical claims that begin "nobody in the Renaissance would have thought ...," especially when what nobody would have thought is something that we prefer to suppress in our own culture. At the same time, it is obvious that nobody would have described the emblem in the terms I have used, or attempted to account for it in the way I have done: neither the critical language nor the concerns of the present are those of 1579, and however much we may undertake to think ourselves back into the past, no amount of historical perspective can erase the history that has formed our sensibilities. Insofar as Elizabeth would have thought of the project she was pursuing in the New World, and (as we tend to forget) much more significantly, energetically and ruthlessly in Ireland, as imperialistic, she would certainly have conceived it as a good thing, not a predatory and morally dubious one. Nevertheless, to presume to explain away her policies on the grounds of a grand historical naïveté, a necessarily insufficient sense of long-term historical consequences, is to indulge ourselves in a degree of condescension that historians can scarcely afford with regard to their subjects. I see no reason not to credit Elizabeth with understanding as much about the implications of her policies as we do about the implications of ours – which is to say, whenever we can say it with hindsight, not very much. History is not something that happened only in the sixteenth century. Renaissance symbolic forms are cultural artifacts, and if they speak to us at all, that is a measure of the extent to which we have been able to recreate the world that made them and to find ourselves in it.

NOTES

1   According to the epigraph engraved on the pedestal of the *Daphne*; see Jean Seznec, *The Survival of the Pagan Gods* (New York, 1953), p. 271.
2   *Ovids Metamorphosis Englished, Mythologized,* and *Represented in Figures,* (Oxford, 1632), p. 35.
3   *The xv. Bookes of P. Ouidius Naso,* ed. (as *Shakespeare's Ovid*) by W. H. D. Rouse (London, 1904), p. 206.
4   *Metamorphosis,* p. 361.
5   William Caxton, *Ovyde Hys Methamorphose* (1480), 10:6.
6   The most thorough discussion of the iconography, though one I disagree with on some central points, is by Raymond Waddington, "The Bisexual Portrait of Francis I," in Jean R. Brink et al., eds., *Playing with Gender,* (Urbana, 1991), pp. 99–132.
7   For a general discussion of the satirical iconography of the reign, see Keith Cameron, *Henri III, A Maligned or Malignant King* (University of Exeter, 1978). The two images considered here are plates 7 and 8, discussed on pp. 78–84.
8   The emblem is discussed in Paul Julian Smith, *The Body Hispanic* (Oxford, 1989), pp. 9, 16–17.
9   The drawing is now in Stockholm; in the catalogue of the 1989 Giulio Romano exhibition in Mantua, it is reproduced and discussed on p. 283.
10   *Dictionarium Historicum, Geographicum, Poeticum* (Paris, 1596), p. 26.
11   *A Choice of Emblemes* (Leyden, 1586), p. 93.
12   *Gloriana* (London, 1987), p. 99.
13   Ibid. pp. 113–14, and figure 112.
14   In the Vulgate, the psalm is numbered 84.
15   See the anonymous pamphlet addressed to Edward VI, *Al Serenissimo Re d'Inghilterra Edoardo Sesto, De portamenti di Papa Giulio III,* 1550, cited by Alessandro Nova, *Artistic Patronage of Pope Julius III* (Garland, 1988), p. 48 n. 57. A photograph of the Villa Giulia stucco is reproduced in figure 28.

16 Neither Hind (I, 285) nor Strong (*Portraits*, p. 113) sees an allusion to the Armada in the print; Yates (*Astraea*, p. 58) does. I am indebted to Peter Hammer for calling my attention to the Cadiz allusion. Hind incorrectly claims the birds are both versions of the phoenix.

17 Cited by Strong, *Gloriana*, p. 96.

18 John Donne, *The Satires, Epigrams and Verse Letters*, ed. W. Milgate (Oxford, 1967), p. 212.

19 Jonson, *The Forest* 10, lines 17–18.

20 Jonson, *Underwood* 88, lines 1–2.

21 Sir Philip Sidney, *The Countess of Pembroke's Arcadia*, ed. Albert Feuillerat (Cambridge, 1912), p. 176.

22 Sir R. Shombergk, ed., *The Discovery of . . . Guiana* (Hakluyt Society, 1848), p. 115.

23 *A Relation of the Second Voyage to Guiana* (London, 1596) sig. F2v.

5 The unauthored 1539 volume in which is printed the *Hecatomphile, The Flowers of French Poetry,* and *Other Soothing Things*

Nancy J. Vickers

Early Modern objects are resistant objects; they tend to promise proximity only to threaten, in the final analysis, insuperable distance. As a student in the early 1970s, I was so drawn to one such object – a French book from the 1530s – that I traveled to Paris to see it. Yet when I finally held it in my hands, it baffled me. It was a tiny volume consisting of three (not entirely) discrete titles. My intent had been to write about just one, but, with the object before me, I puzzled over what to do with the others. The available options seemed either to ignore them (the usual course) or to reveal their inevitable participation in an integrated totality. Nothing in my training had prepared me to meet a "thing" as hybrid as a textual unit without a single genre, title, or author.

Twenty years ago scholarly wisdom argued that in the absence of a presiding genius, of an authorial subject so unified as even to correct proof, such textual groupings were to be taken as random. Thus a considerable number of Early Modern books were not to be identified as "works" at all. They were mere patchworks sewn together by entrepreneurs who chanced upon textual scraps; they were early print versions of manuscript gatherings that formed "books" as potentially unsystematic as any given owner's occasional holdings. A critic in search of an autonomous subject could only conclude that while the parts of such a collection might conceivably signify (if, for example, an elusive author could be tracked down), the collection as a whole – the actual object that sixteenth-century readers held in their hands – did not.

Thus nineteenth- and twentieth-century scholarship had generally treated the volume's three parts independently: it had deported one and dismembered the others. The book opened with a prose "part" – a monologue translated from Italian – that had long since been excised from the French cultural tradition and returned to the complete works of its Italian author.[1] The two subsequent and poetic "parts" – both collective anthologies of lyric – had either been ignored, fragmented, or reorganized in the name of coherence (be it generic, topical, or

166

authorial).[2] To the extent deemed possible, constitutive poetic "members" had been assigned (and misassigned) to namable corpuses.

This chapter attempts a return to this specific Early Modern object – to the tiny volume – by resisting any desire to fixate upon an autonomous Renaissance subject. Claiming no exceptional status for the book in question, I seek only to view it differently. To that end I will focus upon the encodings of the printed artifact itself – its title page, its textual parts, its rubrics and prefaces, its woodcuts – with an eye to discerning how such textual gestures of self-staging reveal the volume's circumstances of production and consumption. I will argue that, as an object signaling multiple cultural affiliations, it must be read neither as perfectly integrated nor as utterly random.

The volume announces itself as tripartite; it is both an aggregate of parts and a single entity. It thus exemplifies the double movement characteristic of tract volumes (volumes made up of "several, usually short, interrelated texts"[3]): its parts are at once independent and allied. "The fact that the texts [of tract volumes] were bound together," Sandra Hindman argues, "suggests that they were read together and thus thought of intellectually as complementary units."[4] The translation of the title page reads only: "Hecatomphile. Sold in the Rue Neuve Notre Dame at the Sign of Sainct Nicolas by Pierre Sergent. M.D.XXXIX." Its verso provides elaboration: "Hecatomphile, which is a composite of two Greek terms, signifying one hundredth love ('centiesme amour'), knowingly adapted to the Lady having in herself as many loves as one hundred other ladies could contain, which are now mentioned. Turned from Italian vernacular into French language. Also the Flowers of French Poetry, and other soothing things. Newly revised."[5] A crude woodcut – the first of fifty-nine – represents Hecatomphile as a woman standing in a theatrical pose; her gaze fixes upon a flower; a small dog scrambles for attention at her feet (fig. 5.1).

The volume's initial text is a dramatic monologue delivered by Hecatomphile, a woman of experience, in what she labels a "theater" (2 recto); she alludes repeatedly to other unspecified entertainments to follow. Her speech, an art of love, is addressed to "virtuous and beautiful" young women (2 recto). Despite the market appeal of the teasing title (could it mean one hundred loves rather than, as the translator has it, one hundredth love?), it is far from libertine. Hecatomphile herself provides clarification; she says that she has better satisfied her desires "with one lover than [she] could have with a hundred" (2 verso). For this reason, she continues, "men of letters, whom [she] has always honored more than ignorant and rustic men, named her Hecatomphile, which means one hundred loves" (2 verso). Indeed, the

Hecatomphile

On les vend en la rue neufue noſtre Dame a lenſeigne
ſainct Nicolas, par Pierre ſergent.   M. D. XXXI X

Figure 5.1   The title page of *Hecatomphile* (Sergent, 1539).

program for female happiness she counsels lies largely in becoming lovingly subservient to an ideal male lover or husband – that is, to a middle-aged scholar of middle means. Neither the Italian author (Leon Battista Alberti, 1404–72) of this ventriloquized speech nor his French translator is named. Editions in both languages were repeatedly printed in the 1530s suggesting that this text was one of the many fashionable items appropriated by the French from the Italians.[6] The French text reproduces, and sometimes glosses, the Italian. For example, it notably adds references to Petrarch – the author who, at least in the mind of the French translator, "ennobled love" through Italian vernacular poetry (2 verso). This specific Petrarchizing gloss puts in play an "ennobling" discursive strain that will repeat, with varying insistence, across the full volume.

The second text, *The Flowers of French Poetry*, follows *Hecatomphile* without an intervening title page or other marked division. An anthology of sixty-seven love lyrics written predominantly in traditional late fifteenth- and early sixteenth-century French forms (quatrains, *huitains*, *dizains*, and *rondeaulx*), the *Flowers* betray thematic and figurative traces of early Petrarchism despite their formal resistance to the sonnet.[7] Some even "turn" Petrarch's verses into French: consider, as example, the song "Being one day alone at the window" ("Ung jour estant seullet a la fenestre," 35 recto – 36 verso) which translates *Rime sparse* 323 ("Standomi un giorno solo a la fenestra"). These poems, which also lack signatures, thus make a parallel move to "ennoble" love though examples now articulated in the French vernacular. Subsequent scholars locate their "authors" at the court of François I; they ascribe the poems to poets such as Claude Chappuys, Marguerite de Navarre, and Mellin de Saint-Gelais. In attributing a full quarter of them to François I himself, June Kane implicitly constructs this specific anthology as the most significant contemporary publication of verse by the King.[8] However, Donald Stone, Saint-Gelais's recent editor, sounds a general and cautionary note; he comments that sixteenth-century manuscripts rather "indifferently attributed the paternity of the same poem to Marot, François I, Chappuys, or Saint-Gelais."[9] Clearly ascribable to a network of poets at the court of France (if not always to an autonomous author), these texts would seem to be the products of a coterie exchange. They are preceded by a second dramatic monologue explaining the anthology from the perspective of the "Disciple of the French *Archipoete*" through a mythologizing account of textual production.

In the Disciple's twenty-eighth year, the fate Lachesis was at work on the "toille" ("tapestry" or "canvas") of his life when "Venus, Pluto, and the world" fought for possession of it. However, merciful Jupiter intervened by urging Minerva to take the "toille" out of their hands and do whatever she pleased with it. She armed herself with her "crystalline shield charged with the Gorgon's head" and conquered the "vile monsters" (Venus, Pluto, and the world) before they succeeded in tearing the "toille" apart. Minerva next asked Mercury to transport the tapestry to the protection of the "beautiful garden of poetry." There the garden's excellent painters enriched it with "pleasing pictures" ("plaisantes pour-traictures"). Thus several "modern masters" ("surpassing Zeuxis, Apelles, and all the classics") came to contribute "these sweetly perfumed flowers" – that is, the "poésies," or poseys, that follow the prologue in the collection. Minerva ultimately returned the richly embellished ta-pestry to the "fatal weaver" ("tessiere fatale") Lachesis, who found it "so well decorated" that she "displayed" the painters' works "to everyone" ("en fait a tous ostension"). In addition, her publicizing gesture also provides instruction; it is meant to be an "impetus" ("aguillon") to imitation for those who would hone their skills in "worldly love" ("amour mondain"). The Disciple concludes by asking us, his readers, to consider what thanks we should offer to the "generous weaver" ("tessiere liberale") without whom we would not enjoy the little flowers: "sans laquelle neussiez jouy des fleurettes."[10]

   Allegory here stages elite production within a traditional enclosed space, one that is, in turn, opened up for view to a broad readership by a "fatal" dispensation. Though in *The Flowers of French Poetry* no authors are named, the poems are preceded not only by little typographic flowers ("fleurettes") but also by manuscript-style indicators that cumulatively situate the texts and mark multiple authorship: "The Disciple begins to describe love in this dialogue"; "Another author defines love"; "Another description of love by the prince of French poets"; "How the most noble and perfect of true lovers defends love ..."; "Another to attract his Lady praises her person"; "A Lady answers," and so on. The poems are thus textually staged as embedded within an aristocratic coterie; they are represented as if they were the overheard snatches of a courtly conversa-tion; they voice both positions and responses (or positions and alternate positions) on the topic of love.[11] Poetry here is figured as a decorative gathering of "mille fleurs,"[12] and this early print collection thus partici-pates in the long-standing tradition of the "anthology" or "florilegium" (the former from the Greek "anthos" ["flower"] and "legein" ["to gather or collect"] and the latter from the Latin "flos" ["flower"] and "legere" ["to gather or collect"]). Clearly of appreciable commercial appeal, French printed variations on this collective format predate *The Flowers of French Poetry* in the form of the late medieval *Garden of Pleasure and Flower of Rhetoric* (*Le Jardin de plaisance et fleur de réthoricque*, 1502) and postdate it in the form of multiple sixteenth-century anthologies

(*The Flower of French Poetry* [*La Fleur de poésie francoyse*, 1543]; *Garden of Honor* [*Jardin d'honneur*, 1545]; and *The Flowers of the Most Excellent Poets of This Time* [*Les Fleurs de plus excellents Poetes de ce temps*, 1599], to name but a few).[13]

In addition, Sergent's 1539 volume closes with a second multi-authored collection classified on the title page only by the supplementary rubric "and other soothing [comforting, joyful, or merry] things" ("et autres choses solatieuses").[14] The very turn of phrase "*autres* choses solatieuses" locates the full contents of the book within the seductive category of "soothing things," of objects which provide "pastime" ("passetemps") and produce "recreation" (refreshment or renewal "by means of some agreeable object or impression"[15]). Implicit here is a world of care from which the book, as a pleasing and frivolous object, distracts the reader. The "other soothing things" specifically here at issue are an assortment of anatomical blazons, of stylistically varied, anonymous poems on the parts of the female body.[16] The blazons flow without transition from the *Flowers*, though their titles and modes of illustration are markedly different from those of the previous poems. Though the anthology's twenty-two blazons resist traditional head-to-toe body ordering, the beginning and the end of the collection are hierarchically marked: the illustrated "Blazon of the Hair" (fig. 5.2) opens this sub-volume, and the unillustrated "Blason du Q [Cul]" ("Blazon of the Ass[hole]") concludes it. "The Blazon of the Breast" (fig. 5.3) and "The Blazon of the Foot" (fig. 5.4) characterize what is found in between. Again, no poems are signed, but communication among them is staged; they simulate a collective and competitive provenance. The "Blason du Q [Cul]," for example, lists virtually every other poem-part in the process of asserting its "lordship" ("seigneurie"). It would therefore seem to participate in a boasting contest between body parts and, by extension, between poems and poets. In addition, the volume's culminating move to the lower bodily stratum wittily literalizes the notion of the "tailpiece" or coda with a closing indicator, a visual and verbal pun enhanced by a typographical gap: "Fin du Q" ("End of the Ass[hole]").

To sketch *Hecatomphile*'s networks of production and consumption, I will depend, for the most part, on qualities manifest in the material book. I will argue that the volume stages itself, first, as the compositional product of a courtly coterie network and, second, as the editorial product of a Parisian printing network. It would thus seduce its purchasers by offering courtly pleasures to a market of aspiring bourgeois professionals. Here I follow the lead of Natalie Zemon Davis in seeking both to "supplement thematic analysis of texts with evidence about audiences that can provide a context for the meaning and uses of books" and to

LES CHEVEVLX

Blaſon des cheueulx.

L   E paranymhe Apollo cheueleux
     Voyant les gens par trop aduentureux
    A collauder tous les membres du corps,
Et quilz neſtoient de beaulx cheueulx recordz,
Deſquelz ſur tous ſen diſoit Dieu pare,
A tout ſoubdain ſes Muſes prepare
Pour en former louange a eulx condigne,
Comme a ceulx la qui font le corps plus digne
Que rien quil ayt, Car ſans cheueulx la Dame
Reſſembleroit vne foreſt ſans rame
Dont incite pour la dame honnorer
Son chef ainſi commencea decorer.
    Cheueulx dorez rayans ſur le ſoleil
Si treſluyſantz quilz font eſblouir loeil
Qui les regarde, & les veoit coulorez
Non pas dor fin, mais encor mieulx dorez
De ie ne ſcay quelle couleur diuine

Figure 5.2 "The Blazon of the Hair" from *Hecatomphile* (Sergent, 1539.

BLASON

Blaſon du Tetin.

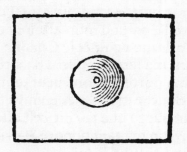

TEtin reffaict plus blanc quung oeuf,
Tetin de ſatin blanc tout neuf,
Tetin qui faitz honte a la roſe,
Tetin plus beau que nulle choſe
Tetin dor,non pas Tetin,voyre
Mais petite boulle diuoyte
Au millieu de qui eſt aſſiſe
Vne Fraiſe ou vne Seriſe
Que nul ne voyt ne touche auſſi,
Mais ie gage quil eſt ainſi.
Tetin donc au petit bout rouge.
Tetin qui iamais ne ſe bouge
Soit pour venir,ſoit pour aller,
Soit pour courir,ſoit pour baller.
Tetin gauche,tetin mignon,
Tetin loing de ſon compaignon,
Tetin qui Portes teſmoignage
Du demeurant du perſonnage.

Figure 5.3 "The Blazon of the Breast" from *Hecatomphile* (Sergent, 1539).

BLASON

Et donne moy ce bien tant precieux.
Ou autrement de toy me pourray plaindre:
Car ie puis bien iuſques au Tetin attaindre,
Loreille entend mon affaire compter,
Leſprit me veult & le Cueur contenter.
Loeil ma ſeruy ſouuent dheureux meſſage
Et ma porte du bon cueur teſmoignage.
La Bouche ma de mes ennuys paſſez
Tant allege que iay dit, ceſt aſſez.
La Main ma tant honore & priſe
Que dire puis, ie ſuis fauoriſe.
Ceſt doncques toy en qui eſt le pouuoir
De ce qui reſte & plus deſire auoir.
Dont te ſupply que ne me vueilles eſtre
Trop rigoreux, mais vueilles moy congnoiſtre
Pour ton amy quant pres de toy ſeray
Te promettant quen riens noffenſeray.
Blaſon du Pied.

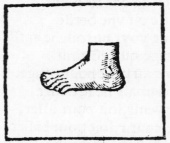

Eulx qui ont fait deᵗ Loeil, Bouche &
Oreille,
Du noble Cueur, du Tetin grant merueille,

Figure 5.4 "The Blazon of the Foot" from *Hecatomphile* (Sergent, 1539).

"consider a printed book not merely as a source for ideas and images, but as a carrier of relationships."[17]

The *Flowers*, for example, signal potential court production by labels that identify their lyric voices as those of "Princes," "Gentlemen," and (rarely) "Ladies." The mythologized figures of their prologue arguably mimic those of François' court, an elite circle constructed to be a "mythology in action."[18] Within that court's discursive codes the patron–poet–king was repeatedly figured as Jupiter; his patron–poet–sister, Marguerite de Navarre, as Minerva. In addition, the "flowers" often meditate on the theme of nobility; they present themselves as textual vestiges of noble leisure activities (love contests, love songs, and love games);[19] they are gathered in such a way as to simulate a courtly conversation. Some of these poems were even set to music and thus participated in an extended and varied entertainment repertory.[20] The very term "entertainment" (from the Latin "inter" ["among"] and "tenere" ["to hold"]) evokes the central socio-political bond forged by a full range of similarly "trivial" activities ascribed to courtiers and court ladies.[21] Though we know little about the Alberti translation, the Court's fascination with all things Italian was legend. Alberti's monologue, moreover, opens with an address to noble young women and closes with the appearance of costumed actors ready for an entertainment to follow. The anatomical blazons were inevitably associated by contemporaries with the "inventor" of the genre, Clément Marot, both a court and a career poet.[22] The volume's non-courtly texts – those by professionals of various stripes – move into the textual mix only in later imprints and editions, like the 1539 volume, which include the added blazon section. Indeed, the volume's insistent anonymity might even constitute a coy and courtly maneuver, a gesture that tantalizes by seeming to make a private society public behind a screen of secrecy.[23] The obsession with attribution – to which most modern readers, as well as most modern editors, seem subject – could itself be an extension of a courtly guessing-game. Nobles were, of course, enjoined not to engage in commerce and thus would resist identification with the new class of career writers who counted on name recognition to sell books. Presenting themselves as reflecting coterie conversations at court, the texts constituting the printed book thus open up those conversations; they offer the cachet of court pleasures to an urban market through the intermediary of another conversation – one between the printers and booksellers of Paris and of Lyon.

Marie-France Piéjus points to ten Parisian or Lyonnais editions of the *Hecatomphile* in the six years between 1534 and 1540; they were first bipartite (just *Hecatomphile* and *Flowers*) and later tripartite

(*Hecatomphile, Flowers,* and *The Anatomical Blazons*).[24] The tripartite 1539 volume described above, then, is a "Newly Revised" ("Reveus Nouvellement") edition with interpolated material. The more numerous Parisian editions have a greater rate of survival. The few extant copies, which reflect the predominant Paris milieu, are formatted in such strikingly similar ways as to suggest a shared notion of the volume.[25] At the level of textual reproduction, a network of printers would seem to be borrowing, buying, or stealing texts and images from one another. To demonstrate this exchange, I will depend upon four Parisian (or probably Parisian) editions:[26] first, a 1534 octavo in the Newberry Library that contains, in its editor's terms, "two little books" (*Hecatomphile* and *Flowers*) and that was published without illustration for the boutique of Galliot du Pré; second, an illustrated 1536 seidecimo volume in the Bodleian Library that contains all three texts and was perhaps printed by Denis Janot;[27] third, a 1536–7 seidecimo volume in the Bibliothèque Nationale et Universitaire de Strasbourg that bears no indication of editor, publisher, or bookseller and that also contains illustrated versions of all three texts (thirty-two blazons); and fourth, the textual unit here at issue, the Bibliothèque Nationale's 1539 seidecimo volume produced for Pierre Sergent. It too is illustrated and contains all three texts (twenty-one blazons). After 1539 the anatomical blazons were augmented and edited to form an independent volume published by Charles L'Angelier (1543) and La Veuve Bonfons (1550), among others.

Following the introduction of the anatomical blazons in 1536 (the year in which Du Pré's 1533 "privilege" on the bipartite volume expired),[28] these multiple producers notably all maintained the same constellation of three texts. Uniformly selecting the same small format, they also consistently produced pocketbooks unsuitable for library shelving but ideal as fashion accessories, as prompts to conversation, and as gifts. Indeed the small number of remaining copies of a text so trendy as to be "sold in every shop" suggests both extensive use and ready disposability.[29] The various editions also display similar patterns of illustration: each works with a limited repertory of repeated images that stand in imitative relationship to one another. Compare, for example, the title page of the 1536–7 edition (fig. 5.5) to that of 1539 (fig. 5.1). These volumes would seem, at the very least, to be conscious of one another.[30]

Let me focus briefly on the only two producers of the *Hecatomphile* that we can now identify with certainty: Galliot Du Pré, active in Paris from 1512 through 1561 and publisher of the bipartite first French edition; and Pierre Sergent, active in Paris from 1532 through 1547 and publisher of the latest extant tripartite edition. Both were booksellers ("marchands libraires") and thus members of the professional class that

Figure 5.5   The title page of *Hecatomphile* (Anonymous, 1537).

dominated Parisian book production. Each indicates his name and his shop's address on his *Hecatomphile*'s title page.

The printing trade in sixteenth-century Paris was divided between two sections of the city:[31] the first, the Rue Saint Jacques, neighbored the University and tailored its product to academic consumption; the second, the Ile de la Cité, targeted a different market. Cité publishing was not a world of production by humanists for humanists but rather of commercial dissemination of some of the humanist lessons, among many other lessons, to an expanded public. Such a gesture generally entailed the use of an accessible, but educated, French vernacular, as well as a delectable display of lavish illustration. Bookshops filled the streets leading to the cathedral of Notre-Dame de Paris; booksellers maintained stalls within the Palais de Justice. Du Pré and Sergent participate in this milieu, as do all other known (or probable) Parisian marketers of this material. Each of the two had a stall in the Galerie du Palais; each was located, at one time or another, on the Rue Neuve Notre-Dame. Early in his career, Du Pré also maintained a boutique on the Pont Notre-Dame, a bridge refurbished by 1512 to include two rows of house-shops catering to fashion-conscious consumers of luxury items such as jewelry, hats, and books.[32]

Du Pré's market has been identified by Annie Charon-Parent as, on the one hand, "legal professionals" ("magistrats") and, on the other, royal officers who frequented both the Palais de Justice and the expanding administrative offices of the realm – all of which converged upon this "quartier."[33] Charon-Parent works both from city geography and from a detailed study of Du Pré's "list" to help evaluate the nature of his audience. She concludes that he served a professional, educated (but not necessarily scholarly) community of officers and functionaries. One third of the list she considered is composed of juridical works; the remainder is made up of translations of classical authors with broad appeal, transla- tions from Italian and Spanish, traditional French texts (including Marot's edition of *The Romance of the Rose* [*Le roman de la rose*], to which I will return), and contemporary authors. Sergent's "list" stresses the last four – the non-professional or leisure – categories. He publishes almost exclusively in French; he seems to specialize in romances, chivalric texts, love literature, and – in a related move – women's literature. For example, he markets inexpensive re-editions of both the female-authored *Sorrowful Sufferings* (*Angoisses douleureuses*) of Helisenne de Crenne and the Sieur de Drusac's misogynist handbook, the *Debates of the Male and Female Sexes* (*Controverses des sexes masculins et feminins*). Many of the same woodcuts reappear across this range of texts. Du Pré, we know, farmed work out to multiple printers and sold through multiple booksellers.

Sergent was part of that same geographical and commercial community, a community that included all probable Parisian printers of this volume and subsequent spin-off texts (Denis Janot, Gilles Corrozet, Alain Lotrian, the families Angelier, Bonfons, Le Petit, and so on). Among this group Sergent seems a popularizer, a consistent producer of smaller and more crudely illustrated (thus cheaper) editions for an arguably less educated market of lesser functionaries and their clients. Compare again, this time with an eye to relative production costs, the title pages of the 1536–7 (fig. 5.5) and 1539 (fig. 5.1) editions.

Though Sergent clearly sells "downmarket," he nonetheless participates in a complexly articulated network of Cité book producers. He shares, or copies, not only the texts but also the woodcuts deployed by his neighbors. For example, he repeatedly uses a seemingly stock image of a painter and his models across his imprints of the *Hecatomphile* and the *Flowers* (fig. 5.6). Like several other images that decorate his text, this woodcut duplicates – even to the point of imitating the border – a 1531 Du Pré illustration for the Marot edition of *The Romance of the Rose* (fig. 5.7). There it represents the story of Zeuxis, the Athenian painter who collected the best parts of the female bodies of Athens to create a composite worthy of figuring Helen.[34] The image then returns in a still more rudimentary woodcut to grace Sergent's edition of Drusac's misogynist *Controverses* (1541), itself a cheaper version of a Denis Janot edition (1540). Here an imagistic repertory corresponds to a textual repertory, and both depend upon related, marketable categories such as fashion, decoration, Italianness, love, leisure, and aristocratic entertainment.

These traditional courtly, and thus feminized, categories constitute a common ground where court and city cultures meet, where "conversations" take place among loosely allied groups of (predominantly) men of different social strata. Neither perfectly integrated nor utterly random, the discrete elements of the *Hecatomphile* editions – themselves so loosely structured as readily to permit inclusions and exclusions – decidedly locate that enterprise under the sign "woman": they open with a monologue by a woman addressed to women; they follow with model texts on how men skilled in "worldly love" might speak to women; they close with a gesture that is at once courtly and popular – the praise of female body parts.[35] The commodified body is, in this case, bound only by a book that is similarly both multiple and integrated. These texts thus clearly participate in France's protracted debate about women ("la querelle des femmes"), a debate that in its late medieval form centered on *The Romance of the Rose* and that, by 1541–2, would engage several anatomical blazoners in a fresh round, the "querelle des Amies."[36] Once

HECATOMPHILE.

dé tamour entier ne merite auſſi que lõ layme dõt bié
heureuſe eſt celle dame qui ayme ſans plus vng amy,
car iamais na leſtomach vuyde de doulx penſemens a-
moureux, de cõtinuelle amytie, & de perdurable lieſſe
Or quãt ce q̃ deſſus eſt dit ſeroit eſtime pour triuolle,
la raiſõ q̃ ie veuil deſduire, ſeroit militãte & condigne.

CHASCVNE regarde par ſoy ſi en tourbe
de requerans lon peut a tous bié ſatiſſaire : cer-
tes il eſt plus difficile que ie ne puis imaginer.
dont qui taſche a chaſcun complaire, ne peult long
temps perſeuerer en amytie pure & loyalle : ie ne
veulx pas dire de tous, mais ſeulement dung de la
bande : car ſi tu veulx employer a blandir chaſcun
de la veue, ceſt infinie ſeruitude : & ſi plus fais a lung
qua laultre, tu metz enuies & rancunes entre eulx
que penſes aymer. Parquoy autour de ta maiſon ſen

Figure 5.6 Woodcut of painter and models from *Hecatomphile*
(Sergent, 1539).

Figure 5.7   Woodcut of painter and models from the Marot edition of
The Romance of the Rose, 1531.

again the "woman question" would be marketed predominantly (though
not exclusively) for the "solace" of hardworking men, the very men
whose aristocratic ambitions would well serve François I's vision of an
expanding and centralized administration.

Such an appeal to the aristocratic pretensions of the upwardly mobile
did not, however, pass unchallenged. That a man of city culture might
well deem the seductions of courtly culture either inappropriate or
dangerous would also be enacted in woodcut and text. When the
consumers of 1539 browsed among the bookstalls of the Cité's Palais de
Justice, they found not only Sergent's "newly revised" *Hecatomphile* but
also a newly published and corrective alternative. Bookseller Gilles
Corrozet and printer Denis Janot had produced *The Domestic Blazons*
(*Les blasons domestiques*), a volume that mimicked the anatomical
blazons in both visual and verbal format but that substituted the parts of
a praiseworthy house for the parts of a praiseworthy female body.

Though Corrozet noted that "houses make cities and cities make a
realm,"[37] the house imaged to open and close his blazons offered country
comfort to city dwellers (fig. 5.8). The pages between the initiating
"Blazon of the House" and the concluding "Honor of the House"

Figure 5.8 "The Blazon of the House" from Gilles Corrozet's *Domestic Blazons*, 1539.

celebrated both <u>architectural units</u> (courtyard, garden, kitchen, bedroom, toilet) and their contents (tables, chairs, beds, mirrors, brooms). The "Blazon of the Chest" (fig. 5.9), for example, described a large box replete with many drawers that were filled with "so many things that it seems impossible to list them" (268). Corrozet nonetheless tried, evoking an array of luxury consumer items worthy of a "queen or a duchess" (265): jewels, miniatures, belt-buckles, bracelets, collars, gloves, mirrors, ivory chessboards, books of hours, and so on. There would clearly be a lady in Corrozet's house, but she would be properly domesticated though marriage and thus form part of the household's adornment:

> When one sees the virtuous lady,
> The servants, and the son, and the daughter
> Such a house is rich and sumptuous,
> And the honor of it belongs to the father of the family.
>
> (273)

Upon concluding his celebrations of houses and household goods, Corrozet's version of the hybrid volume added both a smattering of love lyrics (thus joining the conversation of the *Flowers*) and a polemical

DOMESTIQVES?   30
Le blafon du
CABINET.

Abinet remply de richeffes
Soit pour roynes ou pour
     duchefles,
Cabinet fur tous bié choifi

Figure 5.9   "The Blazon of the Chest"
from Gilles Corrozet's *Domestic
Blazons*, 1539.

poem "Against the Blazoners of Body Parts" which he illustrated with a
now familiar image (fig. 5.10). He thus positioned his text as a moralizing
corrective to a specific category of fashionable publications.[38] In contrast
to this concluding vision of the poet turned courtly painter who decorates
his canvas ("toille") with the tantalizing flowers of French beauty,
Corrozet opened his *Domestic Blazons* with the image of the poet as a
middle-aged scholar of middle means (fig. 5.11). The "domestic blaz-
oner" (staged as Corrozet himself) introduced his work by assuming the
form of a traditional clerk in his study, one who aggressively defines his
interests as other than libertine. His preface to the volume proposed that
potential purchasers take the text up "joyfully" so that "if [said purcha-
sers] were not well housed in fact, [they] would be in writing no less
worthy of being read than the [house] of being possessed" (227). The
"writing" in question would, of course, also need to be "possessed,"
though the relative cost of the compensating material substitute (the
book) was better tailored to the means of most passers-by than was the
house. Postulating greater solace in the pleasures of houses than in the
pleasures of women, *The Domestic Blazons* stands as a revealing complement to the *Hecatomphile*. As objects assembled in the image of their
consumers' varied desires, they materially shape those desires in the
process.

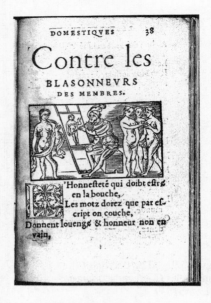

Figure 5.10 "Against the Blazoners of Body Parts" from Gilles Corrozet's *Domestic Blazons*, 1539.

Figure 5.11 "Gilles Corrozet to the Readers" from Gilles Corrozet's *Domestic Blazons*, 1539.

NOTES

1 Here a standard reference tool, the *Critical Bibliography of French Literature*, provides a telling example. As a "natural" effect of adhering to canonical definitions of influential Italians as either "trecentisti" (fourteenth-century authors) or "cinquecentisti" (sixteenth-century authors), it silences any gallic echoes the monologue might have had. Its fifteenth-century author, an intervening "quattrocentista" (Leon Battista Alberti), simply passes unnoticed. See Richard A. Brooks, ed., *A Critical Bibliography of French Literature* (rev. edn., 6 vols., Syracuse, 1985), II, pp. 703–14.

2 Scholarly labor on these texts has predominantly focused on attribution to specific authors and thus on inclusion in volumes of "complete works." Some texts are included in genre-based anthologies (such as collections of Renaissance lyric) or in theme-based anthologies (such as collections of works about women).

3 Sandra Hindman, "The Career of Guy Marchant (1483–1504): High and Low Culture in Paris," in Hindman, ed., *Printing the Written Word: The Social History of Books, circa 1450–1520* (Ithaca and London, 1991), p. 71.

4 Ibid. p. 72. The *Hecatomphile* is notably a "tract volume" in which the two or three imprints (depending upon the edition) are listed on the title page (or on its verso); the texts are thus understood to have formed a volume as printed. Other "tract volumes" assemble imprints selected by individual buyers who, in turn, have them bound together. See ibid. p. 82.

5 The French reads: "HECATOMPHILE, CE SONT DEUX DICTIONS GRECQUES Composees, signifiant, Centiesme Amour, sciemment appropriees a la dame ayant en elle autant damours que cent autres dames en pourroient comprendre, dont a present est faicte mention. Tournee de Vulgaire Italien en langaige Francoys. Ensemble, Les Fleurs de Poesie Francoyse, Et autres choses solatieuses. Reveus Nouvellement." All page references to this edition (Paris, 1539) will be indicated in parentheses in the text. All translations are my own.

6 For example, there were at least five Venetian editions (some attributing authorship to Boccaccio) in the decade between 1524 and 1534; an English translation, *Hecatomphila: The Arte of Love, or Love Discovered in a Hundred Severall Kindes*, was printed by Peter Short in London in 1598.

7 The debate over the date of the first French sonnet is summarized (with bibliography) by François Rigolot, "1536, Summer: The Sonnet," in Denis Hollier et al., eds., *A New History of French Literature* (Cambridge, Mass. and London, 1989), pp. 171–4.

8 In her edition of François I, *Oeuvres poétiques* (Geneva, 1984).

9 In the "Introduction" to Mellin de Saint-Gelais, *Oeuvres poétiques françaises*, ed. Donald Stone, Jr. (2 vols., Paris, 1993–), I, p. xi.

10 For the full prologue, see *Hecatomphile*, pp. 25 verso – 26 verso.

11 My understanding of this text as "conversation" has benefited from reading the first chapter ("'Turning Sonnet': The Politics and Poetics of Sonnet Circulation") of Wendy Wall's *The Imprint of Gender: Authorship and Publication in the English Renaissance* (Ithaca, 1993), pp. 23–109.

12 I allude to the traditional floral background (or "fond mille fleurs") of tapestry.

13 On such collections see Frédéric Lachèvre, *Bibliographie des recueils collectifs de poésies du XVIe siècle* (Paris, 1922).

14 My translation is adapted from Randle Cotgrave, *A Dictionarie of the French and English Tongues*, (London, 1611; rpt. New York, 1971); and Edmond Huguet, *Dictionnaire de la langue française du seizième siècle* (6 vols., Paris, 1928–67).

15 I cite the *Oxford English Dictionary*'s definition of "recreation." The vocabulary of "solas," "passetemps," and "recréation" is characteristic of the period's collective anthologies of lyric; see, for examples, Lachèvre, *Bibliographie des recueils collectifs*, pp. 33, 36, and 51–5.

16 Subsequent scholarly attributions would argue that a few poets were included in both collections; most were not.

17 In *Society and Culture in Early Modern France* (Stanford, 1965), p. 192. Though Davis's specific goal (to "understand the connections between printing and the people") differs from my own, she usefully redirects the ways we approach book–objects. Davis compares her observations to those of Elizabeth L. Eisenstein who speaks of print fostering "cross-cultural interchange" between previously "compartmentalized systems," p. 192.

18 See André Chastel, "Fontainebleau: Forms and Symbols," in *Fontainebleau: Art in France 1528–1610* (Ottawa, 1973), I, p. 243.

19 On the relationship of courtly games and Petrarchism, see François Lecercle, "La culture en jeu: Innocenzo Ringhieri et le pétrarquisme," in Philippe Ariès and Jean-Claude Margolin, eds., *Les jeux à la Renaissance* (Paris, 1982), pp. 185–200.

20 For example, Jannequin had already set Marot's "Blazon of the Breast" to music by April of 1536. See Daniel Heartz, *Pierre Attaingnant, Royal Printer of Music: A Historical Study and Bibliographical Catalogue* (Berkeley and Los Angeles, 1969), p. 285.

21 Castiglione's *Book of the Courtier* (1528), a highly visible text at François' court and in early French publishing, insistently uses the critical Italian verb "intertenere" to describe the proper activities of courtiers and court ladies. Cotgrave's early French–English dictionary defines "recueil" (a term often labeling lyric anthologies) as "a collection, gathering, reaping; also, a intertaining, or welcoming" (*Dictionarie*).

22 Marot is defined as "inventor" of the genre by the editor of *Les blasons anatomiques du corps fémenin* (Paris, 1543), p. 97 recto. For a study of the history of the genre, see Alison Saunders, *The Sixteenth-Century Blason Poétique* (Bern, Frankfurt am Main, Las Vegas, 1981).

23 On stagings of secrecy in relation to courtly sonnets and miniatures, see Patricia Fumerton, *Cultural Aesthetics: Renaissance Literature and the Practice of Social Ornament* (Chicago and London, 1991), pp. 67–110.

24 In Jean-Pierre Guillerm, Luce Guillerm, Laurence Hordoir, Marie-France Piéjus, eds., *Le miroir des femmes: moralistes et polémistes au XVIème siècle* (Lille, 1983), pp. 173–4.

25 For extended description and illustration, see Alison Saunders, "Sixteenth-

century Collected Editions of Blasons Anatomiques," *The Library* 31 (1976), 351–68.

26 I thus rely on the Du Pré bipartite edition and the only three extant tripartite editions according to Saunders, ibid. pp. 352–8.

27 On the identification of Janot as printer, see ibid. p. 352, n. 4.

28 The French "privilege" was an early form of copyright. George Hoffmann argues that regulations forbidding the renewal of a "privilege" serve as an impetus to the creation of "new" texts through variation and augmentation of bestsellers. See "The Montaigne Monopoly: Revising the *Essais* under the French Privilege System," *PMLA* 108, 2 (1993), 311.

29 I cite an epistle attacking the anatomical blazoners by François Sagon, in *Les blasons anatomiques du corps fémenin*, p. 133.

30 The printers and booksellers at issue in this essay also consistently "shared" printings. François Juste, who seems to be the central producer of the *Hecatomphile* texts in Lyon, had a history of working with Du Pré.

31 The description that follows is drawn largely from the work of Annie Charon-Parent: see "Le monde de l'imprimerie humaniste: Paris," in Henri-Jean Martin and Roger Chartier, eds., *Histoire de l'édition française* (4 vols., Paris, 1982), I, pp. 237–53; see also her book (based on the example of Du Pré), *Les métiers du livre à Paris au XVIe siècle* (Geneva, 1974).

32 For the Pont Notre-Dame, see *David Thomson, Renaissance Paris: Architecture and Growth 1475–1600* (Berkeley and Los Angeles, 1984), pp. 73–4. Building upon the work of Michel Simonin, George Hoffmann describes how contemporaries referred to the bookstalls and shops of the Ile de la Cité as fashionable "boutiques de nouveautés," in "About being about the Renaissance: bestsellers and booksellers," *Journal of Medieval and Renaissance Studies* 22 (1992), 83–4.

33 Charon-Parent, "Le monde de l'imprimerie humaniste: Paris," p. 244. Charon-Parent's identification of the Cité's book market is confirmed beyond the example of Du Pré by A. H. Schutz, *Vernacular Books in Parisian Private Librairies of the Sixteenth Century According to the Notarial Inventories* (Chapel Hill, 1955), p. 5. Schutz inventoried two owners of the *Hecatomphile*, a royal officer and a notary, p. 52.

34 See François Lecercle, *La Chimère de Zeuxis: Portrait poétique et portrait peint en France et en Italie à la Renaissance* (Tübingen, 1987).

35 To briefly situate this assertion of the "crossover" status of male fascination with female body parts, consider, on the one hand, its courtly validation in the opening pages of Andreas Cappellanus, who in defining love notes that the lover "begins to think about the fashioning of the woman and to differentiate her limbs ... and to pry into the secrets of her body, and he desires to put each part to its fullest use," in *The Art of Courtly Love*, trans. John Jay Parry (New York, 1969), p. 29; and, on the other, Mikhail Bakhtin's assertions regarding the intrinsically popular status of anatomical blazons, in *Rabelais and his World*, trans. Hélène Iswolsky (Cambridge, Mass. and London, 1968), pp. 426–30.

36 The debate is summarized (with bibliography) by Lawrence D. Kritzman, "1542. The Neoplatonic Debate," in Hollier et al., *A New History of French Literature*, pp. 187–9.

37 "Le Blason de la Maison," in A. de Montaiglon, ed., *Recueil de poésies françoises des XVe et XVIe siècles* (12 vols., Paris, 1857), VI, p. 227. My translations of Corrozet are based upon this readily available edition. Page references appear in parentheses in the text.
38 On the moralizing drift of the domestic blazons and their status as a "deliberate antidote" to the anatomical blazons, see Saunders, *The Sixteenth-Century Blason Poétique*, pp. 212–18.

6   Dematerializations: textile and textual properties in Ovid, Sandys, and Spenser

Ann Rosalind Jones

About 1654 Diego de Velázquez painted a canvas later called *Las Hilanderas* (*The Spinners*) or *La Fabula de Aragne* (*The Fable of Arachne*) (fig 6.1). The two titles given to this painting after Veláquez's death signal the hierarchical habit of thought that divides artistic work into separate spheres, a "low" realm of quotidian, habitual labor and a "high" realm of mythology, pictorial grandeur, and allegorical reading. The title *The Spinners* addresses the foreground of the painting. Barefoot and poorly dressed, working in semi-darkness, surrounded by raw wool and a basket for the finished yarn on the viewer's right and a pile of finished fabrics on the left, three women card (comb), spin, and wind wool. The title *The Fable of Arachne* refers to the background where, on a raised platform rather like a brightly lit stage set, there is a scene of elegantly dressed women, including a figure in a classical helmet who is looking at a tapestry. The two titles (and subjects) of the painting name the process by which spun, woven, and stitched objects – objects belonging to material culture in its most literal sense – have been the site of an ideological division: on the one hand, "meaningless" manual labor; on the other, the elevated world (literally elevated in the painting) of interpretation. The titles of the painting thus represent the process through which a physical substance – the wool yarn produced by women's labor – and the object made from it – a tapestry – can be dematerialized into transcendent symbols.

Spinning wool was largely a cottage industry in Early Modern Spain, where highly valued merino sheep were herded south and then back north each year in a migration carefully controlled by a powerful network of guilds (the "Mesta"), which also supervised the production of woollen cloth, according to strict rules governing shepherds' care of flocks and city men's work in clothmaking workshops.[1] Yet wool yarn, the basic substance required for work in cloth and tapestry workshops, was produced by poor women working at home, with or without the spinning wheel at which Velázquez's white-coiffed older spinner sits.[2] Earlier in the painter's career, he had depicted other poor workers.

Figure 6.1   Velázquez, *Las Hilanderas* or *The Fable of Arachne*.

Examples include the aged egg-stirrer of *Old Woman Cooking* and the young housemaid pounding garlic in *Christ in the House of Mary and Martha*, genre paintings in which he used peasant models and focused on the physical processes and everyday objects of domestic life: a clay bowl, a brass mortar and pestle.[3] Throughout the nineteenth century, *The Spinners*, too, was read as a late *bodegón* or genre painting.[4]

However, by 1654 Velázquez had become a court painter. The title *The Fable of Arachne* was assigned to the painting in a 1664 inventory of the possessions of a Spanish nobleman and courtier, Don Pedro de Arce;[5] sometime before 1711, when the painting was willed to the royal collections, it had been expanded by the addition of painted canvas strips on all four sides, including a top panel depicting a golden arch (fig. 6.2).[6] The background scene of the painting, like the expansion of the canvas after it left Velázquez's studio and the title it was given by a seventeenth-century collector, led later critics to emphasize the more elaborate textile form represented in the painting – tapestry – and to argue that the brightly lit scene in the background represents Athena judging Arachne's tapestry.[7] This kind of classical topic, it has been argued, would have accredited Velázquez as a learned humanist painter rather than a mere craftsman. The painting has been read, accordingly, as a statement of the superiority of art to craft.

Such interpretations subordinate the laboring women to the role of suppliers of mere "stuff," the raw material from which Athenan,

Figure 6.2 Velázquez, *Las Hilanderas* or *The Fable of Arachne*, expanded version.

Arachnean, and painterly *oeuvres* were made. Yet later criticism of the painting stresses its metaphysical implications more than the painter's labor itself does. Why, it seems fair to ask, did Velázquez juxtapose the two kinds of activities? Why did the scene of the spinners originally take up so much of the lower plane of the painting and contain details so much more distinct – the figure of the woman winding wool and dressed in white, for example – than those in the recessed scene of the tapestry viewing?

The painting is not realistic, in the sense that it represents an actual workshop. During the seventeenth century, tapestries were mainly imported into Spain from the Low Countries or made in workshops supervised by Flemish designers. Although a small tapestry workshop was active in Madrid in the late sixteenth and early seventeenth century, first established in the Calle Santa Isabel by a tapestry master named Antonio Ceron, it was a man's workplace: Ceron employed four weavers and eight apprentices.[8] Art historians of the early twentieth century, following the 1772 inventory of Madrid's royal holdings, accepted its identification of the Santa Isabel tapestry workshop as the setting for the painting. However, textile practice in the 1650s, particularly the exclusion of women from men's workshops, makes such an assumption dubious. In tapestry workshops throughout Europe, wool yarn spun by women in private work spaces was typically bought from merchants operating in public markets, who sold such yarn to dyers or directly to the masters of ateliers; they, in their turn, brought it into their workshops for use by male weavers.[9] It is highly unlikely that women spinners would have occupied the same factory space as male tapestry weavers.

Rather, Velázquez seems to be juxtaposing two physically separate stages of the process, the production of yarn and the display of the finished tapestry, in a way that insists on the importance and the interest of the women's work. He includes no male weavers; his play with the texture of the wool, in tufts, yarn, and balls, and the sheen with which he depicts the rapid spinning of the wheel are virtuoso touches. And although the canvas sets the scene of the elaborate finished cloth above the shadowy foreground in which wool is made into yarn, it was a later painter or painters who gave the background scene the architectural frame of golden vault and round window (the oculus) – as it has been art critics of the twentieth century who have assigned the painting the allegorical meaning of a celebration of artistic genius over manual labor. Madlyn Kahr, for example, reads the painting as emphatically subordinating the physical labor depicted in its foreground:

> If we look upon *Las Hilanderas* not as expository prose but as poetry, the picture transmits a message with brilliant clarity: art exists to remind us that there is something beyond our earth-bound daily labors. While it occupies physically but a small part of the world, art is more vivid, more colorful, more exciting – thus, in a sense, larger than life. Art is sublimation. It heightens sensibility, expands consciousness. And though life ends, art endures.[10]

This dematerialization of the painting, read as a statement of the transcendent value of art as antidote to "earth-bound daily labors," misrepresents it even more than other critics' arguments that it belongs among Velázquez's mythological paintings rather than his *bodegones* or genre paintings: it downplays Velázquez's obvious interest in the women's craft in order to privilege high art as the domain of great male painters depicting wealthy noblewomen and female divinities. Kahr reduces the scene of the women spinners to a support for the real center of the painting: "In *Las Hilanderas* the graceful arc of the foreground group as a whole is like a garland, a frame for the jewel-like radiance of the area that fills the upper central part of the canvas."[11]

Yet the painting is itself an object: oil on canvas, a material also made by women in its first stages. Women grew, soaked, combed, and spun the flax from which painters' canvas was made.[12] They also sewed strips of canvas together when painters wanted a larger field for their labor than single pieces of the textile permitted. Antonio Palomino, a historian of the Spanish court in the days when Velázquez worked there, wrote a treatise on oil painting, *El museo pictorico y la escala optica*, in which he explains this gendered division of labor: "Sewing the canvas is more women's work than men's, [so] it is necessary for the artist to tell them which stitch they must use to join the pieces."[13] Who, then, performed the practical labor of joining the new strips of canvas that now frame Velázquez's painting before it was willed to the royal collection in 1711 – the frame that added the golden arch invoked when critics praised the painting as a glorification of art over craft?

In contrast to Velázquez's canvas itself, later readings of the painting emphasize female allegories over female labor as a physical and social fact. The subordination of such labor to moralized and otherwise transcendental interpretation is not just a product of modern art history, however. It has an immense tradition of its own in Renaissance reception of classical literature, in male writers' persistent appropriation and transformation of women's textile work. In order to understand what the painting as object means, then, we will briefly trace the literary tradition which, if it did not produce the interpretive problem posed by the canvas, did supply the mythological title for Velázquez's painting.

Ovid's *Metamorphoses*: Arachne *textrix*

Like Velázquez, Ovid foregrounds the material processes of spinning and weaving in Book 6 of *The Metamorphoses*. He opens his narration of the myth of Arachne with Athena's perspective: having heard the Muses' account of the Pierides, whom they turned into magpies for daring to compete with them as story-tellers, the goddess "turns her mind to the fate of Arachne."[14] Yet the tale that follows pits the goddess and the mortal woman equally against each other, with a close focus on weaving as manual technique shared by both women. Ovid introduces Arachne, the daughter of parents of low birth, as famous throughout Lydia for her skill as spinner and embroiderer. He describes her spinning in detail and uses a painterly metaphor to emphasize her artistry as an embroiderer:

> sive rudem primos lanam glomerabat in orbes,
> seu digitis subigebat opus repetitaque longo
> vellera mollibat nebulas aequantia tractu,
> sive levi teretem versabat pollice fusum,
> seu pingebat acu; scires a Pallade doctam.
>
> (6. 19–23)

(whether she was winding the rough yarn into a new ball, or shaping the stuff with her fingers, reaching back to the distaff for more wool, fleecy as a cloud, to draw into long soft threads, or giving a twist with practiced thumb to the graceful spindle, or embroidering [painting] with her needle: you could know that Pallas had taught her.)

These acquired skills prompt Arachne to call on Athena to compete with her, in a challenge to divine power and to age hierarchy. Athena appears to the girl disguised as an old woman, gray-haired and tottering on a stick, but Arachne refuses divine and generational order alike: "Why does your goddess not come herself? Why is she avoiding this contest?" When Athena throws off her disguise, the nymphs and local women looking on fall to their knees in worship, but Arachne refuses to apologize to the goddess; she is too eager to win the prize. Ovid uses the adjective "stolida" (1. 50) to describe Arachne's greed, a word that has the connotation of "rude" or "uncultivated."

Yet his description of the action that opens the contest, each woman's dressing of her loom, attributes extraordinary nimbleness to mortal and goddess alike. Because he has presented Arachne as the possessor of textile skills so vividly in the earlier passage, and because no superhuman power is implied in his closely focused narrative of the technique whereby vertical warp and horizontal weft are set up by both pairs of skilled hands, his first lines on the contest stress the human skill displayed in loom-work:

> haud mora, constituunt diversis partibus ambae
> et gracili geminas intendunt stamine telas:
> tela iugo vincta est, stamen secernit harundo,
> inseritur medium radiis subtemen acutis,
> quod digiti expediunt, atque inter stamina ductum
> percusso paviunt insecti pectine dentes.
>
> (53–8)

(Without delay they both set up the looms in different places and they stretch the fine warp upon them. The web is bound upon the beam, the reed separates the threads of the warp, the woof is threaded through them by the sharp shuttles which their busy fingers ply, and when shot through the threads of the warp, the notched teeth of the hammering slay [comb] tap it into place.)

In Ovid's narrative, Arachne's defiance of her divine superior in no way undermines her skill. Rather, the material details and precise vocabulary the poet uses to pin down the actions of women working at the loom can be read as a kind of appreciatively competitive salute to the weavers' skill. His imagistic, alliterative language provides a verbal counterpart to their manual virtuosity.

Each woman's tapestry represents scenes that imply a particular view of the relations between gods and mortals and also between men and women. Athena's web supports divine order – her own. Her subject is the moment at which Athens was named after her, the result of her triumph in a contest that pitted her against her brother Neptune. Their rival claims to be the patron deity of Athens are judged by the rest of the gods, headed by Jove as king of the gods, "a royal figure." Athena represents herself in her masculine military mode, with spear, helmet, and aegis, although the images she sets at each of the four corners of her web identify her with female divine power: Juno is specified as the agent of a Pygmy queen's transformation into a crane and the Trojan Antigone's change into a stork. In the central judgment scene, Athena represents herself giving Athens the olive branch, signifying peace and fertility, to convince the city to choose her over her brother. Ovid concludes his description of her tapestry by mentioning the olive branches she weaves into its border.

However, Athena's actions in regard to Arachne are neither just nor peaceful. Arachne's tapestry is flawless; Ovid tells us that neither the goddess nor Envy could find anything to criticize in it. Yet Athena, rather than giving the prize where it is due, envies Arachne's "success," tears the girl's cloth to pieces, and hits her four times on the head with a spindle. When Arachne hangs herself out of indignation at this treatment, the goddess uses Hecate's potions to return her to life, partly out of pity, Ovid says, but also to set her up as a monitory example for generations to come: "hang there still," she says, and declares that all her kin to come shall also exemplify "the law of punishment." As defender of divine justice, Athena produces a four-square, symmetrical textile art to support heavenly order and to take credit for the stability of the city that chose her as patron. Yet her behavior toward Arachne contradicts the principles that her tapestry upholds.

Recent critics have argued that Ovid puts a subversive spin on his version of the myth not only by making Arachne win the contest, contrary to earlier versions of the story, but also by treating her tapestry more sympathetically than Athena's.[15] By setting the mortal woman's work after the goddess's tapestry, the poet gives Arachne's text the last word; and through the sheer quantity of Arachne's twenty-one images of male gods transforming themselves into beasts in order to rape mortal women, he allies himself with the irreverent weaver. He uses Arachne as a narrator within the narration, as a medium through which he can depict celestial crimes ("caelestia crimina," 1. 131) yet – at least in theory – escape the kind of judgment Athena imposes on such blasphemous representation.[16] Although Ovid ends the story by leading his heroine to a suitable dire end, the theme of her work as weaver has supplied him with a double opportunity: to expose the undignified sexual exploits of the gods and to compose verbal tapestries himself – that is, to write skillful ecphrases of textile skill. He rounds off his representation of Arachne's web by describing its border in two lines that bring closure both to the weaver's work and to his own. Arachne's border represents the ivy that was an emblem of poetic fame:[17]

> Ultima pars telae, tenui circumdata limbo,
> nexilibus flores hederis habet intertextos.
>
> (127–8)

(The last part of the web, surrounded with a narrow border, contains flowers intertwined with ivy, woven together.)

Ovid, then, figures Arachne as a self-made woman, distinguished not by place of birth or rank but by command of her craft. His detailed description of her tapestry also demonstrates that her skill and sense of design are fully equal to Athena's. Both interweave colored and golden threads so subtly that the blending is invisible (61–6); each works out a form of composition perfectly suited to her subject, one classically balanced, one tumultuous and crowded. Even the final lines of the episode do justice to the art of Arachne, surviving as a spider:

> in latere exiles digiti pro cruribus haerent,
> cetera venter habet, de quo tamen illa remittit
> stamen et antiquas exercet aranea telis.
>
> (143–5)

(the slender fingers clung to her sides as legs; the rest was belly. Still from this she even spins a thread; and now, as a spider, she exercises her old-time weaver-art.)

Ovid leaves his reader warned of the gods' power to punish presumptuous mortals, but also reminded of the continuing virtuosity of weaving as ancient and modern *métier*.

Athenan reading: George Sandys's commentary on Arachne

Ovid's version of the myth was radically reinterpreted by George Sandys in his immense commentary, *Ovid's Metamorphosis Englished, Mythologized, and Represented in Figures*. Drawing on a range of intervening discourses, Sandys expands and cleans up the narrative by citing other classical texts; he provides allegorical rather than materialist interpretations of the myth by selecting from a range of ancient and Early Modern symbolic conventions; and he hierarchizes the rapport between the tapestries and their makers by reversing the relative significance of frame and center. Sandys's moralized Ovid sides unequivocally with Athena. The humanist commentator assembles a network of "information" that repositions Arachne as political, moral, and gender outlaw and dismisses her craft as female folly.

A central agenda in Sandys's commentary is to extol Athena as a representative of political, as well as divine, order. What Ovid represents as an almost equal battle between two female characters at war with the shuttle Sandys reads as a profound threat to class and gender order. One way he justifies the outcome of the contest is by elevating Athena above both the human and the female condition. In a syncretic explanation of the story of Athena's birth from Zeus' forehead, he cites patristic commentary on the relationship between the three persons of God (Father/Son/Holy Ghost), reading the Greek goddess in relation to the Christian Father/Son dyad: "Pallas is taken for the Intelligence of Jupiter (A notion, as some Authors report, derived from Tradition, of the second Person)."[18] That is, as male divinity is to savior son, so Greek father of the gods is to a daughter who is pure mind, freed by this symbolic genealogy from any taint of the feminine. In this way Sandys can make the punishment of Arachne represent the reassertion of masculine or at least androygnous godliness over female presumption.

Sandys's expanded version of the contest between Athena and Neptune adds a specifically political dimension to the history of the goddess's city. He draws on another myth related to the founding of Athens: the competing deities' response to the citizens' vote to choose a divine patron:

The *Athenians* therefore put it to the Balloting: where the men were for *Neptune*, and the women for *Minerva*; who carried it by only one pebble. Whereupon incensed *Neptune* surrounded most of their territories: ... but after appeased by thus punishing the women: That they should have no voice in publique decrees, that their children should not carry their names, nor themselves be called *Athenians* ... *Neptune* was more easily reconciled to Minerva, both having in *Athens* one Temple, wherein an Altar was erected to *Oblivion*. (218)

In this election the gender gap is total, but its effects are surprising. The bond reestablished between the divine brother and sister is made possible by the denial of political, familial, and civic rights to women; and although the temple is built to celebrate the male and the female siblings' willingness to forget their previous enmity, its name implies that this wrong to women will be forgotten, as well. In contrast to Arachne's tapestry, which assures that posterity will remember gender injustice in the form of male gods' rapes of mortal women, the chapter Sandys adds to Athenian history paradoxically justifies the denial of the women citizens' vote as the basis of harmony for the "democratic" city.

Sandys further transforms Ovid's text by adding details to the four monitory "roundels" of Athena's tapestry to suggest that two royal women deserve punishment not only for their presumption but for specifically feminine faults.[19] He imposes a monarchical framework based on European norms on the tale of the African (Pygmy) queen, informing his readers that she ascended to the throne only through a genealogical mishap; he continues the critique by saying that her foolish subjects encouraged her in her vanity. It is hard not to hear in Sandys's lines an oblique attack on female monarchs in general, that "monstrous regiment of women": "She, the male line failing, became the Queen of that nation: adored by her subjects, as if more than mortall, for the excellency of her features. Wherewith she pleased her selfe so much, that shee began to neglect the service of the Gods" (218). Sandys criticizes Antigone of Troy as a princess justly punished by linking her vanity to a comical picture of an overweening species of bird: "The third Oval presents the transformation of Antigone . . . into a stork, for presuming to prefer her beauty before *Juno*'s. The metamorphosis well suiting with a proud and talkative woman: for this foule, though a stranger to all music, so affects her untunable creakings that she claps her wings in her own plaudite" (219). Nothing in Ovid suggests that the Trojan princess was punished for being too talkative, but Sandys draws on his association of female vanity and loquacity to affirm the appropriateness of the metamorphosis. He draws, as well, on bestiary lore to underwrite Juno's justice: the wife of heaven's king reduces anomalous female rulers to foolish fowl.

Sandys reads Arachne not as a craftswoman or an artist but as a class upstart, and her allies as malcontents intent on disrupting social hierarchy. "Profane Arachne," he writes, insisting on the distance separating mortals and divinities, "sets forth the rapes and adulteries of the gods" (220). He revises Ovid's remark that Envy found nothing to reproach in the tapestry ("non illud carpere Livor / possit opus" ["Envy could find no fault in that work"] [129–30]) by assigning a new motive to Envy: the goddess rightfully censors an act that typifies underlings' pleasure in hearing gossip about their superiors: "Minerva teares in peeces what envy could not but commend, because it published the vices of great ones, and beats her with the shuttle to chastise her presumption" (221). Ovid's concluding comment, that the outcome of the contest caused a furor throughout Lydia and beyond, is taken by Sandys as evidence of the inconstancy of the common people. He concedes Arachne's skill as a weaver only in connection with the mob tendency always to make a martyr of a member of the lower orders: "The common people who envy the eminent, and pitty those whom they envied in adversity, storme at the ruine of so excellent an artizan" (221). According to this reading, Arachne deserves punishment as a traitor because she reveals the secrets of the gods and stirs up sentiment against her betters.

Sandys combines both kinds of accusations – that Arachne is dangerous as an unruly woman and as a political agitator – in his final comment on the frame she weaves for her tapestry: "These personages, with the places, being woven to the life by Arachne, she incloseth the web with a trail of Ivy; well suting with the wanton argument and her owne ambition. [Ivy is] worne in garlands at lascivious meetings; and climing as ambitious men, to compass their owne ends with the ruine of their supporters" (221). To justify his diagnosis of Arachne's frame as symptomatic, Sandys appeals to classical representations of revelry: the ivy garland at the drinking festival. Yet he excludes other possible explanations, for example the association of ivy with poets. A recent editor of *The Metamorphoses*, William Anderson, suggests that Ovid links poetic endeavor generally and his own in particular with Arachne's ivy by assigning her border motif an aesthetic prestige that equals Athena's olive branch.[20] But Sandys, focusing on the vine as a destructive parasite, narrows down the range of meanings that ancient and contemporary discourses assigned to ivy. A deeply ambivalent symbol in the Renaissance,[21] ivy could signify and condemn amorous languor: in Barthélemy Aneau's *Picta Poesis* (1552), a tree trunk covered by ivy represents a man destroyed by the lust of his female lover.[22] Yet it could also figure amorous devotion and political loyalty: in England, Robert Dudley addressed an impresa to Queen Elizabeth in which he was figured as a vine clinging to an obelisk, with a motto affirming their mutual interdependence: "te stante virebo" ("you standing, I will flourish").[23] Sandys's concern for law and order, however, forecloses all readings except the one that condemns Arachne's ivy as evidence of her ambition and envy.

Sandys counters Arachne's woven images by disembodying them: he interprets Jove's rapes as monitory or ennobling allegories. The swan's seduction of Leda, for example, demonstrates that "Pitty introduceth Love: Beauty, and the harmony of the tongue (expressed by the Swan) his prevailing solicitors" (220); Jove's deception of Alcmena, whom he seduced by disguising himself as her husband, is radically decorporealized: "Jupiter signifies the vertue of the minde, and Alcmena fortitude: [they therefore become] the parents of *Hercules*, or noble achievments" (220). However, his final strategy is a shift to *ad feminam* argument: he points to Arachne's ivy border as proof that her argument is "wanton." The logic of Aneau's emblem, in which the vine represents the effeminating effect of a woman's lust upon her lover, may enter into his thinking here, but the crucial issue is libel and censorship. Arachne's publishing of "celestial crimes" is a crime in itself. However skillful she may be as a weaver, she oversteps the bounds when she exposes male gods' sexual adventures to mortal view. To displace lust from Jove, Neptune, Apollo, and Bacchus onto the mortal woman, Sandys reads Arachne's narrative against her, as a revelation of her character rather than the character of the gods. His treatment of the mortal weaver repeats the strategy of judges in modern rape trials who interpret a woman's accusation of a man as proof that *she* is prey to indecent fantasies. Wanton actions by men, divine or mortal, are transformed into signifiers of the wantonness of the woman who exposes them.

Sandys's commentary on Ovid, through which the English humanist reforms a pagan text by putting its heroine on trial, is not merely idiosyncratic; it typifies conservative reaction to the political anxieties of Sandys's era. He condemns Arachne's story-telling as *lèse-majesté*; he interprets the nymphs and neighbor women who support her as anarchic protesters putting dangerous rumors into circulation. He also revalues her final gesture, the ivy skillfully interwoven with flowers, to support a verdict of female ineptitude. His last move is to efface Arachne as textile worker by allegorizing her metamorphosis into a spider in a way that supports a final dismissal of the woman's craft: "uselesse and worthlesse labors are expressed by the spiders web" (221). The virtuosity attributed to both contestants in Ovid's weaving war is rewritten by the seventeenth-century commentator as trivial textile fiddling. The material labor of weaving and the story the weaver pictures forth are displaced by the commentator's allegories, which elaborately transform material sign into metaphysical signified.

Spinners and stitchers in Spenser: textile, textual, and domestic order

In *Muiopotmos* and Sonnet 71 of the *Amoretti*, Edmund Spenser focuses closely on images of textile work. In *Muiopotmos, or the Fate of the Butterfly*, he rewrites the Arachne story as mock epic, setting the butterfly Clarion in a duel against Arachne's son Aragnoll. Reversing Ovid's revision of the outcome of the women's contest, Spenser has Athena win by weaving a dazzlingly beautiful butterfly into her tapestry; envying such skill, Arachne turns into a spider out of sheer spite, and her son Aragnoll inherits her grudge against butterflies, the referent in nature of the sign that defeated his mother. Spenser's plot allows Athena to triumph in her aspect as judge and punisher, even though it removes the violence from the encounter between Arachne and the goddess: Arachne's own envy, not Athena's magical power, brings about her transformation. Violent rivalry is assigned instead to the masculine characters, Clarion and Aragnoll, and Spenser also shifts

Arachne's skill as a weaver to the male villain: Aragnoll uses his web to trap and kill Clarion. If Spenser wrote this mock epic to criticize foolish courtiers, as Robert Brinkley has recently argued, he was shifting Ovid's focus on the two women weavers still further onto contemporary issues of concern to men, displacing the combat between Athena and Arachne onto newly invented male rivals.[24]

Nancy Miller, in a study of the processes through which male theoreticians working in philosophy and literary criticism have identified with the figure of Arachne, points to a typical omission in this kind of cross-gendered performance: "the discourse of the male weavers rhetorically stages 'woman' without in any way addressing women."[25] Such a movement from female textile work to male-authored textual play occurs in *Muiopotmos*, too, even though Spenser displays a concrete, appreciative knowledge of the techniques of embroidery and clothmaking as they were performed by women and men of his time. In his ecphrasis of Athena's butterfly, he draws his audience close into the surface of the tapestry by dwelling on details of texture as well as design:

> Emongst those leaves she made a Butterflie,
> With excellent device and wondrous slight,
> Fluttring among the Olives wantonly,
> That seem'd to live, so like it was in sight:
> The velvet nap which on his wings doth lie,
> The silken downe with which his backe is dight,
> His broad outstretched hornes, his hayrie thies,
> His glorious colours, and his glistering eies.
>
> (329–36)[26]

Athena's butterfly, composed of velvet and silk thread rather than wool, sounds more like an embroidered than a woven figure. The highly detailed stanza foregrounds it in a way that recalls the multi-perspectival design of late sixteenth-century embroidered images, which often juxtapose an immense butterfly or flower with smaller human figures, a disproportion partly explicable by the fact that Englishwomen often combined designs from different pattern books, mixing different scales in a single piece of embroidery.[27]

Toward the end of the poem, describing the fiendish skill with which Aragnoll constructs his web as butterfly trap, Spenser composes a stanza dense with references to embroidery and the textile industry. Framing the names of textiles produced by male weavers with descriptions of women's domestic stitchery, he first invokes domestic knitting, then turns to the public sphere of the international cloth trade, mentioning "dieper" ("d'Ypres"), the fine gauze made in Flanders, and damask, the heavy linen woven in the Netherlands in patterns imitating the scrollwork on

Damascus sword blades. He ends by describing the three-dimensional stumpwork (embossing) and looped crewel stitch of late Elizabethan home embroidery:

> Not anie damzell, which her vaunteth most
> In skilfull knitting of soft silken twyne,
> Nor anie weaver, which his worke doth boast
> In dieper, in damaske, or in lyne;
> Nor anie skil'd in workmanship embost;
> Nor any skil'd in loupes of fingring fine,
> Might in their divers cunning ever dare,
> With this so curious networke to compare.
>
> (361–8)

Yet it would be a mistake to see such allusions as signs of a materialist focus through which Spenser does homage to spinners, stitchers, and weavers. Rather, the refused similes in this passage logically subordinate actual clothworking practices to the poet's fantastic mock-epic plot: the male spider outspins all women knitting at home and all male weavers at work in commercial clothmaking. The Early Modern textile vocabulary produces a comical, anachronistic effect that emphasizes the fictional inventiveness of the chivalry-parodying new myth. Textile references here center attention less upon the manual skill of embroiderers and weavers than upon the abundant vocabulary of the poet.

The external frame of the poem, a dedicatory epistle to Lady Carey (not the Elizabeth Cary who wrote *Mariam*, but a younger woman related to Spenser's family), similarly reveals a disparity between decorative surface and enacted message. Spenser's compliment positions him as humble servant to an elevated lady:

Most brave and bountifull La[dy]: for so excellent favours as I have received at your sweet handes, to offer these fewe leaves as in recompence, should be to offer flowers to the Gods for their divine benefites. Therefore I have determined to give my selfe wholly to you, as quite abandoned from my selfe, and absolutely vowed to your services. (p. 412)

Yet to the extent that the trivial topic of "this smal Poëme," as Spenser calls it, and its references to embroidery are assumed to appeal to Carey's feminine interests, the poet places her even as he places himself beneath her. His dedication of a light, playful text to a woman reader affirms gender conventions: the poet offers a bagatelle to a lady, a parody of epic tossed off by a man who has proved, with the publication of the first part of *The Faerie Queene* the previous year, that he can write the real thing. (It can be argued that his dedication of this text to Elizabeth I and his representations of her in it likewise reverse the polite conventions of patronage.) Spenser's mastery of the epyllion as genre is put to the same effect as his expertise in the jargons of domestic and artisanal craft: both position him above the categories in which he performs with such playful ease.

The poet appears to be working in a more intimate context in Sonnet 71 of the *Amoretti*, but here, too, he puts a woman in her place. By this point in the sequence, the poet's beloved has ceased to reject his advances, and in Sonnet 71 he is clearly shifting from his earlier Petrarchan posture of humble entreaty to a role as husbandly advisor, instructing the lady in the duties of Protestant marriage. The sonnet plays on a piece of embroidery ("drawne worke" means canvas through which thread has been pulled) described by the speaker as the work of his once resistant fiancée. In a stitched satire of his relentless pursuit, she represented him as a spider and herself as a bee:

> I joy to see how in your drawen worke,
>   your selfe unto the Bee ye doe compare;
>   and me unto the Spyder that doth lurke
>   in close away to take her unaware.
> Right so your selfe were caught in cunning snare
>   of a deare foe, and thralled to his loue:
>   in whose streight bands ye now captived are
>   so firmely, that ye never may remove.
> But as your worke is woven all above,
>   with woodbynd flowers and fragrant Eglantine:
>   so sweet your prison you in time shall prove,
>   with many deare delights bedecked fyne.
> And all thensforth eternall peace shall see
>   betweene the Spyder and the gentle Bee.[28]

Jocularly, the poet acknowledges that the woman's embroidery tells the truth: like a benign Aragnoll, he did indeed lay out a web to catch her.

Again like Aragnoll, the male combatant appropriates the woman's textile skill as his weapon in a contest of representation. Against the woman's sampler that exposes the man's will to power, the poet sets a revised image of his cunning as true love. Through the kind of recuperative reading we have seen in Sandys and in *Muiopotmos*, the woman's fabricated object and the narrative worked into it are transformed by the man's restatement of what they mean. In Spenser's first reading of his fiancée's embroidery, he acknowledges that the spider's web figures the prison – the "streight bands" – of married duty. However, he embroiders this prison into a paradise by opposing the frame the woman gave to her needlework to the mocking portrait she stitched in its center, of the predatory lover as arachnid. The sonnet relocates the decorative floral border of the woman's embroidery as the structural premise of the man's argument. In Spenser's reading, his lady's vines symbolize marital harmony and fertility; therefore she has stitched a message that contradicts her central vignette of the spider and the bee.

The poet's revision of the woman's text is consolidated by his turn to a larger audience. In the couplet, Spenser expands the domestic framework in which embroidery is carried out to include a public of onlookers whom he invites to celebrate the union he has produced from discord: "all" the world, in the future, will see uninterrupted harmony between the married couple. Like Athens's Temple of Oblivion, this final prediction constructs a triumphant monument to unity that obliterates the resistance the woman has sewn into her representation of courtship as predatory manipulation. The rhetoric of the sonnet buries the distinct, even opposed, figures of the cunning spider and the wary bee under epithalamial blossoms; and by publishing the sequence, Spenser insures that his masterful reinterpretation will endure long after he and his lady – and her embroidery – have been buried. The tone of the poem suggests a certain equality between speaker and hearer: the poet descends cheerfully into the woman's frame of reference, he freely admits his crafty designs on her, he offers her a dwelling "bedecked" with alliterative delights. Yet the unity celebrated in the public scene at the end of the poem is an exact poetic equivalent of the Elizabethan marriage contract: husband and wife are one body, and the husband is its head. The male poet's eloquence reverses the meaning of the woman's handiwork, effaces its material reality in favor of a Protestant ideology of marriage, and fixes how the sampler – and she – will be read by posterity.

I will end with a return to Velázquez's canvas. *The Spinners* has been read not only as an ethereal treasure asserting the superiority of art to craft but also as the winning move in a contest among men. Jonathan Brown, analyzing the details of the tapestry in the background, builds on earlier critics' recognition that the fluttering cupids and waving woman are copied from Titian's *Rape of Europa*, a painting Velázquez would almost certainly have seen in the royal Spanish collection.[29] Arachne, that is, gestures not toward her own masterpiece but toward a man's. Brown argues that Velázquez treated the subject in this way in order to raise his own status as a painter. By stopping the narrative before Athena changes Arachne into a spider, the tapestry scene focuses on the moment when the mortal woman's weaving is seen to equal that of the goddess. The implication is that human artistry is divine: "Titian is equated with Arachne, and Arachne could paint like a god" (253). Brown argues that Velázquez allied himself in this way with Titian, earlier the favorite painter of both the Spanish kings who later employed Velázquez because

Titian had been honored with gifts and titles by both kings. He suggests further that Velázquez imitated Titian's *Europa* to insist on his own merit as a painter, which had been challenged by court officials refusing his petition for entry into a military order reserved for noblemen. The free, broad strokes with which he treats the spinning figure, particularly, assert the freedom and verve of the artist over the mere craftsman – or, here, the craftswoman. In Brown's interpretation, then, an upward displacement of gender and of material occurs in the substitution of Titian's *Europa* in oil for Arachne's scene in wool.

Velázquez's women spinners have also been metamorphosed from textile workers to divine or political symbols through allegorical readings more recent than Sandys's. Several art historians argue that the old woman represents Athena as goddess of the craft of weaving; others have disregarded the women assisting the spinners at either edge of the canvas by focusing on the number of the three central figures, arguing that they stand for the three Fates; some Spanish commentators argue that they represent the vices of the Prince or the virtues of obedient subjects.[30] Other twentieth-century critics, however, rather than emblematizing the spinners, have emphasized their status as laborers as an important part of the painting's meaning. Gustav Cavallius, a Swedish critic, ends his exhaustive structuralist analysis of the painting with some surprisingly historically oriented remarks. Stressing the deliberate ambiguity of the juxtaposition of realistic work scene and mythological tableau, he writes, "One is prone to consider the degree to which [the meaning of the painting] is veiled as the result of a confrontation between a strong, innovating mind and a rigid self-preserving society, a society which at the same time calls for complex artistic expression as it suppresses extended innovation and subversive insight into reality."[31] Comparing *Las Hilanderas* to Velázquez's earlier painting of Vulcan and four smiths at his forge, Cavallius points out that the "theme of class antagonism is implicit in both pictures." Yet, he suggests, such antagonism is toned down by the spinners' industriousness and the interested gaze of the young woman in white, who looks upward in the direction of the aristocratic interior scene. Thus the painting is in some ways complicit with "the pacification of the working class in the name of a common (national) interest ... The picture as a whole gives no hopes for the future" (p. 179).

Joseph-Emile Muller also remarks on the contrast between the class identity of the spinners and the status of the women examining the background tapestry:

The "poetic" atmosphere of the area where the finished work of art invites admiration provides a contrast to the prosaic nature of the workplace itself. There is a similar opposition in the characters. While the weavers are sitting upright or bent over their work, according to their tasks, and neither their faces or garments are in any way glamorized, the women on the dais have all the elegance of the idle rich. It is immediately apparent to which class each group of women belongs.[32]

Muller concludes, however, with Cavallius, that the painter intended no revolutionary critique: "But there is no reason to believe that Velázquez is deliberately contrasting the situation of the working women with that of the aristocracy in order to make a point about social equality ... For him [the scene] is simply another facet of life, which he considers with his habitual sympathy and seriousness" (228–9).

Whatever principles, dematerializing or materialist, have been invoked in readings of Velázquez's canvas, his art participates in the spinners' craft in the most material way. Women's work on flax made linen thread, which was woven into canvas; women's work on wool produced the yarn that was woven into tapestry – before a painter's work in oil produced an image of weavers. To make possible a reconstruction of the anonymous, industrious subjects who set the warp and woof, a history of art and of its interpretations needs to begin, with Velázquez, in the actual worked texture of the objects themselves.

Now!

NOTES

1 I would like to acknowledge help with this piece from several colleagues who bridge disciplinary divides: Margreta de Grazia, Craig Felton, Maureen Quilligan, and Peter Stallybrass. I owe special thanks to my research assistant at Smith College, Cameron Tims, who made sense with unfailing equanimity of diverse electronic indexes, art-historical search systems, and quirky photograph collections during a year of shared work.
   On the wool industry in Spain, see James La Force, Jr., *The Development of the Spanish Textile Industry* (Berkeley, 1965) and K. G. Ponting, *The Wool Trade, Past and Present* (Manchester, 1961), ch. 3.

2 For women's role as suppliers of woollen yarn throughout Europe, see Alice Clark, "Textiles," in *The Working Life of Women in the Sixteenth Century* (2nd ed. London, 1982), ch. 4, and Bridget Hill, "Women's Work in the Family Economy," in her *Women, Work and Sexual Politics in Eighteenth-Century England* (Oxford, 1989), in which she discusses the shift of spinning and weaving from women's to men's work. For the Spanish situation, see Marta Vicente i Valentin, "El treball de la dona els gremis a la Barcelona del segle XVIII (una aproximacio)," *Pedralbes* 8 (1988), 267–76.

3 For Velázquez's genre paintings, see Jonathan Brown, *Velázquez, Painter and Courtier* (New Haven: Yale University Press, 1988), ch. 1 and plates 11–26. See also his discussion of Dutch models for the interplay of genre and religious subjects in Velázquez, pp. 16–21. Thanks to Craig Felton for alerting me to the foreground/background issue in Velázquez's predecessors, particularly Pieter Aertsen.

4   The art historian who initiated the view of *Las Hilanderas* as a genre painting was Carl Justi, in *Diego Velázquez und sein Jahrhundert* (2nd edn., 1903).

5   The art historian who discovered the title the painting was given in the inventory of Don Arce's collection was Maria Caturla, "El coleccionista madrileño Don Pedro de Arce, que poseyó 'Las Hilanderas,' de Velázquez," *Archivo Español d'Arte* 21 (1948), 292–304.

6   The painting went to the royal collections in the will of the ninth duke of Medinaceli, as Vicente Lleó discovered in 1985 (cited in Brown, *Velázquez*, p. 253, n. 34; p. 302).

7   The argument that the background scene represents Athena and Arachne began with Enriqueta Harris, *The Prado: Treasure House of the Spanish Royal Collection* (London, 1940), p. 85. Two other critics, working independently, also identified the fable of Arachne as the subject of the painting: Diego Angulo Iñiguez, "Las Hilanderas," *Archivo Español d'Arte* 21 (1948), 1–19, and Charles de Tolnay, "Velázquez' *Las Hilanderas* and *Las Meninas* (An Interpretation)," *Gazette des Beaux Arts* 35 (1949), 21–38.

8   On Ceron's workshop, see W. G. Thomson, *A History of Tapestry* (2nd edn., London, 1930), pp. 236–7, and Albert F. Calvert, *The Spanish Royal Tapestries* (New York, 1921), p. 11.

9   For a history of how tapestries commissioned by the Spanish court were produced in the Low Countires, including how wool and silk were dyed for Wilhelm Pannemaker's Brussels workshop, see Calvert, *Spanish Royal Tapestries*, pp. 32–6.

10   Madlyn Millner Kahr, *Velázquez: The Art of Painting* (New York, 1976), p. 211. De Tolnay ("*Las Hilanderas* and *Las Meninas*"), basing his argument on Neoplatonic art theory from Renaissance Italy, similarly claimed that the painting elevates fine art over manual craft (pp. 27–32). Maurice Sérullaz, in contrast, reads the painting as a statement that "Art and Craft – the two groups under Athena's domain – are inextricably linked, in theory as in practice," in Kahr, *Velázquez* (New York, 1981), p. 154.

11   Kahr, *Velázquez*, p. 209.

12   On linen fiber as a women's product, see La Force, *Spanish Textile Industry*, pp. 23–5, and on its production throughout pre-industrial Europe, William Miller, "The Linen Manufactures of the Olden Time," in Alex J. Warden, *The Linen Trade* (3rd edn., London, 1967). Warden also includes descriptions of various stages of linen-making (e.g., "Flax Culture," pp. 3–40). Gervase Markham, in *The English Huswife* (London, 1615), offers detailed instructions for growing, treating, and spinning flax as a household activity.

13   Antonio Palomino y Velasco, *El museo pictorico y la escala optica* (3 vols., Madrid, 1715–24); trans. Zahira Veliz, in *Artists' Techniques in Golden Age Spain: Six Treatises in Translation* (Cambridge, 1986), p. 148.

14   I have used the Loeb edition of Ovid's *Metamorphoses*, ed. and trans. Frank Justus Miller (3rd edn., rpt. Cambridge, Mass., 1984), II, pp. 289–99.

15   The argument that Ovid revised the myth in directions sympathetic to Arachne is made by William S. Anderson throughout the notes to his edition of *Ovid's Metamorphoses, Books 6–10* (Norman, Okla., 1972). He suggests that Athena's punishment of Arachne is made to seem unjust (p. 151), and he comments, on the two tapestries, "As can be recognized, the composition

of the goddess' work is flawlessly classical, perfectly centered, balanced, and framed, highly moral and didactic in content ... Inasmuch as Ovid refuses to give it the victory, he may – having probably changed the story to produce this ambivalent result – be suggesting the value of Arachne's kind of composition: freer, more mannered, more dramatic and distorted, less specifically didactic" (p. 160, note to lines 70–102).

16 Frederick Ahl, considering Ovid's eventual banishment from Rome, points out that the poet in fact did not escape punishment and takes this parallel as further evidence that Ovid allies himself as creator with Arachne: "Arachne is Ovid's artistic double in several ways. The kinds of motifs she represents are very similar to ... the heavenly tales Ovid himself tells. And she, like Ovid, suffers for her outspoken criticism" (*Metaformations: Soundplay and Wordplay in Ovid and Other Classical Poets* [Ithaca, 1985], p. 227). François Rigolot similarly points out the parallel between weaver and poet in an article on the relevance of the Arachne story to Louise Labé: "Ovid certainly suggests here a parallel between the work of Pallas' maidservants and that of the poet: the text which is written (textus: from texo, I weave) presents a highly significant analogy to the weaving of a fable" ("Les 'sutils ouvrages' de Louise Labé, ou: quand Pallas devient Arachné," *Etudes Littéraires* 20 [Autumn, 1987], 45–6; my translation).

17 Anderson points out that ivy was "regularly associated with poets" (*Metamorphoses, 6–10*, p. 167, note to lines 127–8) and suggests, "Possibly Ovid is seeking a floral symbol with connotations to rival those of Minerva's olive."

18 *Ovid's Metamorphosis Englished, Mythologized, and Represented in Figures by George Sandys* (Oxford, 1632), ed. K. K. Hulley and S. T. Vandersall (Lincoln, Nebr., 1970), p. 217.

19 Anthony Brian Taylor cites several examples of Sandys's tendency toward misogynist interpolations in his study of Sandys's use of Arthur Golding's translation of Ovid, "George Sandys and Arthur Golding," *Notes and Queries* 33 (September 1986), 389–90.

20 Anderson, *Metamorphoses, 6–10*, p. 167. See n. 17 above.

21 For an extended discussion of contrasting meanings assigned to ivy as an emblem, drawing on a trans-European range of emblem books, see Beverly Ormerod, "The Ivy Emblem in Scève's *dizain* 150," *Australian Journal of French Studies* 17, 1 (January–April 1980), 58–64.

22 Aneau's emblem is cited by I. D. McFarlane in his edition of *The "Délie" of Maurice Scève* (Cambridge, 1966), in the introductory note to an emblem depicting ivy climbing a wall (p. 201); he names Dorothy Coleman's dissertation ("The Emblems and Images in Maurice Scève's *Délie*," Glasgow University, 1961) as his source.

23 Cited by Richard McCoy, *The Rites of Knighthood: The Literature and Politics of Elizabethan Chivalry* (Berkeley, 1989), pp. 40–1.

24 Robert Brinkley, "Spenser's *Muiopotmos* and the Politics of Metamorphosis," *English Literary History* 48 (Winter 1981), 668–76.

25 Nancy K. Miller, "Arachnologies: The Woman, the Text and the Critic," in Miller, ed., *The Poetics of Gender* (New York, 1986), p. 271. For an acute analysis of ways in which women writers have taken up spinning/weaving/writing analogies, see Elaine Hedges, "The Needle or the Pen: The Literary

Rediscovery of Women's Textile Work," in Florence Howe, ed., *Tradition and the Talents of Women* (Urbana, Ill., 1991), pp. 338–64.

26 Quotations from *Muiopotmos* are from *The Yale Edition of the Shorter Poems of Edmund Spenser*, eds. William A. Oram, Einar Bjorvand, Ronald Bond, Thomas H. Cain, Alexander Dunlop, and Richard Schell (New Haven, 1989).

27 For illustrations of varying proportions in the same piece of needlework, see Rozsika Parker, *The Subversive Stitch: Embroidery and the Making of the Feminine* (London, 1984; rpt. New York, 1989), plates 49 and 50.

28 Quotations from *The Amoretti* are also from *The Yale Edition of the Shorter Poems of Edmund Spenser* (see n. 26).

29 Brown, *Velázquez*, p. 252. The critic who first identified the Titian detail was Charles Ricketts, *The Art of the Prado* (Boston, 1907), p. 182.

30 The interpretation that the white-kerchiefed old woman represents Athena is offered by de Tolnay and Iñiguez. The argument that the three spinners stand for the three Fates appears in Cean Bermùdez (*Historia de arte de la pintura*, 1925) and Ortega y Gasset (*Velázquez, Goya and the Dehumanization of Art*, trans. Alexis Brown [London, 1972]). The political readings are, respectively, by José M. de Azcárate, "La alegoría de 'Las Hilanderas'," in *Varia Velázqueña: Homenaje a Velázquez en el III centenario de su muerte* (2 vols., Madrid, 1960), I, pp. 344–51, and Santiago Sebastian, "Nueva lectura de 'Las Hilanderas,' La emblematica come clave de su interpretación," *Revista "Fragmentos"* 1 (1984), 45–51.

31 Gustav Cavallius, *Velázquez' "Las Hilanderas": An Explication of a Picture Regarding Structure and Associations*, Acta Universitatis Upsaliensis, Figura, new series 1, 11 (Uppsala, 1972), p. 177.

32 Joseph-Emile Muller, *Velázquez* (London, 1976), pp. 227–8.

Part III

Appropriations

Maureen Quilligan

Because a slave is a boundary case for the relationship of a human
subject to a reified object, slavery is a crucial case to bring up in any
discussion of the constitutive relations between subjects and objects. It
also happens that the Renaissance was a time for the renascence of
slavery in the economics of many western European powers (if not
actually in Europe itself). Not often thought of as sharing with antiquity
this particular aspect of economic organization, the Renaissance is more
usually regarded as a time of the birth of the free and autonomous
individual. Yet, if we push some of Fredric Jameson's arguments about
genre to their logical conclusions, we might better understand how the
Renaissance was rightly named for a rebirth of some classical forms,
including slavery. Given Jameson's understanding of genre, we may see
how, in its concern for spiritual freedom and human labor, *Paradise Lost*
may be doing the work that *epic* poems usually do, to wit, mediating the
contradictions (that is, the internally irrational elements) of a slave
economy, particularly as slavery became an important element in the
nascent capitalist economy of Renaissance England's growing overseas
trade. While it will be difficult even to articulate the range of problems
raised by such a global suggestion in a brief discussion, it will be useful to
begin by asking what the relationship of this particular Renaissance epic
was to the history of pan-Atlantic economic activity during the Renaissance.

In *The Political Unconscious*, Fredric Jameson observes that "genre is
essentially a socio-symbolic message"; in other words, "form is imma-
nently and intrinsically an ideology in its own right." When a form is
"reappropriated and refashioned in quite different social and cultural
contexts," Jameson explains, "this message persists."[1] In other words,
the real contradictions of the first historical moment for which the genre
was designed to provide an imaginary solution may continue to supply a
shape for ensuing potentialities of the form. Thus, in Jameson's example,
the point of origin for romance as a genre was that moment when
marauding bands of soldiers finally joined forces and formed themselves

into a cohesive class, the feudal nobility: romance is thereby the genre which insists that the alien enemy is not "other," but the same as oneself.[2] Romance thus takes the older contrast between good and evil in the *chanson de geste* and shows how two enemies can recognize each other as being part of the same group. The typical plot of romance provides this solution when an unknown hostile knight, often in disguise, is bested in a contest and asks for mercy by telling his name, "at which point," Jameson argues, the knight is "reinserted into the unity of the social class" and "he becomes one more knight among others and loses all his sinister unfamiliarity."[3] From this formal viewpoint epic might be seen as the diametrical opposite of romance: epic is that genre which, in making the "same" into an "other," allows one group to fight, conquer, and subject an enemy. It is the genre of nation-building when the construction has imperial purposes. David Quint makes a parallel argument when he proposes that the instituting moment for epic is Virgil's transformation of a "recent history of civil strife into a war of foreign conquest" in the *Aeneid*, that is, the turning of the same into an other.[4] Christopher Kendrick also applies Jameson's thesis to epic and makes a more narrowly Marxist claim that epic as a genre was designed to speak to the contradictions experienced by Greek and Roman societies which relied on the imperial conquest and subsequent enslavement of subject peoples. Epic, in other words, is the genre of the slave mode of production.[5] Kendrick argues that the "peculiar attachment of fate to military action may ... be linked to slavery ... for the classical mode of production ... required a perpetual replenishment of its basic labor force, chiefly manifested ... as the need for foreign conquest" (108).

It is not difficult to see, for instance, how Satan's heroic questing plot to conquer the New World in *Paradise Lost* could be the narrative of "heroic gesture" Kendrick finds characteristic of epic, and indeed many have noticed that Satan is a parody of the classical conquering hero. While Satan argues that he refuses to be enslaved by God, his whole rhetoric oscillates between the poles of liberty and submission, and his revenge is to conquer and enthrall Adam and Eve. Patricia Parker makes his colonialist enterprise explicit when she argues how at the moment that, "stupidly good," Satan gazes on Eve, "we encounter a text which mediates between the realm of the male gaze and the moment of 'wonder' before a feminized New World: for Satan's whole voyage to Eden, and voyage upon Eve, brings with it all the associations of an Exodus to this Earthly Paradise ... a voyage with purpose not just to wonder at but also to colonize."[6] We shall return to a related moment of New World gazing in the poem, but it is important to understand how Adam and Eve are not merely victims to be enslaved in Satan's narrative, but how, in being themselves lords of creation, they inhabit a problematic hegemony over creation. Their sexual partnership is the singular instance of productive private property in the poem: "mysterious law, true source / Of human offspring, sole propriety / In Paradise of all things common else" (4.750-2). Such "sole propriety" is implicitly constructed as a mutual ownership which may be perfectly appropriate to their proper unfallen relations. Yet the gendered difference of their work – specifically Eve's future physical labor in the production of children (and especially when cursed, as we shall see) – outlines a fundamental distinction between manual and intellectual labor crucial to the discourse of slavery.[7] If there may be no object in this first prelapsarian private property, no immediate owner and owned, then the introduction of children promises to instate a hierarchical difference of propertied beings, especially when this offspring is seen, as it so often is in the poem, to be a group of workers.

Although Kendrick emphatically understands slavery to be generic to epic, he never asks what part *actual* slavery might have had to play in the mercantilist developments of the economy of Cromwell's Commonwealth. If we ask such a straightforward historical question, we do not merely switch registers from genre theory to history, we also become able to ask how the epic "ideologeme" (in Jameson's phrase) which mediates the contradictions of classical slavery may persist into *Paradise Lost* – how, for example, in celebrating the heroism of the enemy's refusal ever to admit defeat (a Hector, a Cleopatra, a Turnus), epic authorizes that enemy's continuing and brutal suppression. To ask this kind of question of epic as a genre is to see how its origins in slave-based societies may have helped to make epic not merely prevalent throughout the Renaissance but, even against Aristotle's example, the genre of highest privilege in Renaissance theory.

In his now classic study of *The Problem of Slavery in Western Culture*, David Brion Davis pointed out one compelling paradox for the Renaissance: "The inherent contradiction of human slavery had always generated dualisms in thought, but by the sixteenth and seventeenth centuries Europeans had arrived at the greatest dualism of all – the momentous division between an increasing devotion to liberty in Europe and an expanding mercantile system based on Negro labor in America."[8] If, in classical slavery, epic mediated the contradictory construction of a heroic free citizenry dependent on the labor of a conquered population of inhuman objects, how much more useful might it be in speaking to this Renaissance dualism? A slave is indeed that object most precisely and diametrically opposed to the human subject because the two share everything (both being human) except for the definition of the one versus the other. As Davis's paradox about the Renaissance clearly implies, the master-subject appears to come into being only *with* the slave-object. The position of slave and master are mutually constituting.

Such a simultaneous operation suggests the possibility that the notion of having property in oneself may have been enabled by the legal concept of having property in another. That is, the self-possession of possessive individualism may in part be enabled by the legitimacy of possessing others as objects.[9]

In an important argument in the *Tenure of Kings and Magistrates*, Milton insists upon a similar case in the immediately and mutually constitutive positions of subject and king. While his argument is against the Presbyterians who objected to regicide, Milton's insistence on the mutual constitution of the two positions also interestingly includes the position of slave. Without the right to depose the king, the subject according to Milton indeed becomes a slave: "to say, as is usual, the king hath as good right to his crown and dignity as any man to his inheritance, is to make the subject no better than the king's slave, his chattel, or his possession that may be bought and sold."[10] The king holds his crown by contractual agreement – or covenant – and if one of the parties refuses to uphold the covenant, in Milton's argument, it dissolves. "We know that king and subject are relatives ... if the subject, who is one relative, take away the relation, of force he takes away also the other relative ... that is to say, the king's authority, and their subjection to it" (292). Milton further makes the power such subjects have to break relations a manifestation of the power they rightfully exercise as heads of their own private families:

they that shall boast, as we do, to be a free nation, and not have in themselves the power to remove or to abolish any governor supreme or subordinate, with the government itself upon urgent causes, may please their fancy with a ridiculous and painted freedom fit to cozen babies; they are indeed under tyranny and servitude, as wanting that power, which is the root and source of all liberty, to dispose and economize in the land which God hath given them as masters of family in their own house and free inheritance. Without which natural and essential power of a free nation, though bearing high their heads, they can in due esteem be thought no better than slaves and vassals born ... (296)

Milton here confers on the subjects the patriarchal privilege of inheritance which he would deny to the king. If the king inherits his right to rule over them as a father then that right abrogates their contractual freedom and makes of them mere slaves. Their right not to have him rule over them is something they inherit as fathers. The slavery and servitude of which Milton speaks may seem merely metaphorical and no actual relation, part of Milton's polemic and not a legal possibility. But in fact, slavery was far more than a metaphor during the Commonwealth.

During the Interregnum slavery became a part of personal experience for some combatants in the Civil War. Such local history may help to make the issue more than a question of genre theory or broad European economic history or mere metaphor. It may also help to bring the problem of actual slavery closer to Milton. The buying and selling of men for money into bonded labor, with a consequent loss of personal liberty, was an issue debated in some detail during the very late days of the Commonwealth government.[11]

On 25 March 1659 a petition was debated in Parliament which concerned seventy-two Cavalier Englishmen "now in slavery in the Barbadoes," requesting intervention on their behalf. The petition describes their treatment in terms that are the Englishman's version of the Middle Passage, the transatlantic voyage into slavery experienced by millions of Africans. The men were

driven through the streets of the city of Exon ... by a guard of horse and foot (none being suffered to take leave of them) and so hurried to Plymouth aboard the ship *John* of London, Captain John Cole, master, where, after they had lain aboard fourteen days, the captain hoisted sail; and at the end of five weeks and four days more, anchored at the isle of Barbadoes, in the West Indies, being (in sailing) four thousand and five hundred miles distant from their native country, wives, children, parents, friends and whatever is near and dear unto them; the captive prisoners being all the way locked up under decks (and guards) amongst horses, that their souls, through heat and steam under the tropic, fainted in them; and they never till they came to the island knew whither they were going.

Being sadly arrived there on May 7, 1656, the master of the ship sold your miserable petitioners, and the others; the generality of them to most inhuman and barbarous persons, for one thousand five hundred and fifty pound weight of sugar apiece, more or less, according to their working faculties, as the goods and chattels of Martin Noell and Major Thomas, aldermen of London, and Captain H. Hatsell, of Plymouth; neither sparing the aged of seventy-six years old, nor divines, nor officers, nor gentlemen, nor any age or condition of men, but rendering all alike in this inseparable captivity, they now generally grinding at the mills and attending at the furnaces, or digging in this scorching island; having nought to feed on (notwithstanding their hard labour) but potatoe roots, nor to drink, but water with such roots washed in it, ... being bought and sold still from one planter to another, or attached as horses and beasts for the debts of their masters, being whipped at the whipping posts (as rogues) for their masters' pleasure, and sleeping in sties worse than hogs in England, and many other ways made miserable, beyond expression or Christian imagination.[12]

It was claimed that these men had all been arrested for fighting in the rebellion at Salisbury and had freely chosen the option of slavery over death – which had been, since classical times, an argument in favor of the humaneness of the institution. Slavery deferred (in that it did not entirely erase the right to impose), or substituted for, death. What so troubled the discussion of this petition in Parliament was the ambiguous pressure of the moment; because the Civil War was already over, it was uncertain if conditions still threatened the death for which slavery would have been a substitute. It was equally difficult to be certain if the men in question had freely chosen slavery. Most pertinently, however, the debaters worried that the political tide would soon turn, and fretted that they themselves might soon face a similar fate, and therefore they argued about setting dangerous precedents. These Parliamentary debaters are actual historical instances of citizens contemplating the possibility of a shift in their position, from freeborn subjects of a commonwealth into the status of mere objects such as the petition makes clear has already happened to other Englishmen. Thus Sir Arthur Haselerigge put the Parliamentary debaters' predicament in 1659: "That which is the Cavalier's case to day, may be the Roundhead's a year hence. Our ancestors left us free men. If we have fought our sons into slavery, we are of all men most miserable" (257). Sir Henry Vane argued "Slavery is Slavery as well in a Commonwealth as under another form," and warned them to "take occasion from these ill precedents to make good laws."[13] Sir John Lenthall also objects: "I hope it is not the effect of our war to make merchandize of men" (256). Although virtually retired as Latin Secretary by this date, Milton was still writing letters for Richard Cromwell in April 1659 and may, indeed, have written a letter for this same John Lenthall a month after this debate.[14]

Parliament ultimately voted to refuse the petition and even to jail the petitioner as a member of the Cavalier cause. This Parliamentary wrangle witnesses through the immediacy of a threatened slavery two seemingly contradictory facts about the relationship between lordship and bondage. The first is the fundamental positional nature of the free and enfranchised member of Parliament, who could be transformed by legal and financial transactions into the thinghood of slavery. Formerly in one position, the debater himself could possibly move into the second. However, the nationalism – if not outright racism – of these debaters (who far more easily sent off Scotsmen and Irish children to the Indies) also points to the heart of the constitutive difference between free subject and slave once the process of transformation is complete. While the freedom of Englishmen may be compromised like that of the thousands of Scotsmen and Irish children Parliament had no qualms about shipping to the plantations to work as slaves there, it may not reify them like the slavery of the African. Thus, for example, one of the debaters, a Mr. Boscawen, argued for the petitioners, pointing out the classic, Roman precedent for the guarantee of citizenship against the possible slippage of position, and warning of the danger should Parliament pass up the opportunity for redressing the wrong.

I am as much against the Cavalier party as any man in these walls ... ; but you have Pauls case before you. A Roman ought not to be beaten. We are miserable slaves, if we may not have this liberty secured to us ... These persons come to justify themselves. *If you pass this our lives will be as cheap as those negroes.* They [the planters] look upon them as their goods, horses, etc., and rack them only to make their time out of them, and cherish them to perform their work. It may be my case. I would have you consider the trade of buying and selling men. (256; emphasis added)[15]

Perhaps because the subject positions of citizen and slave are slippery in the extreme in this case, Mr. Boscawen is quick to reify the position of slave as firmly as he can by grounding it in race. Because they have been bought and sold, that is, have been subject to cheapening, "those negroes" are not recognized as men and have become objects. The horror for the Parliamentarians is to contemplate their own transformation to this position. Mr. Boscawen wants to make it impossible for Parliament to leave the Englishmen in slavery and thus marks a boundary-line of objectness, grounding it in racial difference.

In a sense, what race does here is to mark the difference between the Englishman who would descend into thinghood by virtue of having been conquered in war and the African who is a slave by virtue of having been sold. Because it is a result of a series of financial transactions, the African slave *trade* has little enough in common with the heroism of martial conquest. When the lord – and the lord's society as an aggregate – has obtained the slave by purchase and not by personal conquest, the possession can hardly be deemed "heroic." An empire which will be built on a slave trade rather than on martial conquest needs a different kind of heroism. Hence Satan, the classical conquering hero, is the *villain* in the poem. The true heroism celebrated by Milton lies elsewhere in a complexly "heroized" labor, differentiated from manual work but which still relies upon its productive powers. The racism of the transatlantic slave trade carried on by England (as well as, of course, other European powers) allows culture broadly to redefine the heroism of work, relegating to the realm of non-human thinghood a manual labor placed beneath the "Good Works" of nascent capitalist entrepreneurs. This is by no means to claim, of course, that Milton's rewriting of classical form in *Paradise Lost* is entirely motivated by such a shift in the slave mode of production, but it is to suggest how some of the generic rearrangements Milton effects may have been as successful as they are because they are so fundamentally compatible with the original ideological function of epic as a genre. Boscawen's argument in Parliament, by placing the emphasis

on the "cheapness" of "those negroes," specifies the fundamentally
financial, and therefore unheroic – i.e. "cheap" – nature of the transaction which defines the African slave.

While the function of racial difference in the Parliamentary debate is
hardly surprising, it does serve to illustrate in a specific piece of
contemporary evidence, how race played a part in differentiating for men
of the time between slavery as classical conquest and as Renaissance
trade. What is also extremely useful to know is that Milton shared his
culture's alignment of blackness to slavery. In the rhetorically high-
pitched concluding last sentence of his earliest pamphlet *Of Reformation*
(1641), for example, Milton had ended with a vision of the punishment of
those who resist reformation: they shall

be throwne down eternally into the darkest and deepest gulfe of Hell, where
under the despightfull countroule, the trample and spurne of all the other
Damned, that in the anguish of their Torture shall have no other ease then to
exercise a Raving and Bestial Tyranny over them as their Slaves and Negroes,
they shall remaine in that night for ever, the basest, the lowermost, the most
dejected, most underfoot and down-trodden Vassals of Perdition.[16]

Here listed as simply a more specific case of the general term "slaves,"
the plural term "negroes" names the absolute status of the most
degraded class of things, those ultimate objects on a level to which
debates in Parliament insist English subjects may not rightfully be
cheapened and which Milton's powerful rhetoric places as the absolute
lowest of the low, debased beneath even the damned. However impossible it may be to wash an Ethiop white, God can make an Englishman
into a negro if he refuses to listen to Milton's counsel for reform. It is
his ultimate curse.

While perhaps none of this is surprising, the speed of the devaluation
of dignified Moors such as Shakespeare's Othello or even the fatherly if
perfidious Aaron to such a Miltonic nadir may shock. Doubtless, the
economic cause of this change lies contained in the Miltonic doublet
indicating the specificity of the Renaissance form of slavery: "slaves *and*
negroes." That, appositively, slaves are negroes and negroes are slaves,
demonstrates how immediately the reification of race by economics had
proceeded. The impetus for European involvement in African slavery
during this particular period of human culture was, of course, very
broadly based in what all of Europe had to gain from the triangular
trade to the New World. Having had a late start in England, however,
the slave trade gathered momentum throughout the seventeenth century,
taking on a particular urgency at mid-century during the Interregnum.

The cause of this urgency was the same force which compelled the deportation policy practiced by Cromwell's government. From a sense of a labor surplus in England due to overpopulation at the opening of the century, there had developed a sense of a labor shortage. This shortage was especially crucial in the New World, specifically in the newly valuable sugar islands such as Barbados (so that "to barbadoe" had become a verb meaning to kidnap someone into slavery).[17] The switch from the cultivation of tobacco to the fantastically more profitable sugar meant the need to put vast amounts of land into cultivation of cane, which required huge capital outlays and a massively increased labor force. It was a convulsive economic need only capable of being met finally by the African slave trade.

The dates of the changes in population for Barbados make it a singular example of what happened to a possession of Britain under Cromwell's Commonwealth.[18] Eric Williams estimates that in 1645, Barbados had 11,200 white small farmers and 5,680 negro slaves; in 1667, the year of the publication of *Paradise Lost* and after the advent of sugar planting – and the Interregnum – there were only 745 white plantation owners and 82,023 slaves. In 1645 the island had 18,130 whites fit to bear arms, in 1687 only 8,300 – martial preparedness of the whites being crucial with such an imbalanced majority of slaves to keep forcefully coerced.[19] The staggering growth of numbers of slaves and the consequent drop in the number of whites indicate not only that the slave trade had been increasing at an exponential rate, but also that the economy was no longer one of small independent (white) proprietors, but of vast plantations run on (black) slave labor.[20] The "triangular trade" was not only profitable because of the direct buying and selling of people between Africa and the West Indies, but also because of the money to be made from the importation of tropical produce into England and – the third side of the triangle – from the manufacture of goods to be exported from England to Africa for the purchase of slaves. One historian estimates that at the end of the seventeenth century the African–West Indian trade accounted for more than one third of all commercial profits in England.[21] Seventeenth-century student of the new economy, Charles Davenant, guessed that one person in the sugar islands, whatever his color, was worth more in profits than seven in England (cited Williams, *Columbus to Castro*, 143–5).

What has this to do with labor in Milton's epic? It is Satan, the leader of the "captive multitude" in hell, himself enslaved to himself, who comes to conquer the new world: his first thoughts are of empire and,

more pertinently, also of population. At his first sight of Adam and Eve
he plots to make them participate in his condition:

> hell shall unfold,
> To entertain you two, her widest gates,
> And send forth all her kings; there will be room,
> Not like these narrow limits, to receive
> Your numerous offspring; if no better place,
> Thank him who puts me loath to this revenge
> On you who wrong me not for him who wronged
> And should I at your harmless innocence
> Melt, as I do, yet public reason just,
> Honour and empire with revenge enlarged,
> By conquering this new world, compels me now
> To do what else though damned I should abhor.
>
> (IV.381–92)

Satan's embrace here is of a so "numerous offspring" that paradise
cannot contain the imagined surplus. Like all slave masters, Satan is after
not only Adam and Eve, but also the population which will derive from
them.

Adam and Eve's progeny are far more usually discussed in terms of
shortage. This labor short-fall haunts both their imaginations but Eve's
in particular, perhaps most appropriately, because she will be the
"producer" of this particular population. It is doubtless because Eve's
problem about labor and her work of reproduction have been occluded
by the far more obvious problems with gender in the poem, that the issue
of work and the differentiation among laborers have remained less
accessible to critical notice. However, the question of distinguishing
different kinds of work becomes a subtly debated issue in the poem. In
Milton's poem, their labor becomes a carrier of more complicated issues
such as the sexual division of labor, the construction of privacy, the
proto-capitalist "rational" organization of workers, and, implicitly, the
function of sheer manual labor in profit-making enterprises, such as had
developed in the New World. Describing the "blind contempt for manual
labor" in the classical economy, Kendrick points out that, "The labor
[that the slave] performed could not be thought of as a form of human
activity" (*Milton: A Study*, 106). Seventeenth-century England is not
imperial Rome, of course, and it is precisely in Adam and Eve's labor
that *Paradise Lost* does the work of providing solutions to the internal
contradictions set up within a nascent capitalist economy by the Atlantic
slave trade: if one obtains slaves not by conquering them in heroic
warfare, but by buying and selling them as commodities, this colonialist
activity must itself be dignified as "work." Unlike the "tedious havoc" of

battle that Milton refuses to call heroic in the anti-invocation of Book IX, it is their labor which characterizes Adam and Eve's activity as purposeful, dignified, and human. Their labor defines their humanity. Adam explains to Eve how important their work is:

> other creatures all day long
> Rove idle unemployed, and less need rest;
> Man hath his daily work of body or mind
> Appointed, which declares his dignity,
> And the regard of heaven on all his ways;
> While other animals unactive range,
> And of their doings God takes no account.
>
> (IV.616–22)

God's accounting of the various labors of mankind distinguishes that species from all other unemployed animals. Daily work is humanly distinctive. It is also not yet entirely distinguished into two kinds of work, manual and mental. Such labor as Adam and Eve perform of both kinds remains, however, crucially incomplete until more hands arrive to augment the force. Until that time, their employment must be daily and, even to Adam at this moment, apparently insufficient.

> Tomorrow ere fresh morning streak the east
> With first approach of light, we must be risen
> And at our pleasant labour, to reform
> Yon flowery arbours, yonder alleys green,
> Our walk at noon, with branches overgrown,
> That mock our scant manuring, and require
> More hands than ours to lop their wanton growth.
>
> (IV.623–9)

Figured as restraint, the activity falls short of its goal of reformation because they have as yet no children to help in the work. The passage more importantly intends, of course, praise of the garden's untended fecundity. The plants grow even without a lot of fertilizer. This generosity is what makes the garden perfect. However, the terms in which the praise is made stresses a lack of laborers, crucially calling them "hands" – the synecdochic body part which represents specifically the manual part of human labor.

This as yet uncreated workforce will, of course, be products of Eve's specifically female labor – she who is hailed consistently as the mother of mankind. Thus, when she makes this as yet unfulfilled element of her own work – this present lack of labor – the reason for her fateful desire to garden separately from Adam, she lodges the labor shortage at a crucial juncture in the poem. She explains to her husband why she wishes to labor separately from him.

> Adam, well may we labour still to dress
> This garden, still to tend plant, herb, and flower,
> Our pleasant task enjoined, but till more hands
> Aid us, the work under our labour grows,
> Luxurious by restraint; what we by day
> Lop, overgrown, or prune, or prop, or bind,
> One night or two with wanton growth derides
> Tending to wild. Thou therefore now advise
> Or hear what to my mind first thoughts present,
> Let us divide our labours.
>
> (IX.205–14)

According to Eve, the more they labor, the more the "work" grows, "work" here being the luxuriating vegetation itself that is stimulated to greater growth by their pruning. The garden itself then is their "work" and so the term can cover the entire spectrum of their relationship to it, their pleasant manual labor functioning as metaphor for all sorts of ethical and humanly distinctive activity in the poem. Yet "labour" is also sheer manual effort itself and we watch it in the process of becoming that more limited thing in Eve's suggestion, while also remaining allied to, but crucially different from, work of "mind." Adam and Eve argue about this labor and in the process of their argument they complicate the idea by differentiating the activities it names: should they work side by side as Adam wants them to (doing exactly the same work) or should they "divide" their labors and work separately as Eve suggests? In Eve's suggestion to "divide" their labors we see a gap open whereby her desire to have them labor in physically separate spaces allows Adam to define that physical separation as an already prior gender difference. Gender begins to mark the division between manual labor and other kinds of work. Thus, while Adam makes the argument that they should continue to work side by side (doing what we must assume are exactly identical physical activities and therefore not distinct according to gender), he uses a strange formulation to describe Eve's very suggestion as itself a kind of work. His characterization opens up the crucial distinction between his work and hers.

> Well hast thou motioned, well thy thoughts *employed*.
> How we might best fulfil the *work* which here
> God hath assigned us, nor of me shalt pass
> Unpraised: for nothing lovelier can be found
> In woman, than to *study household good*,
> And *good works* in her husband to promote.
>
> (IX.229–34, emphasis added)

The difference Adam institutes here between doing "good works" and "studying household good" delineates a division of labor according to gender. While it may not provide an exact distinction between mental and manual labor, it does outline a difference between husband's and woman's work. Although, somewhat paradoxically, Eve's work is "study" – sheer thoughtfulness – her thinking on these matters is part of her womanly work, that is, care for an enclosed domestic space ("household") which includes her husband's well-being. Adam's distinction constructs a specifically gendered boundary between their work which shared (or even Eve's spatially separate) gardening does not. In reserving for himself a theologically resonant "Good Works," Milton has Adam, in a quite classical way, relegate to the woman the privacy of a derogated *economics*, "household good" being, simply, an English translation of the Greek term. Because Adam's ultimate point is that they will be better off if they continue to perform an undifferentiated physical labor, side by side, doing, presumably, identical work, we see the paradoxical and subtly introduced inequality of gender invade their "equal" work.

As it evolves, Adam and Eve's debate about gardening continues to stage the argument as a contrast between two different ways of conceiving of labor: that is, between work as an economic activity and work as a theological issue. According to Eve, she and Adam should work separately because they do not work efficiently together and do not earn enough in a specific amount of time. Speaking from her purely economic perspective, "Our day's work" she says is "brought to little" and "the hour of supper comes unearned" (IX.225). It is this very notion of "earning" a daily reward which Adam attacks in his redefinition of what it is they are, in fact, doing. Arguing theologically against her proto-capitalist model of wage-labor, Adam explains that their work is, instead, organized by a beneficent Lord in terms of a feudal arrangement of service.

> Yet not so strictly hath our Lord imposed
> Labour, as to debar us when we need
> Refreshment, whether food, or talk between,
> Food of the mind, or this sweet intercourse
> Of looks and smiles, for smiles from reason flow,
> To brute denied, and are of love the food,
> Love not the lowest end of human life.
> For not to irksome toil, but to delight
> He made us, and delight to reason joined.
> (IX.235–43)

Eve's feminine tendency to fall is here seen in its economic register: Adam's correction of her desire for efficiency labels as post-lapsarian her proto-capitalist program (whereby she trades labor of the body for "earnings" and food as a reward for efficient work). Laboring and eating are distinct and separate activities for Eve – as they are, of course, for anyone who works "outside" the home. For Adam, they are part of the same activity, there being no distinction between the times at which they happen, nor the place. Their conversation thus ominously (for the. reader) anticipates the curse that Adam, after he sins, will be forced to earn his bread by the sweat of his brow.

The conjuncture of their conflicting economic organizations is not merely a surface feature of the text which recalls an issue that we, with historical hindsight, may realize traces out the long-term future development of England's economy. The transition from feudalism to capitalism has remained a highly contested topic in Marxist economic theory, as it is, of course, a fundamental question in any historical accounting of the change from some earlier period to the Modern.[22] It is a staple argument of feminist history that an invidious impasse for the devaluation of women's work was that moment when the development of capitalism cut the home off from the workplace, not merely alienating the worker from his labor but ensuring that female ("unpaid") household work would have no value in the new economy, unlike the disposition of work in the feudal household which was a place both of production and consumption.[23] Yet such a set of differences was not merely a slowly evolving set of economic possibilities; they appeared in far more crucial conjunctures in the new colonies than in England where labor structures evolved far more slowly. The problem of how to organize labor in the colonies, *ex nihilo*, as it were, is perhaps most familiar to us from mainland North American history – with our stories of the ultimately egalitarian ethic in Jamestown where, finally, even gentleman had to do manual labor if they wanted to eat. In Barbados, to take a single example, some of the earliest arrangements for the ownership of land had been exclusively feudal grants, which, when they failed to make a profit, were thereafter replaced by numerous small proprietorships owned by released indentured servants. Finally, when the land ran out and indentured servants could no longer be rewarded with land, these proprietorships evaporated and huge plantations, based upon negro labor, took over.[24] It is impossible to overstate the significance of such a competition among the various ways of organizing labor in the New World: one might say that the Civil War in mainland North America was fought out over the contradictions posed to a society by the intermixture of an economy based upon small proprietorships with huge slave labor plantations. Yet the question remains as to how the problematic organization of labor in the New World might have had a cultural impact in England at the time – and how this impact would have left its trace on Milton's epic.[25]

Although they are more interested in intellectual than in manual labor and therefore do not, unfortunately, take up the question of slavery at all, Nancy Armstrong and Leonard Tennenhouse still make an important argument about the relationship between the North American colonies and the metropolitan center in England: cultural influence, they argue, not only moved in one direction, out from the center to the colonial periphery, it also flowed backwards, from colonial periphery to metropolitan core.[26] Relying on the arguments of Benedict Anderson about the formation of new communities out of a broadly shared pan-Atlantic literacy, they insist that new forms of identity and indeed the peculiarly modern concept of "intellectual labor" itself came into being in the colonies and were reimported back to the metropole. *Paradise Lost* is for them a representative element in this new community not only as a product consumed by its members on both sides of the Atlantic, but also because it presents an awareness of "the sudden visibility of labor and an economic definition of the nation as part of a larger revolution in consciousness" (102). Armstrong and Tennenhouse agree that the conflict about labor as it is worked out in the epic lies in the gendered difference between Adam and Eve's preferences about gardening; Eve's "protestant" bourgeois house-holding is opposed, in their terms, to Adam's "aristocratic" mode of conspicuous display (akin to what I have termed his "feudal" sense of service). They also understand the conflict about gardening to establish a distinction between two fundamental categories of labor: "The categories of labor that organize the new world are defined by the most fundamental distinction of all: between those who work only with their bodies and those whose labor is invisible because it is intellectual" (112). Eve's gender allies physical labor with reproduction while Adam's invisible labor is that which services a new identity.[27]

In focusing purely on the intellectual labor of writing undertaken by the new literate individual, Armstrong and Tennenhouse unfortunately neglect the important category of manual labor which has been spun off from Adam and Eve's activity. What happens to physical work in the New World? Someone does it. What happens to the staggering profits created by the so-called "Sugar Islands"? It may overstate the case to argue, as Eric Williams does, that sugar island profits provided the capital which fueled the industrial revolution, but it is true that in the seventeenth century the island of Barbados was widely understood to be far more valuable than all of the mainland colonies put together.[28] So too, the organization of actual manual labor in the historical New World was a point debated at some length around the time of *Paradise Lost*. The debate included explicit arguments in favor of African slavery.

In 1645 George Downing (for whom Downing Street in London is named) had written to John Winthrop in Massachusetts:

> If you go to Barbados, you shall see a flourishing Iland, many able men. I beleive they have bought this year no lesse than a thousand Negroes, and the more [the planters] buie, the better able they are to buye, for in a year and halfe [the slaves] will earn (with God's blessing) as much as they cost ...
> A man that wil settle ther must looke to procure servants, which if you could gett out of England, for 6, or 8, or 9 yeares time, onely paying their passages, or at the most but som smale above, it would do very well, for so therby you shall be able to doe something upon a plantation, and in short tim be able, with good husbandry, to procure Negroes (the life of this place) out of the encrease of your owne plantation.[29]

Armstrong and Tennenhouse understand Eve to represent non-intellectual labor because of her association with physical reproduction – her sexuality as mother of mankind. By her differentiating gender, Eve helps to install the difference between her physical work and Adam's "invisible" and intellectual "Good Works" which are like the work, moreover, which any reader consuming the text of *Paradise Lost* for his private and personal "profit" might do (113). Yet Eve is far more centrally associated in the poem with manual labor because of her concern with the shortage of actual workers. Her question about gardening is: how should they organize labor before the other workers arrive? Her question is not merely quaint or one of Milton's more opportune importations for imagining how life in paradise might have been in all its details. George Downing goes through a similar set of calculations in his letter to John Winthrop when praising the profit to be made in the actual New World, first with indentured servants, and then with slaves.

The islands of the West Indies make their explicit appearance in the poem not in the immediate context of slavery but as exemplars of the fallen innocence Columbus confronted when he found native Americans dressed in feathers. With this mention of Columbus – one of only two historical figures to be explicitly named in the entire poem – Milton corrects the discoverer's notorious error in mistaking America for India, and native peoples for Indians. Quite properly Milton calls these people "Americans" when he explains how the formerly innocent and naked Adam and Eve clothe themselves with leaves from a specific kind of tree:

> not that kind for fruit renowned,
> But such as at this day Indians known
> In Malabar or Deccan spreads her arms
> Branching so broad and long, that in the ground
> The bended twigs take root, and daughters grow
> About the mother tree ...

> those leaves
> They gathered, broad as Amazonian targe,
> And with what skill they had, together sewed,
> To gird their waists: vain covering, if to hide
> Their guilt and dreaded shame; O, how unlike
> To that first naked glory. Such, of late
> Columbus found th' American, so girt
> With feather'd cincture; naked else and wild,
> Among the trees on isles and woody shores.

(IX.1101–18)

The phrasing is ambiguous. Is the American naked or not, fallen or not? While clearly different from the Indians (who would be clothed), this singular creature is either found by Columbus (and compared to him) in an unclothed state, and therefore like "that first naked glory," or, "wearing a cincture of feathers," and therefore the same as fig-wearing, fallen Adam and Eve. However long the sentence with its vague antecedents holds in suspension the fallen or innocent nature of the American, this singular native must in the last analysis be dressed. Thus, like fallen Adam and Eve, the genitals of this person would be covered, and hence the gender goes unmentioned. For this American in particular, sexual difference is erased in a representative singularity, the singularity of the figure contrasting with the paired appearance of Adam and Eve in their innocence. Nakedness is shameful after the fall precisely because it reveals sexual difference, and sexual difference – in all its multiple resonances – is what "causes" the fall in Milton's poem.

The opposition between nakedness and being clothed, is, of course, a dichotomy similar to the constitutive difference between slave and master. One does not understand nakedness without the concept of being clothed. While we remain in ambiguity, before the sentence finally resolves itself, we assume that the American is indeed unfallen, and therefore *like* that first naked innocence. In this understanding it is then Columbus, fully clothed, who inhabits the quintessential fallen perspective, and who stands confronting the American as if the discoverer were himself a Satanic character – just as we first see Adam and Eve's nakedness through Satan's eyes. We do not, of course, see Adam's nakedness. Rather, the allure of Eve's body is installed in front of, as it were, what would seem to be a description of Adam's masculine beauty in terms of a Greek statue (his "Hyacinthine locks" almost explicitly recall Hellenistic statuary). Eve's wanton tresses and later, her "swelling breast naked" meeting Adam's, distract all readers from what might be a far more problematic vision of Adam's nakedness. It is as if we were being protected from reenacting the primal scene of Ham's curse.

Slavery is, of course, the curse for seeing the father's nakedness. As Michelle Frank has suggested, the presence in the poem of distinctly African slavery is connected to the moment of confrontation between Columbus and the American by way of this reference to nakedness. The· mention of the story of Ham comes in the midst of the grinding necessity of history recounted by the last two books, specifically when the "race" of Ham is cursed for shaming their father by seeing his nakedness – just as Adam and Eve are, finally, cursed in seeing their own.[30] The curse on Ham's descendants is thus a specialized version of the curse on the human race:

> Yet sometimes nations will decline so low
> From virtue, which is reason, that no wrong,
> But justice, and some fatal curse annexed
> Deprives them of their outward liberty,
> Their inward lost; witness the irreverent son.
> Of him who built the ark, who for the shame,
> Done to his father, heard this heavy curse,
> *Servant of servants*, on his vicious race.
>
> (XII.97–104; emphasis added)

If Ham's curse is to be enslaved through the generations of "his vicious race," it is as a curse a more intense replication of Adam's punishment to labor for his sin against the Father. If the metaphorical fact of enslavement is never far from Milton's arguments about freedom throughout the prose arguing liberty for his freeborn English readers, and while Milton's use of the word "race" here only means family, the curse of slavery begins to become racial because it is inherited – similar to original sin – in the final history of the poem. Milton's poem imagines the complications inherent in the duality between slave labor and free labor as a set of gendered relations, themselves forming a dichotomy constitutive of relations between the new subject and a redefined object of control, both the woman and the slave, those who do the physical labor of reproduction and production. Gender also makes a more fundamental distinction between the slave and his master, for the slave is that category of person with whom the master would never think of allying himself through the gift of a woman. As a non-human object, the slave could never receive the valuable possession of a woman from the master, thereby cementing some human bond between them. The idea of bondage utterly negates the possibility of that kind of connection.

As epic, *Paradise Lost* is a poem best poised to offer an imaginary solution to the real contradictions inherent in a nascent capitalism based in part upon the expansion of slavery in the New World. No longer the result of conquest but of trade, such slavery becomes necessarily racial, not legitimated by the fateful accident of war but by an inheritable curse. Newly profitable because of expanded markets, such slavery is valuable but unheroic – at the same time, however, enabling an increasing number of metropolitan subjects to live the life of a gentleman, exempt from the necessity of manual labor, freed to do the job of intellectual labor within a new pan-Atlantic literate community.

We might well suspect that other Renaissance epics, members of that genre of highest privilege during the period, may be answering the great need felt across western Europe for some cultural instrument by which each nation could make sense of that vast shared and competitive imperialist project which was the exploitation by Europeans of the human and material wealth of three entire continents: Africa, and North and South America.[31] Satan's plot of enslavement and self-thralldom overwhelms Adam and Eve's free labor and transforms their carefully differentiated work into a system into which slavery is admitted of necessity. The penultimate image of the poem, before Adam and Eve wander out into the world to find their place of rest, is of:

> evening mist, [which]
> Risen from a river o'er the marish glides,
> And gathers ground fast at the labourer's heel,
> Homeward returning.
>
> (XII.629–32).

The heel remembers the prophecy of the protoevangelum when it is promised that the heel of the Woman's seed will crush the serpent's head. However, that it is a *laborer*'s heel is important, for the term crucially recalls all the curses and the complicated relations among them: Adam's – that he must labor by the sweat of his brow; Eve's – that her labor in birth will be painful; and Ham's – that his descendants' labor will be enslaved.

NOTES

1 Fredric Jameson, *The Political Unconscious: Narrative as a Socially Symbolic Act* (Ithaca, 1981), p. 141.
2 Ibid. p. 118.
3 Ibid. pp. 118–19.
4 Quint, *Epic and Empire: Politics and Generic Form from Virgil to Milton* (Princeton, 1993), p. 23. Quint does not derive this insight from Jameson, however, instead insisting that the equation of power and the very possibility of narrative is the defining feature of the genre of epic; he locates two different forms of the genre in the winners' epic and the losers' epic.

5   Christopher Kendrick, *Milton: a Study in Ideology and Form* (New York and London, 1986), pp. 106–11.

6   Patricia Parker, *Literary Fat Ladies: Rhetoric, Gender, Property* (London, 1987), p. 148.

7   Kendrick's argument – which does not take up gender at all – focuses on the change in the subject: " 'possessive individualist' possession expresses in pure fashion the general commodification of labor that marks the constitutive moment of the capitalist subject – the point at which it distinctly separates itself from the normative subject of post-feudalism which was still largely defined by its immediate relationship with its means of production. It *rewrites* feudal possession by breaking with it, casting possession in terms of the individual's control over his only remaining means, his bodily powers" (*Milton: A Study*, p. 64).

8   Davis, *The Problem of Slavery in Western Culture* (Ithaca, New York, 1966) p. 108.

9   Recent arguments such as Stephen Greenblatt's in *Renaissance Self-Fashioning* (Berkeley, 1980) and Catherine Belsey's in *The Subject of Tragedy* (London, 1983) usefully insist on the construction of subjectivity as an opposition to some constitutive other.

10 *John Milton* ed. Stephen Orgel and Jonathan Goldberg (New York, 1991), p. 279.

11 Eric Williams, *From Columbus to Castro: A History of the Caribbean, 1492–1969* (New York, 1970), p. 101.

12 Leo Francis Stock, ed., *Proceedings and Debates of the British Parliaments Respecting North America* (5 vols., Washington, 1924), I, p. 249.

13 So too Henry Vane prefers to overlook a previous enmity, and to recognize a principled commonality: "I do not look on this business as a Cavaliers business; but as a matter that concerns the liberty of the free-born people of England. Slavery is Slavery as well in a Commonwealth as under another form." Vane furthermore warns his fellow members to be "as vigilant against the royalist party as you can but if you find the liberty and property of the people of England thus violated, take occasion from these ill precedents to make good laws" (p. 256).

14 *Complete Prose Works of John Milton*, ed. Douglas Bush, John Diekhof, J. Millén French et al. (New Haven, 1953), V, pp. 872–3.

15 Mr. Noell, one of the slave traders, defends the practice as indentured servitude: "I trade into those parts … I indent with all persons that I send over. Indeed the work is hard, but none are sent without their consent. They were civilly used and had horses to ride on … It is not so hard as is represented to you; not so much as the common husbandman here. The work is mostly carried on by the negroes" (p. 250).

16 *Complete Prose*, I, p. 617.

17 Eric Williams, *Capitalism and Slavery* (New York, 1944), p. 6.

18 I am indebted to Michelle Frank for first pointing out the importance of Barbados as a context for understanding the issue of racism and slavery in *Paradise Lost* in a seminar paper, University of Pennsylvania, Fall, 1989.

19 Williams, *Capitalism and Slavery*, p. 23.

20 Milton had argued that polygamy would be good for agricultural help

because it would increase the population and ease the labor shortage. *Complete Prose*, V, p. 367.

21 Williams, *From Columbus to Castro*, p. 153, citing Charles Davenant, guesses "commercial profits" at 36%. Thomas Dalby estimated that one person in the islands was worth 130 times more than one in England (Williams, *Capitalism and Slavery*, p. 53). The sugar colonies were far more valuable than mainland colonies; in 1669 Josiah Child wrote:

> The people that evacuate from us to Barbados, and the other West India Plantations do commonly work one Englishman to ten or eight Blacks; and if we keep the trade of our said plantations entirely to England, England would have no less inhabitants, but rather an increase of people by such evacuation, because that one Englishman, with the Blacks that work with him, accounting what they eat, use and wear, would make employment for four men in England whereas peradventure of ten men that issue from us to New England what we send to or receive from them, doth not employ one man in England.

22 For the debate see Rodney Hilton, ed., *The Transition from Feudalism to Capitalism* (1976; rpt. London, 1978).

23 Alice Clark, *Working Life of Women in the Seventeenth Century* (1919; rpt. London, 1982); for a critique of Clark's oversimplified model of the transition from feudalism to capitalism, see the "Preface" and appended bibliography by Miranda Chaytor and Jane Lewis, pp. ix–xlii. See also Roberta Hamilton, *The Liberation of Women: A Study in Patriarchy and Capitalism* (London, 1978), pp. 24–6. For further discussion of the problem of the transition from feudalism to capitalism in feminist history (and more bibliography) see "Introduction," in Margaret W. Ferguson, Maureen Quilligan, and Nancy J. Vickers, eds., *Rewriting the Renaissance: The Discourses of Sexual Difference in Early Modern Europe* (Chicago, 1986).

24 Vincent T. Harlow, *History of Barbados, 1625–1685* (New York, 1926), pp. 16–17.

25 John Locke's pivotal theorizing about the relationship between labor and property, published fourteen years after the second edition of *Paradise Lost*, suggests an interesting context; Locke takes up the issue "Of Property" directly after a section "Of Slavery." The exemplification of the famous maxim on the relationship between labor and property is suggestively in touch with West Indian realities. Thus,

> Though the Earth, and all inferior Creatures be common to all men, yet every Man has a Property in his own Person. This no Body has any Right to but himself. The labor of his Body, and the Work of his Hands, we may say, are properly his. Whatsoever he removed out of the State that Nature hath provided and left it in, he hath mixed his Labour with, and joyned to it something that is his own, thereby makes it his Property. (John Locke, *Two Treatises of Government*, ed. Peter Laslett [Cambridge, 1960], II, articles 16–17).

Locke interestingly computes the value of such labor in comparison to land in America: "if all the Profit an Indian received" were computed it would not be one thousandth that of land that is properly worked (p. 316). Locke's first frame of reference in this section is also persistently the West Indies; Locke specifically mentions tobacco and sugar as exemplary crops which are, of course, native to the West Indies.

> For 'tis labour indeed that puts the difference of value on everything; and let any one consider, what the difference is between an Acre of Land planted with Tobacco or Sugar, sown with Wheat or Barley; and an Acre of the same Land lying in common, without any Husbandry upon it, and he will find, that the improvement of labour makes the far greater part of the value. (p. 314)

While Locke is of course talking about West Indian conditions at a slightly later point, it is probable that Milton's frame of reference for the New World would not have been so very different.

26   Nancy Armstrong and Leonard Tennenhouse, *The Imaginary Puritan: Literature, Intellectual Labor and the Origins of Personal Life* (Berkeley and London, 1992), p. 197.

27   The new individual whom Armstrong and Tennenhouse herald is, rather paradoxically, a female whose literate Englishness survives immersion within the alien environment of non-British Indians and whose writing of a captivity narrative announces the existence of the new discourse produced by the autonomous individual who has no other cultural authority for writing than the exercise of this "Englishness."

28   Williams, *Capitalism and Slavery*: "In 1697 Barbados, with its 166 square miles, was worth more to British capitalism than New England, New York and Pennsylvania combined" (p. 54).

29   Collections of the Massachusetts Historical Society, 4th series (Boston, 1863), VI, pp. 537, 539.

30   For the contemporary association of black skin color with the curse on Ham, see "George Best's Discourse," in Richard Hakluyt, ed., *The Principal Voyages* (12 vols., Glasgow, 1904), VII, pp. 263–4; Sir Thomas Browne, "Of the Same" in *Pseudodoxia Epidemica* (Oxford, 1981), pp. 518–19. For a discussion of the curse in the Arab world, see David Brion Davis, *Slavery and Human Progress* (New York, 1984), pp. 42–3.

31   For a discussion of the *Lusiads* which lends some weight to this suggestion, see Quint, *Epic and Empire*, p. 105.

Margaret W. Ferguson

This essay was initially composed for a conference that occurred in October 1992, 500 years after Columbus landed on the Bahamian island he would name San Salvador, the English would later rename Watling, and the native inhabitants called Guanahani. Reflecting on that historically contested occasion and on its quincentennial anniversary, I seek to yoke the famous but still culturally mystified figure of Columbus with a female figure who has re-emerged into historical visibility partly as a consequence of revisionary feminist scholarship that has taken place during the last fifteen years in the US and UK academies, scholarship which has begun to penetrate various territories heretofore occupied most visibly by white men. The female figure upon whom I am focusing here poses some thorny questions for academic scholars, especially those who call themselves feminists, working in first-world educational institutions today. Though much feminist "recovery" scholarship has had an obliquely celebratory dimension (it is of course genuinely exciting, not to mention narcissistically gratifying, to find examples of brilliant literate women like Aemilia Lanier and Elizabeth Cary in an arena of literary study that had seemed, until recently, nearly empty of female writing subjects), I focus here on Aphra Behn partly because she dramatizes, among other things, the need for anti-celebratory labors. She shows, in particular, the need for skepticism about our own psychic investments in our objects of study, especially, but not only, when those objects have the allure of being historical female subjects endowed with some degree of power or agency – Queen Elizabeth, for example, or a writer like Behn.

My chief aim in linking Behn with Columbus at the outset is to look again, and from an oblique but I hope interesting perspective, at the paradigm of discovery and conquest which Columbus and many of his male successors articulated in terms of a masculine penetration of a feminized landscape. Behn invites a reconsideration of this paradigm, which has been brilliantly analyzed by Louis Montrose,[1] because she seems to have been the first European woman to write a first-person narrative – like Columbus's journals, a disturbing mixture of fact and fiction about her encounter with a part of the New World and its inhabitants. By the time she wrote – nearly 200 years after Columbus – America included not only the people Columbus called Indians but enslaved Africans as well.

Born around 1640 in social circumstances her biographers still debate, Behn journeyed with her family to the then-British colony of Guiana in the early 1660s; her father, most likely an adoptive father, was supposed to assume the governorship of the colony. Instead, he died at sea, leaving Aphra Behn to her own devices during a colonial sojourn that may have lasted anywhere from two months to four years.[2] Nearly thirty years later, and almost two decades after the English had lost Guiana to the Dutch in a move Behn deeply regretted (according to the treaty of Breda in 1667, the English traded Guiana for Manhattan), she wrote about her South American experiences – and, in particular, about her friendship with a noble black prince who rebelled against his slave status and was brutally executed as a result – in her novella *Oroonoko, or the Royal Slave*. Her youthful colonial journey, which some early twentieth-century critics argued was a product of her imagination and plagiarizing talents but which most modern scholars accept as having in fact occurred (there is documentary evidence of her presence in the colony from the acting governor who despised her!), also informs her obliquely autobiographical play set in the North American colony of Jamestown and entitled *The Widow Ranter or the History of Bacon*. This play, probably written in 1688, as was *Oroonoko*, was not published or staged until 1690, the year following Behn's death.

Behn's late works about the New World prompt me to ask the following question: what difference does it make to our understanding of Early Modern ideologies of gender when a woman's (written) voice gives a version of the paradigm of New World appropriation I mentioned earlier – the paradigm according to which a European male subject voyages to a New World he describes as a feminized Edenic object, a locus of desire, ripe for penetration? What happens when that act of appropriation, which includes the appropriation of non-European voices for the purposes of a story, comes from a female European subject – who happens to be English, of uncertain social estate, and a supporter of the House of Stuart? I want to look at Aphra Behn standing, as it were, and writing as an heir of Columbus, looking still at a feminized Edenic landscape but looking at it, and at its inhabitants, through eyes conditioned by not only her gender but also her nationality, by her inscription in a particular stage of the colonial enterprise, and, last but not least, by what we might call professional or educational formation, which in Behn's case entailed depending for her living not only on her "female pen," as she calls it, but also on the institution of the theater.

Let me make it clear that I am *not* primarily interested in assessing what difference Behn's gendered perspective on the New World, in conjunction with other constituents of her multiple subject positions, made to the history of colonialism *per se*. The short and brutal answer to that question would be very little, if any, despite the desire on the part of some feminist scholars to celebrate Behn's novella as an influential document in the early history of the abolition movement.[3] There is no doubt that Behn's portrait of the noble Oroonoko, his beautiful wife Imoinda, and their unhappy fates at the hands of hypocritical white Englishmen did influence abolitionist sentimental discourse, as Laura Brown has shown;[4] but there are strong reasons for not crediting humanitarianism as a major cause of abolition. Moreover, there are significant limits to – and contradictions in – Behn's apparently sympathetic attitude toward her noble enslaved Africans, not to mention toward the natives whom she sometimes distinguishes from and sometimes conflates with the Africans. A major limit to Behn's sympathies has to do with ideologies of social status: if she laments the unjust enslavement of Oroonoko and Imoinda, partly because like many seventeenth-century English women she saw analogies between the slave's plight and that of the unhappily married wife, she extends no sympathy to lower-class Africans, whom she presents as "naturally" cowardly. She signals their imputed baseness by a color distinction that may surprise readers conditioned by modern forms of racism: they are brown whereas Oroonoko and Imoinda are ebony black.[5]

A second limit to Behn's critical stance appears in a move of ideological containment that strikes me as interestingly parallel to a move Milton makes in *Paradise Lost*: both authors, one a Royalist, the other a Republican, implicitly underwrite the slave trade pursued by Cromwell as well as by the Restored Stuarts. Milton and Behn both follow Francis Bacon's tactic in "On Plantations." The tactic consists of idealizing a benignly "English" form of agricultural plantation while demonizing – in Milton's case literally – a greedy mercantile form of colonialism which both Bacon and Milton associate with mining the earth for gold. Milton's portrait of Satan as a merchant adventurer smelling Eden's spices and eager for spoil (*Paradise Lost* Book IV) contrasts with the epic vision of God as a father who makes his human creatures "stewards" or good "husbands" of a very fertile (wifely) garden and who offers his creatures, through Raphael, the chance to come home to the metropolis – eventually – if they obey his "easy yoke." Behn offers a similar ideologically charged contrast between a Satanic merchant, a sea-captain who betrays Oroonoko into slavery, and the benign absolute monarch to whom she addresses two elegiac "advertisements" for Guiana's beauty and riches. Behn's willingness to criticize the unjust enslavement of noble black princes but not the system of colonial appropriation which fundamentally fueled the slave trade provides us with ample reason not to romanticize her; but I would also warn against the temptation of feeling morally superior to her, especially if one entertains Eric Williams's powerful though by no means uncontested argument, in *Capitalism and Slavery*, that "abolition of the slave trade and emancipation of the slaves in the British colonies were driven not by philanthropy or humanitarianism but by economic forces within England."[6]

Although the primary question I am posing in this paper concerns Behn's effect on a *model* of colonial history rather than her effect on that history's course, the distinction, as Michel de Certeau suggests in his meditations on the peculiar structures of Western historiographical practice, is neither absolute nor ideologically innocent,[7] especially since the gendered model of appropriation Montrose has analyzed for the sixteenth century arguably continues to do consequential ideological work in modern times, for instance in some of the justificatory arguments that US politicians made recently for the importance – to Mexicans' own "development" – of the so-called free trade agreement (NAFTA) with Mexico's hardly "freely elected" current government. In any event, to begin to assess the small but not insignificant deviations Behn makes from the "penetration" model, as we might call it, I want to compare her version of a central metaphor of colonialist description – the New World as Eden – with passages in Columbus's letter about his first voyage and in Milton's *Paradise Lost*. Each of these passages represents a paradigmatic scene of looking at the bodies of those who inhabit, but are soon to be dispossessed of, a paradisal landscape. In each passage, a paradox or contradiction arises concerning the binary opposition between nakedness and clothedness; moreover, in each passage that paradox points to conceptual and moral problems about who is fallen and what fallenness entails. It clearly entails something different for women and men, and Behn's passage helps us see that the difference has to do with the idea of ornament and beyond that, with the problem of *luxury*.

In his letter to Gabriel Sanchez describing his first voyage, a text published and translated repeatedly from 1493 onward, Columbus details the riches of Española with (dare I say) fairly naked lust to possess the island's spices and gold; and he goes on to remark that the people of Española "all go naked, men and women, as their mothers bore them, although some of the women cover a single place with the leaf

bore them, although some of the women cover a single place with the leaf
of a plant or with a net of cotton."[8] One might initially take the
subordinate clause simply as a qualification of the main clause, but I
want to suggest that there are significant economic, moral, and even
theological issues lurking in the apparently trivial problem of how a
totalizing proposition (all go naked) can conjoin with a gendered exception which requires us, logically, either to reconceive nakedness as something other than an all-or-nothing notion or to wonder whether the
subclass of women somehow does not fully belong to the general
category "all natives." Two illustrators of Columbus's letter dramatize
the problem: one (fig. 8.1), from an illustrated version of the letter
published in 1493, shows the native women as naked in the sense of
absolutely unclothed; a second (fig. 8.2), from a 1495 edition of Dati's
version of the letter, depicts them as cinctured around the "single place"
with leaves.

Milton offers a complex analogue to this paradox when in Book IV of
Paradise Lost he initially describes Adam and Eve as "clad" only in
"naked majesty" (290) but, fourteen lines later, describes Eve but not
Adam as in effect partially clothed:

> She as a veil down to the slender waist
> Her unadorned golden tresses wore
> Dishevelled, but in wanton ringlets waved
> As the vine curls her tendrils, which implied
> Subjection.
>
>   (304–8)[9]

The Miltonic narrator, whose perspective has interestingly blended with
Satan's here (recall that it is through Satan's tormented eyes that the
entire Edenic primal scene unfolds), clearly creates a male subject
position for the reader–voyeur, who is teased, even titillated, by having
his gaze directed not to the lower part of the female body, as we would
expect, but to her breasts instead. The passage merits more discussion
than I can give it here (and might initiate a discussion of the Miltonic
narrator's very labile sexual perspective in other contexts that suggest
colonialist encounters – for instance the scene in Book V when a
gorgeously feathered Raphael visits Adam and Eve and folds his middle
set of wings around his waist, and presumably his loins, before joining
them for that uncooked dinner served by a naked Eve for whom the
angel is pointedly said *not* to feel lust). My point here is that Milton
revises a statement about a general human nakedness into the "exception" of a specifically gendered veiling, which modulates subsequently

Figure 8.1   "Insula Hyspana," illustration from Columbus's letter to Gabriel Sanchez: "La lettera dell'isola" (Basel, 1493).

CLalettera dellifole che ha trouato nuouamente el Re difpagna

Figure 8.2 Title page of Giuliano Dati's poetical paraphrase of Columbus, "Lettera dellisole" (Florence, 1495).

into an insistence on the visibility of both Adam's and Eve's private parts; this visibility is, however, occluded for the reader by the typically Miltonic mediating language of negation and temporal contrast:

> Nor those mysterious parts were then conceal'd,
> Then was not guilty Shame.
>
> (IV.312–13)

Milton's language, which draws here on the noble savage trope so central to colonialist discourse, works to create a split subject position – between desire and guilt – for the male narrator and implied male reader;

the language works also to give epistemological and moral force to a perception of difference considerably more subtle than we find in Columbus's vacillation between condescending praise for the "good" Indians' naïve generosity and invective against the "bad" Indians' cannibalism.[10] Milton's text suggests that one cannot grasp ontological difference – for instance the difference between fallen and unfallen being – simply by means of a binary opposition (naked: them / clothed: us); one must rather disrupt somehow the perceiver's ordinary conceptual categories so that an idea of nakedness that is *also not* nakedness can come, however partially, into existence. Even in Milton's linguistic practice, however, a sophisticated conception of difference comes decked in the now-familiar model of the woman as an object of desire *between* men.

In Behn's version of the Edenic scene, we encounter, in contrast, a narrator–viewer who occupies both a male subject position – constituted by her status as English, white, a collector of exotic objects, and an author wielding a pen – and a female subject position constituted not only by her historical gender but also by her connection with an institution, the theater, that had long been tainted, as women themselves were, by its association with the realm of ornament, with "superfluous things,"[11] with excessive desires. The connection with the theater, moreover, is dramatized in the passage in question with reference to another and equally interesting cultural institution, the "Antiquary" or "Cabinet of Curiosities."[12] The passage occurs immediately after the narrator has claimed an eye-witness veracity for the history she is about to relate and has promised not to "adorn" the narrative "with any accidents, but such as arrived in earnest" to Oroonoko. She now breaks her word, as she is to do again and again in the novella, with the chutzpah of the classical Cretan liar, whose paradox takes the form, "All Cretans are liars. I am a Cretan." Behn in fact digresses fulsomely, in what can only be called an embellishment on the subject of adornment, about the marvels of a world to which neither she nor her African hero are native.[13] Having made a problematic distinction between the black Africans, whom the English "make use of to work in our Plantations of Sugar," and native Indians with whom the English live "in perfect harmony, without daring to command 'em," she goes on to describe how the English trade with the Indians for marvellous birds, and for prodigious snake skins which she compares, for her metropolitan readers, to

one that may be seen at his Majesty's Antiquary; where are also some rare Flies, of amazing Forms and Colours, presented to 'em by my self; some as big as my Fist, some less; and all of various Excellencies, such as Art cannot imitate. Then we trade for Feathers, which they order into all Shapes, make themselves little short Habits of em, and glorious wreaths for their Heads, Necks, Arms and Legs, whose Tinctures are unconceivable. I had a Set of these presented to me, and I gave 'em to the King's Theatre, and it was the Dress of the Indian Queen, infinitely admir'd by Persons of Quality; and was unimitable. (p. 2)

That very headdress is evidently reproduced in an eighteenth-century engraving said to represent the famous actress Anne Bracegirdle (1674–1748; see fig. 8.3). The engraving portrays her, ironically, not playing the heroine of Dryden's *The Indian Queen*, the play of 1664 set in Mexico to which Behn is referring in the passage, but rather playing Semernia, the North American Indian Queen of Behn's own (posthumously produced) *The Widow Ranter*.[14]

I shall return to this image and to Behn's interesting textual gesture of advertising her own connection with the "King's Theatre." For the moment, I want to consider her subsequent description of the Indians' skill in creating ornaments. She mentions the beaded aprons

they wear just before 'em, as *Adam* and *Eve* did the Fig-leaves ... They thread these Beads also on long Cotton-threads, and make Girdles to tie their Aprons to, which come twenty times, or more, about the Waste, and then cross, like a Shoulder-belt, both ways, and round their Necks, Arms, and Legs. This Adornment, with their long black Hair, and the Face painted in little specks or flowers here and there, makes 'em a wonderful Figure to behold. (pp. 2–3)

After this elaborate description of ornament and paint on the natives' bodies, which is followed by a moment of striking gender-asymmetry – a sensuous description of the women's reddish, smooth, soft, and sleek skin – Behn returns to, but also radically alters, the analogy between the Indians and Adam and Eve:

though they are all thus naked, if one lives for ever among 'em, there is not to be seen an undecent Action, or Glance: and being continually us'd to see one another so unadorn'd, so like our first Parents before the Fall, it seems as if they had no Wishes, there being nothing to heighten Curiosity; but all you can see, you see at once, and every moment see; and where there is no Novelty, there can be no Curiosity.

In this passage, Behn repeatedly, almost dizzyingly, contradicts herself on a number of points: on the issue of whether the natives are naked or not, she insists so elaborately that they are both, and compares them so explicitly both to the fig-leaved and to the unfallen Adam and Eve, that one suspects she is writing with a very large tongue – or pen – in her cheek. Her doubled reference to Adam and Eve exposes, I think, a problem that lurks at the heart of the Edenic metaphor in Early Modern literature; her text therefore clarifies aspects of the ideological work done by the paradoxical descriptions of the natives as both naked and not naked in all three examples I've adduced. If the natives are naked, then

Figure 8.3   Mezzotint engraving by W. Vincent, probably of Anne Bracegirdle in the role of the Indian Queen Semernia in Behn's *The Widow Ranter*.

they are not only like Adam and Eve *before* the fall, but we, the colonists, are either superfluous to their blissful state or, worse, like Satan, filled with greed and desire to destroy it. If, however, the natives, and especially the native women, are cinctured around the genitals, then they are like Adam and Eve after the fall, and we can legitimate our profit-taking desires under the guise of bringing Christian salvation to the heathen. On the third hand – and this is the one I think Behn not only exposes but extends – if we see the natives, *pace* Aristotle's law of non-contradiction, as at once innocently naked and ornamentally covered, then we deflect attention from the ethical and theological problems of our presence in an Edenic place onto something that seems to link the natives with us via a desire for something we might paradoxically name a "necessary luxury." That concept, an emergent ideological construct which differed in significant ways from the concept of luxury defined (almost always in morally negative terms) by classical, Jewish, and Christian thinkers, was fostered by developments in the expanding market. Behn had a more capacious and less morally disapproving grasp of this brainchild of capitalism, the *necessary* luxury, than did many of her male contemporaries including mercantilist thinkers who continued to see luxury under the sign of *sin* and to associate it with female desire – arguably thereby displacing onto the ever-convenient weaker sex some of their own anxieties about the moral implications of the market's expansion.[15] Perhaps because as a woman and as a playwright Behn was doubly implicated in the process of re-defining luxury for new historical conditions, she offers a very interesting perspective on the question.

The concept of luxury impinges on moral, economic, political, and psycho-sexual domains during the Early Modern – that is, early imperialist – era.[16] Voltaire would suggest in the eighteenth century that luxury is an ahistorical phenomenon, whether as a subjective human desire or as the object thereof: luxury, he wrote, "is a thing that has been always despised and always loved" (quoted in Sekora, *Luxury*, p. 6). My argument here, however, is that the concept of luxury has a distinct though complex history which is distinctly (though again complexly) related to economic and political histories. To assess the significance of Behn's articulation of a significant change in the conceptualization of luxury, a change that involves, broadly speaking, loosening luxury from its status as a sin or moral error by implicitly defining it as a playful or *aesthetic* phenomenon, we need to consider two facets of the traditional notion of *luxuria* described by John Sekora (and further homogenized and thus oversimplified in my summary of Sekora's "history of ideas" narrative). First, for many classical, Jewish, and Christian authors, luxury was *the* foundational sin, the cause of war according to Socrates, and, according to Plato's report, of such dubious cultural "superfluities" as poetry and the theater as well. Luxury also caused the decline of Roman civic virtue, according to Sallust and other Latin writers; and it was moreover the root cause of the fall from the biblical Eden. In Saint Ambrose's interesting assessment of the effects of that fall, "luxury is slavery" (*De officiis ministrorum*, quoted in Sekora, *Luxury*, p. 21). Second, there is, according to Sekora, "more consistency in the personification of luxury than with any other chief sin. With the major exception of *The Faerie Queene*, almost all personifications of luxury are feminine" (p. 44); she is portrayed by writers and artists from Prudentius through Cellini as a beautiful woman driving a splendid chariot.

Luxuria – the personification and objectification of a desire seen traditionally both as the cause of great evil and as prototypically female – plays a major if still under-analyzed role, as I have suggested, in Early Modern debates about the virtues and vices (or less moralistically, the pros and cons) of what came to be known as mercantilism. Early defenders and conceptualizers of mercantilism like Thomas Mun continually reprove the British consumer for upsetting the balance of trade by a taste for foreign luxuries,[17] and the author of *Britannia Languens, or a Discourse of Trade* of 1680 was much exercised with the ways in which the English merchant and shopkeeper might "avoid Trading in Foreign Consumptive Goods."[18] Moreover, as Louis Landa has shown in a fascinating article on Pope's portrait of Belinda, English guilds and economic writers blame women in particular for their extravagant tastes. In *The Weavers' Complaint Against the Calico Madams* (1719), for instance, the fashionable lady is denounced for her desire for "foreign trumpery" rather than good English wool; and in two numbers of a London newspaper that was entitled *General Remarks on Trade*, Charles Povey decries the losses England incurs by importing – from France – a series of goods clearly marked as feminine or effeminate: "fans, girdles, masks, looking glasses, feathers, pins, needles, and tortoise shell combs."[19] The huge irony of such invectives against female luxury – a phrase that denotes, as I have suggested, both an excessive desire and the objects thereof – is that the transformation of ostensibly "superfluous" desires into needs was at the very heart of the expanding international capitalist system with its thriving trade in items like tobacco, sugar, and slaves – "goods" that were all publicly criticized, from their first appearance in Britain, as morally evil but which all became "necessary luxuries" over time. At the very time when mercantilists were arguing strenuously for a so-called "free" market, unhampered by royal monopolies (or, perversely, by colonial production),[20] the female and her always-already excessive desire seems to become a locus for male writers' expressions of desire for restraint and control on the system of exchange for profit. If the problem of luxury is at the heart of the transition from a feudal to a capitalist mode of production – and the efforts to rationalize and justify the transition – it is fair to say that luxury comes on the scene of Renaissance cultural and economic debate not only gendered female but also often looking like a theatrical apparition.

The theater, indeed, like the royal curiosity cabinet, played an important role in extending Luxuria's sway to – and from – the New World. When Behn offers flies – by which I think she means butterflies rather than the buzzing type of insect – to the King's Kunstkammer and a feathered headdress to his theater, she dramatizes the ways in which both of those relatively new European institutions were coming to function as showcases for New World luxury objects, and also – in the case of the theater at least – as sites for displaying, *as* objects and for profit, the exotically garbed and painted and tattooed bodies of non-Europeans who were brought to the stages of European cities, and also European courts, to work in a highly paradoxical and still insufficiently understood fashion. Unlike the Africans and Indians pressed into manual slave labor in American mines and sugar plantations, persons of color who worked in various European theatrical spaces, among them public stages, royal entries, and courtly masques, labored at "playing" fantasized versions of themselves while displaying their bodies – and the fruits of their weaving and feather-working skills – for Europeans' pleasure. Jody Greene has recently argued, however, that in some cases these non-European performers may also have used their experience as objects of the European gaze to pursue their own personal and military aims, aims of the native *subject*, that is, which were not fully known to Renaissance Europeans and are also imperfectly known to modern scholars.[21]

In the early years of European colonialism, voyagers frequently brought Native Americans back to Europe; among the causes of the practice mentioned by Christian Feest in *Indians in Europe* were desires to give "living proof" of the voyage, to "arouse the curiosity of those who might fund or participate in future voyages," and to "cultivate interpreters."[22] It is very unlikely that any of the early Indians crossed the Atlantic voluntarily (Feest, p. 614); the Aztec man represented in fig. 8.4, for instance, was brought as booty by his people's conqueror, Cortés, to the court of Charles V.[23] It is by no means certain, however, what economic and legal arrangements obtained for later Amerindian and African performers in Europe. Some small fraction of the former group, Jody Greene has argued, may have chosen to come to Europe, or come at the behest of their own fathers or tribal chiefs. Acknowledging the difficulties of evidence and interpretation that attend such an

Figure 8.4 Watercolor by Christoph Weiditz representing an Aztec man with a parrot at the court of Charles V in 1529.

argument (to what extent, for instance, are we to *believe* those travelers "who claim that their captives were actually volunteers" [Greene, "New Historicism," p. 175]?), Greene usefully cautions against assuming too quickly (as she thinks many New Historicists have) that (most) Amerindians were simply "displayed" in Europe like the objects collected for curiosity cabinets. Yet in her eagerness to criticize a critical tendency to write as if the Native Americans had no agency in their visits to Europe, Greene arguably neglects some of the tricky political implications of her own position, which at times risks making the "conquest" of America into an "encounter" ultimately beneficial to the Indians.[24] The waters we are sailing between subject and object are ideologically stormy. Moralizing polemic, at this point in the uneven development of "New World studies" within the field of Renaissance studies, often risks conjuring the parable of the mote in the brother's (or sister's) eye.

We know too little about both the subjectivities of non-Europeans who worked on European stages and the objective conditions under which they worked: what was the economic and legal status of those Indians and Africans who played in gorgeous costumes for aristocratic and common viewers such as those who witnessed Henri II's entry into Rouen in 1550?[25] Were they slaves and if so, according to what laws? Did the laws of various countries and theatrical institutions treat Indians and Africans differently? A case of 1569 had determined that slave status (apparently, in general) would not be recognized in the "pure air" of England, for instance; but as Folarin Shyllon observes, in *Butts* v. *Penny* of 1677 a diametrically opposed opinion – here specified as pertaining to negroes – was upheld. The legal opinion that blacks could be considered "merchandise" (because they were "infidels," which would also apply to most Native Americans) was in turn reversed (or rather, in Shyllon's phrase, "not countenanced") by Sir John Holt of the Court of the King's Bench, who declared in various late seventeenth-century cases, culminating in *Smith* v. *Brone & Cooper* of 1701, that "as soon as a Negro comes into England, he becomes free; one may be a villein in England but not a slave."[26] Judge Holt's view may or may not have been shared by the judge who decided a case of 1687 mentioned in passing by Eric Williams, a case "involving an Amerindian, 'a monster in the Indies,' who had been exhibited in England for profit."[27] Was the "exhibition for profit" illegal on the grounds that the Indian could not be treated as chattel in England's pure air? I do not yet know the answer to this question, and Eric Williams gives me little help in pursuing it; he provides no annotation on the case or the court in which it was brought. This seems somehow ironic, given that Williams mentions this case in the course of discussing the "silence" of the seventeenth-century intelligentsia about the economic aspect of slavery. Modern literary scholars who seek to become less silent about the economics of slavery need not only curiosity but also money and time to comb English and other European countries' legal records if we want to account more precisely for the nature of the work represented in visual examples of "exotic" performers such as the following: Filippo d'Aiglié's drawing of Indians and Europeans dancing in a 1650 performance of the ballet *Il Tabacco* in Turin, at the court of Christine, Duchess of Savoy (fig. 8.5); and a painting by an anonymous artist of an elaborately befeathered African in the *Grand Ballet et Comédie des Nopces* [*sic*] *de Pélée et Thétis* performed at the French court in 1654 (fig. 8.6)"[28]

Because of the gaps in our (or at least my) current knowledge of a mode of work which seems, *pace* Greene, very much like a form of slavery located in theatrical rather than plantation or mining spaces, we encounter, when we look at these European representations of European spectacles featuring non-European performers (as well as Europeans dressed to look like exotic "others"), a vertiginous hall of mirrors that shuttles us, as viewers, back and forth between problems of objectification and (hypothesized or fantasized) subjectivity. Within this eerily postmodern space of simulacra, we can however draw a conceptual link between, and perhaps thereby construct something like a little knowledge about, these depictions of exotic performers on European stages and the image reproduced above, allegedly showing Anne Bracegirdle in the role of an Indian Queen wearing a feather headdress. The white actress (as you can see if you turn back to fig. 8.3) is tended by exotic plumed children who combine characteristics of Amerindians and Africans in a conflation typical of the so-called discourse of primitivism;[29] and the detail of the feathers adorning both the actress and her attendants works, I think, to suggest that despite the contrasting heights and colors of the figures depicted here – and the difference in social status signaled by those contrasts – there is nonetheless some ideologically important kinship among these figures. The mode of kinship is paradoxical but intriguing, since it resides in the fact that all of these figures are *not* what they seem. A white Englishwoman is playing an American (red- or "tawny"-skinned) Indian and black African children are playing that Queen's presumably Indian attendants. The significance of theatrical illusion is underscored, I think, by the ornamentation of humans with feathers, "clothes" appropriated, as it were, from creatures of another species. That species was enormously admired, both in American and European cultures; in many of the cultures homogenized by the very terms "Amerindian" and "European," birds were often associated with the divine or superhuman. In this connection, marvellous "grand Perroquet" forming the "coiffure" of the Frenchman playing an "Indian

Figure 8.5   Filippo d'Aiglié's drawing of Indians and Europeans dancing in a scene from the ballet *Il Tabacco* performed in 1650 in Turin, at the court of Christine, Duchess of Savoy.

Academistes de Chiron.   Le Roy.   Mᵗˢ Sainctot.
Bontemps: Cabou. Les Sʳˢ Mollier, Bruneau, Langlois...
Baptiste, le Vacher, Beauchamp, deForge, et Dolinet. ∞...

Figure 8.6 Painting of African or "Moorish" dancer playing "Le Roy" in the *Grand Ballet et Comédie des Nopces de Pélée et Thétis*, performed at the French court in 1654.

drummer" in an engraving by François Chauveau (Paris, 1670) after a drawing by Charles Perrault (Fig. 8.7).[30] Yet birds also comprise, in European mythologies, a species some of whose members are reviled and associated with danger and error: bird feathers allow Daedalus to indulge his son Icarus' hubristic desire, for instance, and the cawing, black-feathered crow was often a symbol, in Renaissance art and literature, for false or servile imitation. Also tarring and feathering was of course a favorite European mode of punishment. The artist seems particularly caught, one might say, in a net of bird symbolism, as an imitator, as a Hermes-like interpreter between divine, human, and demonic realms, and, of course, as someone who relied on a pen made from a feather in order to write at all.

Feathers work, in Behn's novella as in the engraving of Bracegirdle as Semernia, to suggest an intriguing but deeply problematic kinship between a white woman and non-white "others," fictionalized as a blend of African and Indian, who meet in a theatricalized space to marvel at each other in a facsimile (but it is only a facsimile) of mutual curiosity and pleasure. Accompanied (and, she suggests, protected from possible danger) by her handsome but effeminized Oroonoko, who has himself lamented his slavery as a condition of being made "like an ape or monkey, a sport for women" (61), the narrator visits an Indian village where the natives are wearing feathers. So, it turns out, is Aphra Behn. Describing not only her own act of looking at the exotic other, but also their act of looking at *her* as an exotic other, she writes that "They were all naked; and we were dress'd ... very glittering and rich" (55); but we learn later, and by now predictably, that the Indians are not really naked (they have paint and girdles and feathers and even mutilations as ornaments to their faces and bodies); and we learn, too, that the narrator is not really dressed, if one defines being dressed according to traditional standards of feminine modesty and in binary opposition to nakedness. "My own Hair was cut short," Behn goes on to remark, "and I had a taffety Cap, and black Feathers on my Head" (55).

Here, particularly through the detail of the "black feathers," which I see as signifying, among other things, her status as a user of a quill-pen and black ink,[31] Behn creates a version of that cross-dressing which Marjorie Garber has analyzed in a section of her book *Vested Interests* wittily entitled "Clothes Encounters of the Third Kind." Garber defines cross-dressing as a third term that is *not* a positive term for a third (androgynous) sex but rather a way of "articulating and describing a space of possibility" and hence of both interrogating and perhaps escaping – albeit temporarily – from various stultifying cultural binaries, including "male vs. female" and "European vs. Other."[32] In this light, it

Timballier et Trompette Indiens

Quatriesme Quadrille

F.C. deli. et sculp.

Figure 8.7   Frenchmen playing "Indian drummer and trumpeter" in the "Carousel" festival of Louis XIV, June 1662. Engraving by François Chauveau (Paris, 1670) after a drawing by Charles Perrault.

is worth mentioning that Behn herself was described as an exemplar of a superior "third sex" in a poem by Daniel Kendrick published to praise (and advertise) Behn's own pastoral poem *Lycidus*, which was published in 1688, the very year *Oroonoko* appeared.[33] The poem praising Behn as a member of a "Third Sex" suggests, however, that there are vested interests of an economic kind (a kind that Garber arguably underplays in her book) infusing and definitely limiting the fluid "space of possibility" created by Behn's playful representation of a scene of fantastic mutual admiration between herself, her black slave (who serves here as a kind of theater manager, providing "entertainment"), and the Native Americans. For in this scene as in the book as a whole, Behn is advertising herself, along with the (regrettably lost) colony and its inhabitants, to metropolitan readers of both sexes and especially to a male sovereign whose gaze she hopes to attract. Her reference to the gift of the feathered headdress serves at once to remind the King and Behn's readers that she is a playwright and imaginatively to substitute a "gift economy" – obtaining between herself and her (desired) patron the King – for the capitalist system of buying and selling commodities in which Behn was in fact operating.[34] In 1688, she was out of favor as a playwright and hence unable to garner the "Third Night" receipts upon which she had mainly depended for her livelihood. Her reference to her own hand as a standard for measuring the exotic "flies" that she gave the King suggests, I would argue, that she is not only a woman with a body worth noticing but also a writer whose "hand" both makes and presents books.

In the book named *Oroonoko*, which Behn explicitly and not without signs of guilt offers as a substitute for the narrative Oroonoko might himself have told (and which she offers more obliquely, I have argued elsewhere, as a symbolic substitute for his dismembered body and that of the unborn child he kills when he kills the pregnant Imoinda),[35] we have a partial representation, partial in both senses of the word, of a cultural system in which actors, white women, Native Americans and Africans of both sexes shared versions of a subject position we might define simply as that of "being on display in and for the market." (Seventeenth-century women writers like Mary Lee Chudleigh and Margaret Cavendish explicitly draw an analogy between the "selling" of women as wives and the selling of men as slaves.)[36] Behn's book also shows, however, that this international economic and cultural system allowed literate white women to assume, along with their "display" position, the positions of author, of collector, and of transporter and seller of exotic objects and images. Such positions, usually reserved for white men, were *partially* available to Behn and virtually never open to the non-white subject–objects of her professional woman's gaze.

NOTES

1 Montrose has analyzed this paradigm in "The Work of Gender in the Discourse of Discovery," *Representations* 33 (Winter 1991), 1–41; see esp. p. 1. According to this paradigm, both the landscape and the inhabitants of the New World are gendered female while the European explorer is, of course, male – and usually, even from the early phase of the conquest, a male in competition with another male for possession of the ostensibly virgin land.

In the initial phase of the conquest, the Spanish competed with the Portuguese, appealing to their mutual father the Pope to adjudicate their dispute; and later, the latecoming English competed with the Spanish, in a phase wonderfully exemplified by Sir Walter Ralegh as analyzed by Montrose. Ralegh's language of description in his *Discourse of the Discoverie of Guiana* (1595) draws on the tradition of the blazon of the female body that Nancy Vickers has analyzed in "Diana Described: Scattered Woman and Scattered Rhyme," *Critical Inquiry* 8 (1981), 265–79. Ralegh uses such metaphorical passages as the famous one about "Guiana" as a "countrey that hath yet her maydenhead" to "convey a proleptically elegiac sympathy for this unspoiled world at the same time that it arouses excitement at the prospect of despoiling it" (p. 12) and also to create a triangular relationship whereby "a masculine writer shares with his readers the verbal construction/ observation of a woman or feminized object or matter; in doing so, he creates a masculinized subject position for his readers to occupy and share" (Montrose, "Gender," p. 13).

2   For different accounts of Behn's sojourn in Guiana see Angeline Goreau, *Reconstructing Aphra: A Social Biography of Aphra Behn* (New York, 1989), pp. 49–69, Sara Mendelson, *The Mental World of Stuart Women* (Brighton, 1987), 23–35. Campbell hypothesizes a six-year visit whereas Mendelson argues for a two-month stay between January and February 1664. For a discussion of the historical evidence pertaining to Behn's visit see Margaret Ferguson, "News from the New World: Miscegenous Romance in Aphra Behn's *Oroonoko* and *The Widow Ranter*," in David Lee Miller, Sharon O'Dair, and Harold Weber, eds., *The Production of English Renaissance Culture* (Ithaca, 1994), p. 155 n. 7.

3   See, for instance, Goreau, *Reconstructing Aphra*, p. 289.

4   See Brown's important article "The Romance of Empire: *Oroonoko* and the Trade in Slaves," in Felicity Nussbaum and Laura Brown, eds., *The New Eighteenth Century* (New York, 1987), pp. 40–61.

5   See Behn, *Oroonoko, or the Royal Slave*, with an introduction by Lore Metzger (New York, 1973), p. 8. All quotations are from this edition.

6   Eric Williams, *Capitalism and Slavery* (Chapel Hill, N.C., 1944), quoted in Barbara L. Solow and Stanley L. Engerman, eds., *British Capitalism & Caribbean Slavery* (Cambridge, 1987), p. 1.

7   See Michel de Certeau, *The Writing of History* (1975), trans. Tom Conley (New York, 1988), esp. the introduction ("Writings and Histories") and ch. 1 ("Making History: Problems of Method and Problems of Meaning").

8   *The Journals of Christopher Columbus*, trans. Cecil Jane (New York, 1989), p. 194.

9   Citations of *Paradise Lost* are from *Milton's Complete Poetry and Major Prose*, ed. Merritt Hughes (New York, 1957).

10 For a brilliant analysis of this ideological binarism in Columbus's writing, see Peter Hulme, *Colonial Encounters: Europe and the Native Caribbean, 1492–1797* (New York, 1986).

11 See Margreta de Grazia's essay in this volume for an analysis of this ideologically charged phrase from *King Lear*.

12 For important discussions of these forerunners of the modern museum see

Julius von Scholosser, *Die Kunst und Wunderkammern der Spätrenaissance: Ein Beitrag zur Geschichte des Sammelwesens* (1908; rpt. Braunschweig: Klinkhardt und Biermann, 1978); Jean Céard, ed., *La Curiosité à la Renaissance* (Paris, 1986); Oliver Impey and Arthur Macgregor, eds., *The Origins of Museums: The Cabinet of Curiosities in Sixteenth- and Seventeenth-Century Europe* (Oxford, 1985); and Steven Mullaney, "Strange Things, Gross Terms, Curious Customs: The Rehearsal of Cultures in the Late Renaissance," in Stephen Greenblatt, ed., *Representing the English Renaissance* (Berkeley, 1988), pp. 65–89. (Also published as ch. 3, "The Rehearsal of Cultures," of Mullaney's *The Place of the Stage: License, Play, and Power in Renaissance England* [Chicago, 1988]). See also Jody Greene, "New Historicism and Its New World Discoveries," in *The Yale Journal of Criticism* 4 (Spring 1991), 163–98.

13 On the idea of the "marvel," see Stephen Greenblatt, *Marvelous Possessions: The Wonder of the New World* (Chicago, 1991).

14 Rosamund Gilder, in *Enter the Actress: The First Women in the Theatre* (1931; rpt. New York, 1960), pp. 167–8, notes that there is no record of Anne Bracegirdle playing the part of Dryden's "Indian Queen" and so surmises either that the Vincent mezzotint engraving is of Anne Marshall (who did play that part) or of Bracegirdle playing in Behn's *The Widow Ranter*. The *Biographical Dictionary of Actors ... 1600–1800*, vol. II, ed. Philip H. Highfill, Jr., Kalman A. Burnam, Edward A. Langhams et al. (Carbondale, Ill., 1973), unequivocally captions its reproduction of the engraving with the phrase "ANNE BRACEGIRDLE as Semernia" (p. 270); but Stephen Orgel has recently suggested, in a personal communication, that the attribution may be problematic. I shall accept it (as does the Harvard Theatre Collection) until I discover evidence to the contrary.

15 In his *Luxury and Capitalism* (1913; rpt. Ann Arbor, Mich., 1967), Werner Sombart demonstrates that the ideological connection between women's "nature" and luxury persists into the twentieth century. The acquisition of luxuries is driven, he exclaims, by the "influence of the women! Even more the influence of the mistress"; women "invent other allurements to increase the comforts of their living rooms and to entrap men there" (pp. 102–3).

16 As Philip Siegelman remarks in his usefully skeptical introduction to Sombart's *Luxury and Capitalism*, the relation between luxury, asceticism, and capitalist development has been probed by writers from Mandeville through Adam Smith, Marx, Veblen, to Galbraith (p. xxiv), with no consensus in sight. In his *Luxury: The Concept in Western Thought, Eden to Smollett* (Baltimore, 1977), John Sekora usefully surveys the history of the idea without, however, adding much to the debate about luxury's relation to capitalism either as "cause" (for Sombert, the desire for luxury, which he generally treats as an atemporal "given" of human nature, "gave birth" to capitalism) or as an effect, or – in a more dialectical view – as both.

17 For an incisive discussion of Mun and other early mercantilists, as well as their opponents, see Joyce Appleby, *Economic Thought and Ideology in Seventeenth-Century England* (Princeton, 1978). See also Eric Williams, *From Columbus to Castro: The History of the Caribbean* (1970; rpt. New York, 1984), p. 40, on invectives against trade in "useless things."

18   Sir William Petyt (?), *Britannia Languens, or a Discourse on Trade* (1680), rpt. in J. R. McCulloh, ed., *Early English Tracts on Commerce* (Cambridge, 1952), p. 421. The passage is cited (along with others illustrating economic writers' anxiety about female luxury and its costs to England) by Louis Landa, "Pope's Belinda, The General Emporie of the World, and the Wondrous Worm," *The South Atlantic Quarterly*, 70 (Spring 1971), 215–35; see 227–8 for the citations from *Britannia Languens*, which Landa describes as "doubtfully attributed" to Petyt.

19   Both the *Weavers' Complaint* and Povey's newspaper essays are cited in Landa, pp. 226–7, notes 18 and 22.

20   See Eric Williams, *From Columbus to Castro*, pp. 164–5 and *passim*, for a discussion of the contradictions in mercantilist ideology and its allowances for metropolitan enterprises to be protected from colonial ones.

21   See Greene's "New Historicism," cited above, n. 12.

22   See Christian F. Feest's epilogue to his collection *Indians in Europe* (Aachen, 1987), p. 614; my quoted phrases are from Jody Greene's summary of Feest's argument, "New Historicism," 175.

23   The picture is discussed in William C. Sturtevant, "First Visual Images of Native America," in Fredi Chiappelli, ed., *First Images of America: The Impact of the New World on the Old* (2 vols., Berkeley, 1976), I, pp. 417–54. On Indians as slaves see John Hemming, *Red Gold: The Conquest of the Brazilian Indians, 1500–1760* (Cambridge, Mass., 1978). As Jody Greene remarks ("New Historicism," n. 24), an account of the Aztecs enslaved by Cortés who eventually ended up performing their acrobatic tricks at the court of Pope Clement VII in Rome may be found in Bernal Diaz del Castillo, *The True History of the Conquest of Mexico*, trans. Maurice Keatinge (London, 1927), II, pp. 498–504.

24   Tzvetan Todorov, whose *The Conquest of America* Greene cites admiringly, has been criticized along just these lines for seeming at times – particularly in his emphasis on and favorable evaluation of European skills of *communication* (literacy) – to justify the conquest as (ultimately) beneficial to the Indians. This critique, which Greene does not cite, seems germane to the work of many Anglo-American scholars currently negotiating the question of their own investment(s) in the topic of early European colonialism. See Deborah Root, "The Imperial Signifier: Todorov and The Conquest of America," *Cultural Critique* 9 (Spring 1988), 197–219.

25   In "New Historicism," Greene counters Mullaney's reading of the Rouen entry in "The Rehearsal of Cultures" (cited above, n. 12) by arguing that the Rouen townspeople, funded by local merchants, relied on Brazilian "actors" who may well have been living in Rouen for some time, who may have come to France voluntarily (though there is no clear evidence for this) and who were definitely not regarded by the French as "monstrous" curiosities because the aim of the entry was not to create (as Mullaney argues) a "detailed mise-en scène of Brazilian culture" but rather "a carefully composed representation of the harmonious trading relations between the French and their Tupinamba associates" – relations that the King was threatening to undermine (Greene, 170).

26   The contradictory cases are discussed by and cited in Folarin Shyllon, *Black People in Britannia, 1555–1833* (London, 1977), p. 17.

27   Williams, *From Columbus to Castro*, p. 207.

28   I am indebted to my colleague Claire Farago for initially directing me to these images and to Liesel Nolan for helping me find the locations of the originals. An English example of a performance dramatizing Indians is the masque, with text by George Chapman and sets and costumes by Inigo Jones, presented on 15 February 1613 to celebrate the marriage of Princess Elizabeth and Frederick, Elector Palatine. As Suzanne Boorsch notes, the characters included "a chorus of Virginian priests" who "sing songs to the Sun but are then urged to worship 'our Briton Phoebus,' that is, James I" (Boorsch, "America in Festival Presentations," in Chiappeli, *First Images*, I, p. 512. For a reproduction of the design for one Indian torchbearer, the only remaining design for this masque, see Stephen Orgel and Roy Strong, *Inigo Jones: The Theatre of the Stuart Court* (2 vols., Berkeley and London, 1973), I, p. 256.

29   For this conflation see David Brion Davis, *The Problem of Slavery in Western Culture* (Ithaca, 1966), p. 480; and Boorsch, "America in Festival Presentations," pp. 505–6.

30   Boorsch discusses the "so-called Indians" (played by French noblemen) in this engraving and remarks on the merging of exotic types effected by the use of a "parrot for a headdress" when the Indian in question is evidently from the East, not from the New World, since the procession of Indians was followed by a brigade of "Americans" led by the Duke of Guise ("America in Festival Presentations," pp. 505–6).

31   For a fine discussion of the links Behn draws between blackness and the writer's tool of ink, see Catherine Gallagher, "The Author–Monarch and the Royal Slave: *Oroonoko* and the Blackness of Representation," ch. 2 of *Nobody's Story: The Vanishing Acts of Women Writers in the Marketplace, 1670–1820*, (Berkeley, 1994).

32   See Garber's *Vested Interests: Cross Dressing and Cultural Anxiety* (New York, 1992), p. 11.

33   For Kendrick's poem see *The Works of Aphra Behn*, ed. Montague Summers (6 vols., 1915; rpt. New York, 1967), VI, pp. 296–8.

34   In "Owning Oroonoko: Behn, Southerne, and the Contingencies of Property," *Renaissance Drama*, n.s., 23 (1992), 25–58, Laura J. Rosenthal argues shrewdly that Behn seeks to deny her own implication in the "commodification of discourse" by depicting an idealized "gift economy" in the African and New World settings of *Oroonoko*.

35   See Margaret Ferguson's essay, "Transmuting *Othello*: Aphra Behn's *Oroonoko*," in Marianne Novy, ed., *Cross-Cultural Perspectives: Differences in Women's Revisions of Shakespeare* (Urbana, Ill., 1993), pp. 15–49.

36   For these and other instances of the "wife–slave" analogy, see my article "Juggling the Categories of Race, Class and Gender: Aphra Behn's *Oroonoko*," *Women's Studies: An Interdisciplinary Journal* 19 (1991), 165 and n. 27; rpt. in Margo Hendricks and Patricia Parker, eds., *Women, "Race," Writing* (London, 1994).

9 Unlearning the Aztec *cantares* (preliminaries to a postcolonial history)

Gary Tomlinson

Whatever else it might do for scholars nurtured in Eurocentric traditions, postcolonialism brings with it enforced, penetrating, and mystifying dialogue. It destabilizes once-solid models of subjectivity and objectivity, breaks down old orders of enclosed selves and separate others. It offers relationism, context, and parallax as means of self-definition and thus hybridizes one subject-situation with others. It is a locale of decentering strategies that travel, these days, under many names: Lyotard's paralogies, the fractal landscapes of Arjun Appadurai's transnational anthropology, Houston Baker's intertwining vernacular discourses, and Homi Bhabha's in-between spaces of enunciation, to rehearse a few.[1]

Something like hybridization inhabits our histories too. A postcolonial historiography pushes into the light of day the challenge of the encounter between historian and past subjectivities. It embraces as part of historical story-telling itself analysis of the negotiations extending between the present-day scrutinizer and the scrutinized past (a past accorded little bargaining power in an earlier historiography and referred to as the historian's "object"). It calls upon the historian to relinquish the notion of a pristine *re*construction of some past reality in favor of a hybrid construction forefronting today's strategies, intents, and desires as well as those of past others.

The move away from the goal of reconstruction is no simple matter, notwithstanding the uneasiness we feel these days at its recollections of earlier historicisms: of objective, scientific retrieval of the past and the Rankean "wie es eigentlich gewesen." The goal of reconstruction is endemic even in histories informed by post-structuralist thinking, histories now long after the "linguistic turn." It is endemic because it is necessary. What we do in thinking historically is in a fundamental way bound up in a quest for authentic knowledge of past actions and intents. To abandon utterly this quest would be to relinquish a developing ideology that has defined western historiography since at least the sixteenth century. This we have found difficult to do.

Still, a postcolonial approach to history complicates the reconstructive

260

urge by joining with it a newly permeable and vulnerable version of the historian's subjectivity projected onto the past. The resulting historical construction is concerned not only with past actors and actions but with why and how the historian makes them thus. It merges history, the study of the past, with historiography, the study of how we study the past. Yet the merger is shot through with productive tension: in emphasizing the meeting in dialogue of historian and historical subject it amplifies the dissonance between the pastness of the things we seek to understand and the presentness of our seeking to understand them. It magnifies the distance between our abiding self-concern and our fearful curiosity about others, opening a space for those others that we cannot fully inhabit. It is a history of the present that never relinquishes its faith in its ability to grasp a distant, other past but that is always undone or undermined by the otherness at its goal.

From this solid but unstable faith, this belief that affirms at once our comprehension and the stark, inaccessible otherness of what we comprehend, a new historical goal emerges: not to recreate a docile past "the way it really was" but to build a past that resists our intellectual attempts to occupy it even while it takes its shape from us – and, moreover, takes only the shape we give it. We build into our histories a keen responsiveness to the evidence of the historical traces we (for our own reasons) select. This responsiveness abides by our own, modern western ways of logical concatenation and sequencing, of causation and narration. It allows, in this abiding western modernity and in the particularity of the traces adduced, only *this* specific story to be told. Yet we also build in our histories an overlay on this modernism that takes the form of the signs of the indelible resistance the traces of others offer to our own ways of knowing. We order those traces into a story, but at the same time we uncover in them a Derridean remainder that undoes the narrative and strikes sparks at the peripheries of our colonizing comprehension. The traces of others empower us to tell tales but do not in the process relinquish their own power; they manifest this power by undermining the tales they enable. In writing postcolonial histories we inscribe at every moment our confident mastery and the unbounded, uncanny ability of others to elude it.

Postcolonial historiography, then, is characterized by a dialogue of complementary comprehension and mystification, of knowledge at once full and thwarted. Yet in a postcolonial history of an overtly colonial encounter – a history of the encounters of Spaniards and Americans in the sixteenth century, to take the example I will be concerned with – this colloquy between historian and past other is not the only prominent dialogue. It is entangled with another one, the one between past actors themselves, between conquerors and conquered, between colonizers and colonized.[2] In this dialogue, too, masterful knowledge of others and others' evasion of knowing mastery stand in productive and tense proximity. Here too the construction of others is at once controlled and elusive. Though this dialogue within the historian's dialogue is no doubt especially marked in a postcolonial history of dramatic encounters (Europeans and Native Americans, Europeans and Africans, etc.), it will also appear in other histories insofar as we can emphasize in them the innate dialogism of human communication. For this reason a postcolonial historiography might be said to be characteristically recursive: its dialogism is compounded, operating along two primary axes, one from our present to an imagined past and another entirely within that past. The decentering, deconstructive potential of its dialogue is raised, so to speak, to the second power.[3]

The juxtaposition in our historical (and other) dialogues of comprehension and mystification, what we might call their constructive uncanniness, emerges repeatedly and with singular force from the space between speech and song. This space maps the distance between utterance marked as normal in a culture and utterance marked in any number of ways as "heightened," for want of a better metaphor. The distance seems to be recognized – if, again, in myriad ways – in all cultures, which is to say that all cultures seem to have discovered in their experiences of language the potential for a graded series of manners of utterance. The gradations typically include such hard-to-delimit things as plain speech, self-consciously formal, rhetorical, or ritual speech, incantation, chant, formalized shouts and cries, and full-fledged song. Worldwide, what we consider the nonspeech portion of this list is not very well served by our relatively recent and culturally limited coinage "music," which, if it includes much not found in most varieties of indigenous song, nevertheless excludes much marked off from many varieties of indigenous speech. But whatever we call heightened, nonspeech utterances, it is repeatedly clear that they make up some of the most captivating, challenging, and unsettling moments in our experiences of others. They are a chief locus for our mystification by others, a primary avatar of the dialogical uncanny. It is likewise clear, from many sources, that this was true for sixteenth-century Europeans in the Americas as well. In this essay I will attempt to give freer reign to such uncanniness than it has until now had by moving with certain Aztec songs along the two chief axes of postcolonial historiography.

Aztec song seems an ideal subject for such an attempt. In the first place, even though (as we will see) it has been weighed down with more than its share of our own unexamined ideological baggage, its palpable, occasionally spectacular, foreignness begs us to look hard at the dialogue we enact with and through it. Moreover, the frankly colonial aspect of its surviving traces distances them in complex ways from the autochthonous reality they ostensibly reflect, highlighting the dialogue between colonizers and colonized. And, not least, all these traces are suffused with the deep uncanniness of others' singing.

The legacy of Aztec song is fragmentary, alienated, and alienating. It takes many forms: depictions of singing and instrumental accompaniment in both precontact and colonial picture-codices; preserved instruments now sitting mute in museum collections; more-or-less accepting, bemused, and confused reports of indigenous singing by Spanish friars and other colonizers; long and short testimonies on the functions of song and dance in indigenous ceremony both in Spanish and in alphabetized Nahuatl, the language of the Mexica and the lingua franca, insofar as one existed, of the Aztec dominion (chief among these are the testimonies in Bernardino de Sahagún's huge protoethnographic survey, the so-called *Florentine Codex*); and a substantial number of song texts transmitted in various manuscripts in alphabetized Nahuatl.

By any measure the most tantalizing document of this legacy is the manuscript entitled *Cantares mexicanos* or *Mexica Songs*, one section of a modest, late sixteenth-century miscellany now in the Biblioteca Nacional of Mexico City (MS 1628bis). It preserves the texts of ninety-one songs in alphabetized Nahuatl. The genesis of the manuscript is obscure, the dating of its contents warmly debated by Mexicanists. Some of its *cantares* clearly date from after the Spanish conquest; others may in some form antedate it; all probably reflect, if in ways difficult to gauge, traditions that reach back to prehispanic times.

The *cantares* have come to bear an extraordinary historiographical burden over the last sixty years or so, especially since the fundamental work on them of Angel María Garibay K.[4] They have been seen as important new evidence for an old interpretation of Mexican culture on the eve of the conquest. This interpretation proposes the existence of a noble, melancholic, stoic, and philosophic facet of Aztec society opposed to its warfare, human sacrifice, and cannibalism. Scholarly scrutiny of the *cantares* has immeasurably helped this interpretation to proliferate. It has encouraged our imagining of fifteenth-century poet–philosopher–rulers in Mexico musing on the ephemerality of mortal existence, rulers like Prince Tecayehuatzin of Huexotzinco, for example, or, signally, King Nezahualcoyotl of Texcoco, likened in recent accounts to Alexander the Great, Lorenzo the Magnificent, and the psalm-singing King David. Some of the *cantares* have been advanced as the work of

Nezahualcoyotl and others like him. Such sage rulers, to quote a recent synopsis of the story by Davíd Carrasco, "preserved honored traditions, produced and read the painted manuscripts, and developed refined metaphors and poems to probe the true foundations of human existence."[5]

Carrasco's refined metaphors are especially significant in the vision of Aztec culture fostered by the *cantares*. Already in the sixteenth century Spanish observers like Sahagún and Diego Durán called attention to the metaphorical nature, the difficulty, the obscurity, and the propensity to conceal idolatry of the indigenous songs they encountered. Garibay more than anyone else transformed this suspicion of native opacity and back-sliding into a poetic virtue. He did so by universalizing the metaphors of the *cantares* to bring them in line with European poetic expectations (in language that recalls no one so much as the seventeenth-century theorist of metaphors Emanuele Tesauro): "The metaphor is the mother of all beauty. In essence it comes to be the nucleus of all poetry ... Nahuatl poems teem with [metaphors] ..." Garibay singled out a particular metaphorical technique that he found to be characteristic of Nahuatl discourse. This device, which he termed *difrasismo* or diphrasis, consists in "joining two metaphors which together yield the symbolic means of expressing a single thought."[6]

Foremost among the metaphors of the *cantares*, and sitting near the heart of the poetic–philosophic interpretation of Aztec culture, is an example of diphrasis. *In xochitl in cuicatl* runs its Nahuatl, meaning roughly "flower and song" and supposedly referring to poetry in particular and the poetic–philosophic mentality in general. For the most important and dedicated proponent of this interpretation of indigenous thought, Garibay's student Miguel León-Portilla, the sages – especially Nezahualcoyotl and his followers in Texcoco – captured in this metaphor a "poetic vision of the universe" that could gain and express "a view of ultimate reality." Their vision led them to question the cult of human sacrifice and to reject the "martial mysticism" of other elements in their society (especially the powerful rulers of Tenochtitlan). It brings them, for us, "near the profoundly human and universal concerns of the sages and philosophers of other times and places." In León-Portilla's writings and those of the many other authors who have followed his and Garibay's lead, *xochicuicatl* provides the perfect liberal humanism for the Aztec empire.[7]

Without prejudice to the achievements and complexity of Aztec society, without doubting the profound fascination it has worked on us, and without even raising the western myths of noble savagery that have always played a part in this fascination and that live on with particular force in the humanistic interpretation, it may be said that the idea of an indigenous philosophy of *xochicuicatl* rests on very thin evidence. Indeed as much has already been said in a growing body of revisionist accounts of prehispanic and colonial Mexican society. Scholars like J. Jorge Klor de Alva, Louise Burkhart, and Serge Gruzinski have challenged analyses of the León-Portilla sort explicitly or implicitly, specifically or generally.[8] James Lockhart and Gordon Brotherston have doubted the ascriptions of particular *cantares* to precontact authors, problematized the notion of indigenous authorship, and questioned the reliability of the chief early source on Nezahualcoyotl's poetic tendencies, Ixtlilxochitl.[9] John Bierhorst has gone so far as to pronounce the whole equation of *xochicuicatl* with poetry an invention of Garibay with no earlier authority.[10]

All these criticisms of the poetic–philosophic interpretation are, I think, well taken. Yet the quality of the evidence at the hermeneutic level of analysis they embody is not my primary concern here. Instead I want to call attention to some ways the manner of preservation of the *cantares* has constrained our view of their nature, their expressive intent, and their makers. I want to scrutinize the way the manuscript's features have conspired with our own assumptions and presumptions to determine a part of our historical lives.

For the collective historical imagination set in motion by the *cantares* in the years since they became objects of serious study has surely been circumscribed by the brute fact of the manuscript's presence; this is true for the most part even of those revisionist scholars who have challenged León-Portilla's interpretation. *Cantares mexicanos* has appeared to us to be nothing less and nothing more than a book of poems. We have started from this seemingly unassailable premise. Yet the premise is not innocent. It carries with it many obvious and some not-so-obvious implications for our understanding and use of the manuscript. We read books; we transcribe and translate their contents; perhaps we scrutinize their physical features. As for poems, we fetishize them with a healthy dose of western aestheticism. We analyze their language, imagery, and form. We install them in canons of "literature" of one sort or another. From within such aesthetic canons we use them as evidence of the expressive aims of past authors and, more broadly, the emotional and intellectual texture of past cultures. Each of these activities has played its role in the construction of the *xochicuicatl* view of Aztec culture.[11]

At the same time the bookishness of the *Cantares mexicanos* has resisted other sorts of uses. The fundamental act of reading takes place within the network of our cultural assumptions about the acquisition of knowledge (a primarily visual process), the nature of language (a dual nature, spoken and written, starting from discrete, relatively little-changing words), its technology (an alphabet), and its relation to things in the world (a representative relation based on conventional, not natural, connections of words to things; two broad kinds of referentiality, literal and figurative). We tap this network every time we read; in unearthing it we recall Derrida's critique of logocentrism and begin to construct a genealogy of western regimens of reading. The other activities mentioned above pose more specific networks of constraint. Varied but compelling disciplinary stipulations are involved in criticism, poetic analysis, paleographical study, and contextual literary history. The limitations of translation, finally, are famous, its philosophical conundrums having stimulated much discussion in the "traduttore–traditore" vein. Yet even these limitations are usually viewed from within a relatively narrow conception of translation's transformative effects, one ill-equipped to address the yawning chasm between Indo-European and Nahuatl expression. (With regard to translating song texts like the *cantares* Gordon Brotherston's warning of 1972 holds true today: "The valences of words in lyrical Nahuatl, especially focal terms like 'xochitl,' are so different from those available in Indo-European grammatical patterns as to make translation a hatchet affair ...")[12] All these things together have compelled us to see the songs in a dim but warmly comforting western light.

Among the strategies for achieving a different view that suggest themselves I will outline two here; they are interrelated and conducive to broad refigurations of Aztec culture. First, we might scrutinize the nature of the scripted Nahuatl word itself. Second, we might ponder those elements of the *cantares* unsusceptible (or little susceptible) to written preservation, most importantly, for my present purposes, the features that distinguish them from speech, their "musical" or – the term I will adopt as a less constricting alternative – their "songish" features.

The written Nahuatl word of the early colonial period is an alienated object, suspended between two worlds and belonging fully to neither. It represents what was a signifying wisp in its unwritten indigenous form, a transiently formed air that was wrenched into a European regime soon after the conquest and preserved by its alphabetization according to the rules of Spanish orthography. From the Mexica viewpoint it must have seemed a familiar thing made radically foreign; every historian of early European encounters with Americans knows stories of indigenous wonder at "speaking books," at alphabetic writing and its apparent power to enable speech, song, and precise recall. From our own perspective and that of the Spanish colonizers it might be thought to be the epitome of a distant and unknown object masquerading as something familiar.

What is entailed in reading such a word as a trace of indigenous culture? Clearly something different from what is involved in reading Milton's or the *National Enquirer*'s or even a trouvère's words as traces of their respective authors and cultures. In reading alphabetized Nahuatl of the early colonial period the space between what we read and its imagined source is qualitatively different from such space in our more usual readings. For the *cantares* do not merely reflect in writing an oral practice, do not (more specifically) crystallize an oral tradition that lived in the midst of a larger context that included notions of fixed authorship and alphabetic writing. They do two things whose implications are less ponderable for us than this. They endow Aztec voices with a certain discrete and stable western subjectivity that has no necessary point of reference within indigenous discourses and ontologies, prehispanic or colonial; that is, they fix by means of the text the authority Foucault famously called an "author-function." (I will return to this point later.) And they inscribe oral practices of a people for whom alphabetic writing was not conceivable.

Writing always effects an alteration of spoken or sung language, of course, a change we tend to imagine as a fixing, solidification, or crystallization. However, in the instance of the *cantares* and other early Nahuatl documents, this solidification is of a sort that could not have been foreseen in prehispanic culture. It granted to the language an independent material volume of a sort that must have been utterly foreign to indigenous linguistic usage. The inconceivability of this particular volume in the Nahua mind – or, put positively, the existence there of other valences between utterance, inscription, and the world – challenges at a deep level expectations of linguistic commonality that are basic to our usual modes of historical understanding.

In saying this I do not intend to endorse general analyses of the differences between oral and written cultures like those of Walter J. Ong and Jack Goody.[13] These, notwithstanding the many insights they yield into relations of speech and writing and perceptions of the world involved in each, are too sweeping, too near to older teleological views, too prone to structuralist reification, and too distant from specific language practices in particular cultural situations to be of much help here.[14] Instead I wish to locate in the meeting of Mexica and Spaniards the borderlines of different manners of linguistic registering of the world and to begin to chart the distances between territories in the larger realm Derrida called *écriture*. When Nahuatl was written in Latin characters its ties to a whole view of reality were subtly undone. It was, so to speak, coerced from one inscriptive territory toward another.

The ties that were thus loosened seem once to have brought prehispanic Nahuatl into intimate contact with the material world. What we might imagine as its ephemeral, immaterial orality, that is, probably seemed to the indigenous speaker something more like a voluminous intersection of numerous worldly realms in the structures of Mexica life. Prehispanic Nahuatl, as Serge Gruzinski has put it, "in addition to expressing itself through oral speech and the written word, ... adopted an architectural, iconographical, choreographical, liturgical, musical, ornamental vocabulary that makes doubtful and inevitably partial any attempt at exegesis in our writing."[15] From this multiplicity of reference, this contact with many realms of reality, indigenous Nahuatl gained its own material semantics distinct from the meaningfulness of European written languages. So we must try to conceive Nahuatl in terms that are for us paradoxical. What seems to us its ephemerality as an unalphabetized language must be understood within the larger context of its worldly materiality, its intimate bond to structures external to speech.

Such worldly contact is evident at the level of fundamental grammatical formations. Nahuatl is an agglutinating language, laden with prefixes, infixes, and suffixes, building up lengthy compound words and stringing them together in various ways to put across messages of syntactic or conceptual complexity. Yet even the most basic kernels of this complex grammar, the units that western linguists present for pedagogical convenience as their stems or roots, are not absolutive or abstract in the sense we are accustomed to from our experience of Indo-European languages. They do not have the semantic generality and neutrality we expect in Indo-European roots. Instead of infinitives, the simplest form of a Nahuatl predicative word already assumes a substantive: *cuica* means not "to sing" but instead "he/she/it sings." Instead of absolute nouns, the simplest form of a substantive includes a predicate: *cuicatl* means not simply "song" but something closer to "it/there is a song." The most basic words are, in J. Richard Andrews's term, "sentence-words," irreducible to absolute grammatical abstraction, and he warns us against eliding this difference in our necessarily westernizing translations.[16] Before European contact such irreducibility must have assured that every Nahuatl utterance reached outward to an external context. It reflects a smaller distinction between the linguistic denotation of things and the actions involving them than we habitually presume and binds both tightly to the world around. It marks a material volume fixed in the language and the perceptual modes underlying it.

The solidification brought about by alphabetic writing fostered in Nahuatl a different sort of materiality than this, one at odds with its autochthonous connectedness to things. It created a materiality of a sort that was at that moment consolidating its already substantial hold on the

European mind and closing out other possibilities: the materiality of an independent, representative linguistic system running parallel to the things it denotes. This kind of materiality distanced Nahuatl from the world. In its written form the language came quickly to seem more a means of representing a reality separate from it (like Latin or Spanish) than a constituent part of reality. The precontact valences pertaining between words and things were altered, twisted toward modern western valences.[17]

Of course Mesoamerican cultures had their own systems of writing. These, as Brotherston has warned, must not be minimized either in some teleology that recognizes only alphabetic writing as effective or in the general logocentric suspicion of writing (or rather transcendental exaltation of speech) to which Derrida has drawn our attention.[18] The complex pictographic systems of Mesoamerican writing, preserved on various monuments, in the few prehispanic painted codices that remain, and, in altered forms, in many colonial documents, seem only to underscore the (for us) paradoxical material immateriality of indigenous Nahuatl. They inscribe the world in a palpable, substantial medium not itself distanced from the things it encodes. Gruzinski has written eloquently of the ritual substance the painted codices assumed in prehispanic times and of the rupture of their bond to the broader world that occurred when, after the conquest, their contents were alphabetized. The transference from painting to writing was in his view precisely a loss of the materiality that bound the codices both to the world and to the ritual speech and song they recorded.[19]

Inga Clendinnen pursues a slightly different line of thought. She describes the indigenous view as one in which the experienced world was made up of ephemeral images of a somewhat more stable and enduring sacred reality behind and beyond them. Thus material things in the world – butterflies, quetzal plumes, obsidian knives, *tamales* – were already images of a more real reality; they had the same ontological status as pictures in the codices. "Our art–nature distinction," Clendinnen writes, "lapses where nothing is 'natural'"; in such a view "our world is not the measure for the 'real,' but a fiction, ... its creatures and things called into transitory existence through the painting and the singing of an elaborate pictorial text."[20]

This formulation smacks of a familiar Platonism – Clendinnen even calls the perceived Mexica world "a representation composed out of representations" (214) – and may seem suspect as an interpretation of a Mesoamerican mentality. However, I believe there are important notions lurking in it, especially the ideas of the equivalent constitutive powers of painting and singing and of the absence in indigenous perceptions of the art–nature dichotomy that has served as the basis for western aestheticism. (Oddly, Clendinnen does not pursue very far the implications of this latter notion; it comes at the beginning of a chapter on Aztec "aesthetics.") We may rescue these ideas and alienate Clendinnen's formulation from its Platonic associations with two related qualifications. First, we might insist on the palpable and substantial, not ephemeral, constructive powers of indigenous singing and painting. Clendinnen herself acknowledges (if she does not lengthily explore) the substantiality of Mexica song when she speaks of native "worlds sung into existence" (349).

Second, more broadly, we might note that Clendinnen's idea of a fictive, made world need not entail its immateriality but could just as easily, in the absence of Platonic ontologies, suggest the opposite. That is, we might see the whole indigenous world – godly and human realms, pictures, words – as pervasively materialized. This would shift Clendinnen's dichotomy of mundane ephemerality versus supramundane solidity toward a fully material, fully voluminous, and (by the way) fully sacred dichotomy somewhat like that envisioned by Brotherston: a dichotomy between material presence and (material) absence, between palpable fulness and privation, between "precious tactile splendour and emptiness."[21] Such a shift would have the advantage of distancing us from the suspiciously familiar, nostalgic, and melancholic version of ephemerality that has, as I noted before, played a large role in interpretations of the *cantares*. It would also seem to be warranted even in explicitly sacred indigenous ceremonies, with their emphasis on *ixiptlayotl*, the incarnation (not "impersonation" or "representation," as it is often described) of deities by chosen humans.[22]

At any rate, whatever the material status of pictures and things and sacred truths, Clendinnen suggests that the relation of pictures and things to one another was intimate in Aztec perceptions. The materiality of quetzal plumes and the materiality of pictographic glyphs were equivalent. This equivalence once more conflates the distance between language and things. It makes the glyphs presentations rather than representations of "real" things. Glyphic writing did not set itself apart from the world it presented but rather was absorbed back into it. Its syntax was the syntax of things, not a separate system by which things might be represented.[23]

In this integrated place in the world, this location in the midst of material entities, glyphic writing resembled spoken Nahuatl. This is true of all three sorts of glyphs Mesoamericanists customarily distinguish: iconographic, depicting persons or objects (for example a ruler, palace, or temple); ideographic, depicting concepts or ideas (a volute coming out of a mouth to connote speech); and phonetic (a glyph for water, "atl," to signify the sound *a*, a picture of a bean, "etl," to signify *e*). It is particularly worth lingering over the case of phonetic glyphs, since scholars have most aggressively assimilated these to western forms of writing. At least by the early colonial period (their prehispanic provenance is unclear) these glyphs functioned in a rebus-like manner, the sounds of the words for things depicted adding up to the desired names of places and persons. In the most teleological view they have sometimes been seen as the first step in a progress that would have led inexorably, even in the absence of European contact, toward western alphabetic abstraction. Gruzinski has rightly cautioned against such Whiggishness.[24] In avoiding it we should note at least one crucial distinction between indigenous phonetic glyphs and European phonemes: the glyphs never relinquish their bond to things in the world. They convey the sound of the word for the thing they depict – water, beans, and so forth – and in doing so they bind the person or place they name to the material entity whose sound-essence they borrow. They are not abstract and unworldly in the manner of the phonemes of Indo-European languages, and in this they enhance rather than undermine the material union of language and the world.

There is every reason to believe that this unity of language and the world and the material immateriality of spoken words embraced also sung words and accompanying sounds. This brings me to my second strategy for loosening the conceptual constraints imposed by the manuscript of the *cantares*: a consideration of the elements that set them apart from speech and written poetry, what I have called their songish elements.

Other than their many selfconscious references to singing, accompanimental instruments, and so forth and some enigmatic sequences of syllables that seem to record percussion cadences for the primary Aztec drums, the *huehuetl* and *teponaztli*, the *cantares* do not inscribe their songish traits. In this circumstance discussion of these traits is, to say the least, difficult. In the face of such inscrutability many interpretations of the *cantares* have chosen simply to leave "musical" matters to one side with only the most peripheral mention. Other accounts have dwelled on the "musical" aspects of the *cantares* separately from their "poetic" features and in general fashion, amassing colonial descriptions of indigenous singing, information on Aztec musical instruments, and so forth in hope of shedding light on performances of such "poems." Some few accounts, finally, have attempted specific interpretations of the percussion cadences – interpretations that, in the absence of much evidence apart from the cadences themselves, range from informed speculation to extravagant historical fantasy and bring little insight to the relations of sung words and percussive accompaniment.[25]

All these treatments, it seems to me, miss a very basic aspect of the *cantares*. They approach these song texts as if "music" and "poetry" are in some way distinct and distinguishable in them. Yet the distinction emerges only as an artifact of the Europeanization of the *cantares* – that is, of the alphabetization and inscription that pries them apart from their sung delivery. This process encourages us to comprehend the *cantares* within a specifically European musicopoetic ideology that we have little reason to think should be relevant. It sets up a hierarchy of poetic words and distinct music, with words the primary means of signification and music only a feebly signifying conveyance for them.[26]

In this treatment of the *cantares* the European-style sovereignty of words as independent, representative entities is not challenged. Therefore the absence of their delivery as song with instrumental accompaniment becomes a superficial loss; we can translate and read the songs and analyze their content with scant attention to their songish features and still reassure ourselves that we possess everything essential. The temptation of such reassurance is great. Even Gruzinski, so perceptive on the nature of indigenous language and the differences between painted and alphabetic transmission, sometimes succumbs to it with only slight resistance. In *La colonisation de l'imaginaire*, for example, he contrasts the *cantares* with pictographic expressions because the *cantares* were "easily fixed" in alphabetic writing with only "a crystallization and a Christianization of the oral tradition" as the result (77). It is as if the crystallization were not a fundamental metamorphosis, as if it did not alter the significance of the *cantares* inevitably and at every point. Here again the nonsongish, western materiality of the *Cantares mexicanos*, its palpable presence as a book of poems, limits our hearing, leading us to push the specifically indigenous sung materiality of its contents to the edges of our thought.

Elsewhere Gruzinski voices a different position, one closer to the subtlety of his analysis of pictography. He suggests the profound mutation involved in the alphabetic crystallization of Nahuatl: "The reduction to alphabetic writing leads one to believe that the medium ... is simply the vehicle of the idea of which it is in fact an integral part, from which it is so indissociable as indeed to be the idea."[27] To view the *cantares* in a modern western poetic guise, apart from their songish nature, does not merely render them less vividly communicative than they once were. It brings about more basic changes. It places them in a paradigm of linguistic significance, a particular vision of the relations of words, music, and the world, that is entirely distant from them. It shifts them, once again, into a foreign province of the realm of *écriture*. It insists upon their ability to speak with unfamiliar accents even while aggressively familiarizing them, even in the absence of singing and instrumental accompaniment (not to mention dance, ritual circumstances, etc.). In doing so it robs them of a chief source of their deep, uncanny otherness and alters dramatically their meanings. To enable the *cantares* to speak in a manner less familiar to us we should seek the conflation suggested by Gruzinski of their medium and their significance – elements that it may only be a western habit, after all, to separate.

In restoring to these songs a foreign voice we should seek also, more broadly, the conflation of language and the world implied in Clendinnen's view of the pictographic codices. Where there is no space between pictures or words and things in the world, neither can there be any separable ontological niche for sung words and their accompanying sounds. These then take a position alongside pictures, words, and material objects. Sung words and the things that came along with them in the Mexica world – the introductory finger-whistling; the deep intonations of the *huehuetl*; the resonant wooden thong of the *teponaztli*; perhaps the rhythmic clatter of rattles, the scratchy whisper of rasps, the wail of conch trumpets; the synchronized kinetics of dance; the torchlit incandescence of jeweled, plumed, flowered, and painted costume – all these things that we insist on setting apart as "music" or in some other category were as fully engaged in immanent material reality as words and pictures, as fully pregnant with sacred truths as any other material things.

Prehispanic cultures have left suggestive traces of the unity of their songs with the world. These are the elaborate volutes extending from the mouths of singing deities pictured in some of the codices. Figure 9.1 reproduces a famous example from the Codex Borbonicus, most likely of Mexica origin from around the time of the conquest.

The interconnected, integrated world-conception of indigenous culture – its conflating force, seen from a European perspective – operates at many levels in this image. First is the contiguity of speech and song. The volute in Figure 9.1 is only a more elaborate version of the speech volutes found in the Borbonicus and other sources. The contrast of plain and ornate volutes seems to convey the differing gradations of formality in verbal utterance I discussed above. However, it does not betoken any simple or rigorous distinction of song and speech since, in the first place, the ornate volutes seem to have been used in some cases to depict rhetorically heightened speech and the plain volutes to depict song and since, in the second place, the complex formality (and even modest tonal

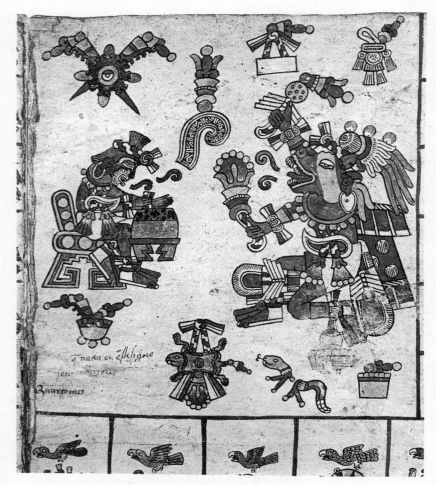

Figure 9.1   Codex Borbonicus, p. 4, detail.

elements) of elite spoken Nahuatl probably narrowed the distance between speech, formal speech, and song all told. Perhaps the most that can be said is that the plain and ornate volutes expressed the unbroken spectrum inhabited by both speech and song at the same time as they registered in various ways graded differences along it.

A second integration evident in the song volutes is the union of song and paint. The paint in the codices was, as I have argued along with Gruzinski, a solid, voluminous presence binding the glyphs to the material things they depicted. It was the medium through which the glyphs took on a materiality equivalent to things outside the codices, through which they came to be presentations rather than representations of the world. The plain and ornate volutes drew song (and speech) into this loop of equivalent substances. From our perspective they seem to materialize song, conflating it with painted substance in the encoding of the world. From the indigenous perspective they probably affirmed a self-evident propinquity of the materialities of paint and song.

In doing so they seem also to have affirmed the material linkage of song to other things that can appear in paint. The third connection evident in the ornate volutes is a particular case of this linkage: they joined song with flowers. In fact the ornate volutes often include indigenous images of flowers; iconographers among students of Mesoamerica have identified particular species thus depicted. The ornate volutes presented speech blossoming. They connected song to another of the material substances basic to Mexica ritual.

The flowers in the volutes may even have had a quite specific ritual significance – and this indicates a fourth material union expressed in the song glyphs. Abraham Cáceres has argued that the flower atop the volute in figure 9.1 is the *heimia salicifolia*, *xonecuilli* in one of its Nahuatl names, one of a number of hallucinogenic plants employed in Mexica ritual to aid the priests in their shamanic contacts with sacred realms.[28] This interpretation is in some of its particulars more than a little speculative, to be sure, but the identification of *xonecuilli* in the song glyph seems well founded. It hints at a sacred reality immanent in the worldly materiality of the glyph. It suggests a final, sweeping embrace that might have operated in this volute, a hallucinogenic embrace of song, flower, and paint as avatars of sacred truths.

The joining of flower and song in painted volutes can be interpreted, then, as a powerful manifestation of the integrated, materialized indigenous world. Yet it also anticipates precisely the "flower-and-song," *xochicuicatl* imagery of the *cantares*, and it might seem to lead us back toward León-Portilla's humanistic interpretation of Aztec culture. So it does, for example, in Cáceres's work.

Instead, I think, it turns this interpretation on its head: rather than confirming it, it has the effect of denying altogether a place for León-Portilla's metaphorical play in indigenous sensibilities. The idea that flower and song could be a metaphor for poetry and for a wider poetic philosophy depends on the perception of flowers and song as distinct, disjunct realms of reality. In a manner basic to all metaphor, that is, it requires an *a priori* separation of things that may then be joined. Yet there is little evidence of such separations in the prehispanic Mexica mentality. They seem to be so many more ghosts of European habits of thought. Instead of disjunction, what we sense in Aztec thought is connection: not a seamless merger of all things into all other things, to be sure – this would negate all difference and with it all perception – but rather a circumscribing of the sorts of differences westerners habitually perceive, within a stricter-than-western integration of things. Our effort should not be to divide Aztec flowers from Aztec song so we can put them together again in a metaphorical emblem. It should be to see, however hazily, a perception of the world in which flower and song were always already connected; in which flower was in contact with song and therefore able to present it in some aspect and song adjacent to flower and likewise able to present it; in which the question of the connections of parts to a whole stood in place of the question of relating unrelated things. Our effort, in short, should be to see a culture not of metaphors but of metonymies. These, not metaphors, might be the useful tools for us to understand a material world seen as a varied, complex, but nonetheless closely integrated whole.

This view pushes us to a reconsideration of Garibay's notion of *difrasismo*. It is a metaphorical notion that needs to be remade in antimetaphorical terms of proximity, participation, and the partial habitation of one thing in another: not *difrasismo* so much as a redoubled *monofrasismo* of a sort we do not easily comprehend. Likewise, and more generally, the whole European discovery of complex metaphors at the heart of Nahuatl discourse, a discovery dating back to earliest colonial times, as I have noted, needs to be questioned. More generally still, the metaphorical foundation of the *xochicuicatl* interpretation of the *cantares* and of Aztec thought as a whole needs to be reimagined. How do the juxtapositions of different (to us, sometimes, distant) objects in these songs function? What is their relation to the world when they are conceived as confirmations of perceived affinities rather than as poetic images spanning distance in unexpected ways? How then do we rethink the world they reflect?

Among writers on Aztec culture Clendinnen comes closest to dissolving western categories that yield metaphors. "The puzzle," she writes,

is to know when [the Mexica] were speaking, as we would say, "merely" metaphorically, and when they were speaking literally, simply describing the world as they knew it to be. In certain tropes, as when maize is invoked as human flesh, we casually take the linked concepts to be so widely separated that we assume we are dealing with metaphor and the cognitive *frisson* of overleaping difference. Then comes the jolting recognition that the Mexica might well have been stating a perceptually unobvious but unremarkable truth: maize was flesh.

Here our parsing of the world is, for a moment, effectively challenged. But still Clendinnen holds out the possibility that the Mexica perceived a duality of literal and figurative relations between language and the world. Still she assumes that the Mexica "lived by" metaphors: "On other occasions," she continues, "... they might well have been 'speaking metaphorically.' In a differently conceptualized world concepts are differently distributed. If we want to know the metaphors our subjects lived by, we need first to know how language scanned actuality."[29]

I would push farther Clendinnen's insights. It seems likely that the duality of literal and figurative language is, all told, a western importation to the Mexica mentality; that the indigenous construction of the world connected things to other things in a network of extraordinary, more-than-western complexity and intimacy; that the expression of one thing in another was, therefore, a real connection – a metonymic one, again, involving the interplay of adjoining parts of a whole; and that the surmounting of distance and difference basic to metaphorical understandings of the world was simply not an issue.[30]

If this carries Clendinnen's view of indigenous metaphor farther than she might take it, it nonetheless affirms her most general thesis about the place of the individual in precontact Mexica culture. Here I return, finally, to the caveat I broached above about the western authorial subjectivity we project onto a text like the *Cantares mexicanos*. Clendinnen argues that the individual subject was a "highly vulnerable social construct" in Mexica life, "made or unmade through a series of public acts." In a manner foreign to emerging Early Modern subjectivities in Europe, the Mexica self was permeable, opening out to fortifying, terrifying, sustaining, and destructive sacred powers and defined by its changing relations to them embodied in ritual. This view of the self originated in conjunction with an eschatology widely dispersed through Mesoamerica that involved a cyclic world order and periodic destructions of the cosmos. The Mexica harped with particular insistence on this eschatology; though they lived in relative abundance, as Clendinnen says, "they represented themselves as ... toiling along a windswept ridge, an abyss on either hand."[31] The fluid Mexica view of individual subjectivity is apparent also in the (to us) vague borders of selfhood in the complex Aztec pantheon, where a deity seemingly distinct and individual at one moment can reemerge as a single aspect of a different deity at another. It is also evident in the permeable borders between sacred and human selves in Aztec ritual, where chosen humans, as I remarked before, became this god or that.[32]

The integrated, metonymic construction of Mexica perceptions I have advocated here sits well with this notion of subjectivity. The permeable boundaries of Mexica selfhood echo and redouble the operative adjacencies at the edges of all things. The self takes its place in the numberless proximities that allow the connections I outlined before among song, flower, paint, words, and world. The "eclipse of subjectivity" Clendinnen finds at crucial moments of Mexica life, the "deep cultural predilection" she perceives among the Mexica "for seeking the sacred through the extinction of self,"[33] is the most basic ritual confirmation of the participation of human flesh and life-force in a cosmos of contact and affinity. It might therefore better be called an expansion or unfolding or dilation of the self than its extinction or eclipse. Mexica woman and Mexica man opened out at every point – just like maize, *teponaztli*, and glyph – to the material world around them.

From this vantage point, finally, we may see clearly some implications of Mesoamerican studies for a postcolonial historiography. The unlearning of the *cantares* I've tried to set in motion here suggests that we need to allow our historical constructions more latitude to reconstruct us, that we need to empower their uncanny otherness. Or, in terms that Myra Jehlen has recently developed, that we need to curtail our authority as historians in the same way we have been willing for some time to curtail the authority of the European colonizers whose accounts we use.[34] This undermining of mastery would then operate on both the axes of postcolonial historiography I discerned at the outset: on the axis between historian and past others as well as on the axis between others within the past. The general problem plaguing even the most enlightened Aztec studies is that their resistance to this curtailment of authority remains largely unspoken and is not made a manifest aspect of a dialogical history. (Note that I do not suggest the possibility of a history without such resistance, only the need for our innate resistance to become part of the stuff we contemplate in our histories.)

The Mexica view of the world is the perfect postcolonial "object" of study because it does something all human "objects" do but in a more radical way: it talks back, remaking itself as speaking subject even as we try to pin it down. Moreover, it talks in a tongue whose foreignness dramatically dismantles the matrices of our emerging understanding. In doing so it effectively denies us the power ever to grasp it fully, to represent completely its otherness.[35] It also defamiliarizes the ways we filter its foreignness through our most basic sorts of categorical grids, our most fundamental choices in dividing up and ordering the external reality that impinges on us. If we could begin to see, hear, and imagine the *cantares* in a way that promotes their reshaping of these conceptual categories, then unlearning the *cantares* might become part of a more general process of unlearning ourselves.

The constraints I've pointed out clustered around the *cantares* constitute, after all, nothing other than what James Clifford has called an "ethnographic allegory," an encompassing narrative we tell ourselves in order to bring near the others we encounter. Our effort should not be to escape such allegories – impossible in any case, as Clifford notes – but to gauge carefully their force and thus, as Clifford says, to "take responsibility for our ... constructions of others and of ourselves through others." In the process we might enable others to bring *us* near, to exercise a power in their dialogue with us that we habitually arrogate to ourselves. In the process, as Clifford puts it, we might "open ... ourselves to different histories."[36]

In recent Mesoamerican studies perhaps the most widely read failure to see other histories is Tzvetan Todorov's interpretation of the Spanish colonization of Mexico, *The Conquest of America*. The book has been criticized, more or less vehemently, from many quarters. Clendinnen, for example, has noted how Todorov reaffirms the outlines of the conquest narrative put in place by Prescott a century and a half ago. Stephen Greenblatt, in his book *Marvelous Possessions: The Wonder of the New World*, has rejected Todorov's central thesis that the Europeans' possession of writing, what Samuel Purchas called their "literall advantage," was the crucial element of an epistemological flexibility that enabled them to triumph over the Mexica. Brotherston has spoken more plainly, ridiculing Todorov's depiction of "native Americans ... as illiterate and therefore mindless, and in any case incapable of recording and reflecting upon their own history for themselves." And Deborah Root has heatedly and lengthily catalogued the narrative strategies Todorov uses that coerce indigenous materials into western molds.[37]

From my perspective Todorov's difficulties manifest just the kind of epistemological straightjacket involved in the misconstrual of the *cantares*. Caught in one of the most pervasive western ethnographic allegories, the allegory of the alphabet and its unsurpassed capability for flexible representation, he cannot see indigenous traces as revealing a different construction of the world abundantly empowered in its own right. He cannot construct a *pictographic* advantage but is bound to see only a crippling pictographic limitation. The crucial difference between European and Aztec languages, I have suggested here, might have to do not with the flexibilities of their graphic versions to adapt to changing contingencies but rather with their differing immersions in the world. The dynamics of the Spanish defeat of Tenochtitlan would then need to be understood not from a perspective that automatically aligns greater efficacy with one of these immersions, but from a multivalent vantage point that struggles, harder than Todorov, to recognize the differing efficacies of each. (Of the powerful efficacy of Aztec discourse and practice, at any rate, there can be no question; they had subjugated wide reaches of the Central American subcontinent in the century before Cortés's landing.) Todorov's version of the conquest embodies a colonizing, controlling, and finally silencing of indigenous voices rather than a postcolonial revision of ourselves in response to their accents.[38]

More subtly, Greenblatt also demonstrates the difficulty we have in curtailing our historiographic authority. To be sure, *Marvelous Possessions* is, unlike *The Conquest of America*, a book mainly about European views, and traveling this narrowed path it avoids many pitfalls that brought low Todorov, Prescott, and others like them. Greenblatt sets himself to analyze European ideas of the New World, their complexities and their limitations, and he does so brilliantly. Yet he cannot evade indigenous voices altogether, and when faced with them he opts for a cautious approach. He writes: "The responses of the natives to the fatal advent of the Europeans survive only in the most fragmentary and problematical form, ... only through the mediation of those Europeans who ... saw fit to register [them]." Such mediation so transforms the indigenous perspective that it comes close to obliterating it: "The few textual traces of Indian responses to the Europeans in the earliest years of contact are precious, but principally because they provide unusually candid and revealing access to the Europeans' own selfconceptions."[39]

There is no question that the traces we have of indigenous societies are mediated through European technologies, histories, and desires. But this mediation does not simply erase their autochthonous features. Traces like the *cantares*, the Codex Borbonicus, or Sahagún's *Florentine Codex* could not have taken the shapes they did without the participation of native voices, after all, whatever the European voices that clamor alongside them. Rather than compromising hopelessly their usefulness for an understanding of indigenous perceptions, the multicultural mediation involved in such sources might draw our attention to itself as the locus of a revised historiography, as the Archimedean point from which our constructions of others and ourselves proceed. Greenblatt raises the complex issues found along my second axis of postcolonial historiography, the axis extending in the past between colonizers and colonized, only to cancel in his caution one of its poles. He ignores the uncanny otherness of indigenous accents rather than engaging with it.

Greenblatt's caution is motivated by that residual yearning to hear clear and pure others I described before. "I catch myself constantly straining to read into the European traces an account of what the American natives were 'really' like," he writes, "but I have resisted as much as I can the temptation to speak for or about the native cultures as if the mediation of European representations were an incidental consideration, easily corrected for."[40] Here the impossibility of authentic reconstruction does not lead into the thickets of dialogical history. Instead, ironically, it obscures our responsibility to converse at all.

Postcolonial historiography (and Greenblatt's own histories, when it comes to the European voices he mostly attends to) takes fuller account than this of our inability to hear others, near or far, speak to us with a pure voice. It places at the heart of our historical methods the pervasive hybridity of our encounters, colonial or otherwise – their messy inter-subjectivity; their habitation of a foggy, dialogical, and essentially linguistic middle-ground between us and them, me and you; their distortion by the static of transmission, their coercion by the *a priori* presence of one or another linguistic matrix, and their bafflement by mystifying difference. In such a history Mexica voices will speak to us anew. They will be heard, paradoxically, to be no different in the nature of their colloquy with us than the most familiar western voices, whatever the vast differences in the things they say. The perfection of Mexica subjects as postcolonial subjects resides, then, in this: that they confront us so dramatically with the vacillation, endemic to all our communicative acts, between distance and familiarity.

NOTES

1   See Jean-François Lyotard, *The Postmodern Condition: A Report on Knowledge*, trans. Geoff Bennington and Brian Masumi (Minneapolis, 1984); Arjun Appadurai, "Disjuncture and Difference in the Global Cultural Economy," *Public Culture* 2 (1990), 1–24, and "Global Ethnoscapes: Notes and Queries for a Transnational Anthropology," in Richard G. Fox, ed., *Recapturing Anthropology: Working in the Present* (Santa Fe, 1991), pp. 191–210; Houston A. Baker, Jr., *Blues, Ideology, and Afro-American Literature: A Vernacular Theory* (Chicago, 1984); and Homi K. Bhabha, "The Commitment to Theory," in Jim Pines and Paul Willemen, eds., *Questions of Third Cinema* (London, 1989), pp. 111–32.

2   In an important statement of 1979 on ethnohistorical method Dennis Tedlock lamented our tendency to ignore this dialogue in our pursuit of "truly aboriginal" views; see *The Spoken Word and the Work of Interpretation* (Philadelphia, 1983), pp. 333–4. The tendency has been redressed in the many recent studies that have taken the interactions of colonizers and colonized as their subject. In Latin American scholarship three such studies of special importance are Nancy M. Farriss, *Maya Society Under Colonial Rule* (Princeton, 1984); Serge Gruzinski, *La colonisation de l'imaginaire: sociétés indigènes et occidentalisation dans le Mexique espagnol XVIe–XVIIIe siècle* (Paris, 1988); and Sabine MacCormack, *Religion in the Andes: Vision and Imagination in Early Colonial Peru* (Princeton, 1991). A monumental new contribution along these lines, which reached me too late for consideration here, is James Lockhart's *The Nahuas After the Conquest: A Social and*

Cultural History of the Indians of Central Mexico, Sixteenth Through Eighteenth Centuries (Stanford, 1992).

3   Or even to the third, as we begin to make dialogues in present-day scholarly and broader communities an integral part of our histories. My sketch of postcolonial historiography remains a wholesale simplification since it does not address such dialogues, which are couched in terms at once ideological (political, disciplinary, etc.) and emotional. Neither does it address the multiplicity of dialogue within each of my general axes, nor the complexity of interaction between them.

4   The manuscript first came to broad scholarly attention in the late nineteenth century, with Daniel Brinton translating some of the songs into English in 1890 (*Ancient Nahuatl Poetry*, Philadelphia) and Antonio Peñafiel issuing a photographic facsimile in 1904 (*Cantares en idioma mexicano*, Mexico). But it was not until the efforts of Leonhard Schultze Jena (*Alt-Aztekische Gesänge*, Stuttgart, 1957) and Garibay (*Poesía náhuatl*, 3 vols., Mexico, 1964–8) that substantial portions of the collection were translated (into German and Spanish respectively). Garibay's interpretation of the *cantares* is embodied chiefly in his *Historia de la literatura nahuatl* (2 vols., Mexico, 1953–4). John Bierhorst's recent edition and translation into English, *Cantares mexicanos: Songs of the Aztecs* (Stanford, 1985), is the first complete translation into any language. His long introduction contains an overview of earlier work on the *cantares*; it also advances a controversial interpretation of them as ghostsongs of a postcontact revitalization movement with scant direct connection to prehispanic Mexica culture. For objections to this interpretation see James Lockhart, "Care, Ingenuity, and Irresponsibility: The Bierhorst Edition of the Cantares Mexicanos," *Reviews in Anthropology* 16 (1991), 119–32.

5   Carrasco, *Religions of Mesoamerica: Cosmovision and Ceremonial Centers* (San Francisco, 1990), p. 79. The poet–philosopher–king portrait of Nezahualcoyotl has deep roots, counting among its earliest sources writings from shortly after 1600 by his descendant Fernando de Alva Ixtlilxochitl. Indeed these writings, especially the *Historia de la nación chichimeca* (ed. Germán Vázquez, Madrid, 1985), are important sources for the poetic–philosophic interpretation all told. Because of Nezahualcoyotl's rulership of Texcoco, across Lake Texcoco from Tenochtitlan, the interpretation has tended to take on a geographical dualism, with philosophical Texcoco playing Athens to martial Tenochtitlan's Sparta (see for example William H. Prescott, *History of the Conquest of Mexico* [New York, n.d.(1843)], Book 1, ch. 6). For the persistence of this dualism in Miguel León-Portilla's writings see below; for its permeation of popular accounts see Gary Jennings's recent (and vast) historical romance, *Aztec* (New York, 1980); for an older novelistic biography of "poet–king" Nezahualcoyotl dependent on Garibay's early work see Frances Gillmor, *Flute of the Smoking Mirror* ([1949]; Salt Lake City, 1983); and for a strongly voiced challenge of the poet–king portrait see Bierhorst, *Cantares mexicanos*, pp. 103–5.

6   Garibay, *Historia*, I, pp. 19, 76. For sixteenth-century references to the metaphors and obscurity of indigenous songs see Diego Durán, *Historia de las Indias de Nueva-España e islas de la tierra firme*, quoted in Garibay,

Historia I, p. 74; and Bernardino de Sahagún, *Florentine Codex: General History of the Things of New Spain*, ed. and trans. Arthur J. O. Anderson and Charles E. Dibble (12 vols., Salt Lake City, 1950–82), I, p. 81.

7   León-Portilla has expressed these views in various writings. For an influential summary version see *Aztec Thought and Culture: A Study of the Ancient Nahuatl Mind*, trans. Jack Emory Davis (Norman, Okla., 1963); for the quotations here see *The Aztec Image of Self and Society: An Introduction to Nahua Culture*, ed. J. Jorge Klor de Alva (Salt Lake City, 1992), ch. 5; for specific stylistic discussion of the *cantares* see "Cuícatl y tlahtolli: las formas de expresión en náhuatl," *Estudios de Cultura Náhuatl* 16 (1983), 13–108, and, in a more popular vein, *Pre-Columbian Literatures of Mexico*, trans. Grace Lobanov (Norman, Okla., 1969), pp. 76–89; and for the most recent framing of his ideas, his critique of John Bierhorst's opposed conception of the *cantares*, and his translations of some of the song texts see *Fifteen Poets of the Aztec World* (Norman, Okla., 1992).

8   See Klor de Alva's introduction to León-Portilla's *Aztec Image*, "Nahua Studies, the Allure of the 'Aztecs,' and Miguel León-Portilla," where he summarizes his own differences with León-Portilla and those of Burkhart and Gruzinski.

9   See Lockhart, "Care, Ingenuity, and Irresponsibility"; Brotherston, "Nezahualcóyotl's 'Lamentaciones' and Their Nahuatl Origins: The Westernization of Ephemerality," *Estudios de Cultura Náhuatl* 10 (1972), 393–408.

10 In *Cantares mexicanos*, p. 17. Inga Clendinnen's *Aztecs: An Interpretation* (Cambridge, 1991) does not figure in this list of revisionist work because it rather too readily accepts much of León-Portilla's *xochicuicatl* aesthetic (see in particular ch. 9). Nonetheless I should say that I consider it the most eloquent and thoughtful overview of its subject since Jacques Soustelle's *La vie quotidienne des aztèques à la veille de la conquête espagnole* of 1955 (trans. as *Daily Life of the Aztecs on the Eve of the Spanish Conquest*, Stanford, 1970). At some points Clendinnen's account approaches the postcolonial perspective sketched here; I will have more to say about her book later.

11 For literary canonizing see Garibay's *Historia*, lengthily concerned with the *Cantares mexicanos*. For a suggestive cultural interpretation of the *cantares* couched, however, from within western aesthetic sensibility see David Damrosch, "The Aesthetics of Conquest: Aztec Poetry Before and After Cortés," *Representations* 33 (1991), 101–20. For formal analysis of the *cantares* see Francis Karttunen and James Lockhart, "La estructura de la poesía náhuatl vista por sus variantes," *Estudios de Cultura Náhuatl* 14 (1980), 15–64.

12 Brotherston, "Nezahualcóyotl's 'Lamentaciones'," 404.

13 See among their many writings on the subject Ong, *The Presence of the Word: Some Prolegomena for a Cultural and Religious History* (Minneapolis, 1981), chs. 2 and 3; and Goody, *The Interface between the Written and the Oral* (Cambridge, 1987), ch. 1.

14 For an intriguing recent musicological use of such dichotomies that does not, however, avoid the hazards of their decontextualized generalization see John Shepherd, *Music as Social Text* (Cambridge, 1991), part 1.

15   Gruzinski, *Man-Gods in the Mexican Highlands: Indian Power and Colonial Society, 1520–1800*, trans. Eileen Corrigan (Stanford, 1989), p. 18.
16   Andrews, *Introduction to Classical Nahuatl* (Austin, 1975); see for instance p. 204.
17   On the degree to which our presumption of the separateness of words and things continues to underpin our narratives of discovery see Mary C. Fuller, "Ralegh's Fugitive Gold: Reference and Deferral in *The Discoverie of Guiana*," *Representations* 33 (1991), 42–64; esp. 45–7. On the solidification of representational linguistic modes in Early Modern Europe see Michel Foucault, *The Order of Things: An Archaeology of the Human Sciences* (New York, 1970), chs. 2 and 3; and Gary Tomlinson, *Music in Renaissance Magic: Toward a Historiography of Others* (Chicago, 1993), ch. 6. For related issues in the development of logic and dialectic see Walter J. Ong, *Ramus: Method and the Decay of Dialogue* (Cambridge, Mass., 1958).
18   See Gordon Brotherston, "Towards a Grammatology of America: Lévi-Strauss, Derrida and the Native New World Text," in Francis Barker, Peter Hulme, Margaret Iversen, and Diana Loxley, eds., *Literature, Politics and Theory: Papers from the Essex Conference 1976–84* (London, 1986), pp.190–209.
19   *La colonisation de l'imaginaire*, pp. 77–8.
20   *Aztecs*, p. 214.
21   "Nezahualcóyotl's 'Lamentaciones,'" p. 402.
22   We should strive to understand literally Soustelle's assertion that in *ixiptlayotl* ceremonies "it was the god himself who died before his own image and in his own temple" (*Daily Life of the Aztecs*, p. 8). In translating the notion of *ixiptlayotl* Clendinnen wavers between a westernizing "god-representation" or "god-image" (*Aztecs*, pp. 77, 99) and the more effectively defamiliarizing "god-presenter" (pp. 104, 110). She summarizes our perceptual problems in dealing with this phenomenon on pp. 251–3. For a good discussion of similar issues in the colonial period see Gruzinski, *La colonisation de l'imaginaire*, pp. 325–6.
23   With regard to Mesoamerican writing and painting Arthur G. Miller has developed this dichotomy of representation and presentation along different lines (see *The Mural Painting of Teotihuacán*, Washington, D.C., 1973, pp. 26–8). He sees the two-dimensionality of Mesoamerican images as "presentational" in opposition to "representational" western perspectival technique. Presentational painting eschews western naturalism and with it the "intermediary step between the painted image and what it represents, i.e., what it symbolizes." It forges a direct, symbolic connection between the image and the idea of what it depicts and is distanced from the world by this unmediated connection ("Teotihuacán painting ... is a presentation whose meaning is *in the image* and not anywhere else ..."). This is a more expressly Platonic view even than Clendinnen's. I would argue that the unmediated connection of image and what it depicts functions, in a world observed in a non-western, fully materialized fashion, to draw image and world together rather than to separate them; the image conveys a part of the world in its iconic, semantic, and material substantiality.
24   *La colonisation de l'imaginaire*, p. 54.

25 For examples of general avoidance of musical matters see Garibay, *Historia*,
    I, pp. 79–83, and Karttunen and Lockhart, "La estructura de la poesía
    náhuatl." Samuel Martí's discussion of the *cantares* in *Canto, danza y música
    precortesianos* (Mexico, 1961), pp. 118–51, is a compilation of primary and
    secondary sources heavily indebted to Garibay's *Historia*; Robert Steven-
    son's *Music in Aztec & Inca Territory* (Berkeley, 1968) is a more thorough
    survey of colonial testimony and organological evidence with, however, less
    to say concerning the *cantares*. Both Martí, pp. 140–8, and Stevenson, pp.
    46–54, offer speculation on the percussion cadences; for a somewhat better-
    grounded attempt to interpret them see Bierhorst, *Cantares mexicanos*,
    pp. 72–9.
26 I have argued elsewhere that alternatives to this hierarchy existed in the
    Early Modern era even within European traditions; see Tomlinson, *Music in
    Renaissance Magic*, ch. 4.
27 Gruzinski, *Man-Gods*, pp. 18–19.
28 "*In xochitl, in cuicatl:* Hallucinogens and Music in Mesoamerican Amer-
    indian Thought" (Ph.D. diss., Indiana University, 1984), ch. 2
29 *Aztecs*, p. 287. Clendinnen's indecisiveness is apparent also in comparing pp.
    143 and 182, where she accepts "metaphors" as pervasive ways all societies
    conceive the world and themselves, with p. 251, where she faces "the
    implication that [a] metaphor might not be metaphor at all." In her
    discussion of the *cantares* Clendinnen pronounces metaphors a basic tech-
    nique of Mexica poetry (p. 215) but also glimpses a less familiar view, where
    she senses "a marvellous concreteness in what we would call 'meta-
    phors'"(p. 220).
30 In *Man-Gods*, p. 21, Gruzinski touches on an insight similar to Clendinnen's:
    "The Nahua perceived totalities," he writes, "even if it meant confusing, as
    sometimes happened, the signifier with the signified, the object with its
    representation." Gruzinski returns to the subject in *La colonisation de
    l'imaginaire*, pp. 325–6, broaching it now as a fundamental indigenous mode
    of perceiving reality and correcting (p. 330) his earlier ethnocentric imputa-
    tion of confusion to the Mexica.
31 *Aztecs*, pp. 143, 29. For the sources of Clendinnen's image see Anderson and
    Dibble, *Florentine Codex*, VI, pp. 101, 125. Here Clendinnen pursues a
    theme raised by Soustelle in his *Daily Life of the Aztecs*. Mexica existence
    was perilous at the most fundamental level, according to Soustelle, for "their
    fragile world was perpetually at the mercy of some disaster" (p. 101). This
    threat configured every ritualized gesture of Mexica society as "a continually
    renewed white-magic operation, a perpetual collective effort without which
    nature itself would be destroyed" (p. 147). "The common task," Clendinnen
    writes in developing Soustelle's view, "was to sustain a social order suffi-
    ciently in harmony with the 'natural' order to exist within it, with women
    and men pursuing their separate and dangerous paths, to maintain human-
    kind's precarious purchase on existence" (p. 209).
32 Clendinnen is particularly eloquent on the permeability of borders between
    sacred and mundane realms and the role of ritual in controlling border-
    crossings; see esp. *Aztecs*, pp. 50–4. She discusses the fluid identities of
    Mexica deities on pp. 248–9.

33   *Aztecs*, pp. 258–9; on the warrior's escape from subjectivity see p. 150.

34   "History Before the Fact; or, Captain John Smith's Unfinished Symphony," *Critical Inquiry* 19 (1993), 677–92; p. 691.

35   Homi K. Bhabha has rightly insisted that even the deepest western critiques of our ethnocentrism (for example Derrida's analysis of logocentrism) do not provide us a neutral ground from which to represent others. See "The Other Question: Difference, Discrimination and the Discourse of Colonialism," in Barker et al. *Literature, Politics and Theory* pp. 148–72; esp. pp. 150-51, 154.

36   James Clifford, "On Ethnographic Allegory," in J. Clifford and George E. Marcus, eds., *Writing Culture: The Poetics and Politics of Ethnography* (Berkeley, 1986), pp. 98–121; see pp. 121, 119.

37   Todorov, *The Conquest of America*, trans. Richard Howard (New York, 1984); Clendinnen, "'Fierce and Unnatural Cruelty': Cortés and the Conquest of Mexico," *Representations* 33 (1991), 65–100, p. 66; Greenblatt, *Marvelous Possessions: The Wonder of the New World* (Chicago, 1991), pp. 9–13; Brotherston, "Towards a Grammatology of America," p. 195; Root, "The Imperial Signifier: Todorov and the Conquest of Mexico," *Cultural Critique* (Spring 1988), 197–219.

38   This is not to question an assertion like Jack Goody's that "human capacities are enhanced by employing various instruments of a material and intellectual kind," for example writing, an alphabet, etc. (*The Interface*, p. 290). This is the sort of generalization, unimpeachable in itself, that stands behind and stimulates an analysis like Todorov's. I wish only to insist that in putting to use such generalizations we habitually underestimate the enhancement of capacities enabled by other people's instruments.

39   Greenblatt, *Marvelous Possessions*, pp. 145–46, 192.

40   Ibid. p. 7.

Part IV

Fetishisms

See Janet Arnold . On Q. Elizabeth's
Wardrobe _____

10   Worn worlds: clothes and identity on the Renaissance stage

Peter Stallybrass

> Over a period of five years from 1608 to 1613, James I bought a new cloak every month, a new waistcoat every three weeks, a new suit every ten days, a new pair of stockings, boots, and garters every four or five days, and a new pair of gloves every day.
>
> Lawrence Stone, *The Crisis of the Aristocracy*

> Between 1530 and 1609, 11,201 people were apprenticed to 11 major companies (including the main victualling companies) in the City of London. During the same period, 19,913 people (nearly *twice* as many) apprenticed with four of the major cloth and clothing companies (the Clothworkers, the Drapers, the Haberdashers, the Merchant Taylors).
>   Between 1550 and 1609, the personnel of the 5 major victualling companies increased by 132%, the Merchant Taylors by 496%.
>
> Steven Rappaport, *Worlds Within Worlds: The Structures of Life in Sixteenth-Century London*

Renaissance England was a cloth society; it was also a livery society. By this I mean both that its industrial base was the production of cloth and the circulation of clothing, and also that cloth was a staple currency. To be a member of any but the poorest of households was to wear livery. It was to be paid above all in cloth. And the companies of London were named to emphasize their central relation to clothes: they were *livery* companies. When a guild member was set free, he or she was said to be "clothed" and to be a free member was technically called "having the clothing."[1] To be incorporated into a household, to be incorporated into a guild, depended upon a transmission of clothes.

But livery has contradictory implications. The word "livery" derived from the Old French *livrance*, which suggests both delivery or distribution (the delivery of clothes from master to servant which marked the latter's subservience) and deliver*ance*, liberation, release (the "freedom" of the guild member, who bought his or her livery and, at the same time, the right to clothe apprentices in his or her household livery). Livery thus conjures up servitude and freedom from such servitude. To oversimplify, livery in a *household* was a mark of servitude whereas livery in a *guild* was a mark of freedom. The servitude of household livery is emphasized by Francis Bacon when he writes of "liveries, tokens, and other badges of factious dependance," and by Milton in *Samson Agonistes*, when the Philistines clothe the defeated Samson "[i]n their state Livery," thus making "thir dreadful enemy thir thrall."[2] Sir Thomas Overbury describes a "Servingman" as "*a creature, which though he be not drunk, yet is not his owne man. He tels without asking who ownes him, by the superscription of his Livery.*"[3] The freedom of guild livery is suggested both by the fact that monarchs and princes adopted it (Prince Henry assumed the livery of a Merchant Taylor and his father, James I, the livery of a Clothworker in 1607)[4] and by the meaning of the word "livery" in relation to the guilds: to wear the livery was to be made free of the City of London (and thus, despite guild regulations to the contrary, to be set free of the guild, since a liveried fishmonger might work in the booktrade, while many of the Skinners Company were in fact drapers).[5]

All forms of livery, though, displayed clothing as a means of incorporation, the marking of a body so as to associate it with a specific institution. As clothing exchanged hands, it bound people in networks of obligation. In societies like ours, dominated by neutral exchanges of money, the construction of bonds, of debts, and of liberties through the physical medium of clothes has appeared increasingly strange. I think this is because, for all our talk of the "materialism" of modern life, attention to material is precisely what is absent. Materials, despite their value, are endlessly devalued and replaced. Marx's critique of capitalism has never been more misunderstood than in his supposed critique of modern materialism.[6] For Marx, the triumph of the commodity betokens the death of the object. What, then, is Marx's critique of the object within capitalism? *Not* that it is fetishized. On the contrary, Marx argues that it is the *commodity* that is fetishized. And what defines a commodity as such always lies outside any specific object, and depends upon the equating of a specific quantity of paper cups with a specific quantity of coal or diamonds or academic books. Capitalism could thus be defined as the mode of production which, in fetishizing the commodity, *fails* to fetishize the *object*.[7] It remains unfortunate, though, that Marx appropriated the concept of "fetishism" from nineteenth-century philosophy and anthropology. He was, of course, right in insisting that the commodity is a "magical" (that is, mystified) form, in which the labor processes which give it its value have been effaced. But in applying the term "fetish" to the commodity, he obscured the true magic by which tribes other than our own inhabit and are inhabited by the objects upon which they work. To restore "true" fetishism would be to value the labor which is absorbed into the object and the labor which we expend in the touching, handling, and remaking of the object. But in capitalist societies, to love *things* is something of an embarrassment. Things are, after all, *mere* things. To accumulate things is not to give them life. It is because things are *not* fetishized that they remain lifeless.[8]

In a cloth economy, such as that of Renaissance England, things take on a life of their own. One is paid not only in the "neutral" currency of money but in material which is richly absorbent of symbolic meaning and in which memories and social relations are literally embodied. But am I right in suggesting that Renaissance England *was* such a cloth economy? After all, wages were paid. But it is rarely fully recognized by literary and theatrical historians that wages were usually a marginal part of the economy. In so far as England had a monetary economy by the late sixteenth century, it was one that still operated primarily through gifts, perks, and favors (what a later society would redefine as corruption). The highest wages for women at court were for the Ladies and Gentlewomen of the Privy Chamber and Bedchamber. In 1589, these women were paid per annum either £33 6s 8d or £20 (of the three Bed Chamberers, Lady Cobham received £20 and Lady Carew and Blanche Parry £33 6s 8d each).[9]

In comparison to wages, livery was a substantial part of the economics of the court. We have no account of what the livery of aristocratic Bed Chamberers cost, but if we dramatically descend the social scale, we find accounts for a woman known as Ippolyta the Tartarian, who was possibly a child, but more likely a midget. In 1564, she was granted as livery a "Gowne & kirtle of damaske gardid withe velvett drawne oute with sarceonett with poyntynge Ribande lined with cotton fustian and linnin Item one other Gowne and kirtle of grograyne chamlett garded with velvett poyntynge Ribande Item one other gowne of clothe And a kirtle of grograyne drawne out with sarceonett as afore ..."[10] The accounts for the *other* items of clothing (smocks, thread, a scarf, a hat etc.), given to Ippolyta that year, have survived, and they amount to £15 8s 10d. Not only does this figure not include the figure for the expenditure on her gowns and kirtles, but it also does not include additional clothing like furs, of which she was given five dozen black coney skins in 1569.[11]

In other words, the livery of Ippolyta the Tartarian must have cost significantly more than the wages of Lady Cobham for a whole year's work. And we can only guess at the cost of Lady Cobham's livery. Nor was the expenditure on Ippolyta in any way atypical. If we turn to the Italian jester, Monarcho, who is mentioned in *Love's Labour's Lost* ("[a] Phantasime, a Monarcho, and one that makes sport / To the Prince"),[12] we find that in 1569, the year of his arrival at court, not only was he granted an elaborate costume but also his gown and jerkin were furred by Adam Bland, the Queen's skinner, with 12 fox skins and 151 lamb skins. In 1574, Monarcho's new gown was furred "with twelve white fox and forty-six hare skins, powdered with sixty black genets tails."[13] In addition to livery, other gifts of clothing to court entertainers were frequent. In 1575, William Shenton, a court fool, received, over and above his livery, "One fetherbedde a bolster: A Coveringe: a peire of Blankettes: two peire of Sheetes: sixe Shirtes: two quilted nighte Cappes and sixe peire of Showes."[14] What recent work like Janet Arnold's on the Elizabethan court demonstrates is that the gift of clothing was the constitutive gesture of social organization. Clothing, indeed, was more binding than money, both symbolically since it incorporated the body and economically since it was less easily convertible than cash. Livery was thus central to the court, as it was to other households and to the guilds.

The London professional theater was situated at the juncture of the court and the city guilds, although both literally and symbolically at a distance from both. It was thus simultaneously related to the "servitude" of household livery and to the "freedom" of guild livery. The training of boy actors, as Stephen Orgel has argued, depended upon an apprentice system and, since there was no theatrical guild, at least some of the shareholders of the company had to gain or retain membership of other guilds so as to act as masters to the young apprentices.[15] This meant that, from a legal point of view, the boy actors were not theatrical trainees but apprentice bricklayers, butchers, drapers, goldsmiths, and so on. At the same time, playwrights and actors alike were drawn in to the elaborate pageants of the guilds. Their presence was particularly striking in the Drapers' company, for whom Anthony Munday wrote *Metropolis Coronata*, Thomas Middleton *Sun in Aries*, *The Triumph of Integrity*, and *The Triumph of Health and Prosperity*, and Thomas Heywood *Porta Pietatis* and *Londini Status Pacatus*. Munday and Middleton are both referred to on title pages as Drapers. Munday also wrote *The Triumphs of Reunited Britannia* and *Troia Nova Triumphans* for the Merchant Taylors, for whom John Webster wrote *Monuments of Honour*. On the title page of the latter, Webster is described as himself a Merchant Taylor.[16]

Indeed, Webster had been admitted to the Merchant Taylors' company through patrimony, his father having been a member, and his brother Edward was also apprenticed to the company.[17] Webster's own estimate of the significance of the Merchant Taylors' pageant in 1624 may be inferred both from the fact that its elaborate costumes and staging meant that it cost "at least ten times all the sum of [his] previous productions" and from its title page motto which he had quoted several times before but never in relation to his own work: "*Non norunt haec monumenta mori*" ("these monuments do not know how to die").[18] Webster, like Middleton, Munday, and Heywood, was thus proudly and actively involved in one of the guilds associated with the clothing trade.

However, if the theaters were intimately connected to the livery guilds, their survival depended upon the fact that the actors wore the liveries of aristocratic households. James I's household included the King's Men, the theatrical company to which Shakespeare belonged. The King's Men received every second year at Easter a livery for each member of the company, consisting of three yards of bastard scarlet for a cloak and a quarter-yard of crimson velvet for a cape. In 1627, the allowance for the cloak was increased from three to four yards, although it remained only three for the Queen's Men until 1630.[19] At one level, this livery was something of a legal fiction. Professional actors were hardly regular members of the royal household, and they earned their most significant income as shareholders in the companies that performed in the public and private playhouses of the suburbs and the City of London. But legal fictions are never *mere* fictions. Being clothed in royal livery, the King's Men were given crucial protection from the City fathers who were constantly troubled by the civil disturbances, the economic disruption, and the immorality which they attributed to this new industry, an industry which utilized both the aristocratic household and the livery guilds even as it clearly violated them.

The theaters, then, incorporated the contradictory implications of livery as both servitude and freedom. Yet, to the theater's critics, it was usually only in so far as the actors were absorbed by their livery into aristocratic households that they could be deemed worthy of respect. John Stowe wrote in his *Annales* for the year 1583:

Comedians and stage-players of former time were very poore and ignorant in respect of these of this time, but being now grown very skilfull and exquisite actors for all matters, they were entertained into the service of great lords, out of which companies were xii of the best chosen at the request of Sir Francis Walsingham, they were sworn the Queenes servants, and were allowed wages and liveries as groomes of the chamber.[20]

Actors were not attacked for their servitude but for their liberties. In so far as they were perceived as "free" men, they were imagined as dangerously transgressive vagrants. Above all, they were attacked for *shifting* liveries, or for shifting from liveried servants to wealthy justices of the peace.

But to *shift* clothes, the actors had to *have* clothes. It is, I believe, because theatrical historians have started with the companies themselves and with the negotiations of actors that they have drawn attention to the extraordinarily lavish outlay on costumes without seeing the full import of clothes in themselves. What I argue here, which will no doubt seem counterintuitive, is that the commercial theater is directly *derived* from the market in clothes. Or, to put it another way, the theater is simply a new and stunning development of the clothing trade.

The centrality of clothes to the medieval guild theater which preceded the professional playhouse has become increasingly apparent in recent years due to the publication of the Records of Early English Drama.[21] The guilds paid for costumes to be made; they hired them, rented them out, stored them, repaired them, dismantled them and reused the cloth for new costumes. In Coventry, the Weavers' Rentgatherers' Book for 1564 records: "Item paid for settyng one of Ihesus sleues ijd"; "Item paid for solyng of Iesus hose jd"; the Drapers' Accounts for 1563 record: "Itm payde for a Coate for god and for A peyre of gloues ffor hym iijs"; "Itm payde for blacckyng of the Sowles facys vjd."[22] On 3 January, the Cappers made an inventory of their costumes and properties, which included:

Itm pylates dublit ij curtaynes the spirate of godes cote godes cotes and the hose pylates heade fyve maries heades one coyffe mary maudlynes goune iij beardes gods head the spirites heade sixe pensils iiij Rolles iij marye boxes one play boke. The giandes head and clubbe pylates clubbe hell mowth iiij standynge iij small stremars adams spade Ives distaffe ij angels awbes one dore for a seate.[23]

A striking feature of these lists is the way in which the things take on a life of their own. God or the Holy Ghost, as much as Adam or Eve, take on a local habitation and a name as a coat, a glove, a beard. As if, beyond any particular performance, the specific items of costume retain not only a specific and enduring financial value (which is carefully noted), but also the vivifying magic which attaches both to a theatrical part and to the figure which the part embodies.

It is, I think, because the costume can endure after the performance is ended that it takes on a curious precedence to the actor, as if through the donning of a costume alone the actor puts on Christ, or Satan, or a Roman soldier, or whomever. Indeed, the guild accounts suggest the ability of the clothes to absorb the very identity of the actors. Sometimes, it is true, we find records like these, from the 1584 Smiths' accounts, paying for a production of the *Destruction of Jerusalem*: "... to Jhon Bonde for playenge of Justus, Ananus, Eliazar and the Chorus, vj s viij d ... to Jhon Hoppers for playenge of Jesus and Zacharyas, iij s."[24] Here,

it is the actual labor practices of the guild members which are attended
to. John Bond, who doubles in four parts, is paid 6s 6d; John Hopper,
who doubles in two, is only paid 3s, despite the fact that one of his roles
is Christ. Yet it is equally or more common to find records in which the
money is paid to what we would think of as a part rather than a person.
Thus, the Chester records of the Smiths, Cutlers, and Plumbers for
Midsummer 1575 record payments to "litle god" of 20d and to "oure
marye" of 18d; and the Coventry accounts of the Drapers in 1572 record:
"pd to god iijs iiijd."[25] More complexly, the Coventry Smiths' accounts
of 1499 record money paid "to Dame Percula for *his* wages" and "to
pylatts wyffe for *his* wages," the formulation insisting both upon the
absorption of the actor into the costume and upon the distance between
male actor and female costume.[26]

The extraordinary expense and care devoted to clothes suggests that
the guild theatricals which both preceded and were contemporaneous
with the professional theaters were organized above all around the
making and maintenance of costumes. What I argue here is that the
professional London companies were equally organized around costumes, but that those costumes were now part of a massive capitalist
development in the circulation of clothing.

For such an argument to be plausible, it is first necessary to understand
just *how* valuable costumes were. To begin with, they were considerably
more valuable than plays. As G. E. Bentley puts it: "Every new play was
a gamble; it might fail miserably and the sum paid its author would
constitute a total loss for the company. A fine costume, on the other
hand, could be used for years and for many different plays, whether the
production for which it had originally been purchased was a long-
running success or a complete failure."[27] In other words, in contrast to
our retrospective view, clothes retained their value better than plays.
New plays cost twice as much to see on opening nights, and though old
plays were constantly restaged, comparatively large sums of money were
spent to rewrite them and keep them up-to-date. Although clothes
needed care and alteration, the materials themselves retained much of
their value. Quite simply, clothes were an enormous investment. As
Bentley notes, "the greatest expense of any company of players in the
period was the purchase of costumes."[28] A play usually cost about £6,
although the prices were gradually pushed up in the seventeenth century.
By comparison, the actor and theatrical entrepreneur Edward Alleyn lists
a single "black velvet cloak with sleeves embrodered all with silver and
gold" as costing £20 10s 6d.[29]

The possession of plays was, of course, crucial to the companies, but
the care with which plays were treated was as nothing compared to the

care lavished upon costumes. The companies acquired specialists, in the form of tiremen or wardrobe keepers, to look after the costumes. In 1634, Thomas Crosfield recorded in his diary that the company at Salisbury Court had seven sharers and two "clothes keepers," Richard Kendall and Antony Dover, and one of the boys' companies seems also to have had two clothes keepers in the early seventeenth century.[30] The clothes keepers were usually tailors or apprenticed to tailors, and no doubt they altered, mended, and sometimes made the costumes. Large sums could be spent on mending alone. In July 1601, Henslowe paid out 6s 7d to repair a tawny coat "which was eatten with the Rattes."[31] In addition to the clothes keepers, we know from a complaint of the Lady Elizabeth's Men in 1615 that Henslowe "apointed a man to the seeinge of his accomptes in byinge of Clothes (hee beinge to have vi[s]. a weeke)."[32] And Henslowe also made independent payments on behalf of the actors to tailors, mercers, a milliner, lacemakers, and a "sylke man."[33] In other words, a new labor force grew up around the theater, created entirely by the value of clothes.

The scale of that value is suggested by Andrew Gurr:

A pair of silk stockings might cost £2 or £4, depending on quality and purchaser. A woman's gown might cost anything from £7 to £20 or more. The Earl of Leicester paid £543 for seven doublets and two cloaks, at an average cost for each item rather higher than the price Shakespeare paid for a house in Stratford.[34]

Gurr's comparative figures are quite staggering. For all we now might think about the price of an Armani suit, it is as nothing compared to the price of a house. Given the value of costumes, it is not surprising that the life and death of theatrical companies were crucially premised upon the accumulation and dispersal of those costumes. When Francis Langley built the Swan in 1586, he spent £300 on new apparel for his players, while Henslowe established Worcester's Men at his new theater, the Fortune, in 1600 by advancing them money for apparel and playbooks.[35] And when Henry Evans established a second boys' company at the Blackfriars, he joined up with Nathanial Giles, Master of the Chapel Children at Windsor, to obtain actors, and with Edward Kirkham, Yeoman of the Revels and in charge of the Revels wardrobe, to obtain clothes, and he later paid out £200 for apparel.[36] If companies collapsed, they made what they could by selling their costumes. Pembroke's Men were in trouble in 1593, and so they sold costumes to the value of £80, which was divided among the six sharers. When Lady Elizabeth's Men fell out with Henslowe in 1615, the financial wrangling was particularly concerning costumes and cloth. Henslowe was accused of having sold "tenn poundes worth of ould apparrell" that was the company's; of having valued apparel, bought from one Rosseter, at £63 when it was really only worth £40; of having held on to arras curtains for which the company had paid £40; of having "taken right gould and silver lace of divers garmentes to his owne use with out accompt to us."[37]

The value of the theatrical companies' investment in clothing is further demonstrated by the clauses they imposed upon the sharers and by the subdivision of costumes when a sharer died. The Articles of Agreement which Henslowe drew up between himself and the actor Robert Dawes specifically state that Dawes shall not

at any time after the play is ended depart or goe out of the [howse] with any [of their] apparell on his body, or if the said Robert Dawes [shall carry away any propertie] belonging to the said company, or shal be cosentinge or privy to any other of the said company going out of the howse with any of their apparell on his or their bodies, he ... shall and will forfeit and pay unto the said Philip and Jacob ... the some of ffortie pounds of lawfull [money of England] ...[38]

The embeddedness of the theater in the circulation of clothes is even more strikingly suggested by the 1635 will of John Shank, one of the King's Men. He begins his will by asserting his double life as actor and as guild member: he is both "one of his Mats: servants the Players" and a "Cittizen and weaver of London." And he requires the company to give his widow £50 for his share of the costumes and books as well as to repay "Sixteene Pounds and Twelve shillings which they owe mee for Two gownes."[39] To control the theater was thus not only to build playhouses but also to own, lend, and sell costumes.

There were multiple connections between theaters and the cloth industries. Francis Langley, for instance, who built the Swan, was a member of the Drapers' Company, and, in 1585, he had been appointed as an alnager to the Court of Aldermen, to check the quality, size, and weight of woolen cloth.[40] And when Edward Alleyn retired from the stage, it was to buy and sell clothes as well as to build and rent theaters.[41] Henslowe himself was a member of the Dyers' Company when he financed the building of the Rose in 1587 and the Fortune in 1600. Shakespeare also had complex familial and professional ties to the cloth trade. His father was a glover and whittawer and "also bought and sold wool on a large scale."[42] It is further worth noting that the first attempt at a "collected" edition of Shakespeare was by Thomas Pavier in 1619: Pavier was originally a Draper, who, along with eleven other Drapers (two of whom also published plays by Shakespeare), was translated into the Stationers' Company in 1600.[43]

We can suggest the centrality of the trade in clothes to the founding of the professional theaters through a brief analysis of the career of Philip Henslowe. Henslowe had a thriving pawnbroking business. Commentators have usually treated this business separately from his theatrical dealings, but pawnbroking was in no sense a sideline for Henslowe. Three sets of his pawnbroking accounts have been preserved, somewhat sporadically covering the years 1593 to 1596. During this period, it seems that Henslowe employed no fewer than four agents to assist him in the business: his nephew Philip, Goody Watson, Mrs. Grant, and Ann No[c]kes. Although the business dealt in items as small as combs, earpickers, and pint pots, the vast majority of items pawned were clothes. There is nothing surprising in this. The records of fourteenth-century Pistoia, for instance, show that clothing was the commonest pledge, "followed by tools, jewellery, arms, bedding and household utensils."[44] As late as the 1950s, in *Some Like It Hot*, Tony Curtis and Jack Lemmon pawn their overcoats even though it is the middle of a bitter Chicago winter, and only when that money has been spent does Curtis try, unsuccessfully, to persuade Lemmon to pawn their musical instruments. Clothes first, tools second.

The pawning of clothes (as well as their theft) is, indeed, constantly referred to in Renaissance drama, sometimes as a central aspect of the plot, sometimes as a mundane aspect of personal finances. Thomas Middleton's *Your Five Gallants* begins in a pawnshop with Frippery (his very name testifying to the importance of clothes in his business) going over his stock of gowns, petticoats, jackets, suits. Indeed the play is full of pawning: Goldstone steals Fitzgrave's cloak and pawns it to Frippery; Tailby, losing at gambling, pawns his weapons, his hat, and his satin doublet; and, at the end of the play, Pursenet gives Tailby the pledge of a gold chain to rent masquing costumes.[45] In Jonson's *Every Man in His Humour*, Brainworm begins by disguising himself as a soldier with clothes purchased from "a *Hounds-ditch* man ..., a broker." He later steals the clothes of Justice Clement's clerk and pawns them to raise cash. And when he promises aid to Matthew and Bobadill, they raise the necessary money by pawning a jewel, silk stockings, and a pair of boots.[46]

But the pawning of clothes depends upon the pawnbroker being sure of a market for them. When Henslowe's pledges were unredeemed, they became his. He sent Goody Watson clothes which he now called "my owne" and required that she sell them at the prices he set.[47] Just how sure Henslowe was of a market in second-hand clothes is demonstrated by the extraordinary sums he was prepared to pay for them. If we recall that the cost of admittance to the public playhouses was 1d, we get some idea of the value of even the smallest items of clothing for which Henslowe lent money: 10s lent "vpon a payer of blacke sylke stockenes of goody streates"; 10s "vpon a velluate cappe"; 6s "vpon a lynynge of shage for A clocke"; 6s "vpon A dublet & a payer of breches ffor A chylld."[48] At the other end of the market, Henslowe lent £3 10s to Mr Crowche "vpon his wiffes gowne"; £5 for "A womones gowne of branched damaske & lyned throwghe wth pincked tafetie & layd wth a lace of sylke and gowld"; £3 10s "vpon A sylke grogren gowne garded wth veluett & lyned wth saye of m^{r}. Burdes"; £4 "vpon ij payer of fyne sheates & a tabell cloth & a towell & a sylke quylte."[49] But the crucial question is *how* Henslowe could be sure of a market for these surprisingly valuable items of clothing.

It seems probable that Henslowe engaged in the sale or renting out of clothes to whomever could afford them, including the professional companies, amateur players at the Inns of Court and city pageants, and members of the audience of these spectacles. It is true that the theaters had special needs which a pawnbroker's ready-mades could not meet. On these occasions, Henslowe subsidized the making of new costumes. In November 1602, for instance, Henslowe lent John Duke £5 for the making of a single satin suit for *Lady Jane*.[50] When the Admiral's Men staged the first part of *Cardinal Wolsey*, Henslowe paid out £35 for costumes and other properties, and he paid another £11 6s for costumes for the second part. And the black satin suit bought for £5 2s for the performance of *2 Black Dog of Newgate* by the Worcester's Men was not reused when they staged *A Woman Killed with Kindness*, for which they bought a new black satin suit for 10s as well as a woman's black velvet gown for £6 13s. Given the cost of clothes, the restaging of an old play saved very little if it required new clothes. When the Admiral's Men purchased the previously performed *Vayvode* in 1598–9, new apparel cost them £17 5s. And Worcester's Men, restaging the Admiral's Men's *Sir John Oldcastle* in 1602–3, paid 50s for revisions to the play but £15 10s for new costumes.[51]

There is no need, though, to suppose that new *costumes* were always made from new *clothes*. Indeed, I believe it is almost certain that Henslowe both rented and sold the clothes which he had accumulated through his business as a pawnbroker to the theaters, as he undoubtedly did to other customers. Moreover, he probably received clothes back from the theater, and marketed them both in a general way and possibly as specific, famous garments attached both to particular roles and to the names of charismatic figures – professional actors like Richard Tarlton,

Will Kempe, Edward Alleyn, and Richard Burbage.[52] My reason for supposing this is that this had happened in the past, there was a market for it, and Henslowe rarely missed an opportunity for making a profit. Given the absence of records, I shall try to give an outline of this cloth-driven theater first by pointing to some anomalies in Henslowe's records and secondly by seeing Henslowe (and the theatrical entrepreneurs generally) as both suppliers and retailers of the clothes which the theater staged.

To start with Henslowe's records. In March 1598, Henslowe and his son-in-law, Edward Alleyn, made a series of inventories of the costumes and properties belonging to the Admiral's Men.[53] To us, they look like impressive lists; the inventory for 13 March includes "13 doublets, 10 suits, 4 jerkins, 20 gowns, 25 capes, and 23 coats."[54] But what is striking about these lists, as Neil Carson has acutely noted, is that "the Company maintained a surprisingly *small* stock" (my emphasis).[55] Moreover, there is no trace of many of the costumes which, according to Henslowe's records, he had sold the company. What had happened to them? It is certainly possible that the sharers occasionally divided the clothes amongst themselves, clothes which they in turn could have given as gifts or resold, rented out or pawned. The actor Thomas Downton, for instance, pawned two cloaks and Henslowe lent him £12 10s to get them out of pawn.[56] But I believe that by far the most likely explanation for the disappearing costumes is that the company gave the clothes back to Henslowe when they had no further use for them or when they were in financial difficulties.

This would explain the puzzling records of September 1602, when Henslowe estimated that the players owed him £718 12s 10d, a truly fabulous sum of money, and one which we have no reason to believe the players could pay. Then, at Christmas, Henslowe scaled down his estimate to £226 16s 8d and an extra £50 lent to Jones and Shaa. And finally, less than a year later, he writes that he was "descarged to them of al deates" except for £24.[57] Carson speculates that the players sold their costumes to raise cash, but I think it is more likely that the debt was never a real one in the first place. Instead, I believe that Henslowe *rented* the costumes to the actors, although, while they were in the actors' possession, he charged them to their account for fear of loss through damage, theft, or fire, in which case the company would be accountable. When the costumes were returned, the debt was cancelled.

Theatrical records are some of the best records we have for the circulation of clothes in Renaissance England. They help us, for instance, to see the relation between the pawning, renting, and recirculation of clothes and the specific oscillations of men and women between their

need to raise ready cash (through pawning) and their need to maintain
and assert status and identity (through buying or renting clothes). When
the theatrical company to which he belonged was about to tour Europe,
Richard Jones wrote to Edward Alleyn, asking for a financial loan to
repurchase his pawned clothes: "J have asut of clothes and acloke [a
cloak] at pane [pawn] for three pound and if it pleas you to lend me so
much to release them J shalbe bound to pray for you so long as J leve,
for if J go over and have no clothes J shall not be esteemed of."[58] The
clothes were the precondition of "estimation." It is not surprising, then,
that Samuel Pepys, when he wanted to have his portrait painted, *rented*
suitably magnificent clothing.[59]

In *The Fable of the Bees*, in the early eighteenth century, Bernard
Mandeville complained that the trade in second-hand clothes had totally
obscured social hierarchy:

> The poorest Labourer's Wife in the Parish, who scorns to wear a strong wholsom
> Frize, as she might, will half starve her self and her Husband to purchase a
> second-hand Gown and Petticoat, ... because, forsooth, it is more genteel. The
> Weaver, the Shoemaker, the Tailor, the Barber, and every mean working Fellow,
> that can set up with little, has the Impudence with the first Money he gets, to
> Dress himself like a Tradesman of Substance. [60]

The expansion in the second-hand clothes trade, though, did not begin in
the eighteenth century but in the London of the 1580s and 90s. And it
depended upon the *overaccumulation* of clothes by pawnbrokers like
Henslowe. The reason for this accumulation is clear enough: as Lawrence
Stone has documented, the late sixteenth century witnessed the explosion
of the London "season," the renting or buying of houses by the gentry in
London, and a phenomenal increase in the speed with which fashions in
clothing changed. Hence, the significance of the epigraphs to this article:
monarchs and aristocrats accumulated and disposed of clothes at an
ever-increasing pace, and there was a rapid increase in the number of
haberdashers and merchant tailors, as well as in imported luxury cloth
(silk, satin, fine linen, lace).

Given their overaccumulation of clothes, pawnbrokers like Henslowe
needed to find new outlets. The theater was such an outlet. It was a
strikingly novel one which solved a particular problem: there were real
limits to what pawnbrokers could do with the most splendid of the
clothes that they had acquired, due to the (admittedly ineffective)
sumptuary laws which regulated what specific classes could wear. We
know, for instance, that Henslowe had acquired clothes from "my lord
Burte," possibly either Baron Willoughby or William Herbert, later Earl
of Pembroke.[61] But unless he could find an aristocratic buyer for such

clothes, he would have had some difficulty reselling them if they were not reclaimed. He thus had to *create* a new market for the materials which he had accumulated. The need for such a new market for aristocratic clothes is indeed suggested by the remarks of the Swiss traveler, Thomas Platter, when he visited England in 1599. He wrote:

The actors are most expensively and elaborately costumed; for it is the English usage for eminent lords or Knights at their decease to bequeath and leave almost the best of their clothes to their serving men, which it is unseemly for the latter to wear, so that they offer them then for sale for a small sum to the actors.[62]

The only thing to doubt in Platter's account is his economic analysis. We know from Henslowe's accounts that clothes made from expensive materials and dyes could be pawned for *large* sums, and there is no reason why servants would have sold their perquisites to the actors for less money than they could have got by pawning them to Henslowe. But the more striking aspect of Platter's account is the suggestion that it was primarily to *actors* that clothes of any station or gender could safely be rented or sold.

When the theatrical companies themselves accumulated costumes, they could then enter into the second-hand clothes trade on their own account. While few records survive from the professional theaters, an earlier record about the Office of the Revels survives. In 1572, Thomas Giles formally complained that the Office of the Revels was renting out its costumes. Giles was right: "yello clothe of golde gownes" had been rented to Grey's Inn and to the Horsehead Tavern; black and white gowns were rented for the marriages of Edward Hind and Mr. Martin; copper cloth of gold gowns were rented for the marriage of Lord Montague's daughter; and red cloth of gold gowns were rented for a tailor's marriage. Giles, in his complaint, attributes an identity to the clothes themselves. He argues that they have suffered from the "soyll of the wereres / who for the most parte be of the meanest sort of mene" and that this was "to the grett dyscredytt of the same aparell."[63] Here, as in the accounts of the guild theaters, the clothes themselves assume an identity, one which comes from their association with the monarchy. The clothes can thus be devalued, soiled by circulation among "the meanest sort of mene."

Giles was himself a haberdasher who lent out clothes and he was thus in competition with the new role of the Office of the Revels in the second-hand clothes trade. His alarm was caused not by the social pretensions of actors but by the extraordinary circulation of clothes which the theater both staged within its fictions and encouraged in its audience. Scott McMillin argues that the number of distinct *roles* in a particular play can be translated as the number of *costumes* required, costumes which within the dramatic fictions are frequently borrowed or stolen. G. K. Hunter notes the "dizzying progress" of costumes in *Look About You* (1600):

Much of the play consists of a frenetic chase in which Skink, a murderer supposed hermit, steals the clothes of Redcap the jailor's son, and is then forced to give up Redcap's clothes to Gloster (also on the run). Dressed as Gloster, Skink then successively steals the clothes of Prince John, Geoffrey the barman, a hermit-conjurer, a falconer, and then a hermit again. In parallel incidents Gloster (as Redcap) appears in his turn as Old Faulconbridge, as a pursuivant and as a hermit. Meanwhile Lady Faulconbridge has become "a merchant's wife" while Robin Hood (in minority) dresses as Lady Faulconbridge.[64]

In *Your Five Gallants*, Frippery, the pawnbroker, is able to transform himself by dressing up in the pledges which he has accumulated: "Let me see now, whose cloak shall I wear today to continue change? ... Bring down Sir Oliver Needy's taffeta cloak and beaver hat – I am sure he is fast enough in the Knight's Ward – and Andrew Lucifer's rapier and dagger with the embossed girdle and hangers ..." Frippery also loans out ladies' clothes to Primero, a bawd, for the reclothing of prostitutes.[65]

If the theater staged the renting out of clothes from pawnbrokers, there is no doubt that it too acted as renter of its own clothes. We do not need to suspect Ben Jonson of pure comic invention when, in *The Alchemist*, he has Face tell Drugger to rent the costume of Hieronimo (of Kyd's *The Spanish Tragedy*) from the players:

FAC.   Thou must borrow,
A *Spanish* suite. Hast thou no credit with the players?
DRV. Yes, sir, did you neuer see me play the foole?
FAC. I know not, Nab: thou shalt, if I can helpe it.
Hieronymo's old cloake, ruffe, and hat will serue,
Ile tell thee more, when thou bringst 'hem.

The costume itself appears an act later, when Subtle announces to Face, "Here's your Hieronymo's cloake, and hat," and it migrates again when Lovewit puts on the costume for his marriage to Dame Pliant.[66] The costume hovers between a fetishized identity from the past (the specific role of Hieronimo) and its new possibilities once it has been appropriated (its generalized nature as a disguise and as a sign of "Spanishness").

The companies' role as traders in second-hand clothes, though, is only a part of the role of the theaters as engines of fashion. For, if the actors provided a constant demand for clothes, so too did the *audiences* who attended the theaters. Before the repeal of the sumptuary laws in 1604, it could be a risky undertaking to wear "unsuitable" clothes, particularly in church or the workplace, where one was most liable to surveillance and arrest. A Fellow of King's College was committed to prison in 1576 after a formal dispute with the Provost, when it was discovered that he was wearing "a cut taffeta doublet ... and a great pair of galligastion hose" under his gown. And it was suggested that an attorney who appeared before the Privy Council in 1592 with a gilt sword, huge ruffs, and other "unseemly apparel" be dismissed from the Court of Common Pleas.[67] But in the theaters, it was virtually impossible to regulate who wore what, whether on stage or off.

This accounts for one of the central attacks upon the theaters: that audiences used the liberty of the theatrical space to rival the actors themselves in their dress. William Harrison noted that "few of either sex come thither, but in theyr hol-dayes appareil, and so set forth, so trimmed, so adorned, so decked, so perfumed, as if they made the place the market of wantonnesse ..."[68] In his *Characters*, Thomas Overbury describes "A Phantastique" as one who "withers his clothes on a Stage, as a Sale-man is forc't to doe his sutes in Birchin-lane; and when the Play is done, if you marke his rising, tis with a kind of walking Epilogue between the two candles, to know if his suit may passe for currant."[69] Henry Fitzgeffrey decries both the unpatriotic luxury of an audience whose fashions come from Turkey, Spain, and France and the extent to which such luxury bankrupts the young gallant, Tissue Slop.

> Vengeance! I know him well, did he not drop
> Out of the *Tyring-house*? Then how (the duse)
> Comes the misshapen *Prodigall* so spruce,
> His year's *Revenewes* (I dare stand unto't,)
> Is not of *worth* to purchase such a *Sute* ...[70]

Attacks upon the acting companies combined a critique of the actors as shape-shifters with an awareness that the theaters staged and marketed new fashions in clothes through actors and audience alike.

I have been arguing that Renaissance London was both a cloth and a livery society and that the theater was a direct and indirect growth out of the trade in clothes. Direct, in that the theatrical entrepreneurs used the theaters as places to stage and profit from the apparel they had acquired either through renting or through purchase. Indirect, in that the players were supported both by their legal status as liveried servants and by their acquisition of aristocratic clothing. But I also began by suggesting that clothes, unlike money, powerfully inscribed *memory*. They did so when new by associating the wearer (if only in his or her memory) with the household or guild to which he or she belonged. (Livery, that is, did not have to be *marked* as such: any "gift" of clothing from master to servant counted as livery in the broad sense – as did food and lodging.) They did so when second-hand by retaining the traces of court, or theater, or just the shape of another body.

If livery, though, was an attempt to inscribe memory upon the body, the theater radically dis-placed memory. It did so, as Stephen Mullaney has finely shown, by translating the rituals of court and city alike from their "proper" locations to the Liberties to the north and south of London, from which distance it could interrogate the solemnities of rule together with an audience which included the politically disenfranchised.[71] It also dis-located those rituals by making them nakedly dependent upon a cash nexus. This dis-location appears even more dramatic if we turn from the court to the church. The church had always been involved in theatrical spectacle, and its vestments had been used in the miracle plays.[72] But the Reformation dramatically altered the church's relation to its own clothes. The majority of the elaborate garments which it owned could no longer be worn. Indeed, the central Puritan controversy of the late sixteenth century was the vestiarian controversy, in which the debate was about precisely what ministers could wear.[73] Not having any use of its own for its sacred clothes, the church rented them out or sold them. Thus, in 1560, the Church of the Holy Trinity, Chester, sold "the best cope and the vestment & appurtenances" to the mayor. But they also sold three vestments for 8s to Thomas Shevynton's son and Thomas Dycher's son "to make players garments."[74] At Chelmsford, the churchwardens hired out clothes to visiting actors for up to £2 19s until 1574, when the wardrobe was sold for £6 12s 4d. The Church of St. Mary the Virgin in Tewkesbury regularly rented out players' costumes between 1567 and 1585, charging between 1d and 5s, depending upon what was taken. Its "players Apparell" consisted of eight gowns, seven jerkins, four green silk caps, eight heads of hair for the apostles, ten beards, and "a face or vysor for the devyll."[75]

The case of the Church of St. Mary the Virgin is, of course, somewhat different from the other cases I have quoted. It was, after all, renting out apparel which had *always* been used for acting. Far more radical in its implications was the restaging of actual ecclesiastical garments upon the secular stage. This is what St. John's College, Cambridge, did in 1540–1, when it turned two green vestments, an old silk cope, and "halfe a decones cote" into theatrical costumes.[76] At King's College, the transformation of clothes from ecclesiastical garb to players' clothes and back again took on a Monty Pythonesque absurdity, when the liturgical garments that had been made into playing gear under Edward VI were turned back into priests' robes under Mary, only, presumably, to be turned back again into players' clothes a few years later.[77]

Most interesting of all in revealing the relations between the church, the second-hand clothes trade, and the professional theater companies is a note by Sir Henry Herbert in his office book:

> I committed Cromes, a broker in Long Lane, the 16 of february, 1634, to the Marshalsea for lending a church robe with the name of JESUS upon it to the players in Salisbury Court to present a Flamen, a priest of the heathens. Upon his petition of submission, and acknowledgment of his fault, I released him the 17 February, 1634.[78]

Given how few records have survived, we should particularly note the fact that the theater was renting clothes from a second-hand clothes dealer. Indeed, Long Lane, where Cromer worked, was recorded by Strype in his additions to John Stow's *Survey* of London as a "Place of Note for the sale of Apparel, Linen, and Upholsters Goods, both Second-hand and New, but chiefly for Old, for which it is of note."[79] But what, of course, is most striking about Herbert's note is the theater's extraordinary inversion of the meaning of an ecclesiastical garment, both in translating it from the sacred realm of the church to the secular playhouse and in appropriating a robe with the name of "Jesus" upon it for the part of a pagan priest. In their assumption of clothes from court and church, the actors put the *meaning* of those clothes in crisis. They thus subordinated the rituals of church and state to the protean play of the marketplace.

In this, the actors accompanied, supported and rivaled that other great early capitalist industry: the printing trade. Like the printing trade, the playhouses depended upon large capital investments. Also like the printers, the actors, once they had achieved the protection of patronage, depended not upon the livery economy of the court but upon the direct collection of money. In other words, whereas the court transmuted money into cloth, thus *material*izing the economic as social relations, the theater transformed cloth into cash, thus opening up a gap between the economic and the social.[80] In this, again, the theater paralleled the print shops, whose single greatest outlay was upon *paper*, which in turn (until the use of wood pulp in the nineteenth century) was dependent upon the residue of cloth. There was, as I noted above, a close relation between the cloth trade and the Stationers' Company: in 1600, twelve drapers were translated into the Stationers, and the fact that they were already working as printers and publishers may have been because of the direct connection between drapery and paper.[81] From rags, the final worn state of clothes and bedsheets, came the sheets upon which Shakespeare, like every other dramatist and writer, was printed.

But if theater and print shop alike were formative in a new monetary economy and, indeed, in the very possibility of imagining an economy unregulated by the "households" of court or guild, they did not simply demystify the hierarchical magics of absolutism, but also created their own magics in their reworking of cloth. In terms of the relation between print and clothes, that magic was still at work in the nineteenth century, and it is wonderfully caught in the fairy tales of Hans Christian Andersen. In "The Rags," for instance, Andersen writes that "[e]ach rag had his history, each could tell his own tale ... Some were domestic rags, others came from foreign countries." The proximity of such diverse rags is the precondition both for the violent magic of the new aggressive distinctions between nation-states and for the dissolution of those distinctions. After a Danish and a Norwegian rag have each boasted of the superiority of their own respective nations, "they were both turned into paper; and as luck would have it, the Norwegian rag became paper on which a Norwegian wrote a faithful love-letter to a Danish girl, while the Danish rag became the manuscript of a Danish ode written in praise of Norway's power and splendour."[82]

This new magic, which metamorphosed clothes into the materials of a new form of literary production, is even more strikingly captured in Andersen's story, "The Shirt Collar." The collar wants to get married, and proposes in the wash to a garter. But she won't tell him her name, so he proposes to the iron, who burns a hole in him, and addresses him disdainfully as "You rag." Finally, at the papermill, the collar says "it's high time I changed into white paper. And that's what happened. All the rags were turned into white paper; but the collar became this very bit of paper we have before us, on which the story has been printed."[83] Andersen restores to the notion of the book, which had become increasingly the "invisible" medium joining the immaterial ideas of the writer to the immaterial mind of the reader, the literal matter of the book and the participation of "literature" in the life-cycle of cloth.

The printed book, like the theater, stands at the intersection of two radically distinct ways of conceiving matter. Book and theater alike wrenched cloth from its place within a system of patronage and reinserted it within a market economy. But from the perspective of that new economy, the theater insisted upon staging the magic of clothes, even as it interrogated the meaning of all magics. Part of the new magic which the theater was constitutive in shaping and popularizing was the magic of *fashion*. That language is energetically and troublingly presented in *Volpone*. In Act III, scene vii, Corvino and Mosca exit, leaving Celia alone with Volpone. Then, as the stage direction reads, Volpone "leapes off from his couch" and proceeds to conjure up an extraordinary vision of polymorphous perversity. His desire for Celia has, he declares, already "rays'd" him "in severall shapes." But now Celia, the fixed star of his gaze, can herself enter into the play of metamorphoses,

> Whilst we, in changed shapes, act OVIDS tales
> Thou, like EUROPA now, and I like JOVE,
> Then I like Mars, and thou like ERYCINE,
> So, of the rest, till we have quite run through
> And weary'd all the fables of the gods.
> Then will I haue thee in more moderne formes,
> Attired like some sprightly dame of *France*,
> Braue *Tuscan* lady, or proud *Spanish* beauty;
> Sometimes, vnto the *Persian Sophie*s wife;
> Or the grand *Signior's* mistress; and, for change,
> To one of our most artfull courtizans,
> Or some quick *Negro* or cold *Russian*.
> And I will meet thee, in as many shapes.[84]

In this exuberant and imperialist vision of fashion, clothes can elide human and animal (Europa and the bull [Jove]), human and divine (Mars and Erycine, Jove and Europa), different nations (French, Spanish, Tuscan, Persian, Russian), different continents (Europe, Asia, Africa), and different classes (the Persian Sophie's wife, a Venetian courtezan).

Such hybridization is made possible, one might say, because of the transformations of the world-system which Venice, where *Volpone* is set, itself helped to initiate. In the process, the aristocracy becomes no more than one possible kind of style: a style which one can adopt or drop according to the extent of one's wardrobe. In Volpone's vision, one might locate a mercantilist view of what capitalism can do. And a new political economy would later provide the conceptual tools through which the new social order would view both itself and its prehistory: tools like "individual," "identity," "choice." Another form of power, though, was equally embodied in the staging of clothes: their power to absorb memory. Yet the ability of clothing to absorb memory is again and again figured as a site of crisis; clothing falls into the wrong hands (the handkerchief in *Othello*, the sleeve in *Troilus and Cressida*), erases distinctions of class and gender (*Lear, Twelfth Night, As You Like It*), signifies falsely (the bloody cloth in *Cymbeline*), does not fit (Macbeth's "borrowed robes"). Shakespeare's plays, indeed, condense the magic of cloth when its meaning is least certain.

Let me try to clarify this point by looking at *Cymbeline*.[85] It is the doltish but dangerous Cloten who, sneering at Imogen's husband, Posthumus, calls him "[a] hilding for a livery, a squire's cloth." Imogen responds to Cloten's insult, not by claiming that Posthumus transcends or is better than his clothes, but by dwelling upon the value that his clothes have for her, particularly now that he is absent:

> His mean'st Garment,
> That euer hath but clipt his body; is dearer
> In my respect, then all the Heires aboue thee,
> Were they all made such men.[86]

All modern editions have followed the second Folio in changing "Heires" to "haires" ("hairs" in F 3 and F 4), but the F 1 reading seems to me equally plausible (although with a quibble on "hairs" and "airs"). The point that Imogen would then be making is that the lowliest clothing that has touched and embraced her lover is worth more than even a rightful heir (Cloten being only the stepchild of the monarch). Touching him, Posthumus's clothes have absorbed him into themselves.

For Cloten, as much as for Imogen, Posthumus's clothes come to embody memory. To take revenge, Cloten plans to take Posthumus's place not only by becoming Imogen's lover but also by assuming Posthumus's clothes. He asks Pisanio: "Hast any of thy late Masters Garments in thy possession?" The suit which Cloten takes is the last one which Posthumus wore before he left England, and, in wearing it, Cloten attempts to erase him. He intends to do this by transforming the meaning of the clothes: "the very Garment of *Posthumus*," that Imogen held "in more respect, then my Noble and naturall person," will be transformed into the clothes of her rapist ("I will execute [the rape] in the Cloathes that she so prais'd"). It is as if the clothes will keep Posthumus, imagined as dead, alive so that he, in the remaining form of his suit, can witness Imogen's rape, while, simultaneously, the suit, and thus Posthumus, will be both defiled and appropriated by Cloten.[87]

Wearing Posthumus's clothes, though, Cloten erases himself. In one of the play's most bizarre jokes, Cloten, dressed in Posthumus's clothes, says to Guiderius: "Know'st me not by my Cloathes?" And yet, in an ironically inverse form, Posthumus is indeed absorbed into Cloten, as Cloten is absorbed into him. When Imogen finds the headless body of Cloten, she says:

> A headlesse man? The Garments of *Posthumus*?
> I know the shape of's Legge: this is his Hand:
> His Foote Mercuriall: his martiall Thigh
> The brawnes of *Hercules*.[88]

The passage is extraordinary, because, seeing the garments of Posthumus,

Imogen reads the body of Cloten as Posthumus. If these are Posthumus's clothes, then this is his hand, and this his leg, foot, thigh, and brawn. No doubt one implication is that Posthumus's betrayal of Imogen has reduced him to an identity with Cloten. But I think that we must also understand how, in the Renaissance, clothes could be imagined as retaining the identity and the form of the wearer. It is Imogen, after all, who would embrace Posthumus's meanest garment, even as that garment had embraced him ("clipt his body"). The garment bears quite literally the trace and the memory of its owner.

Cymbeline, though, like the theater as a whole with its "borrowed robes," makes the question of the *ownership* of clothes profoundly problematic. Clothes and bodies merge and separate in perverse and vagrant fashion. While Posthumus's suit migrates from him to Cloten, Posthumus himself migrates to Italy, or, in terms of the theatrical spectacle, into "these Italian weedes," which align him with the treacherous courtiership of Iachimo and of England's invaders. Returning to England again, he "disrobe[s]" himself, thus distancing himself from Iachimo, and redresses to appear, like Cymbeline's outlaw sons, as "a *Britaine* Pezant."[89] Here, as Jean-Christophe Agnew puts it in a different context, "to re-dress [is], in effect, to redress."[90] The scene, though, in which Posthumus makes this last transformation simultaneously stages cloth, not as a guise which can be shifted without trace, but as memory, the living embodiment of a dead past. Posthumus's very first line is "Yea bloody cloth, / Ile keep thee," as he holds the cloth which Pisanio has sent as a token of his killing of Imogen.[91] It is as if the "Senselesse Linnen" of Posthumus's handkerchief as he parted from Imogen at the beginning of the play has been incarnated, now that she is dead, as the sentient material of the cloth which has "clipt" her.[92] Having killed Imogen, Posthumus is forced to learn the value of the trace: the dearness of the "mean'st Garment." He will keep the bloody cloth.

There is a further unsettling twist. The bloody cloth bears a purely theatrical stain, invented by Pisanio. Imogen is not dead, the blood is not her blood, and it is clear that the cloth is in no way connected with her. This returns us to the point we mentioned above: the theater seems to stage cloth as the site of a crisis, in which meaning is simultaneously profoundly asserted and denied. It can be asserted so powerfully because clothing *could* carry the absent body, memory, genealogy, as well as literal material value.

Nowhere is this more apparent than in the care with which specific items of clothing are transmitted in wills. At one level, and particularly among the aristocracy, the leaving of clothes is an assertion of the power of the gift-giver and the dependency of the recipient. Such is the chilling implication of the Earl of Dorset's bequest of his wife's own clothes to her in 1624: "'Item I doe give & bequeath to my deerlye beloved wife' all her wearing apparel and such rings and jewels as were hers on her marriage and the 'rocke rubye ring which I have given her.'" His own apparel, Dorset divided amongst his servants, with the exception of some rich apparel which he left to his brother and one embroidered suit delivered to Captain Sackvill.[93]

The will of Dorset's wife, Anne Clifford, on the other hand, is far more detailed and moving in its association of clothes with memory: she leaves to her grandchildren "the remainder of the two rich armors which were my noble father's, to remaine to them and their posterity (if they soe please) as a remembrance of him." And to her "deare daughter," she leaves

my bracelett of little pomander beads, sett in gold and enamelling, containing fifty-seven beads in number, which usually I ware under my stomacher; which bracelett is above an hundred yeares old, and was given by Philip the Second, King of Spaine, to Mary, Queene of England [and by her?] to my greate grandmother, Anne, Countesse of Bedford: and also two little peices of my father and mother, sett in a tablett of gold, and enamelled with blew; and all those seaven or eight old truncks and all that is within them, being for the most part old things that were my deare and blessed mother's, which truncks commonly stand in my owne chamber or the next unto it.

Finally, Anne Clifford left

[t]o Mrs. Elizabeth Gilmore (whoe formerly served me for many yeares together) 20l. and my fugard sattin mantle lyned with a white furr mixt, with haire collar; and to her daughter, Mrs. Elizabeth Kelloway, 10l., and my best riding coate of haird colloured sattin ... My weareing apparell to my servants, and my linnen to my daughter. 100l. to be bestowed in mourning blacks att my death for some of my frinds and servants.

Here, the transmission of clothes is a transmission of wealth, of genealogy, of royal connections, but also of memory and of the love of mother for daughter (the trunks which she gives to her own daughter contain "old things that were my deare and blessed mother's, which truncks commonly stand in my owne chamber or the next unto it").[94]

It was not only aristocrats who bequeathed their clothing with such care. A typical legacy of a master upon his death was the gift of clothes to his apprentice. Augustine Phillips, an actor and sharer in the King's Men, left bequests upon his death in 1605 not only to fellow sharers like Henry Condell and William Shakespeare, but also to the boy actor who had trained under him: "Item, I give to Samuel Gilborne, my late apprentice, the sum of forty shillings, and my mouse-colored velvet hose, and a white taffeta doublet, and black taffeta suit, my purple cloak, sword, and dagger, and my bass viol."[95] Bequests of clothes recur in actors' wills. Thomas Pope, another actor in the King's Men, wrote in his will in 1604: "I give and bequeath to Robert Gough and John Edmans all my wearing apparel, and all my arms, to be equally divided between them."[96] William Bird, a leading actor in the Earl of Pembroke's Men and then with the Lord Admiral's Men, wrote on 30 January 1623: "I doe bequeath vnto my eldest sonne William Byrd my Ash cullor suite and cloake of cloth laced with sattin lace ... I give and bequeath vnto my third sonne Thomas Burde my Ash cullor suite and cloake trimmed with greene silke and siluer lace."[97] Philip Henslowe himself, while he traded professionally in second-hand clothes, participated in the circulation of material ghosts – the clothes of his dead brother, Edmond, who left him "a gold ring with a pearl, and a black cloak."[98] The clothes are preserved; they remain. It is the bodies which inhabit them which change.

Memories are literally *worn*. That is quite explicit in Renaissance wills, even when new clothing and jewelry is called for. Jewelry (and in particular rings) were, in fact, the most frequent form of explicit memorial. The actor, Thomas Bass, left money in his will in 1634 to nine friends to buy "each of them a Ring of the value of tenn shillings a peece to weare in remembrance of him."[99] Similarly John Hemminges, the sharer in the King's Men, bequeathed "vnto every of my fellowes and sharers his Mats servants ... the somme of tenn shillinges apeece to make them ringes for remembrances of me." But William Browne left twenty shillings to his company "to buy them blacke ribbons to weare in remembrance of me." And the buying of memorial clothes is clearly implied in Nicholas Tooley's will of 1624: "Item I doe giue vnto her [Mrs. Cuthbert Burbage's] daughter Elizabethe Burbadge als Maxey the summe of tenn pounds to be paied vnto her owne proper hands (therwithall to buy her such things as shee shall thincke most meete to weare in remembrance of mee)."[100]

What are the implications which we can draw out from the wills which bequeathed clothes? First, clothes have a life of their own; they both *are* material presences and they *encode* other material and immaterial presences. In the transfer of clothes, identities are transferred from an aristocrat to an actor, from an actor to a master, from a master to an apprentice. Such transfers are, of course, staged within the theater in the many scenes where a servant dresses as his or her master, a lover dresses in the borrowed garments of another lover, a skull inhabits the clothes which have survived it. In *Twelfth Night*, brother is transformed into sister and sister into brother through the costume identified as Cesario/Sebastian. We here move closer to the narrower meaning of "transvestism" as that term is used today to imply cross-gendering. But what I want to emphasize is the extent to which the Elizabethan theater, and the culture more generally, was fixated upon clothes in and of themselves. This fixation was part of a larger interest in what Arjun Appadurai has called the "social life of things."[101]

In the Renaissance professional theater, though, the social life of these particular things is a life of rupture and crisis. With the transmission of clothes, there is a transmission of identity, but a transmission which is staged as constantly undoing the mutual dependencies materialized in the gift of cloth. In Act IV, scene iv of *Troilus and Cressida*, Troilus gives his sleeve to Cressida as a token of his love. In the first line of the first scene of the play, Troilus had said "I'll unarm again."[102] There, he took off his armor; here, he "unarms" again, but it is something both literally and symbolically closer to his own arm, his own flesh, his own identity, which he takes off and gives away. When Cressida, herself given away by Troy, gives away the sleeve to Diomedes, the transaction is so prominent as to have disturbed editors, who have added stage directions so that, to quote the Arden editor, the sleeve does not "change hands with ludicrous frequency."[103] But it is precisely the extraordinary *value* which has been attached to the cloth and which is embodied within it that accounts for the complex back-and-forth exchange of it. As Cressida says of the sleeve, in Q1, "He that takes that doth take my heart withal," or, in the Folio, "He that takes that, rakes my heart withall."[104] Q1 captures the magical power of a piece of clothing to absorb its wearer; F1 captures the power of clothing to dispossess its owner's self when the clothing is transferred. Into the sleeve which passes from hand to hand, which has no secure owner or origin, are woven the identities of both Troilus and Cressida. Diomedes, who wears the sleeve on his helmet, appropriates both lovers. And in imagining destroying Diomedes, Troilus imagines destroying the token of himself:

> That Sleeue is mine, that heele beare in his Helme:
> Were it a Caske compos'd by *Vulcans* skill,
> My Sword should bite it.[105]

Troilus, in fighting Diomedes, attacks his own sleeve, and hence himself. The material of cloth matters so much because it operates on, and undoes, the margins of the self.

Troilus and Cressida may also remind us of the curious *erotic* charge which attaches so frequently to the transmission of clothes in the Renaissance. And if this eroticism comes sometimes from the specific relation of a piece of clothing to the remembered lover (Imogen's attachment to Posthumus's clothes), it can equally spring from the hybridization of bodies made possible by the circulation of clothes: the boy in woman's dress; the woman in man's clothing; the adulterous lover in the husband's garments; a man or woman's body sexualized by a transposition of class. In Middleton's *The Widow*, Martia, a woman, cross-dresses as Ansaldo. It is the "man" Ansaldo to whom Phillippa is violently attracted. But, as Susan Zimmerman observes, the attraction is to a "man" indeterminately dressed, since s/he has been stripped of her clothes down to a shirt: "I think it was a shirt," says the maid;

> I know not well
> For gallants wear both [i.e. shifts or shirts] now-a-days.[106]

Phillippa proceeds to dress Martia/Ansaldo in an old suit of her husband's. It is as if the eroticism comes not from the body "beneath," but rather from the shifting, clothed surfaces. The eroticism of these surfaces, though, is established by the fetishized oscillation between sameness and difference, between Martia/Ansaldo imagined as man/woman, lover/husband, cuckolder/cuckolded.

I will conclude with *Hamlet*, returning a final time to the contradictory engagement of the Shakespearean theater in the staging of an economy of clothes. In particular, I want to look at Hamlet's father, the Ghost. The first problem with the Ghost is that no one knows how to address the apparition. To Marcellus, Barnardo, and Horatio, the Ghost is "it": "speake to it *Horatio*"; "Marke it"; "It is offended." But to Hamlet, the Ghost, dressed in his father's armor, cannot be "it" although it is only questionably "he":

> Ile *call* thee *Hamlet*,
> King, Father, Royall Dane.[107]

But, despite the identity of name, *this* Hamlet, called "father," bears no resemblance to the son. I mean this quite literally. The son wears an inky cloak and suit of solemn black; the father wears, or we might almost say *is*, were it not for his raised visor, a suit of armor. Not any suit of armor but "the very Armour [Hamlet] had on" when he fought with Fortinbras.[108] Now it is precisely such suits of armor that were transmitted as the markers and, indeed, creators of genealogy. It was "the remainder of the two rich armors which were my noble father's" that Anne Clifford left to her grandchildren, "to remaine to them and their posterity (if they soe please) as a remembrance of him."

This is a play, though, in which there will be no such legacy. If Hamlet takes upon himself the Ghost's demand, if he reiterates, and reverses, his father's conflict with Fortinbras, if he is buried as a soldier with "[t]he Souldiours Musicke, and the rites of Warre," he never becomes his armored father.[109] Indeed, when Hamlet returns from England he writes to Claudius in a curiously ambiguous phrase that he is "*set naked on your Kingdome.*"[110] It seems, in other words, as if Hamlet gets ever more distant from the armor which his father wears. In putting an "antic disposition" on, Hamlet becomes the fool or court jester. And it is the court jester, Yorick, not his father, whom Hamlet most fondly recalls: "he hath borne me on his backe a thousand times: And how abhorred in my Imagination is, my gorge rises at it. Heere hung those lipps, that I have kist I know not how oft."[111] The lips that he has kissed: the lips not of the father but of the jester.

One striking feature of Alleyn's list of the costumes of the Admiral's Men in 1598 is a list of "Antik sutes." It is not entirely clear whether "antik" here means antique or belonging to the jester, since the two words were usually written alike. Perhaps "antik" means both, since the list includes both cloth of gold and of silver and "will somers cote."[112] Will Sommer was Henry VIII's fool, so that, if the suit truly belonged to him, it was both "antique" and "antic," a memorial to the power of the fool to reach out with his mocking legacy into the present. Though Yorick is dead, his skull memorializes the legacy he leaves, a legacy which includes the "antic disposition" which Hamlet, his illegitimate heir, puts on. In striking contrast to *The Spanish Tragedy*, where the ghost returns gloatingly to conclude the plot, the Ghost of *Hamlet* simply disappears after Act III. One might say that the ghost of the jester displaces the ghost of the soldier–king.

However, if we are to believe the so-called "bad" Q1, the soldier–king had been displaced even before Act III. In the bedchamber scene, as Hamlet berates his mother, the stage direction reads "Enter the ghost in his night gowne."[113] Nearly all editions delay this entry by a single line, the line where Hamlet says: "A King of shreds and patches."[114] Moved, the line can only refer to Claudius (especially if, as in many modern productions, the Ghost is still wearing armor). But in its earlier position in Q1, Q2, and F1 alike, the line seems to hover between the mock king who rules and the dead king who returns, no longer clad in complete steel, but in a robe of undress, a nightgown. "A King of shreds and patches": possibly, at least, the father, like the son, *as* jester, denuded of his armor, yet still "[m]y Father in his habite, as he liued."[115]

Whichever reading or staging we supply, I hope to have shown that clothes are central to what is staged, that, indeed, if we do not understand the clothes, we do not understand the action, or the actors, or the theater, or the social formation. And I have argued that the Renaissance theater, far from reproducing the orderly transmissions of a cloth economy, obsessively staged the misunderstanding of clothes, clothes as a site of crisis from which nostalgia for a lost time of splendid armor could offer no reprieve. On the Renaissance stage, the transmission of cloth figures the formation and dissolution of identity, the ways in which the subject is possessed and dispossessed, touched and haunted by the materials it inhabits.

NOTES

1   William Herbert, *The History of the Twelve Great Livery Companies of London* (2 vols., 1834–7; Newton Abbot, 1968), II, p. 60.

2   Francis Bacon, *The historie of the raigne of King Henry the seventh* (London, 1622), p. 58; John Milton, *Samson Agonistes*, in Merritt Y. Hughes, *John Milton: Complete Poems and Major Prose* (New York, 1957), p. 590, lines 1616, 1622.

3   Sir Thomas Overbury, *A wife now the widdow of Sir T. Overbury ... Whereunto are added many witty characters* (London, 1638), "A Servingman," G.

4   John Nichols, *The Progresses, Processions, and Magnificent Festivities of King James I* (4 vols., London, 1828), II, pp. 141, 132.

5   Herbert, *The History of the Twelve Great Livery Companies*, II, p. 300.

6   See Karl Marx, "The Fetishism of the Commodity and Its Secret," in *Capital*, vol. I, trans. Ben Fowkes (New York, 1976), pp. 163–77; for Marx's assertion of the *necessity* of "alienation" in the positive form of the imbuing of objects with subjectivity through our work upon them and of the imbuing of the subject with objectivity through our materializations, see his *On James Mill*, in David McLellan, ed., *Karl Marx: Selected Writings* (Oxford, 1977), pp. 114–23.

7   The centrality of objects in *pre*capitalist economies should be clear from Marcel Mauss, *The Gift: Forms and Functions of Exchange in Archaic Societies*, trans. Ian Cunnison (New York, 1967).

8   On the movement of objects in and out of commodification, see Igor Kopytoff, "The Cultural Biography of Things: Commoditization as Process," in Arjun Appadurai, ed., *The Social Life of Things: Commodities in Cultural Perspective* (Cambridge, 1986), pp. 64–91. On the history of the concept of fetishism, see the important articles by William Pietz on "The Problem of the Fetish," *Res* 9 (1985), 5–17; 13 (1987), 23–45; 16 (1988), 105–23. See also his "Fetishism and Materialism: The Limits of Theory in Marx," in Emily Apter and William Pietz, eds., *Fetishism as Cultural Discourse* (Ithaca and London, 1993), pp. 119–51.

9   Janet Arnold, *Queen Elizabeth's Wardrobe Unlock'd* (Leeds, 1988), pp. 101–2.

10 Ibid. p. 107.

11 Ibid. p. 107.

12 William Shakespeare, *Love's Labour's Lost*, in Charlton Hinman, ed., *The First Folio of Shakespeare: The Norton Facsimile* (London, 1968), TLN 1080 (iv. i. 99). Unless otherwise noted, all quotations from Shakespeare are from this edition and references are to its Through Line Numbers (TLN), followed by act, scene, and line numbers in parentheses from *The Riverside Shakespeare*, ed. G. Blakemore Evans (Boston, 1974).

13   Arnold, *Elizabeth's Wardrobe*, p. 106.

14   Ibid. p. 105.

15   Stephen Orgel, "Call Me Ganymede: Shakespeare's Apprentices and the Representation of Women," *Impersonations: The Performance of Gender in Shakespeare's England* (Cambridge, forthcoming).

16   See M. C. Bradbrook, *John Webster: Citizen and Dramatist* (New York, 1980), p. 180.

17   Bradbrook, *Webster*, p. 1.

18   Ibid. p. 166.

19   Gerald Eades Bentley, *The Jacobean and Caroline Stage* (7 vols., Oxford, 1941), I, p. 247.

20   John Stow, *Annales*, continued by Edmund Howe (London, 1615), p. 697.

21   On the crucial dramatic significance of costumes and changes of costumes in the guild theaters, see Richard Southern, *The Staging of Plays before Shakespeare* (London, 1973), particularly pp. 132–42; and David M. Bevington, "'Blake and wyght, fowll and fayer': Stage Picture in *Wisdom*," in Milla Cozart Riggio, ed., *The "Wisdom" Symposium*, Papers from the Trinity College Medieval Festival (New York, 1986), pp. 18–38. I am above all indebted to Stephen Orgel's work on costumes and the theatre in *Impersonations*. To my shame and regret, I did not come across Jean MacIntyre's *Costumes and Scripts in the Elizabethan Theatre* (Edmonton, 1992) until after I had completed this chapter. However, I would direct the reader to this important book.

22   R. W. Ingram, ed., *Coventry*, Records of Early English Drama (Toronto, 1981), pp. 226, 224.

23   Ibid. pp. 334–5.

24   Ibid. p. 308.

25   Lawrence M. Clopper, ed., *Chester*, Records of Early English Drama (Toronto, 1979), p. 105, and Ingram, *Coventry*, p. 259.

26   Ingram, *Coventry*, p. 93.

27   G. E. Bentley, *The Profession of Dramatist in Shakespeare's Time, 1590–1642* (Princeton, 1971), pp. 88–9n.

28   G. E. Bentley, *The Profession of Player in Shakespeare's Time, 1590–1642* (Princeton, 1984), p. 88.

29   Andrew Gurr, *The Shakespearean Stage 1574–1642* (2nd edn., Cambridge, 1980), p. 178.

30   Bentley, *The Profession of Player*, pp. 91, 90.

31   R. A. Foakes and R. T. Rickert, eds., *Henslowe's Diary* (Cambridge, 1961), p. 184.

32   Walter W. Greg, ed., *Henslowe Papers* (London, 1907), p. 90.

33   Foakes and Rickert, *Henslowe's Diary*, pp. 168–9, 178, 179, 180, 169–70, 179, 185–6, 97, 133; Neil Carson, *A Companion to Henslowe's Diary* (Cambridge, 1988), pp. 38–9.

34   Gurr, *Shakespearean Stage*, p. 13.

35   Ibid. pp. 44, 47.

36   Ibid. p. 50.

37   Ibid. pp. 57–8.

38   Greg, *Henslowe Papers*, p. 125.

39   Bentley, *The Jacobean and Caroline Stage* (Oxford, 1941), III, pp. 646–7.

40   William Ingram, *A London Life in the Brazen Age: Francis Langley, 1548–1602* (Cambridge, Mass., and London, 1978), pp. 51–65.

41   Bentley, *The Profession of Player*, p. 5.

42   E. A. J. Honigmann, "'There Is a World Elsewhere': William Shakespeare, Businessman," in Werner Habicht, D. J. Palmer, and Roger Pringle, eds., *Images of Shakespeare*, Proceedings of the Third Progress of the International Shakespeare Association, 1986 (Delaware, 1988), p. 40.

43   See Gerald D. Johnson, "The Stationers Versus the Drapers: Control of the Press in the Late Sixteenth Century," *The Library*, 6th series, 10, 1 (1988), 16.

44   Carson, *A Companion*, pp. 22–3.

45   Thomas Middleton, *Your Five Gallants*, in A. H. Bullen, ed., *The Works of Thomas Middleton* (8 vols., London, 1885), vol. III, 1.1.1–113; 4.4.2–6; 2.3.238–41, and 274–7; 4.8.277–80.

46   Ben Jonson, *Every Man in His Humour* (acted 1598, 1616 text), in C. H. Herford, Percy and Evelyn Simpson, eds., *Ben Jonson*, (11 vols., Oxford, 1954), vol. III, 3.5. 31–2, 4.9.45–50.

47   Carson, *A Companion*, p. 23.

48   Foakes and Rickert, *Henslowe's Diary*, pp. 151, 149, 151, 158.

49   Ibid. pp. 159, 259, 152, 156.

50   Ibid. p. 219.

51   Roslyn Lander Knutson, *The Repertory of Shakespeare's Company, 1594–1613* (Fayetteville, Ark., 1991), pp. 35–7.

52   See Carson, *A Companion*, p. 52: "[C]lothing was a readily marketable commodity in which there was an active second hand trade. There may, therefore, have been a fairly rapid turnover of lavish costumes that could be identified with a particular role or play."

53   Greg, *Henslowe Papers*, pp. 52–5; Foakes and Rickert, *Henslowe's Diary*, pp. 316–25.

54   Carson, *A Companion*, p. 52.

55   Ibid. p. 52.

56   Foakes and Rickert, *Henslowe's Diary*, p. 73.

57   Ibid. pp. 207, 209–10; Carson, *A Companion*, p. 29.

58   Greg, *Henslowe Papers*, p. 33.

59   Robert Latham and William Matthews, eds., *The Diary of Samuel Pepys* (Berkeley, 1983), VII, p. 602. See also Beverly Lemire, *Fashion's Favourite: The Cotton Trade and the Consumer in Britain, 1660–1800*, Pasold Research Fund (Oxford, 1991), p. 15.

60   Bernard Mandeville, *The Fable of the Bees: Or Private Vices, Publick Benefits* (Oxford, 1957), pp. 127–8.

61   Foakes and Rickert, *Henslowe's Diary*, pp. xxii–xxiii.

62   Clare Williams, *Thomas Platter's Travels in England, 1599* (London, 1959), p. 167.

63   Albert Feuillerat, *Documents Relating to the Office of the Revels in the Time of Queen Elizabeth I* (Louvain, 1908), p. 409.

64   Scott McMillin, *The Elizabethan Theatre and the book of Sir Thomas More* (Ithaca, 1987), pp. 53–5. G. K. Hunter, "Flatcaps and Bluecoats: Visual

Signals on the Elizabethan Stage," *Essays and Studies* (1980), 39–40. I am indebted to Hunter's important essay throughout this piece.

65 Bullen, *Middleton*, vol. III, 1. 1. 317–23.

66 Jonson, *The Alchemist*, in Herford *et al.*, *Jonson*, vol. V, 4. 7. 67–73, 5. 4. 68, 5. 3. 84–8. I am indebted to Michael Warren for drawing this passage to my attention.

67 N. B. Harte, "State Control of Dress and Social Change in Pre-Industrial England," in D. C. Coleman and A. H. John, eds., *Trade, Government and Economy in Pre-Industrial England: Essays Presented to F. J. Fisher* (London, 1976), p. 147.

68 Quoted in Andrew Gurr, *Playgoing in Shakespeare's London* (Cambridge, 1987), p. 234.

69 Overbury, *A wife*, M4; Gurr, *Playgoing*, p. 228.

70 Fitzgeffrey, *Satyres: and Satyricall Epigrams: With Certaine Observations at Black-Fryers* (London, 1617), F2v; Gurr, *Playgoing*, pp. 231–2.

71 Steven Mullaney, *The Place of the Stage: License, Play and Power in Renaissance England* (Chicago, 1988).

72 Glynne Wickam, *Early English Stages, 1300–1660* (New York, 1963), II, part 1, "1576–1660," p. 37.

73 M. M. Knappen, *Tudor Puritanism: A Chapter in the History of Idealism* (Chicago, 1939), pp. 187–216.

74 Wickham, *English Stages*, p. 3.

75 Audrey Douglas and Peter Greenfield, eds., *Cumberland, Westmoreland, Gloucestershire*, Records of Early English Drama (Toronto, 1986), pp. 335–9.

76 Alan H. Nelson, ed., *Cambridge*, Records of Early English Drama (Toronto, 1989), I, p. 123. On the circulation of vestments and costumes, see Stephen Greenblatt, *Shakespearean Negotiations: The Circulation of Social Energy in Renaissance England* (Berkeley, 1988), pp. 112–14.

77 Ibid. I, p. 189; II, p. 756.

78 Bentley, *The Profession of Dramatist*, p. 179.

79 John Stow, *A Survey of the Cities of London and Westminster ... Corrected, Improved, and very much Enlarged by John Strype* (London, 1720), Book 2, p. 122.

80 See Jean-Christophe Agnew, *Worlds Apart: The Market and the Theater in Anglo-American Thought, 1550–1750* (Cambridge, 1986), pp. 17–56.

81 See Johnson, "The Stationers Versus the Drapers": "What originally attracted these drapers to the book-trade is not clear. Perhaps there was an affinity between their trade and the importation and sale of paper" (p. 5).

82 Hans Christian Andersen, *Eighty Fairy Tales*, trans. R. P. Keigwin (New York, 1982), p. 454.

83 Ibid. pp. 229–31.

84 Jonson, *Volpone*, in Herford, ed., *Jonson*, vol. V, 3. 7. 221–33.

85 On clothes in *Cymbeline*, see David Bevington, *Action Is Eloquence: Shakespeare's Language of Gesture* (Cambridge, Mass., 1984), pp. 63–4.

86 Shakespeare, *Cymbeline*, TLN 1111–14 (2. 3. 133–6).

87 Ibid. TLN 2039–40, 2051–3, 2059–60 (3. 5. 123–4, 135–6, 142–3).

88 Ibid. TLN 2350, 2630–3 (4. 2. 81, 308–11).

89 Ibid. TLN 2879–81 (5. 1. 22–4).

90 Agnew, *Worlds Apart*, p. 35.
91 *Cymbeline*, TLN 2858 (5. 1. 1).
92 Ibid. TLN 272 (1. 3. 7).
93 George C. Williamson, *Lady Anne Clifford, Countess of Dorset, Pembroke, and Montgomery, 1590–1676: Her Life, Letters and Work* (Kendal, 1922), · pp. 460, 462.
94 Ibid. pp. 467, 468, 469.
95 Bentley, *The Profession of Dramatist*, p. 20.
96 Ibid. p. 130.
97 S. P. Cerasano, "New Renaissance Players' Wills," *Modern Philology* 82, 3 (1985), 300–1.
98 S. P. Cerasano, "Revising Philip Henslowe's Biography," *Notes and Queries*, 230 (1985), 68.
99 Bentley, *Jacobean and Caroline Stage*, III, p. 631.
100 Ibid. III, pp. 644, 637, 649.
101 Appadurai, ed., *The Social Life of Things*.
102 *Troilus and Cressida*, TLN 36 (1. 1. 1).
103 Ibid. TLN 3049–96 (5. 2. 65–106); *Troilus and Cressida*, ed. Kenneth Palmer, The Arden Shakespeare (London and New York, 1982) p. 273.
104 *Troilus and Cressida*, TLN 3069 (5. 2. 82).
105 Ibid. TLN 3166–8 (5. 2. 169–71).
106 Bullen, *The Works of Thomas Middleton* V, 3. 3. 24–8; see Susan Zimmerman, "Disruptive Desire: Artifice and Indeterminacy in Jacobean Comedy," in Susan Zimmerman, ed., *Erotic Politics: Desire on the Renaissance Stage* (New York and London, 1992), pp. 50–1.
107 *Hamlet*, TLN 54, 55, 63 (1. 1. 45, 43, 50), TLN 629–30 (1. 4. 44–5).
108 Ibid. TLN 76 (1. 1. 60).
109 Ibid. TLN 3900 (5. 2. 399).
110 Ibid. TLN 3054–5 (4. 7. 43–4).
111 Ibid. TLN 3374–6 (5. 1. 185–9).
112 Greg, *Henslowe Papers*, pp. 53, 54.
113 William Shake-speare, *The Tragicall Historie of Hamlet* (London, 1603), G 2v (3. 4. 101).
114 *Hamlet*, TLN 2483 (3. 4. 102).
115 *Hamlet*, TLN 2518 (3.4.135).

I have incurred many debts in the writing of this piece: to the Folger Library, Barbara Mowat in particular; and to Arjun Appadurai, Meg Jasten, Scott McMillin, Phyllis Rackin, Marion Trousdale, and Michael Warren. Above all, I am indebted for comments to Margreta de Grazia, David Scott Kastan, and Stephen Orgel.

11　The Countess of Pembroke's literal translation

Jonathan Goldberg

Mary Sidney, Countess of Pembroke, has received high marks for her translation of Petrarch's *Trionfo della Morte*. Robert Coogan, for example, in an essay surveying and assessing the role of the *Trionfi* in the English Renaissance, notes that while hers was the last translation undertaken in the period – it was done sometime in the 1590s, in all likelihood – it is, he writes, "the finest translation of this triumph in the English language." By finest, Coogan means that it excels in "accuracy"; "each *terzina* in Mary Sidney literally translates the corresponding *terzina* in Petrarch," he goes on to say.[1] Coogan depends in his essay on judgments reached earlier by D. G. Rees, who, in a consideration of translations of the *Triumph of Death* from the Renaissance through the nineteenth century, had found Mary Sidney's superior to all others. "Hers is in fact an exceedingly literal translation," Rees wrote, going on to praise its "close adherence to the original."[2] These are views shared by Gary Waller, the contemporary critic who has often praised the *Triumph of Death*; endorsing Coogan's description of the poem as "the most triumphant poem of the early Renaissance," adherence to the original is also what Waller finds remarkable, so much so that he both cites Rees and then repeats the same words without putting quotation marks around them; he too claims, to quote him, that "the most outstanding technical feature of the Countess's translation is her reproducing Petrarch's original stanzaic pattern."[3]

These views of the countess's accomplishment could seem unexceptionable, yet they raise questions that I would address here. Indeed, the questions perhaps have begun to suggest themselves simply in the account that I have been giving, for there is, among the critics of the poem, an uncanny sense of *déjà lu*, as if, that is, they were reading each other, and not Mary Sidney's poem. Echoes, inside and outside of quotation marks, seem to recycle the same words and thoughts, to have decided on criteria which need only be restated, in whomever's words, for their truth to be apparent. Reading these critics, the chronology I have offered – in which Rees has priority of place – is virtually supplanted by the recirculation of the terms of praise that makes such priority a secondary question: what matters is the fact that the countess excels at translation, excels thanks to her literality, her accuracy, her adherence to a great original. This matters so much that Waller can both quote Rees and then use the same words without quotation marks, making them his own. So much, in fact, that Waller's sentences are repeated, word for word, in three different locales, in the introduction to his edition of Mary Sidney's poems, in his biography of her, and in his pages on her in his volume entitled *English Poetry of the Sixteenth Century*. Of course his reuse of the same words – letter for letter – does not come with quotation marks around them; they are his words after all – and Coogan's and Rees's too, as we've seen.[4]

The sign of propriety in his recirculation of the same words is precisely what is denied Mary Sidney, a troubling fact when one adds that Waller's work on her behalf has been done, increasingly so in the last decade, in the name of feminism. Yet there is not even a moment in which the gendered suppositions governing the praise of literal translation have been noted, that the original is placed in the paternal position – as if there could be no question but that Petrarch's words were his own, no reason to question his originality or priority – while the translator is a dutiful daughter or wife, faithfully adhering, and tied to a role that Waller calls *reproduction*. Yet, as I've been hinting already, chasing the round robin of critical estimations and echoes, reproduction – even faithful reproduction – could evacuate the terms of priority, opening possibilities of ownership precisely in the lack of self-sameness that citation – even literal citation – makes possible. Where even the issue of technical mastery of interlinked *terza rima*, with its imbrication of rhymes, might speak not so much to the matching of Petrarch as to the intertangled effects to which I have been alluding. Effects, I would hasten to add, that cannot be thought of in the hierarchies that invidiously characterize the relation of original and translation, of adherence and reproduction.

Literal translation supposes that there is something literally there in Petrarch, something so self-identical that it could simply be faithfully reproduced. In that light, it is worth noticing two quite different assessments of what Mary Sidney sought in Petrarch's triumph. For Margaret Hannay, in her recent biography, *Philip's Phoenix*, by translating the *Triumph of Death*, Mary Sidney could place her voice in Laura's and find strength in Laura's declaration in the poem that the relation that had seemed to exhibit Petrarch's mastery had, in fact, been mastered by Laura, whose withdrawals and refusals, whose very silences, had produced their effects in him. "In delightful irony," Hannay writes, "the passive mistress proves to have been in control of her ardent lover";[5] Hannay reads Petrarch's poem to find it giving voice to a voice that displaces the poet's, presenting, as she puts it, "the Petrarchan situation from Laura's point of view" (108). Virtually the opposite conclusion is reached by Mary Ellen Lamb in her study of *Gender and Authorship in the Sidney Circle*; she finds the poem frankly "disturbing" for embracing a voice that speaks its own destruction: it is, after all, the dead Laura that Petrarch gives a voice to speak a self-abnegation empowered by an almost suicidal passivity.[6] The refusals that tell in Hannay's account are strikes against her in Lamb's. This may be how women found a voice in the period, Lamb contends, and for that reason it is worth recognizing the strategy of speech *in articulo mortis*, but no woman would want to endorse that speaking position. Indeed, it might be said that, in some measure, Hannay agrees; her discussion of the poem occurs at the opening of a chapter devoted to how those who sought the countess's patronage wrote about her. The *Triumph* is taken as a kind of paradigmatic version of those encounters, in which men are given voice to write the countess by the power she has – a power that does not entail the kinds of entitlements within the written sphere that her would-be suitors had. The countess's patronage was, after all, highly circumscribed; wealthy and powerful as she was, much depended on her position as wife to the Earl of Pembroke; after his death, poets stopped importuning her. Hannay is able to construe her life as a series of heroic encounters in part because she is far less troubled by what Lamb sees: the cost of such success.

Seeing that, however, Lamb's account of the poem enacts the very erasure that she finds so disturbing, and, in that respect, her argument echoes Hannay's, but now from the opposite direction, for while Hannay ultimately treats the poem as an instance of how the countess empowered others, Lamb empties the poem of the countess by arguing that she subscribed to the lethal effects of the effacements of a Petrarchan poetics that only simulates, at best, any sphere for female subjectivity. Either way, the poem, and the countess, disappear. But into what? One answer that might trouble these suppositions: into a Petrarch whose *Trionfo della Morte* either simulates his mastery or achieves it, into an original, that is, whose self-sameness is split by the representation of the relationship between lover and beloved. But what then would it mean literally to translate this divided text? Would the only access to the text lie along the gendered lines in which the countess is in the position of Laura? Can she simply be in that position when she is writing the poem? Must one conclude, as Waller does balefully in his most recent account of the countess, that "she was a woman, written by men," a death sentence if there ever was one?[7] Or that if she was a woman writing as a man, that must mean some fundamental betrayal of and to her gender? Wouldn't such conclusions ascribe to the original a determinate power that might itself fall into question even in this most literal of translations, if, that is, one were to argue that even literally to rewrite the poem could locate the countess's hand at a site of original duplication? And if, in Petrarch, the effect of displacement, of giving voice to Laura, serves to enhance only the poet's power, can one deny that Mary Sidney is the poet – is the author – of her *Triumph of Death*?

In asking these questions, I follow Ann Rosalind Jones, who has argued in *The Currency of Eros* for a difference that would inevitably be there even in the most faithful adherence to an original, the difference that gender will make. However powerful the discourses of gender in the Renaissance were in their attempts to keep women chaste, silent, and obedient (to cite the usual formula), they were not all-powerful, and the very existence of writing by women is one sign of that fact. To make the woman and her writing disappear into the male text or into male-dominated society means to be giving more power to men than they had. "Women were interpellated by the Nom/Non du Pere," Jones writes, "but they were not interpellated into a tragic female speechlessness," and one reason for that, as Jones argues, was that the texts on which they modeled their own were not themselves seamless; nor was the social imperative to silence women without a contradictory element: the solicitation of the participation of women in the construction of the social, the hegemonic process described by Gramsci.[8] Even were Petrarch's poem the very monument to male accomplishment and mastery that it is taken to be, for Mary Sidney to rewrite it faithfully word for word would nevertheless mean for her to have rewritten it. Still, to take up the position of writing her own demise, to find voice only at the point of death, might call these arguments into question. Here one can turn to Wendy Wall's account of how that rhetorical position could empower, for, as Wall suggests, in a close examination of Isabella Whitney's "Wyll and Testament" and a tradition of women's writing to which it can be allied, the representation of oneself in that state of dispossession could be just that: a site of representation rather than one of identification, and a site moreover so riven with contradictions about person, place, and time – since one speaks, and yet is dead, since one takes possession at a moment of dispossession, since one occupies a temporality split between a future that one will never occupy and a present one is evacuating – that the contradictions, rather than being annihilative, are productive.[9] Among other things, as Wall suggests, these contradictions occasioned by speech at the last moment can serve to reflect upon and to critique the limits of women's speech, and therefore to transgress them. The very extremity of the situation of writing as a woman is enacted and, in some measure at least, overcome. Isabella Whitney writes a last will and testament and does not die; Mary Sidney writes in the voice of a Laura who can claim power after death, but Mary Sidney goes on living.

Granting these arguments, it would then be possible to distinguish between Petrarch's assumption of his own dispossession by the voice of Laura and Mary Sidney's occupation of that voice, to measure thereby the ruses of power as well as the enablements that occur on either side of the divide of gender. So doing, one might still be in the position of assuming that the only site of identification – of identification and disidentification, at one and the same time – was determined by gender, that it was to Laura that the countess looked to find her voice. Yet she writes "I" in the poem not only there but also as she assumes the voice of the mourner, the voice inscribing the loss of another. And that position, the assumption of the voice of mourning, as everyone who has written about the Countess of Pembroke agrees, impels all her writing. In 1586, and within the space of some six months, Mary Sidney's father, mother, and brother died, and it was especially the death of Sir Philip Sidney that mobilized her: her major project was the completion of the psalm translation left unfinished at his death, the piecing together of the two versions of the *Arcadia*, and their publication. (She also oversaw the publication of *Astrophil and Stella* and the *Defense*.) Hannay's description of the stance taken in the *Triumph of Death* also governs her thesis about Mary Sidney's career as a whole: that she occupied vis-à-vis her brother the position that Laura takes up in relation to Petrarch in the poem. Nonetheless, her *Triumph of Death* must also be a poem of mourning for Philip Sidney. This places the countess in the position of Petrarch. Gary Waller comes to something like this point; having argued for the faithful adherence of translator and original, he continues by extending that relationship to the adherence of brother and sister; for him it is inescapable that the power and pathos of Mary Sidney's triumph represents her continued act of mourning for the brother with whom she so insistently identified.[10] Waller follows the countess literally when he represents her as the dutiful follower making whole what Sidney had left maimed, and Hannay's rewriting of that claim is a powerful one; she counters that such signs of devotion and subservience mask the very creation of Sir Philip Sidney that was the Countess of Pembroke's accomplishment. Hannay balks, as well, at the identifications for which Waller argues, and not surprisingly, for his arguments recirculate the suppositions of Aubrey, that the relationship of brother and sister was incestuous.

"Given the Sidneys' piety and their unembarrassed affection for all members of their family, the charge of incest is preposterous," Hannay disposes of the claim in a note.[11] Preposterous is a nice word; it suggests some of the unstated anxieties in Hannay's quick rebuttal: it mixes up before and behind in ways that might render gender identification indeterminate; it mixes before and after, the very work of incest, but also of all retrospective constructions, which is as much as to say, all the activities of consciousness; it also makes guilty what was at first innocent. Which is to say: the charge is preposterous because it is true.[12]

To think about the identification of the countess and her brother – without, I hasten to add, endorsing Aubrey *literally* – one might follow Judith Butler's theorization of how one comes to have a gender position: the assumption of gender is troubled at the start since it rests upon identifications with lost objects, and the presumption of a single and determinate and self-identical gender position only testifies to the impossibility of such an acquisition, gender resting upon and mourning the loss of that singularity, founded upon desires for and identifications with those not necessarily of the same sex to which one is assigned.[13] Mary Sidney's empowerment as a writer seems to have been coincident with the death of Sir Philip Sidney; moreover, the choice of Petrarch would seem in some measure to acknowledge the role of her brother, the English Petrarke, upon her. Which is not to voice again the notion of her faithful subservience to him or to the literary model he represented; rather, to suggest that in her *Triumph of Death*, Mary Sidney occupies both positions, as Petrarch and as Laura, and that Sir Philip Sidney is written into the poem in both parts as well. Indeed, the poem could be said also to be rewriting *Astrophil and Stella*, much as Petrarch's triumph rewrites his *Canzoniere*. If the countess's poem is a faithful translation, it faithfully translates these complex routes of identification, across literary texts, across sites of imitation, across sites of identification that cross gender identification as well, or that, more finely, relocate gender as an unstable and less fully determined site.

To make this point, as I've said, is not to endorse Aubrey's salaciousness, and not, I hope, to echo Waller, for whom too, incest turns out to be a secret (even from herself, Waller opines) that reflects upon the countess's "disturbing" female sexuality.[14] Yet, to criticize these positions is not to take up Hannay's portrait of a pious and desexualized countess either. Indeed, I would argue that I follow Hannay, if not literally, in reading the countess's active piecing and putting together of her brother as an act of phallic enhancement that becomes further legible within the preposterous logic of incestuous, cross-gender identification. Something like this has been argued by Jonathan Crewe in his suggestion in *Hidden Designs* that the secret that historicism has failed to uncover in *Astrophil and Stella* is the love of Philip and Mary Sidney.[15] As Crewe argues, once one grants that Stella is a screen, numerous possibilities of dissimulation are put in place. Indeed, as Crewe suggests, the absolutely unspeakable might involve a host of desires, including the possibility that Stella stands in for a man. Crewe's point here finds an odd echo in a throwaway line of Mary Ellen Lamb's when she suggests that one could theorize the possibility of women finding voice in the sixteenth century in much the way that Foucault describes the emergence of homosexual identity in the nineteenth century; that just as the sites of disempowerment gave discursive space to the newly emergent homosexual identity so too one might find women's voices emerging from what was said in the attempt to silence them and keep them in their place.[16] As Lamb argues, though it is a point she wishes to repudiate, much as does Hannay, the site involves an identification of women's voices with their sexuality. This is, admittedly, undeniably, misogynist and projective; yet here it seems to me that the response made by Hannay and Lamb – which is to deny sexuality because it has been so written – seems to me mistaken. And not least if the sexuality involved does not support normative and regulatory regimes, indeed it could be a site that undermine the mechanisms of normality. Incest violates the taboo that maintains the proprieties of reproduction. If one were to read the emergence of Mary Sidney's voice as transgressing the proprieties of gender, as occupying the territory of, and indeed even inventing the site of male (dis)empowerment, then her faithful and literal translation, I would argue, reproduces the social and the literary precisely by evacuating the linchpin that ties those things together. Hers is a reproduction outside the domain of compulsory heterosexuality, and it makes legible a range of desires lodged within and also on the surface of the social. As Crewe suggests in *Trials of Authorship*, incest is not to be read as the "dirty secret" (98) but as co-extensive with the constitutiveness of the social; such a point continues the line of argument that Ann Jones offers: we are dealing here with the most active solicitation of women for the construction of the social, the fullest engagement of desire, the transgression of the boundary between licit and illicit that founds and troubles the licit and the normative and that renders it *preposterous*.

For, as Kenneth Thorpe Rowe suggested, despite himself, in the classic 1939 article supposed to have laid Aubrey's claims forever to rest, incest is the most ordinary story one can tell.[17] Aubrey, to recall the passage, recounts that he had "heard old gentlemen say that they [Philip and Mary Sidney] lay together" and that "the first Philip earle of Pembroke was begot by him, but he inherited not the witt of either brother or sister." Rowe contends that such storytelling reflects upon Aubrey as "innocent – but also salacious" (592). Thus, Rowe continues, it took little more than some wine and the "process of association" to put together his tale: "Philip Sidney dearly loved his sister and was much at Wilton; perhaps he lay with her there. Someone remarked, from the association of names, and thinking loosely of family resemblance, not of direct descent, that Philip Herbert inherited not the wit of his mother nor of his uncle Philip; shortly, Philip Herbert was begot by his mother's brother" (593). In following his processes of association, producing the startling conjunction of the preposterous and the obvious, Rowe forgets to mention one further piece of evidence that might lead in the same direction, and along the same trajectory of disidentification, the possibility of reading literally the letter prefacing the *Arcadia*;[18] there, to recall the passage, a text written only for the countess, only to her, is taken also to be the maimed child that she and her brother have produced together, she, as it happens, in the more active position, soliciting and desiring – "you desired me to do it, and your desire to my heart is an absolute commandment," he at first the reluctant father and then a kind of male mother who has delivered a child that is characterized by its "deformities," indeed is called a "monster," not merely for what it is as it came out but as much for what "came in"; this monstrosity bears her name and wears her livery. The letter traffics in gender crossing, unnatural desires and their offspring, crossing boundaries that hint at (if they do not explicitly name) incest, sodomy, and bestiality. The work Sidney characterizes as that of an "offender" he nonetheless also offers as a token of the writer's love; indeed, of one "who doth exceedingly love you," and it is a question whether the excesses of the letter are not precisely of the kind that makes impossible the kind of argument against Aubrey that Rowe seeks to marshal.

Not, as we've seen, that Rowe disbelieves everything; indeed he has no trouble believing another story Aubrey tells:

She was very salacious, and she had a Contrivance that in the spring of the yeare when the stallions were to leape the mares, they were to be brought before such a part of the house, where she had a vidette to looke on them and please herself with their Sport; and then shee would act the like sport with *her* stallions. One of her great gallants was crooke-backt't Cecill, earle of Salisbury.

"What is recorded in the first part of the passage," Rowe writes, "does not appear to be unconsonant with the frank Renaissance attitude toward nature and beauty"; Aubrey's age was less frank – "therefore," Rowe concludes, "the conclusion by way of inference" (594). The conclusion about the countess and her brother, however, is rather more literal when Aubrey moves from the voyeuristic scene to endorse what old men have said. The missing connection is there in the slip from her stallions to her gallants, or it is as soon as we supply the missing signifier; as Michael Moon has suggested to me all one needs to get from the horses to Philip is the Greek etymology of his name. Cross-species sex, sex between brother and sister; joined in the signifier, put into the mouths of old men – is this Socrates lecturing Phaedrus on the horses of the passions, or are these the old men that, as Katherine Duncan-Jones suggests in her recent biography, Philip Sidney was so good at pleasing?[19] When Aubrey proceeds from the horses to Sir Philip by way of imagining the countess having sex with the aged Cecil, we need only recall how assiduously Philip sucked up to Leicester and to Walsingham, not to mention his mentor Languet. It is then within the normative and scandalous routes of the homosocial, along the lines of power and patronage, that one might begin to locate the love that dares not speak its name in Mary Sidney's writing, and not least so when she does nothing more than faithfully insert herself into these circles.[20]

One more testimony might be added here, and with it we return to the terms of the relation of original and translation with which I began, John Donne's poem on the Sidneian psalms which points to the union that Mary and Philip achieved as their way of reproducing a division and doubling in the source.[21] David's psalms, Donne writes, were already a double and divided text, written by a "cloven tongue" (9), and it was only through a further "cleft" (12) that the spirit of divided and doubled David met in brother and sister, "Two, by their bloods, and by thy Spirit one" (14). As Crewe reminds us, spirit is a perfectly equivocal term, and the attempt to translate this union to an elsewhere, to a dephysicalized site – much like the site of the phoenix and the position of spiritual unity beyond gender for which Hannay argues – is belied by the choice of the word.[22] The "two that make one" (17) in Donne is a union in spirit and blood, in spirit that is the efflorescence of blood that has not been expended in vain; it makes, Donne, says, an "Organ" (16), and more than a musical instrument is meant, more than the toy that brother and sister traded across the Arcadian pages. Like the Nom/Non du Pere, or the Phallus that is its signifier, it goes on beyond their deaths. So, Donne concludes, have the translators been translated. Literally; for however etherealized Sir Philip and Mary Sidney are now, they exist in the only site in which we can be certain that they ever were coupled – here, now, where ink is their blood and spirit and the page their making.[23] Literally, materially, translated, reproduced. On those triumphant pages which we must, at last, however briefly, open.[24]

To notice, for instance, that the speaker of The Triumph, the "I," is never gendered; true, in Petrarch's version as well, there is no mark of gender throughout the first part of the *Trionfo*; but, as the second section begins, the speaker is, insistently, a man, *uomo* (2.3, 20); as insistently, the speaker in the countess's triumph remains simply an "I," its gender never marked. And the effects of this? In the first part, the speaker who bears no mark of gender – and, since this is the countess's poem, is therefore implicitly marked as female – begins by describing a "gallant Ladie" (1) and "hir chosen mates" (14), and it is within this entirely female world that an "I" first appears, noting yet another woman on the horizon, one in black "such as I scarcelie knowe" (32), who arrives and seems to address the speaker of the poem:

> Thow Dame, quoth she, that doeth so proudlie goe,
> Standing upon thy youth, and beauties state,
> And of thy life, the limits doest not knowe.
>
> (1.34–7)

The effects of this address are multiple: the lines identify the speaker of the poem as the about-to-be-dead lady or as the one who desires that condition – a few lines down an "I" in the poem reports that she will "thank who shall me hence assoile" (54). One effect of this, then, when we return to Petrarch's version of the poem, is that the speaker is put in the position of Laura. That this crossing is possible has something to do with how Laura appears in the poem, for instance when one notices that she dies at least three times in the first part of the poem – she seems to be dead when the poem starts, seems to be dead after the woman in black appears, seems to be dead again when her company can do nothing for her at the end of the first part of the poem, when she ascends to heaven – which is, one might have thought, where we were to begin with. When she returns in part 2, it is to announce that the speaker of the poem, not she, is dead (a point to which I will return shortly). These prevarications make her the very site of that passage across limits that are continuously being violated, transgressed, crossed beforehand and afterwards in ways that can only be re-marked rather than marked once. All of this, I would suggest, helps the countess to cross the line as well as she comes from the start to occupy the position both of Petrarch and of Laura, and to occupy them in the unmarked "I." This is not the only direction in which the cross-identification works, however, for, at the end of the poem, the last question the speaker poses to the dead beloved is to ask when they will be united. The answer is, devastatingly, "Thow without me long time on earth shalt staie" (2.190). The limits remain, therefore, unknown, the desired transgression of part 1 refused. Yet in her identification with that still-living speaker, the countess identifies herself, and this remains transgressive, if not a violation of the ultimate ontological border; for the final crossing by way of identification with Petrarch cannot fail to position Sir Philip at the site of the dead lady.

The liabilities of cross-identifications, of marks that are re-marked and yet remain indeterminate and unmarked, can be seen at the close of the address to the "Dame," or rather can be seen precisely because where the address closes and where it is responded to are impossible to tell. Some twenty lines after the speech begins, the line that announces "replide then she" (51) could as easily be referring to the line that comes before as to the one that comes after. What comes before, in fact, is a line that says "To this, thow right or interrest hast none" (49), and it is exactly the case that which of the two – the lover or the beloved, the one alive or the one dead – is in this state of dispossession is only furthered when one cannot tell who says the line, whether it begins the reply or ends the speech. And the line, of course, only makes this situation all the more dizzying by itself announcing the very state of dispossession. Thus one cannot know whether it is the speaker or the one spoken to who is so dispossessed. Moreover, if it is the lines that follow that constitute the reply – "This charge of woe on others will recoyle" (52), they begin – those lines recoil even further when one notes, following Rees, and therefore following everyone who has commented on the faithful literalness of the countess's translation, that here the translation errs: what is translated as "others" is, in Petrarch, a reference to the speaker himself.[25] And the effect of this so-called mistranslation? A further displacement along the lines of gender; for the others on whom this death recoils are the host of ladies that form the squadron around this doubled figure of the dead, the wished-for dead, the over and again and not yet dead – a figure who, I would add also, is at moments in the poem inextricable from the very figure of Death, the woman in black first sighted and not recognized. Lines of cathexis are opened here that heighten a female–female erotics to be found from the very opening lines of the poem in which the "I" of the poem may be read as a woman speaking of and to other women as her "chosen mates" (1.13). This displacement along the lines of single-sex identification furthers the scandal of the crossing and cross-identification that the poem undertakes.

Such displacement is marked again, insistently so, as the second part opens, when the "I" of the poem refuses to call itself man, but is insistently and only "I."

> That night, which did the dreadfull happ ensue
> That quite eclips't; naie rather did replace
> The Sunne in skyes, and me bereave of view.
>
> (2.1–3)

"And me" bereaves the poem of the line describing the I as "come uom cieco" (2.3). The blind man blinded, eclipsed, replaced. Replaced is not in Petrarch's version, and it marks the site of translation, as the blind man becomes this visionary. This marks and remarks the crossings of the second section, when Laura appears to Petrarch to tell him that she lives, and he is dead, when she takes over the mastering function of passively leading him to the revelation of their shared love. Read as his writing, these crossings dissimulate his occupation of every writing position; but read as the countess's crossing out of and replacement of the speaker position so that she is both him and her, another "strange passion" – to recall the phrase the countess uses elsewhere to characterize her relationship to her brother – is revealed.[26] It's there perhaps even more palpably in the first part of the poem, when the speaker stops a digression that seems to have gotten out of hand, one about the futility of heroic lives wasted. Read in Petrarch's poem, voiced in his voice, the digression is, at best, a self-pitying gesture, but word for word, when it is in hers, the digression comes all too close to revealing whose futilely heroic death is covered by the figure of the dead lady, especially if one notes that, unlike Petrarch, the countess attributes courtesy (1.146) as well as beauty to the figure; the mourned beloved can only be her brother, wasted in the wars, and the pained stop to the digression is the virtual announcement that what seems out of place in the poem is all too literally its subject.

These lines could be set beside the other place where the countess, it is claimed, mistranslates; not surprisingly, it is a moment when she speaks of her own desires when she should be speaking of his:

> If lyking in myne eyes the world did see
>   I saie not, now, of this, right faine I am,
>   Those cheines that tyde my heart well lyked me.
>
>   (2.127–9)

Where she says "my heart," Petrarch puts his.[27] The chains around her heart are the ones she tied and ties around his. This crossing occurs at the end of a particularly dense and complex section of the poem, one in which the line between speakers is continually crossed, so much so that when "silence foulde[s] / Those rosie lips" (41–42) they seem to go on speaking, and when "I" reports "my eare possest" (54) with the desire to cross the line,

>   with spirit readie prest,
>   Now at the furthest of my living wayes,
>
>   (52–3)

that "I" is then compared to another who is marked as male, as if the "I" were not – that is, if he speaks the lines in which the "happless he" is described, but it might be that his ear is possessed with her unmarked voice. For, as usual, after that speech, an "I" appears, and, as usual, it renders retrospectively impossible the determination of voice, even as it renders indeterminate who speaks in the position of that "I." Moreover, it is in this possessed state that the speaker's "failing-sight" (61), dying or going blind, gives access to a voice that belongs to a woman who seems just to have appeared: "Well, I hir face, and well hir voice I knewe," this blinded, ear-possessed speaker declares, "who oft did thee restraining, me encyte" (2.63), and the woman so entirely known either is or is not the woman to whom he has been speaking all the while, or is the woman who has never stopped speaking, no matter whose voice we think we hear or see. So apprehended, she appears to be another woman, or at any rate, a site of new recognition. Yet who is this other woman, this screen? Is it Stella, and is the countess now declaring that her refusals only produced the countess's further encitements to refuse and grant at once? It should be noted that twice during the speech of the recognized, unnamed woman, she insistently compares herself to a man who has come to the end of his life and embraces it with as much joy as a man who returns home from exile. She is that man (2.72, 74), and the pathos of his/her "onelie ruth" is that the return home does not include the one spoken to. This change in gender identification is something that does not happen in Petrarch's version, and something that further allows the cross-identification of the dead woman in the poem with Astrophil/ Philip. That is, if it does not occur a bit later in faithfully translated lines – in which the other woman seems to have become Laura, or to have become the countess without a screen, and in which the male beloved now has her brother's name, or at least the name that insisted itself – the insistence of the letter – in Aubrey's account. That is to say, he is called a "wanton steede" (98), she the brake; he runs a "race" guided by the alternating current of "kinde acceptance" and "sharp disdaine," the application of the spur and bit. In Petrarch's poem, the usual dynamics that are called Petrarchan are split between the speaker and his dead lady; and in the countess's they are reunited:

> Never were
> Our hearts but one, nor never two shall be:
> Onelie thy flame I tempred with my cheere;
> This onelie way could save both thee and me.
>
> (2.89–91)

The one-ly way of the poem is its truth, and the point of arrival of this section of the poem is that moment of so-called mistranslation with which I began, and which might now be seen to be as faithful as anything else in the poem. "Through fiction, Truth will neither ebbe nor flowe" (2.147), the countess writes, "my love dares speak no more" (150), and having said that, goes on speaking, crossing all the lines.

It only remains to be said that the lines to be crossed are ones we put there – I think, for instance, of the quotation marks around speeches that modern editors attempt in Petrarch's text, but to little avail.[28] If his indeterminations of voice may be signs of a desired masculine appropria-tion, the countess's unmarking of ownership of voice, her occupation of and crossing over of the marks of identification, carries the same but utterly different meaning. Such is the triumph of the Countess of Pembroke's literal translation. It comes without quotation marks.

NOTES

1 Robert Coogan, "Petrarch's *Trionfi* and the English Renaissance," *Studies in Philology* 67 (1970), 306–27; p. 324 cited.
2 D. G. Rees, "Petrarch's 'Trionfo della Morte' in English," *Italian Studies* 7 (1952), 82–96; p. 83 cited.
3 Gary F. Waller, *English Poetry of the Sixteenth Century* (London, 1986), p. 159. Compare this with his discussion of the poem in his "Introduction" to *The Triumph of Death and Other Unpublished and Uncollected Poems by Mary Sidney* (Salzburg, 1977), pp. 12–14, and in his *Mary Sidney, Countess of Pembroke: A Critical Study of Her Writings and Literary Milieu* (Salzburg, 1979), pp. 144–50.
4 On the logic of citationality and iterability, I depend upon Jacques Derrida's classic 1971 essay "Signature Event Context," and his subsequent exchange with John Searle, conveniently gathered (though without Searle's reply) in Jacques Derrida, *Limited Inc* (Evanston, Ill., 1988).
5 Margaret P. Hannay, *Philip's Phoenix* (New York, 1990), p. 109.
6 Mary Ellen Lamb, *Gender and Authorship in the Sidney Circle* (Madison, 1990); the poem is discussed on pp. 138–41, where the judgment that it is "disturbing" is reached.
7 Gary F. Waller, "The Countess of Pembroke and Gendered Reading," in Anne M. Haselkorn and Betty S. Travitsky, eds., *The Renaissance English-woman in Print* (Amherst, 1990), p. 343. For a similar account in which the countess is reduced to a position of silence that the critic teases into speech, see Waller's "Struggling into Discourse: The Emergence of Renaissance Women's Writing," in Margaret P. Hannay, ed., *Silent But for the Word* (Kent, Ohio, 1985), pp. 238–56; see pp. 245–6, for example, for an account of the countess's writing couched entirely in the negative ("she wrote no prose romance ... She wrote no original drama ...); "it is the critic's responsibility to make those silences speak" (p. 247), Waller concludes, not noting that the critic has also produced the silences.
8 Ann Rosalind Jones, *The Currency of Eros* (Bloomington, Ind., 1990), pp. 2–3.

9   Wendy Wall, "Isabella Whitney and the Female Legacy," *ELH* 58 (1991), 35–62.

10 "It [the translation of Petrarch] reflects, one might speculate, her own deeply idealized love for her brother, the impossibility of its consummation and the realization that his poetic inspiration for her is the only real and lasting fruit of her love," Waller writes in his biography, *Mary Sidney*, p. 144, concluding that Laura's final farewell to the poet may be "expressive of Mary's own farewell to her brother" (p. 150).

11 Hannay, *Philip's Phoenix*, p. 259 n. 41. Waller has reviewed his original account of the incestuous relationship between brother and sister in his biography of Mary Sidney (p. 100) in "Gendered Reading," pp. 335–6. Mary Ellen Lamb also balks at Waller's account in *Gender and Authorship*, pp. 69–71.

12 For further thoughts on the logic of the preposterous, see Lee Edelman, "Seeing Things: Representation, the Scene of Surveillance, and the Spectacle of Gay Male Sex," in Diana Fuss, ed., *inside/out* (New York, 1991), pp. 93–116, and Jonathan Goldberg, *Sodometries* (Stanford, 1992), pp. 4f, 180f, 184, 188, 192.

13 I summarize the arguments of the second chapter of Judith Butler, *Gender Trouble* (New York, 1990).

14 Commenting in his *Mary Sidney* on lines of a dedicatory poem to her dead brother accompanying the psalm translation, Waller finds them "personal and disturbing" (p. 99), indeed "peculiarly personal" marks of "intense intimacy": "It is as if a veil is being lifted very briefly, unwillingly, even unconsciously. Her love for her brother passes even her own understanding. With caution, we may recall Aubrey's speculation ..." (p. 100).

15 Jonathan Crewe, *Hidden Designs* (New York, 1986), pp. 76–88, who notes Waller's "dirty" version of the open secret of the relationship of brother and sister. For Crewe's further thoughts on the powerful social logic of incest, see his account of the relationship of Margaret More Roper and Sir Thomas More in his *Trials of Authorship* (Berkeley, 1990), pp. 79–100.

16 Lamb, *Gender and Authorship*, p. 18.

17 Kenneth Thorpe Rowe, "The Love of Sir Philip Sidney for the Countess of Pembroke," *Papers of the Michigan Academy of Science Arts and Letters* 25 (1939), 579–95; citations from Aubrey as quoted by Rowe.

18 Sir Philip Sidney, *Arcadia*, ed. Maurice Evans (Harmondsworth, 1977); the prefatory letter appears on p. 57 in this edition. I am grateful to Charles Barker for discussion of this text.

19 Katherine Duncan-Jones, *Sir Philip Sidney: Courtier-Poet* (New Haven, 1991); see, e.g., her description of Sidney as "the darling of so many older men" (p. 42), or her conclusion that "friendships with older men were what Sidney was best at" (p. 254). For further thoughts on Duncan-Jones's account of Sidney's relations with men, see my review of her biography in *Lesbian and Gay Studies Newsletter* 19, 2 (July 1992), 22–4.

20 For another instance of this, see the letter of the Countess of Pembroke to Sir Tobie Matthew reproduced in Hannay, *Philip's Phoenix*, p. 199; the letter is about manuscript circulation, and in it, the countess recalls that she has forgotten Sir Tobie's "Other-self," his friend George Gage, and then

comments on her pleasure that "two so worthie, and so well-paired Friends" include her in their circle. The countess's attitude here gives the lie to Hannay's remark that she would have "resented Nashe's accusation that Harvey courted Sidney as a *Cyparissus* or *Ganimede* (sig. O3v). Accusing Harvey of homosexual impulses toward Sir Philip was not the way to endear himself to Sidney's family" (140).

On the relations between the homosocial and the homosexual in the Elizabethan period, the best guide remains Alan Bray, *Homosexuality in Renaissance England* (London, 1982), although the term homosocial and its relevance to the Renaissance is best explored in the chapter on Shakespeare's sonnets in Eve Kosofsky Sedgwick, *Between Men* (New York, 1985). See also Goldberg, *Sodometries*, including the discussion of the Countess of Pembroke's writing there (pp. 81–101) and J. Goldberg's "Introduction" to *Queering the Renaissance* for more general considerations of the relations between gender, sexuality, and writing in the period (Durham, N.C., 1994).

21 Jóhn Donne, "Upon the Translation of the Psalmes by Sir Philip Sydney, and the Countesse of Pembroke his Sister," in Helen Gardner, ed., *Divine Poems* (Oxford, 1978), pp. 33–5; line numbers are provided in my text.

22 See Crewe, *Trials of Authorship*, p. 179 n. 10.

23 Cf. Beth Wynne Fisken, " 'To the Angell spirit ...': Mary Sidney's Entry into the World of Words,'" in Haselkorn and Travitsky, *Renaissance Englishwoman in Print*, pp. 263–75, particularly her comments on blood and ink on p. 269, and her conclusion that "through her writing Mary Sidney forged a bond with her brother that his death could not sever" (p. 272).

24 Citations of "Triumphis Mortis," from Ferdinando Neri, ed., *Rime e Trionfi di Francesco Petrarca* (Turin, 1966), pp. 555–69; book and line numbers are provided in my text. The Countess of Pembroke's "The Triumph of Death" is similarly cited from Waller, *The Triumph of Death*, pp. 67–79.

25 "Here she has treated 'altri' as masculine plural, failing to realize that it is of course singular and is an allusion to Petrarch himself," Rees, "Trionfo," p. 85.

26 "To thee pure spirite, to thee alones addres't," in Waller, ed. *The Triumph of Death*, pp. 92–5, l. 45. It is these lines that led Waller to his incestuous speculations.

27 Mistaking a second person singular for first person, as Rees notes, "Trionfo," p. 85.

28 See, e.g., *The Triumphs of Petrarch*, trans. Ernest Hatch Wilkins (Chicago, 1962).

12   Remnants of the sacred in Early Modern England

Stephen Greenblatt

He drew a paper from his pocket and read:

Lourdes
Basses-Pyrénées
France

Sir,

A rat, or other small animal, eats of a consecrated wafer.
1. Does he ingest the Real Body, or does he not?
2. If he does not, what has become of it?
3. If he does, what is to be done with him?

Yours faithfully
Martin Ignatius MacKenzie
(Author of *The Chartered Accountant's Saturday Night*)

Mr. Spiro now replied to these questions, that is to say he replied to question one and he replied to question three. He did so at length, quoting from Saint Bonaventure, Peter Lombard, Alexander of Hales, Sanchez, Suarez, Henno, Soto, Diana, Concina and Dens, for he was a man of leisure.

(Samuel Beckett, *Watt*)

Martin Ignatius MacKenzie's questions repeatedly surface, like a traumatic fantasy or a very bad joke, in the bitter polemical exchanges between Catholics and Protestants in the sixteenth century. They articulate a powerful current of anxiety about what was for Renaissance subjects the most significant and endlessly fascinating of Early Modern objects: the sacramental bread of the Supper of the Lord. The answers that Beckett's Mr. Spiro scrupulously provides suggest that the questions were anything but novel or unique to Renaissance Christianity: here, as so often, the obsessions of Early Modern Europe have ancient roots. The polemical antagonists of the Reformation and Counter-Reformation eloquently bear out Marx's dictum that "the tradition of all the dead generations weighs like a nightmare on the brain of the living."[1]

We could use the Eucharistic controversies of the period to insist upon the historical distance from ourselves of the quintessential Early Modern object and, by extension, the psychological distance from ourselves of the Renaissance subjects who dwelt with such passionate, even violent, intensity upon this object. There has, after all, been a long debate between those who argue that the roots of modernity lie in the Renaissance and those who argue that the modern world originated in the Enlightenment. The latter would no doubt argue that the objects that actually define the onset of modernity, the objects that are the precursors of our own, are those studied and classified by Linnaeus or Alexander von Humboldt and not those inherited from medieval theology by Luther or Bellarmine. However, I would like to pick up another strand of my opening quotation – the fact that it comes from Beckett – and suggest that there is a link between the Eucharistic wafers that obsessed Renaissance subjects and the object that most exemplifies postmodernity, what Slavoj Zizek calls "the sublime object of ideology."[2]

For Zizek, the sublime object of ideology is what Lacan termed the Real: at once a hard kernel resisting symbolization and an entirely chimerical entity, impossible to grasp except by tracking its traumatic effects. The object most worthy of theoretical reflection, the object around which the subject is structured, is precisely the one that, while it continually invites the overwhelming desire to see, seize, and digest it, cannot in fact be securely located, measured, inventoried, or experienced in any of the ways that we normally associate with objects. Without the Real there can be no symbolic order: in one sense, the Real *precedes* symbolization which serves to feed off its primordial fullness, carving up its incomprehensible wholeness into consumable units of meaning. Yet in another sense the Real is the excess that always escapes this process of meaning-production and is therefore produced by it, since it can only be known in and as such excess.

For Renaissance England, the sublime object of ideology is a piece of common baked bread. The language that surrounds this object is in certain ways strikingly similar to Zizek's Lacanian rhetoric. Primordial wholeness, wounds, excess, the thing which at once precedes and exceeds symbolization, the intertwining of intense pleasure with equally intense grief or lack, the coincidence of opposites: virtually all of the terms used to describe the indescribable – the Real that is both out of our grasp and the basis for everything that we are – are terms that not simply resemble but rather emerge from the fevered attempts in the late Middle Ages and Early Modern period to theorize the Eucharist. At the same time, both

Catholics and Protestants repeatedly note the simple ordinariness of the sacramental object. What is a great mystery is a great banality, a prime piece of the everyday. It was possible to argue about the physical composition of the bread (as it is possible for human beings to argue about anything): in the Bay of Rio in the 1560s Huguenots and Catholics quarreled bitterly about whether the wafers could be made of manioc flour. Yet for the most part even those who disagreed about everything else were in accord that the sublime object, the sign of the Real and the Real beneath the sign, was an overwhelmingly familiar one: "These signes considered nakedly in and by themselues," writes William Bradshaw, "are not of any great force to stirre vp any great reuerence to the receiuing of them, because there is no one thing in the world more ordinary then eating of bread, and drinking of wine."[3] Bradshaw was an extremist who got into trouble with the authorities because of his association with the Puritan exorcist John Darrell, but very similar thoughts about the Eucharist were expressed by Church of England divines and by recusant Catholics.

It could be argued that the words of the consecration – in the Vulgate version, "Hoc est corpus meum" – conferred upon the ordinary bread its sublimity, and hence that the sublime object was a function of mystical language and not banal matter. Yet even here what is most striking is the almost embarrassing simplicity, the insistent ordinariness, of the formula. Some theologicians gamely proposed that Jesus had spoken "hard words," a quasi-technical term for words which defy understanding unless interpreted by authority. The problem, of course, is that the words in question, "This is my body," seem dismayingly straightforward: as Edward Dering impatiently asked, "Is there any obscuritye in these wordes?"[4] Yet, as so often happens, straightforwardness comes to possess its own form of obscurity, and Jesus' sentence became the focus of a bewildering variety of interpretations and a contentious debate.

At times this debate focused on the neuter demonstrative pronoun *hoc*. Orthodox Catholics, eager to show that Christ was corporeally present in the Eucharist, argued that *hoc* could not possibly refer to *panis* (bread), since the latter was of the masculine gender, while *corpus* was neuter. The argument seems strange, since the historical Jesus presumably spoke in Aramaic rather than in Latin or Greek, but Vulgate had long acquired something like scriptural authenticity. Indeed the Council of Trent decreed in 1546 that "the Vulgate approved through long usage during so many centuries be held authentic in public lectures, disputations, preachings and expositions, and that nobody dare or presume to reject it under any pretext."[5] Hence the Catholic priest William Bishop writes in 1607 that "It is false to say that this word (*Hoc, This*) doth demonstrate bread:

for it is of a different gender from it, both in *Latin* and *Greeke*." Bishop adds that if Jesus had said "that bread had beene his body, his word was so omnipotent, that it had beene of force to make it his body"; that is, even if *hoc* at the beginning of Jesus' sentence had referred to bread, by the time the sentence was complete, that bread would have turned into flesh.[6]

English Protestants sometimes countered with historical or philological arguments. Hence George Joye observes the close resemblance between the Lord's Supper and the Passover Seder, a meal at which bread is blessed, broken, and distributed to the participants. When you compare "the olde passouer with the newe," Joye writes, "ther is in ether of them syche lyke composicion of wordis, siche affinite and proporcionn in speche, syche symilitude and propertie in them bothe, the newe so corresponding in all thingis the olde, that the olde declarethe the newe."[7] But more often Protestant apologists used grammatical and logical arguments. First, in the words of Andrew Willett, *hoc* "is vsed substantiuely, not adiectiuely, and signifieth as much as 'this thing,' and therefore is put in the neuter gender: neither is it so strange or vnusuall a thing ... to demonstrate some thing in sight in such generall termes, not naming the thing." Second, if Jesus did by *hoc* refer to his body, as the Catholics claim, "there should be a tautologie or idle repetition of the same thing, as if he had said, this body is my bodie."[8] To the claim that the omnipotence of God's word transformed representation into reality – that *hoc* turned from bread into body in the very speaking of the sentence – Protestants pointed to passages where no such transformation had occurred: the Papists, writes Thomas Becon, say, "'Christ's calling is making. Christ called the bread his body; therefore is it made his body.' I answer again: Christ called himself a 'vine,' a 'door,' a 'shepherd,' and called his heavenly Father a 'ploughman': is Christ therefore made a natural vine, a material door, a rustical shepherd, and his Father an husbandman of the country?"[9]

Becon's examples, tirelessly reiterated in the polemics of the sixteenth century, point to the central Protestant argument about the consecration formula, an argument that centers not on *hoc* but on *est*. Following the suggestion of the Dutch humanist Cornelius Hoen, Zwingli adopted the view that *est* meant *significat*. By this reading, the Eucharistic formula was a trope, specifically, in Calvin's influential analysis, a metonymy in which "the sign borrows the name of the truth that it figures."[10] For the Reformers then the figurativeness of language, its ability not to mean what it appears to say, is the key to a correct understanding of Scripture. Never perhaps has so much depended upon a figure of speech: in trope we trust. There are, Beza said flatly, only two possibilities: "either transubstantiation or a trope."[11]

Many English Reformers embraced the Zwinglian position. Thus, for example, George Joye wrote in 1533 that Jesus' words "This is my body" are exactly like his words "I am the door and the vine": they are figures of speech.[12] Likewise, in the same year, John Frith observed that an "alepole is not the ale it selfe which it doth signifie or represent." A person who seeks salvation in the "outward sign" of the sacrament is like a thirsty man who tries to "goe and sucke an alepole, trusting to get drinke out of it."[13] Frith's irony points us to the fact that change in the understanding of the sacramental word – from literal to figurative, from "is" to "signifies" – is simultaneously and necessarily change in the understanding of the sacramental object.

Is such a change in the understanding of the object tantamount to a change in the object itself? It could be argued that the object itself simply remains what it always was and that the transformations are strictly verbal. However, this is to embrace one side of the controversy, the Protestant side that refused the distinction between substance and accidents and declared that the material bread in the Supper of the Lord was never more or less than material bread. For Catholics, however, the consecrated bread was actually something other than bread. The wonder of its transformation into flesh was compounded by the wonder that the communicants did not actually see it and taste it as flesh. That they did not, it was sometimes suggested, was a consequence of divine charity: hence Rastell argued that in the Mass a change in the substance of the bread had actually taken place and that we should be able to see the body "with our bodily eyes, except divers causes were to the contrary, of which this is one, lest some horror & lothsomenes might trouble us, if it were geaven in visible forme of flesh ... unto us." And Harding noted that the form of wine remains, covering the blood, "ut nullus horror cruoris sit, that there might be no abhorring of bloude ... Thus the bread and wine are changed in substance and yet kepe stil their olde outwarde formes."[14]

Catholics could cite, in confirmation of these claims, stories of those who were actually granted the vision or taste of the real presence. One such story, related in an anti-Protestant tract by an English Jesuit of the late sixteenth century, concerns an English gentlewoman who traveled to Rome for the Jubilee Year. Upon her arrival, the woman went

to Father Parsons, who was her Confessor: and he administring vnto her the blessed Sacrament (which in the forme of a little Wafer, hee put into her mouth) obserued shee was long chewing, and could not swallow the same: whereupon he asked her, whether shee knew what it was shee receiued? She answered, Yes, a Wafer. At which answer of hers, Father Parsons beeing much offended, he thrust his finger into her mouth, and thence drew out a piece of red flesh, which after was nailed vp against a post in a Vespery or priuate Chappell within our Lady-Church: and though this were done about some twenty yeeres since or more, yet doth that piece of flesh there remaine to bee seene, very fresh and red as euer it was.[15]

By the early seventeenth century this pious story could be quoted by the Protestant John Gee as an example of the manifest absurdity of Catholic propaganda. For Gee the gentlewoman's description of the object in her mouth – "a Wafer" – is the only sane and honest one. The consecrated bread has been transmuted from meat to metonymy. These are the views not only of radical Reformers but of principal architects of the Church of England. Communion continued to be given only to those who knelt down, but the 1552 *Book of Common Prayer* included a rubric that disclaimed any act of adoration in kneeling:

Whereas it is ordeyned in the book of common prayer, in the administration of the Lord's Supper, that the Communicants knelyng shoulde receyve the holye Communion: which thynge beyng well mente, for a sygnification of the humble and gratefull acknowledgyng of the benefites of Chryst, geven unto the woorthye receyver, and to avoyde the prophancion [*sic*] and dysordre, which about the holye Communion myght else ensue: Leste yet the same kneelyng myght be thought or taken otherwyse, we dooe declare that it is not ment thereby, that any adoracion is doone, or oughte to bee doone, eyther unto the Sacramentall bread or wyne there bodily receyved, or unto any reall and essential presence there beeyng of Christ's naturall fleshe and bloude.[16]

For Thomas Cranmer the words of the consecration are not to be taken literally: "This manner of speaking is a figurative speech: for in plain and proper speech it is not true to say, that bread is Christ's body, or wine his blood." We do not "eat Christ with our teeth grossly and carnally," Cranmer writes, for Christ is in heaven, sitting by God's side; rather, the sacramental bread and wine are "tokens, significations, and representations."[17]

Cranmer's terms, which are central to English Protestantism, point us to two observations that link the sublime object of Early Modern ideology to the period's language and literature: first, most of the significant and sustained thinking in the period about the nature of linguistic signs, and particularly about figuration, centered on or was deeply influenced by Eucharistic controversies; and second, most of the literature that we care about from this period was written in the shadow of these controversies. To these observations, I want to add a third more speculative one: the significance of the Lord's Supper for the literature produced in Protestant England lies less in the problem of the sign than in what I will call *the problem of the leftover*, that is, the status of the material remainder. Cranmer argues that in Jesus' words at the Last

Supper "must needs be sought out another sense and meaning than the words of themselves do bear." That sense and meaning leads away from the literal bread and wine, away from carnal eating and toward a spiritual feast. But what then is the point of the stuff that serves as a token of the Savior? Why should Jesus have chosen such insistently material objects to serve as the signs of his flesh and blood? And what are we to make of the vulnerability of these objects, the fact that they can be chewed, digested, vomited, dropped on the ground, left to rot?

We return to Martin Ignatius MacKenzie's questions, questions that haunted a discourse obsessed by the yoking of the holy to the embarrassments of matter. "If a Mouse chance to creepe into your pixe," asks Andrew Willet, "and fill her hungry belly with your god-amight, what is it that the Mouse feedeth vpon?"[18] Thomas Becon writes contemptuously that according to the Catholics

not only the godly and faithful eat the body of christ in the supper, but also the ungodly and misbelieving; yea, the cats, rats, mice, dogs, owls, flittermouses, and such other unreasonable creatures, whether they be birds, or four-footed beasts, or serpents, &c., if at any time it so chance that, through the negligence of the priest, it be so left that they devour it.[19]

The host-eating mouse is a way of insisting on the inescapable, untransformed materiality of the elements of the Mass and hence a polemical weapon against Catholic doctrine. That doctrine claims, reports Willet, that "the body of Christ goeth downe into the stomacke, but no further: but when the formes of bread and wine begin to be corrupted there, the body of Christ goeth away" (516). Such distinctions may reflect a subtle Aristotelian understanding of the relation between substance and accidents, but they are, in Willet's view, patently falsified by ordinary experience: when a priest drinks too much of the consecrated wine and gets drunk, he asks, is it the "accidents" of the wine that are making him light-headed? Catholics obviously found this mockery blasphemous: the sacred Eucharist, writes the recusant priest Thomas Wright, is "a most Maiesticall & diuine obiect," one worthy of the highest veneration.[20] Protestants responded with intensified contempt, dwelling not only on the contents of the mouse's intestines but of human excrement: can God, Willet asks, be chewed, digested, and "cast out into the draught" (518)?

These contemptuous sallies come close to ridiculing the sacrament itself, even as they attempt to ridicule only the Papists. Yet the Reformers were driven to take the risk in order to counter what they regarded as the still greater risk of idolatry. The material elements themselves must not be venerated. Why keep them at all? The answer, Cranmer suggests, is that God, knowing our childishness and our weakness, intended us to experience the physicality of the bread and wine in order to help confirm our inward faith. The sacrament enables us, as he puts it bluntly, to experience "a sensible touching, feeling, and groping" of Christ: "the eating and drinking of this sacramental bread and wine is, as it were, a showing of Christ before our eyes, a smelling of him with our noses, a feeling and groping of him with our hands, and an eating, chewing, digesting, and feeding upon him to our spiritual strength and perfection."

Cranmer's "as it were" is an acknowledgment in the midst of his insistently literal language of the figurative nature of this experience. It is the mark of an uneasy meeting: the conjunction of gross physicality and pure, abstracted spirituality, of Body and Word, of corruptible flesh and invulnerable ghost, of rotting corpse and majestical ruler. We have another name for this meeting when it assumed an apparently secular form: we call it *The Tragedy of Hamlet*.

NOTES

1   Marx, *The Eighteenth Brumaire of Louis Bonaparte*, in *The Marx–Engels Reader*, ed. Robert C. Tucker (New York, 1972), p. 437.

2   Slavoj Zizek, *The Sublime Object of Ideology* (London, 1989). Zizek defines the sublime object as "a positive, material object elevated to the status of the impossible Thing" (p. 71).

3   William Bradshaw, *A Direction for the Weaker Sort of Christians, Shewing in What Manner they Ought to Fit Themselves to the Worthy Receiving of the Sacrament* (London, 1609; 4th edn. 1615), p. 28.

4   John E. Booty, *John Jewel as Apologist of the Church of England* (London, 1963), p. 151.

5   Quoted in W. Schwarz, *Principles and Problems of Biblical Translation* (Cambridge, 1955), p. 10; cf. Stephen Greenblatt, *Renaissance Self-Fashioning: From More to Shakespeare* (Chicago, 1980), pp. 94ff.

6   Anon. [William Bishop (priest)], *The Second Part of the Reformation of a Catholike Deformed (An answere unto M. Perkins Advertisement)* (1607), p. 25. See, similarly, Nicholas Sanders, *The Supper of our Lord Set Foorth in Six Bookes* (with a seventh book) (Louvain, 1565).

7   *The Souper of the Lorde* (1533), based closely on Zwingli's 1526 treatise *On the Lord's Supper* (probably by George Joye). Appendix A of *The Answer to a Poisoned Book*, in *The Complete Works of St. Thomas More*, ed. Stephen Foley and Clarence Miller (New Haven, 1985), XI, p. 323.

8   Andrew Willet, *Synopsis papismi, That is, a Generall View of Papiestrie* (London, 1600), p. 511.

9   Thomas Becon, *The Displaying of the Popish Mass*, in Becon, *Prayers and Other Pieces*, Parker Society 17 (Cambridge, 1844), p. 271.

10 "Nous rejetons donc comme mauvais expositeurs ceux qui insistent ric à ric au sens littéral de ces mots: Ceci est mon corps, Ceci est mon sang. Car nous

tenons pour tout notoire que ces mots doivent être sainement interprétés et avec discrétion, à savoir que les noms de ce que le pain et le vin signifient leur sont attribués. Et cela ne doit être trouvé nouveau ou étrange que par une figure qu'on dit métonymie, le signe emprunte le nom de la vérité qu'il figure"; Calvin, *Consensus Tigurinus* (1549; the French translation, cited here, was published in 1551 and entitled "L'accord passé et conclu touchant la matière des sacrements, entre les ministres de l'église de Zurich et maître Jean Calvin, ministre de l'église de Genève"). Quoted in Bernard Cottret, "Pour une Sémiotique de la Réforme: Le *Consensus Tigurinus* (1549) et la *Brève résolution* (1555) de Calvin," *Annales ESC* (1984), 268. In *Brève résolution* (Geneva, 1555), Calvin writes similarly: "mais selon que l'Écriture parle partout des sacrements, que le nom de la chose signifiée s'attribue au signe, par une figure qu'on appelle métonymie, qui vaut autant comme transport de nom" (p. 268).

11   Quoted in Jaroslav Pelikan, *Reformation of Church and Dogma (1300–1700)*, in Pelikan, *The Christian Tradition: A History of the Development of Doctrine* (5 vols., Chicago and London, 1984), IV, p. 201.

12   For another example (out of many), see John Hooper writing against Stephen Gardiner's Catholic position: "Christ callid hymselfe a dore Ioan. 10. a vyne Ioan. 15. and yet was nether dore nor vyne except ye undrestond by a dore the only gate into heaven, and by the vyne the lycure of grace that confortithe every troblyd conscience and quensith thyre and displeasure of god the father against us for our synnes. So lyke wice in these wordes, Hoc est corpus meum, there is none other thyng to be understood by them, but the bread representyd unto his apostles," quoted in Booty, *John Jewel*, pp. 150–1.

13   *The Souper of the Lorde*, p. 325; John Frith, *A Boke made by Johan Fryth*, (1533), quoted in C. W. Dugmore, *The Mass and the English Reformers* (London, 1958), p. 99.

14   Rastell and Harding, quoted in Booty, *John Jewel*, pp. 154, 158.

15   The story is attributed to "I. Markes Iesuite, in a book of his written of late, and intituled, The Examination of the new Religion, page 128" and is cited in John Gee, *The Foot out of the Snare: with a Detection of Sundry Late Practices and Impostures of the Priests and Iesuits in England* (London, 1624), pp. 28–9.

16   Quoted in J. P. Boulton, "The Limits of Formal Religion: The Administration of Holy Communion in late Elizabethan and early Stuart England," *London Journal* 10 (1984), 139. This rubric was dropped in the 1559 *Prayer Book*.

17   Cranmer, *Defence of the True and Catholic Doctrine ...*, in *The Work of Thomas Cranmer* (Appleford, UK, 1965), pp. 144–5.

18   Willet, *Synopsis papismi*, p. 516.

19   Thomas Becon, *A Comparison Between the Lord's Supper and the Pope's Mass*, in Becon, *Prayers* p. 378.

20   Thomas Wright, *The Disposition or Garnishmente of the Soule to Receiue Worthily the Blessed Sacrament* (Antwerp, 1596), p. 1.

Part V

Objections

13   The insincerity of women

Marjorie Garber

> Reflect on the whole history of women: do they not have to be first of all and above all else actresses? Listen to physicians who have hypnotized women; finally, love them – let yourself be "hypnotized by them"! What is always the end result? That they "put on something" even when they take off everything.[1]
>
> Woman is so artistic.
>
> Nietzsche, The Gay Science

Imagine the scene.

Beatrice-Joanna, rummaging in her new husband's closet, is desperate about the impending wedding night, since she has yielded her virginity, under duress, to the aptly named DeFlores. Now she fears discovery and disgrace.

DeFlores, at her bidding, has secretly murdered Alonzo de Piraquo, her father's choice, the man to whom she was first engaged, so that she is now free to marry Alsemero. To confirm the deed, DeFlores has cut off his victim's finger with its ring and brandishes it before her in triumph. Welcome to the "other scene." *The Changeling* is not a play that will hide castration under a bushel.

Thinking to buy him off with gold, Beatrice-Joanna is dumbfounded to learn that DeFlores expects instead a sexual reward. "Y'are the deed's creature," he tells her (3.4.137). The "deed" here is, prospectively, both sex and murder. He is implacable in his demand:

> Can you weep fate from its determin'd purpose?
> So soon may you weep me.
>
> (161–2)

And he is coolly knowing. He anticipates, in fact, that she will enjoy herself, despite her demurrals. "Las, how the turtle pants," he grins at her,

> Thou'lt love anon
> What thou so fear'st and faint'st to venture on.
>
> (169–70)

So here is Beatrice-Joanna, on the night of the wedding, convinced that her husband will detect her deflowered condition and denounce her. What remedy? Luckily for her, Alsemero has gone for a walk in the park, leaving the key in the closet door. It is only a moment's work to open it. And what does she see? Alsemero's pharmacy, "A right physician's closet," as she describes it, "set round with vials" (4.1.20–21), and a book of experiments called *Secrets in Nature* open upon the table. Her worst fears are confirmed by the table of contents.

> "How to know whether a woman be with child or no."
> I hope I am not yet; if he should try though!
> Let me see: "folio forty-five." Here 'tis;
> The leaf tuck'd down upon't, the place suspicious.
> "If you would know whether a woman be with child or not,
> Give her two spoonfuls of the white water in glass C – "
> Where's that glass C? O, yonder, I see't now – "and if she be with child,
> She sleeps full twelve hours after, if not, not."
> None of that water comes into my belly:
> I'll know you from a hundred.
>
> (26–36)

This pregnancy test, as the Revels editor N. W. Bawcutt notes, bears some resemblance to a test contained in Thomas Lupton's *A Thousand Notable Things of Sundry Sorts* (1579): "If you would know whether a Woman be conceived with Child or not, give her two spoonfuls of Water and one spoonful of Clarified Honey, mingled together, to drink when she goes to sleep; and if she feels Gripings and Pains in the Belly in the night, she is with child; if she feel none, she is not."[2]

However, for Beatrice-Joanna, the worst is yet to come – "ten times worse," as she declares. For the next experiment offers advice on "How to know whether a woman be a maid or not."

> If that should be applied, what would become of me?
> Belike he has a strong faith in my purity,
> That never yet made proof; but this he calls
> A merry sleight, but true experiment, the author Antonius Mizaldus.
> Give the party you suspect the quantity of a spoonful of the water in the
> glass M, which upon her that is a maid makes three several effects: 'twill
> make her incontinently gape, then fall into a sudden sneezing, last into a
> violent laughing; else dull, heavy, and lumpish.
>
> (40–9)

Bawcutt's note informs the reader that, although Alsemero is apparently consulting Mizaldus's *De arcanis naturae*, "there are no passages in it resembling those quoted by Beatrice." Such tests are, however, very common in the scientific literature of the period, he observes, ultimately deriving perhaps from Pliny's *Natural History*;[3] and in another collection by Mizaldus, a sixteenth-century French scholar and compiler of scientific knowledge, virginity and pregnancy tests are given, two of which involve the ingestion of liquids by the woman being tested, "though," as Bawcutt reports, "in none of them are her reactions those described" in Middleton and Rowley's play. "The fantastic nature of the virginity test," he concludes, in language that is worth our noting, "makes it seem very probable that Middleton devised it himself and then fathered it upon Mizaldus."

"Fathered it upon Mizaldus." The editor's note here makes explicit the implicit link between glass M and glass C. For what would be the economic and political usefulness of "scientific" tests for virginity and pregnancy? Manifestly, to ensure the legitimacy of offspring. A wise father – and the bridegroom Alsemero is described by Beatrice-Joanna, despairingly, as a "wise man" who will detect her secret – will want to know his own child. Thus a materialist reading of the contents and effect of "glass M" in *The Changeling* will take the agency of the letter – M for maid – at its word. The test is a test for virginity, the commodification of the well-born bride and her expected children, part of a nobleman's marriage bargain. In the next moments Beatrice-Joanna – and the audience – will witness a graphic demonstration of the efficacy of that test, as in desperation she hits upon a plan to employ a changeling, sending her waiting-woman Diaphanta in her place to Alsemero's bed.

First, however, she must be sure that Diaphanta is herself a "maid" – an identification the waiting-woman puts in doubt by volunteering with alacrity to take her mistress's place. "Y'are too quick, I fear, to be a maid" (93), observes Beatrice pointedly, and she proposes an "easy trial." Both of them will drink from glass M. The results are just what she fears – and hopes. She herself feels no effect, but Diaphanta produces all the appropriate symptoms, and in the prescribed sequence. She gapes ("there's the first symptom. And what haste it makes / To fall into the second" [107–8]), then sneezes, then laughs ("Ha, ha, ha! I am so – so light / At heart! Ha, ha, ha! – so pleasurable! / But one swig more, sweet madam" [112–14]), and finally grows "sad again" (115). "Just in all things and in order," observes Beatrice-Joanna ruefully,

> As if twere circumscribed; one accident
> Gives way unto another.
>
> (110–12)

The bargain between them is struck: Diaphanta, convinced that her mistress is afraid of sex and wants someone else to describe it to her before she tries it, is to have "the bride's place, / And ... a thousand ducats" (125–6), while Beatrice-Joanna prepares to slip into the bed at midnight, after the supposed defloration has occurred.

Glass M, then, would seem to be as aptly and transparently named as the deflowerer DeFlores. If we ask Malvolio's question from *Twelfth Night*, "What should that alphabetical position portend?" as he ponders a similarly enigmatic letter "M," we may if we like rest content with a version of Malvolio's answer – "why this is evident to any formal capacity. There is no obstruction in this" (*TN* 2.5.117–20). M stands for "maid" and "maidenhead." Drinking glass M's contents reveals, to the skilled scientific eye, the unmistakable symptoms of virginity.

But does it? Alsemero clearly thinks so, but then Alsemero, while no Malvolio, is a somewhat hapless and inattentive observer, for all of his vaunted experience and knowledge. He is an investigator with an answer already in mind as he conducts his experiment, and, like many such investigators, he finds his desired result.

We may recall that the Revels editor, who found precedents in the scientific literature for the pregnancy test of glass C, regarded the "virginity test" of glass M as "fantastic" in nature, and noted that "in none of the tests" in Mizaldus's works – including tests "Mulierem corruptam ab incorrupta discernere" and "Noscendi ratio an mulier sit virgo integra & intacta an non" – "are her reactions those described in ll.48–50": that is, first gaping, then sneezing, then laughing, then falling into a fit of melancholy.

What if we were to ask, then, not "what is the agency of the letter M" but, rather, of what are these things symptoms? Or, even, of what are they *supposed to be* symptoms? In other words, what is being tested here? And what is being displayed?

Let us consult some putative experts, some latter-day Mizalduses. "I maintained years ago that the dyspnoea and palpitations that occur in hysteria and anxiety neurosis are only detached fragments of the act of copulation." This is Freud, describing the patient known as Dora, one of whose chief symptoms was "dyspnoea," or shortness of breath. He notes Dora's "concern whether *she* might not have over-exerted herself in masturbating – an act which, like [her father's copulation with her mother], led to a sexual orgasm accompanied by slight dyspnoea – and finally came a return of the dyspnoea in an intensified form as a symptom."[4] Dyspnoea; shortness of breath. Not always, perhaps, with open mouth – but to "gape" is also to gasp, with pain or pleasure. " 'Twill make her *incontinently* gape" says the symptom book describing the effects of glass M. This is stage one.

And now to stage two, the telltale sneeze.

Sneezing had been associated with omens and the supernatural at least since Aristotle.[5] In the early seventeenth century the physician William Harvey took special note of the sneeze reflex as an involuntary reflex *in women*, and compared it to labor pains: "the throes of childbirth, just as sneezing, proceed from the motion and agitation of the whole body."

Harvey tells the story of a young woman patient who fell into a coma during labor and could not be roused. "Finding that injections and other ordinary remedies had been employed in vain" to rouse her, he "dipped a feather in a powerful sternutatory [that is, a substance, like pepper, that induces sneezing] and passed it up the nostrils. Although the stupor was so profound that she could not sneeze, or be roused in any way, the effect was to excite convulsions throughout the body, beginning at the shoulders, and gradually descending to the lower extremities."[6] The impulse to sneeze is deflected or displaced physiologically into convulsions, which here facilitate a healthy completion of labor. In Harvey's description these convulsions, "roused" by the sternutatory, appear to mimic the involuntary spasms of sexual orgasm. Notice, however, that the woman feels nothing, neither pain nor pleasure. It is the (male) doctor who produces these effects, without her conscious participation, or even her knowledge.[7]

In the early days of psychoanalysis, with its emphasis upon hysteria and the body that unconsciously speaks its symptoms, the sneeze again figured memorably as a sign. Here is Freud's collaborator Joseph Breuer: "Sexuality at puberty appears," he writes, "as a vague, indeterminate, purposeless heightening of excitation. As development proceeds, this endogenous heightening of excitation, determined by the functioning of the sex-glands, becomes firmly linked (in the normal course of things) with the perception or idea of the other sex."[8]

To explain the ways in which repressed sexual feelings are acted out in "hysterical" symptoms, Breuer instances a particular physiological event:

I will select an extremely trivial example – the sneezing reflex. If a stimulus of the mucous membrane of the nose fails for any reason to release this preformed reflex, a feeling of excitation and tension arises, as we all know ... This everyday example gives us the pattern of what happens when a psychical reflex, even the most complicated one, fails to occur. (*SE* 2: 206–7)

However, for Freud sneezing and sexual energy are not merely analogous. Freud had, he said, "begun to suspect" his patient Dora of masturbating when he heard her complain of gastric pains, since, according to his friend Wilhelm Fliess, "it is precisely gastralgias of this character which can be interrupted by an application of cocaine to the 'gastric spot' discovered by him in the nose" ("Fragment," *SE* 7: 78).

The famous "gastric spot" – we could call it a G spot – was, Fliess thought, a seat of sexual passion, and he and Freud corresponded avidly about "the therapy of the neurasthenic nasal neurosis." Freud referred to Fliess surgery patients, both male and female, who evidenced "a suspicious shape to [the] nose" or other symptoms indicative of masturbation.[9] So sex, desire, is seated in the nose. (The recurrent popularity of both cocaine and snuff as pleasurable stimulants attests to the enduring autoerotic *jouissance* of the sneeze.)

Furthermore, it is worth noting that, at about the same time that the sneeze was being regarded by Freud and Breuer as suspiciously sexual, sexy sneezes were also occurring in literature and film. *Studies on Hysteria* was published in 1893. In 1891 Thomas Hardy described, in *Tess of the d'Urbervilles*, the effect of Tess's beauty on Angel Clare:

> Clare had studied the curves of those lips so many times that he could reproduce them mentally with ease; and now, as they again confronted him, clothed with colour and life, they sent an *aura* over his flesh, a breeze through his nerves, which wellnigh produced a qualm; and actually produced, by some mysterious physiological process, a prosaic sneeze.[10]

The juxtaposition here of the lips, the "*aura*," and the sneeze, however the latter is dismissed as "prosaic," tells its own story. The body – here the body of the neurasthenic male Angel – speaks.

Meanwhile, the pioneers of film technology were recording the sneeze as a visual document of involuntary pleasure. *Fred Ott's Sneeze* was one of the earliest test films made by the Edison Laboratory, in 1893–4. The short film record (eighty-one frames) of a man in the act of sneezing has been celebrated by film historians as Edison's first film, the first film to use an actor, and the first cinematic close-up.

Yet in fact the initial impetus to film a sneeze specified a *female* subject. The idea for the film came from a journalist for *Harper's Weekly*, bored with the dull topics of previous experiments in film, who wrote to Edison suggesting the possibility of a "nice looking young person to perform a sneeze," explicitly a woman "in the act of sneezing."[11] Ott, a young laboratory technician with a flowing mustache, was chosen by Edison as a substitute, for reasons of convenience.

The original idea of a "pretty young woman who would have lent prurient interest to the involuntary comic action of a sneeze," as Linda Williams notes, indicates the way in which "technicians of pleasure," "from Charcot to Muybridge, from Freud to Edison," solicit for their science "further confessions of the hidden secrets of female pleasure."[12]

"The animating male fantasy of hard-core cinema," maintains Williams, might be described as "the (impossible) attempt to capture visually this frenzy of the visible in a female body whose orgasmic excitement can never be objectively measured ... the woman's sexual pleasure is elicited involuntarily, often against her will" (Williams, 50). When *Fred Ott's Sneeze* appeared as a series of photographs in *Harper's Weekly*, it was accompanied by a text that analyzed in detail the ten stages of "this curious gamut of grimace," a sequence that seems cognate in some ways to Alsemero's – or Mizaldus's – four-stage sequence of female involuntary pleasure.

Freud's and Breuer's observations about panting and sneezing are taken from some of their earliest work. Interestingly, however, it was to very similar questions about sexual pleasure and displaced physiological response that Freud recurred in his last years, and, indeed, in his journal jottings just before his death.

"The ultimate ground of all intellectual inhibitions and all inhibitions of work," he wrote on 3 August 1938, "seems to be the inhibition of masturbation in childhood."

But perhaps it goes deeper; perhaps it is not its inhibition by external influences but its unsatisfying nature in itself. There is always something lacking for complete discharge and satisfaction – en attendant toujours quelquechose qui ne venait point – and this missing part, the reaction of orgasm, manifests itself in equivalents in other spheres, in *absences*, outbreaks of laughing and weeping ... , and perhaps other ways. Once again infantile sexuality has fixed a model in this. (Emphasis in original)[13]

Gaping, sneezing, laughing – and finally melancholy sadness. For this last symptom, perhaps, we do not need the testimony of psychoanalysts to augment that of the poets: *Post coitum omne animal triste est.* Yet in fact the relationship between orgasm and sadness, hypnosis, and sleep is repeatedly noted in the psychoanalytic literature. Thus Breuer insists that "the sexual orgasm itself, with its wealth of affect and its restriction of consciousness, is closely akin to hypnoid states" (*SE*, 248); "in orgasm thought is almost completely extinguished" (*SE* 2: 200).

In a letter to Fliess, Freud finds "Instructive!" (the ejaculatory punctuation is his own) the story of a young woman who – according to her wealthy lover – had "from four to six orgasms during one coitus. But – at the very first approach she is seized with a tremor and immediately afterwards falls into a pathological sleep; while she is in this she talks as though she was in hypnosis, carries out post-hypnotic suggestions and has complete amnesia for the whole condition."[14] Later Freud would write in his "Three Essays on Sexuality" that in infants "sensual sucking involves a complete absorption of the attention and leads either to sleep or even to a motor reaction in the nature of an orgasm."[15]

Of what, then, might this sequence of diagnostic symptoms in *The Changeling* be indicative? A list of symptoms, detailed from Mizaldus's "The Book of Experiments, Call'd Secrets in Nature," that Bawcutt found "fantastic," and that seem, indeed, to have more than a little to do with fantasy? They are not, in fact, the telltale signs of virginity, but rather of *orgasm*. Not the commodification and ownership of women, as virgins, as mothers, but rather the intangibility of desire.

Here again is Sigmund Freud, writing to Fliess in the early days of psychoanalysis about the case of one "Frau P. J.," aged twenty-seven, who was suffering from feelings of oppression, anxiety, and abdominal discomfort. The tone in this letter, as in many of Freud's communications with Fliess, is man-to-man, self-congratulatory, much – to strain the comparison a little – like Alsemero's confident assertions to his friend Jasperino. "What I expected to find was this. She had had a longing for her husband – that is, for sexual relations with him; she had thus come upon an idea which had excited sexual affect and afterwards defence against the idea; she had then taken fright and made a false connection or substitution."[16] And from the same account:

I then asserted that before the attack there had been thoughts present to her which she might not remember. In fact she remembered nothing, but pressure [on her forehead] produced "husband" and "longing." The latter was further specified, on my insistence, as longing for sexual caresses ... There was certainly something besides this: a feeling in the lower part of the body, a convulsive desire to urinate. – She now confirmed this. The insincerity of women starts from their omitting the characteristic sexual symptoms in describing their states. So it had really been an *orgasm*. (Emphasis in original)

Notice the astonishing scientific "detachment" of this last pair of assertions. "The insincerity of women starts from their omitting the characteristic sexual symptoms in describing their states. So it had really been an *orgasm*."

The male doctor here detects – and shares with his male friend – the woman's secret, and thus her power. "Insincerity" seems a harsh word for the concealment of symptoms; Freud's response in fact appears overdetermined, both by his own agency in producing this result (the pressure of his hands on her forehead, an early aspect of the treatment of his neurotic patients, later discontinued) and by his desire to *know* what he cannot know except through her confession and confirmation. "So it had really been an *orgasm*."

Freud and Alsemero, in fact, are fellow physicians in this quest for certainty and power over the stories told by women's symptoms. One curious paradox of Alsemero's glass M is the fact that it produces, or is expected to produce, orgasmic effects in *virgins, and not in women of sexual experience. Should we not expect the opposite to be the case?* Furthermore, contemporary physiology held that female orgasm was necessary for conception.[17] Why then are the orgasmic symptoms in Middleton's and Rowley's play not elicited by glass *C* (for "child") rather than by glass M? The answer to both questions, I think, is that glass M – the detection of a virgin – represents the fruits of a male fantasy, the fantasy of the male doctor/lover as at once the inventor and the scientific investigator of female pleasure. Glass M, like the whole pharmacopoeia so carefully locked away by Alsemero for his private use, is in fact a fantasy projection of the lover's power. He will elicit signs of sexual pleasure in their most manifest form from a woman who knows sexuality, and physical love, only through him. Just as Freud knows better than Dora (or even the married Frau P. J.) what pleasures her body betrays, so Alsemero's drugs test his power, not, or not only, Beatrice-Joanna's response.

Let us now consider what happens in *The Changeling* once Beatrice-Joanna learns, by precept (Mizaldus's book) and example (Diaphanta's display of "symptoms") how to respond to the contents of glass M.

The plot has reached a crucial juncture. It is still the night of the wedding when Alsemero is advised first of Piraquo's murder and then of a private conversation between Beatrice-Joanna and DeFlores. "The very sight of him is poison to her," Alsemero protests (4.2.98), but once again the borderline between "poison" and "remedy" appears to have been breached. Beatrice-Joanna has pleaded her "fears" as a "timorous virgin" (117–18) and has asked to come to her husband's bed modestly in the dark. Can she be lying? Has she betrayed him with DeFlores? Discovery, exposure, and denunciation lie apparently just around the corner. Is DeFlores a *pharmakeus* (magician, sorcerer) or a *pharmakos* (scapegoat)?

Good empiricist that he is, determined to find the truth, Alsemero sends immediately to his closet for "A glass inscrib'd there with the letter M" (114) and offers it to his bride. Her response, aside, has all the horror of classic melodrama: "The glass, upon my life! I see the letter" (130); "I am suspected" (131). Yet, forced to drink, she produces all the appropriate symptoms, in the right order – gaping, sneezing, laughing, melancholy. As she confides to the audience,

> th'effects I know,
> If I can now but feign 'em handsomely.
>
> (137–38)

Alsemero is completely won over, convinced that she is "Chaste as the breath of heaven, or morning's womb" (149–50). His faith in her is tied to his faith in science, and, indeed, to his own sexual expertise – for, as he notes confidently to a male friend, glass M "ne'er missed, sir, / Upon a virgin."

What Beatrice-Joanna learns in Alsemero's pharmacy, and turns immediately to her own use, is "what every woman knows": how to fake it. She produces the symptoms, the simulacra of orgasmic response, that delight her husband and confirm his apparent mastery of her. When she does so, Alsemero clasps her to him: "thus my love encloses thee" (150).

The Changeling is a play about the pleasure and danger of woman's desire. In the complex dynamics of its heterosexual power relations, the power to withhold becomes the power to control. Beatrice-Joanna romanticizes her feelings about the dashing Alsemero ("This was the man meant me!" [1.1.84]), but she finds in DeFlores the frisson of involuntary response:

> I never see this fellow but I think
> Of some harm towards me; danger's in my mind still,
> I scarce leave trembling of an hour after.
>
> (2.1.89–91)

Her ruse to employ him to dispatch her inconvenient fiancé ("men of art make much of poison. Keep one to expel another. Where was my art?" [2.2.46–7]; "Why, put case I loathed him [. . .] / Must I needs show it? Cannot I keep the secret / And serve the turn upon him?" [2.2.66–9]) leads inexorably to a relationship in which loathing and desire are intertwined and finally beyond her control. "I have kissed poison" for your love, she tells Alsemero (5.3.66), but it is never finally clear whether for Beatrice-Joanna there is any real difference between danger, trembling, loathing, and desire.

With Alsemero, however – the idealized lover, the longed-for husband, the handsome romantic lead, Ashley Wilkes to DeFlores's sinister Rhett Butler – she is, paradoxically, in control, once she learns, from his own pharmacy, how to simulate the throes of passion.

Here, then, is our question: is there any difference between centering a play on woman's desire and centering it on woman's ability to fake it? Which is more threatening?

Recall once more Freud's apparently unfeeling judgment on Frau P. J. (her name itself, to a modern reader, so evocative of bedtime): "The insincerity of women starts from their omitting the characteristic sexual symptoms in describing their states. So it had really been an *orgasm*."

Hollywood mogul Sam Goldwyn gave this famous advice to aspiring actresses: "The most important thing about acting is sincerity. If you can fake that you've got it made." From the analyst's couch to the casting couch, from the "insincerity" of concealing sexual responsiveness to the "sincerity" of faking it, the fear, and the excitement, is of a woman's sexual pleasure. Woman's orgasm is Freud's "dark continent," as well as Mizaldus's "secret of nature." Female pleasure is the unknown and unknowable, the other, less masterable and controllable answer to the question Freud poses over and over again, in different forms, throughout his work: "What does a woman want?"

It is hardly a new question.

Ovid's famous story about Tiresias, who was asked whether men or women had greater pleasure in sex, is part of the same obsessive inquiry. How could a man ever know? Tiresias was drawn into the dispute between Juno and Jove because he had been both woman and man. Once, having seen snakes coupling, he struck them apart and was instantly turned into a woman. Seven years later he saw them again, struck them again, and was changed back into a man. His answer, that women had more pleasure than men, pleased Jove and displeased Juno, who struck him blind; Jove then, since he could not undo this curse, gave to Tiresias second sight, power to know the future. Thomas Laqueur points out that "Ovid's account would become a regular anecdote in the professorial repertory, told to generations of medieval and Renaissance students to spice up medical lectures," and comments trenchantly that "One might translate the question more specifically as 'which sex had the better orgasm.'"[18]

Was Tiresias himself a changeling? No one more so. In fact he makes a cameo appearance in Middleton's and Rowley's play, in the voice and person of the feigned madman Franciscus, who has entered Alibius's madhouse in order to seduce Alibius's wife. The scene is constructed, with some pertinence, as another "pharmacy," with Lollio, Alibius's assistant, cast for a madman's moment in the role of the *pharmakon*, who offers both "poison" and "remedy."

> FRANCISCUS. Come hither, Aesculapius. Hide the poison.
> LOLLIO. Well, 'tis hid.
> FRANCISCUS. Didst thou never hear of one Tiresias,
>   A famous poet?
> LOLLIO. Yes, that kept tame wild-geese.
> FRANCISCUS. That's he; I am the man.
> LOLLIO. No!
> FRANCISCUS. Yes; but make no words on't, I was a man
>   Seven years ago –
> LOLLIO. A stripling I think you might –
> FRANCISCUS. Now I'm a woman, all feminine.

LOLLIO. I would I might see that.
FRANCISCUS. Juno struck me blind.
LOLLIO. I'll ne'er believe that; for a woman, they say,
   has an eye more than a man.
FRANCISCUS. I say she struck me blind.

(3.3.62–77)

Why does Tiresias' answer anger Juno? Because female pleasure is shameful? Or because a woman's pleasure is her secret – and her power?

Can she fake it? And thereby deny her partner the pleasure of her pleasure? How can her partner ever know? For orgasm, *jouissance*, is – as Jacqueline Rose deftly describes it – "what escapes in sexuality."[19] Thus Lacan recurred to Freud's unanswered question, "What does a woman want?" by evoking Bernini's St. Theresa as a model for *jouissance*. "What is her *jouissance*, her *coming* from?" he asks.[20] Thus, too, in discussing Mallarmé's *Mimique* Derrida identifies the "supreme spasm," the orgasm of Columbine as mimed by her husband, Pierrot, as a double miming. "I'm going to tickle my wife to death," Pierrot declares, and for Derrida the "spasm" is also the "hymen," that word that paradoxically incorporates virginity and marriage.[21] Gayatri Spivak saw clearly that this was for Derrida a scene of faked orgasm, in which the male actor appropriates the language of a woman's desire. "The faked orgasm now takes center stage. The Pierrot of the pantomime 'acts' as the woman 'is' ('Pierrot is [plays] Columbine') by faking a faked orgasm which is also a faked crime."[22] Is it worth noting that the boy actor playing Beatrice-Joanna likewise "fakes[s] a fake orgasm" from the ambivalent double position of transvestite theater, a man playing a woman playing a trick on a man? So perhaps we are dealing not – or not only – with the "insincerity of women," but also with the intrinsic and instrumental insincerity of theater. With the mimesis of mimesis itself.

Female orgasm as mimesis, as an act or an acting out, poses a special problem. How can a lover tell the difference between origin and imitation, between the "fake" and the "real"? And, once again, which is more threatening?

Aristotle as a scientist was not interested in female pleasure, or in female orgasm; it did not fit into his theories.[23] Debates about the role, if any, of the clitoris, and about the necessity of pleasure for procreation appear from time to time in the writings of medieval and Renaissance physicians.[24] Aphrodisiacs for women were seldom mentioned in the herbals, and then they were recommended for use by unsatisfied husbands with recalcitrant wives.[25] Laqueur suggests that in the eighteenth century and after, "the routine orgasmic culmination of intercourse became a major topic of debate."

The assertion that women were passionless, or alternatively the proposition that, as biologically defined beings, they possessed to an extraordinary degree, far more than men, the capacity to control the bestial, irrational, and potentially destructive fury of sexual pleasure; and indeed the novel inquiry into the nature and quality of female pleasure and sexual allurement – all were part of a grand effort to discover the anatomical and physiological characteristics that distinguished men from women. Orgasm became a player in the game of new sexual differences. (Laqueur, 150)

The histories of medicine and sexual sociology appear to offer an either/or choice, between the fantasy of women possessing no desire and the fantasy of women as eros embodied. But more disconcerting remains a third possibility: that women are somehow in control of the sexual rhetoric of desire. Women may lack desire – and therefore stand aloof and untouched by the circuit of courtship, blandishment, arousal, and possession which is the economy of sexual mastery. Or they may act in pursuit of their own desire. Or they can fake it. With no one the wiser but themselves.

Here, for example, is the sage counsel of a nineteenth-century French physician, Auguste Debay, whose manual on the physiology of marriage went through an astonishing 153 editions from its original publication in 1849 to 1880.

O wives! Follow this advice. Submit to the demands of your husband in order to attach him to you all the more. Despite the momentary aversion for the pleasures he seeks, force yourself to satisfy him, put on an act and simulate the spasm of pleasure: this innocent trickery is permitted when it is a question of keeping a husband.[26]

If the Victorian Englishwoman had been exhorted to close her eyes and think of England, her Gallic counterpart, with the future of her marriage rather than the Empire in mind, was to keep her eyes open for theatrical opportunity, for simulation and innocent trickery. All this ostensibly in the service of "keeping a husband," preserving the basis of her own social legitimation and economic dependency. Marital truth here depends upon theatrical falsehood, "permitted" – once again – by an authorizing doctor. In Debay's formulation the satisfaction is imagined as entirely the husband's. The woman's pleasure is in her status, not in her bed.

Twentieth-century sex manuals, especially those from the "free to be me" seventies and eighties, stress the usefulness of rehearsal. Here, for example, with theatrical coaching and stage directions included, is a passage from an American self-help book entitled *Becoming Orgasmic: A Sexual and Personal Growth Program for Women* (first published in 1976):

We call this exercise Role-Playing Orgasm. What we'd like you to do is to fantasize about a wild orgasm and act it out.

Set aside thirty minutes to one hour. Begin one of your self-pleasuring sessions in the usual way. The first time, begin role-playing orgasm after you've pleasured yourself for a while but *before* you become extremely aroused. Move around, tense your muscles, lie very rigid, do some pelvic rocking, make noises – do whatever seems really extreme to you. Moan, scratch, pummel the bed, cry – the more exaggerated the better. Stop pleasuring yourself if you want, or continue while you have your "orgasm." You will probably feel awkward doing this the first few times, but it will become easier with practice. Remember the way you act is not really the way you would or should act. For this exercise, pretend to be the star in your own orgasmic fantasy![27]

In a chapter called "Orgasm – Yours, Not His," "J," the author of *The Sensuous Woman*, notes that she has "never met a woman yet who didn't occasionally fake it," and stresses the theatricality of faked orgasm, which she calls "The Sarah Bernhardt" maneuver. "J" also emphasizes the importance of rehearsal: "To become a fabulous fake, study again every contortion, muscle spasm, and body response that lead to and make up the orgasm and rehearse the process privately until you can duplicate it." "Women have been faking since time began," she informs us, cautioning against "ham[ming] it up too much" ("then he really will suspect you're acting") and, above all, against telling the truth. "You must *never, never* reveal to him that you have acted sometimes in bed. You will betray a trust shared by every other female in the world if you do."[28] In this case the presumed homosocial compact among women enforces the "success" of heterosexual relations.

Dr. Ruth Westheimer, "author, psychologist, and media personality," has a different concern about "The Perils of Faking It," since to pretend to be satisfied is to forego real satisfaction. Yet she too sees the congruence between theater and sexual fakery. In a "typical case" of a "lady [who] had never experienced orgasm" although she had been impressed by women thrashing about on the movie screen in the throes of ecstasy, Dr. Ruth's client was manifestly "a good actress," because her husband "never had an inkling that she was faking it." In this case the cure, facilitated through the intervention of a sex therapist, was the one proposed by the authors of *Becoming Orgasmic*, a variant of Beatrice-Joanna's observation and imitation of Diaphanta. The woman learned to masturbate, thus discovering for herself the sensations of pleasure, which she could then reproduce by guiding her husband's hand over her body.[29]

The desire to control a woman's orgasm, and to know when it occurs, has mobilized the agency of the letter. Beyond Middleton's (or Alsemero's) glass M and glass C lie, for example, the elusive G spot, or Grafenberg spot, as well as the erotic advice of "J," the author of *The*

Sensuous Woman, and "M," the author of *The Sensuous Man*. Sexologists from Kinsey to Masters and Johnson to Ladas, Perry, and Whipple have sought to describe, delimit, and pin down the female orgasm. Was it clitoral? Vaginal? "Blended"? How could you tell when a woman had one? Consider the case of sex researcher John D. Perry, who attempted to replicate the research of Masters and Johnson on women's muscle contractions. Perry asked a number of male college students who the sexiest women on campus were, and then invited them – without explaining how he got their names – to become research subjects. One agreed.

She passed with flying colors a written test of sexual interest and demonstrated good control over her sexual musculature. They then put her to the test in the lab. "At first, during masturbation, her PC [urinary] muscle showed normal, expected increases in tension. But as she became more aroused, suddenly PC muscle activity ceased. The laboratory technicians assumed that their research subject was taking a break – until the remote signal light flashed that the woman was having an orgasm."[30] This unexpected datum, together with "subjective reports from many women" who claimed that they had experienced more than one kind of orgasm, "our own laboratory evidence that some women achieved what they claimed were satisfying orgasms *without* the characteristic contractions of the orgasmic platform," and "the undeniable fact of female ejaculation, especially in response to G spot stimulation" (147) led the sex researchers to revise their understanding of female sexuality completely. Notice here the conjunction of "subjective reports," women's "claims," and "undeniable fact." Despite all the data, it was upon claims and reports that these scientific findings had, necessarily, to be based.

Is this experiment another example of the "insincerity" of women? How much pleasure does a woman get, and how?

"While the mechanics of an orgasm may be known, it is still a sensation, and like all sensations it's subjective," writes the author of an article called "Evolution of the Big O," in the popular science journal *Discover*. "As a result, its existence can't be demonstrated or disproved by empirical measures. That unhappy truth becomes especially clear when evolutionary biologists turn their attention to the female orgasm – which they do with unseemly fascination. Even human lovers have to take their lady's word for it. How much more ineffable, then, must be the coital consciousness of Madame Marmoset."[31]

The Big O. When something hits the Renaissance G spot, what is often told is a story of "O." Thus in the final discovery scene of *The Changeling* an incensed Alsemero dispatches DeFlores after the woman he labels, in fury, a "crying crocodile."

        – Get you into her, sir.
    I'll be your pander now; rehearse again
    Your scene of lust, that you may be perfect.

                                    (5.3.113–15)

From the "closet," behind the stage, there now issue ambiguous cries.

> BEATRICE (*within*). O! O! O!
> ALSEMERO. Hark! 'Tis coming to you.
> DEFLORES (*within*). Nay, I'll along for company.
> BEATRICE (*within*).   O, O!
> VERMANDERO [Beatrice-Joanna's father]. What horrid sounds are
> these?

                                    (5.3.139–141)

The nonplussed father, Vermandero, hearing his daughter's cries, finds them mysterious, unrecognizable. "What horrid sounds are these?" "O! O! O!" Are these the sounds of enforced sexuality, of rape and injury? Or the voice of the woman moved beyond control? The omnipresent Renaissance "die" pun, the simultaneity of sex and death, is in this episode more than usually literal and vivid, not an implication but an enactment, a passionate outcry. Remember Alsemero's scathing epithet "crocodile," his brusque instruction to "rehearse" the "scene" of sexual passion. Even here it is not possible to tell what Beatrice-Joanna feigns, and what she feels.

We might usefully compare this final moment, embedded in a Jacobean tragedy, with what is perhaps the *locus classicus* of histrionic "faking it" for the 1980s: Rob Reiner's 1989 film *When Harry Met Sally . . .* , with a witty, streetwise screenplay by Nora Ephron. In the climactic scene, set in a New York deli, Sally (Meg Ryan) takes Harry (Billy Crystal) to task for his casual ways with women.

HARRY. I don't hear anyone complaining. I think they have an okay time.
SALLY. Because they . . . (*rotating hand gesture signifying orgasm*)?
HARRY (*truculently*). Yes, because they . . . (*rotating hand gesture signifying orgasm*)
SALLY. How do you know they really . . . (*rotating hand gesture*)
HARRY (*indignantly*). What are you saying, that they fake orgasm?
SALLY. Most women at one time or another have faked it.
HARRY. Well they haven't faked it with me.
SALLY. How do you know?
HARRY. Because I know.
SALLY. I forgot, you're a man. All men are sure it hasn't happened to them and most women at one time or another have done it, so you do the math.
HARRY. You don't think I could tell the difference?
SALLY. (*faking orgasm, as all heads in the restaurant turn*). Mmmmm . . . Yes . . . right there . . . Yes, yes yes yes YES!!!"

A pause. She lifts one corner of her mouth and grins at him, then casually picks up her fork and resumes stabbing at her salad. Harry looks at her steadily, while everyone around them draws a deep breath. Everyone, that is, except a middle-aged woman – played by Rob Reiner's mother, Estelle – seated a few tables away, who beckons to the waiter and tells him, deadpan: "I'll have what she's having."

"I'll have what she's having." But what she's having is a fake orgasm.

In Middleton's and Rowley's play the father, who has attempted to control his daughter's marriage and thus her desires, finds the sounds of a woman's passion indecipherable and "horrid." In Reiner's film the mother – and we might note that practically everyone who has seen the film has somehow learned the "real" identity of the customer in the deli – listens, recognizes, and desires the woman's "passion," even (or especially?) if that "passion" is only a pretense. "I'll have what she's having." But what if she's having us on?

The potions and philtres in Alsemero's pharmacy, like the book of recipes he follows, are designed to decipher, and thus to control, women's bodies and women's pleasure. By learning to fake the responses of pleasure, Beatrice-Joanna, like Sally Albright in the film, re-takes control of the relationship, and of the scene. Yet, as all the self-help manuals suggest, to fake pleasure may be the first step in attaining it. Or – and this is more to the point – it may become a pleasure in itself.

When Beatrice-Joanna shifts her mimetic attention from Alsemero's book to Diaphanta's symptoms she shifts from text to theatricalization, from script to stage. In both the written and the acted models she finds, and takes, the cues for passion.

The particular case of orgasm only serves to epitomize the power that actors derive more generally from this "female" capacity to withhold, to dissimulate, to test the boundaries of the real.

Furthermore, these scenes in which, instead of faking an orgasm, characters fake the faking of an orgasm exhibit something intrinsic to the nature of theater. Isn't the frisson an audience feels both in *The Changeling* and in *When Harry Met Sally* ... related to this intrinsic paradox of performance, that in acting only the fake is real?

Nor (is it needless to say?) are women the only ones who fake it on or off the stage, when the occasion arises. Martin Sherman's 1979 play *Bent*, with its central scene of two homosexual men in a Nazi prison camp, unable to touch or even look at each other, brought to simultaneous orgasm by language as they stand facing the audience, is a theatrical *tour de force*. Compare this onstage fake realness to the commercial phenomenon of telephone sex, its erotic power dynamic linked, fiber-optically, to questions of authenticity, sincerity, and arousal, offering an example of the disparate pleasures of faking it in the real world.

In a rather different performance register, how does the cliché "money shot" of pornographic film, with its evidence of "real" ejaculation by men, put in question protocols of imitation and sincerity? If the ejaculation is "real" and the "passion" is faked, is the actor, male or female, in the position of Beatrice-Joanna?

As we have seen, there is a special theatrical "insincerity" in orgasm enacted on the stage, in precisely the space where grounded scientific knowledge and secure anatomical reference are by the nature of the genre put in question. What is "female orgasm" when mimed by a boy player? "Female," in the context of drama and performance, reveals itself, once again, as a position in a structure rather than an aspect of anatomical – or even cultural – destiny.

From Dr. Freud to Dr. Ruth the "insincerity of women" has been seen as an ambivalent asset, a poison needed to effect a remedy. It turns out, though, that the poison is its own remedy, the remedy its own poison. The representation of female pleasure is itself a changeling. The existence of the possibility of fakeness protects the privacy and control of pleasure. Perhaps this was the secret that Juno was so angry at Tiresias for disclosing.

NOTES

1   "*Dass sie 'sich geben,' selbst noch, wenn sie – sich geben*. Literally: that they 'give themselves' (that is to say, act or play a part) even when they – give themselves." Friedrich Nietzche, *The Gay Science*, trans. Walter Kaufmann (New York, 1974), p. 317 and n.

2   Thomas Lupton, *A Thousand Notable Things of Sundry Sorts*, The Fifth Book, No. 56 (1579; rpt. 1814), p. 43. Thomas Middleton, *The Changeling*, ed. N. W. Bawcutt, Revels Plays (Cambridge, Mass., 1958), p. 69n.

3   Pliny, *Natural History*, xxxvi.19, trans. Philemon Holland (1601), II, p. 589. Antonius Mizaldus (1520–78), *Centuriae IX. Memorabiliam* (1566): *Centuriae* VI, 54, "Experiri an mulier sit grauida" (Frankfurt, 1613), p. 127; *Centuriae* VII, 12 and 64, "Mulierem corruptam ab incorrupta discernere" (Frankfurt, 1613), pp. 141–2, 154; "Appendix secretorum experimentorum antidororumque contra varios morbos," p. 253, "Noscendi ratio an mulier sit virgo integra & intacta an non." Robert Burton, as Bawcutt notes, is dismissive of the entire notion: "To what end are all those Astrological questions, *an sit virgo, an sit casta, an sit mulier*? and such strange absurd trials in *Albertus Magnus, Bap. Porta, Mag. lib. 2, cap.21*, in *Wecker, lib. 5, de secret.*, by stones, perfumes, to make them piss, and confess I know not what in their sleep; some jealous brain was the first founder of them."

(*Anatomy of Melancholy*, Pt. III, Sec.3, Memb.2; ed. A. R. Shilleto [1983], III, p. 327.)

4   "Fragment of an Analysis of a Case of Hysteria" (1905 [1901], in *The Standard Edition of the Complete Psychological Works of Sigmund Freud* (24 vols., London, 1953), VII, p. 80. Subsequent references to these volumes will be indicated by the abbreviation *SE*.

5   "For a man inhales and exhales by this organ [the nose], and sneezing is effected by its means: which last is an outward rush of collected breath, and is the only mode of breath used as an omen and regarded as supernatural." *The Works of Aristotle*, ed. W. D. Ross, vol. II, *History of Animals* (*Historia animalium*), trans. D'Arcy Wentworth Thompson, reprinted in Great Books of the Western World: no. 9, ed. Robert Maynard Hutchins (Chicago, 1952), p. 14 (492b, 5).

6   *De generatione animalium* in *The Works of William Harvey*, ed. and trans. Robert Willis. (New York, 1965), p. 534.

7   Nasal stimulation as a test for fruitfulness was also recommended in the eighteenth century. The author of *Aristotle's Last Legacy* reports that "some make this experiment of a woman's fruitfulness":

They take myrrh, red florax, and such odoriferous things, and make a perfume of it: which let the woman receive into the neck of the womb, thro' a funnel; if the woman feel the smoak ascend to her nose, then she is fruitful; otherwise barren.

Others take garlick, and beat it, and let the woman lie on her back upon it, and if she feel the scent thereof to her nose, it is a sign of fruitfulness. (*Aristotle's Last Legacy* [London, 1776; rpt. New York and London, 1986], p. 30)

8   Josef Breuer and Sigmund Freud, *Studies on Hysteria*, in *SE*, II, p. 200.

9   *The Complete Letters of Sigmund Freud to Wilhelm Fliess, 1887–1904*, trans. and ed. Jeffrey Moussaieff Masson (Cambridge, 1985), pp. 45–8. The notorious case of Emma Eckstein, on whom Fliess operated with disastrous results, was the most dramatic of these surgical interventions on the nose. Eager to acquit his friend of culpability in the botched operation, Freud wrote to him a year after the surgery, "I shall be able to prove to you that you were right, that her episodes of bleeding were hysterical, were occasioned by *longing*, and probably occurred at the sexually relevant times [the woman, out of resistance, has not yet supplied me with the dates]"; p. 183.

10 Thomas Hardy, *Tess of the d'Urbervilles* (New York, 1981), p. 148.

11 Gordon Hendricks, *Origins of the American Film* (New York, 1972), p. 91.

12 Linda Williams, *Hard Core: Power, Pleasure, and the "Frenzy of the Visible"* (Berkeley, 1989), p. 53.

13 "Findings, Ideas, Problems" (1941 [1938]), in *SE*, XXIII.

14 Sigmund Freud, Letter 102 (to Fliess), 16 January 1899, in *SE*, I, p. 277.

15 "Three Essays," in *SE*, VII, p. 180.

16 Sigmund Freud, "Extracts from the Fliess papers," Draft J (1950 [1892–9]), trans. Eric Mosbacher and James Strachey, in *SE*, I, p. 217.

17 Thomas Laqueur, *Making Sex: Body and Gender from the Greeks to Freud* (Cambridge, 1990), pp. 45–46, 49–52, 66–8.

18 Laqueur, *Making Sex*, pp. 43, 257n. Ovid, *Metamorphoses*, 3.323–31.

19 Juliet Mitchell and Jacqueline Rose, eds., *Feminine Sexuality: Jacques Lacan and the Ecole Freudienne* (New York, 1982), p. 52.

20 Jacques Lacan, *Encore: Le seminaire XX, 1972–73* (Paris, 1975). Mitchell and Rose, *Feminine Sexuality*, p. 52.

21 Jacques Derrida, "The Double Session," in his *Dissemination*, trans. Barbara Johnson (Chicago, 1981), p. 201.

22 Gayatri Chakravorty Spivak, "Displacement and the Discourse of Woman," in Mark Krupnick, ed., *Displacement: Derrida and After*, (Bloomington, 1983; 1987), p. 175.

23 Aristotle, *Generation of Animals*, Loeb Classical Library (Cambridge, 1958), 2.4.739b1–20. Laqueur, *Making Sex*, pp. 47–8.

24 Danielle Jacquar and Claude Thomasset, *Sexuality and Medicine in the Middle Ages*, trans. Matthew Adamson (Princeton, 1988), p. 46.

25 Thomas G. Benedek, "Beliefs about Human Sexual Function in the Middle Ages and Renaissance," in Douglas Radcliffe-Unstead, ed., *Human Sexuality in the Middle Ages and Renaissance* (Pittsburgh, 1978), p. 108.

26 Auguste Debay, *Hygiène et physiologie du mariage* (153rd edn., Paris, 1880). See esp. pp. 17–18, 92, 94–5, 105–9. Erna Olafson Hellerstein, Leslie Parker Hume, and Karen M. Offen, eds., *Victorian Women: A Documentary Account of Women's Lives in Nineteenth-Century England, France, and the United States* (Stanford, 1981).

27 Julia R. Heilman and Joseph LoPiccolo, *Becoming Orgasmic: A Sexual and Personal Growth Program for Women* (New York, 1976, 1987), p. 91.

28 "J," *The Sensuous Woman* (New York, 1969), pp. 180–1.

29 Ruth Westheimer, *Dr. Ruth's Guide to Good Sex* (New York, 1983), pp. 45–6.

30 Alice Kahn Ladas, Beverly Whipple, John D. Perry, eds., *The G Spot: And Other Recent Discoveries about Human Sexuality* (New York, 1982), p. 143.

31 Karen Wright, "Evolution of the Big O," *Discover* (June 1992), 56.

14   Desire is death

Jonathan Dollimore

I am concerned with the perverse dynamic in western culture which binds together desire, death and loss (mutability), and especially the belief that desire is in a sense impossible, which is to say that it is driven by a lack inherently incapable of satisfaction; it is, at heart, contradictory: the very nature of desire is precisely what prevents its fulfillment.

In our own time this "impossibility" at the heart of desire has become an increasing preoccupation in various strands of critical theory, especially psychoanalysis. Jacques Lacan for example claimed to find in the most desperate affirmation of life the purest form of the death drive; declared that it is from death that existence takes on all the meaning it has; theorized desire as lack, absence, and impossibility. Yet we can also find something similar in the writing of Michel Foucault, albeit in a more historicized form. Throughout his work there are cryptic, lyrical, paradoxical speculations on how we *live* death – how, that is, its changing face organizes our identity, language, sexuality, and future. In the final pages of *The Order of Things*, just before the notorious conclusion that "man" is an invention of recent date, soon to be erased "like a face drawn in the sand at the edge of the sea," he speaks also of "the Death that is at work in [Man's] suffering, the Desire that has lost its object ..."[1] A few years later, he would make this connection between death, identity, language, and lack: "It is quite likely that [the approach of] death – its sovereign gesture, its prominence within human memory – hollows out in the present and in existence the void toward which and from which we speak."[2] These perceived links between death, desire, and language connect revealingly with what, in modern theory, is variously called the subversion, the death, or the decentering of the subject. Modern theory is especially indebted to three earlier intellectual episodes in this displacement of the autonomous subject: first, the Hegelian dialectic which locked the subject into its other; second, the Marxist insistence that social being in all its contradictions determines consciousness; third, the Freudian contention that the ego is imprisoned, and forever being ruined, by the unconscious.

369

Yet before all these, and influencing them, what subverted the subject of western culture was the perceived impossibility of desire. Lucretius, in a text published more than 2,000 years ago, declared of sexual desire that it is "the one thing of which the more we have, the more our breast burns with the evil lust of having." Crucially, for Lucretius, desire becomes impossible – i.e., the frustration which it experiences is an internal necessary condition of itself (rather than being, for instance, the consequence of the contingent unattainability of the object of desire), such that "Lovers' passion is storm tossed, *even in the moment of fruition*, by waves of delusion and incertitude"; and because "*from the very heart* of the fountain of delight there rises a jet of bitterness that poisons the fragrance of the flowers" (my emphasis).[3] A kind of living death which will eventually become a sense of desire *as* death in which (to recall the theme of this volume) death will have everything to do with the object, yet always from the position of the desiring subject, which is to say one subjected to death, experiencing the impossibility of desire, and thus the perpetual inadequacy or even, paradoxically, the irrelevance of the object. Shakespeare's *Sonnets*[4] and *Romeo and Juliet*[5] will be the eventual focus of an argument which of necessity begins elsewhere and earlier, and ends much later, with Freud.

One of the most influential founding narratives of desire's impossibility – an influential text for Freud and Lacan – is the famous allegory in Plato's *Symposium*[6] of how sexual desire, originating in traumatic division of perfect wholes, became an experience of incompleteness, loss, and lack which ruined identity. And so severely, that desire henceforth becomes an experience haunted by death. Originally, says Aristophanes in the *Symposium*, there were three sexes: male, female, and hermaphrodite. Each was a self-sufficient whole, with two organs of generation. They were formidable and hubristic creatures who even dared to attack the gods. To weaken them, Zeus cut each in half. Thereafter each half yearned for its severed other half. This is why we now only desire what we lack, and why desire is a striving back to an early state of unity. Even when reunited the creatures died in each other's arms.

Here then, splitting or dividing is the founding principle of desire; desire originates in a division which is a kind of death, and its experience is one of loss and lack. Desire becomes an experience of present/projected lack rooted in present/remembered loss, somewhere between past loss and future lack, and always finally unrealizable. These three conceptions of desire – its paradoxical intimacy with death, its experience as loss and lack, and its being beyond fulfillment, are intimately related, and nowhere more so than in those early Christian ascetics who were influenced by Plato, but also departed from him, often radically so, and in ways which would be even more significant for the western tradition. They drive death even further into desire, and intensify the perverse and paradoxical dynamic binding the two.

It is well known that these Christians stressed the renunciation of desire. For Gregory of Nyssa, not only sexual love but all the joys of life – wealth, youth, affection, glory, power, renown – are haunted by a "smoldering grief" (On Virginity).[7] Now this grief is not merely what we feel when these joys end, as of course they must; rather, joy actually produces and intensifies this grief. Further, joys of life do not merely fade; rather they turn into their own opposites. This is because death is at work at the heart of life itself. Again, not death simply as eventual demise, but death as a devastating, living mutability which overdetermines life with a terrible sense of loss and even, or especially, before anything has actually *been* lost. Thus we behold a lover only to realize that his or her beauty will come to nothing. This *eventuality* is lived as an *ever-present reality* – a vivid tormenting sense of the skull beneath the skin: "in place of [the beloved] he now beholds, there will be bones, disgusting and ugly, with no trace, no reminder, no remains of this present blossoming" (14–17, 27). Desire, sexuality, and even sexual difference are, for Gregory, what permit death to thrive inside life. Therefore, to renounce them is to achieve a state in which "the power of death is somehow shattered and destroyed" (49).

Now, as Peter Brown reminds us in *The Body and Society*, such writers sought not the repression of the sexual drive *as such*, but rather to be released from the devastating effects of death, mutability, and time *on* desire, and *as* desire: these things at once engender desire and render it impossible. And of course death and mutability were starkly present at that time: this was a society, Brown tells us, "more helplessly exposed to death than is even the most afflicted underdeveloped country in the modern world";[8] for the population of the Roman Empire to remain even stationary it appears that each woman would have had to bear an average of five children. So ascetic preaching threatened to overturn the traditional structures of that society; its demand for sexual renunciation was regarded as a brief for social extinction. To dismiss this aspect of early Christian history as entirely due to a squeamish attitude to the body is just ignorant. Without doubt, these early Christians were, in their own way, socially and sexually dissident.

Early Modern

Their vision of desire as at once impossible and a kind of death is everywhere present in the literature of the Early Modern period, especially in the anarchic excess of Jacobean tragedy. In some of these plays the death/desire dialectic is present not just as a theme, but as a principle of dramatic structure and psycho-social identity, as the dynamic which simultaneously drives and disintegrates the world. Often hilariously so – as one Brown University student has brilliantly glossed the sensibility of *The Revenger's Tragedy*: "is that a skull in your pocket or are you just pleased to see me?"[9]

But *why* the intensified preoccupation with death and mutability? John Kerrigan suggests that it is because of the intervention of mechanical time, of the clock.[10] This was indeed a factor, but the preoccupation was already there in existing and earlier concepts of time. If we think of the surrealist's stopped clock, at once explicable, melancholy, and utterly mysterious, it seems modern. And it is, but it is also evoking the same mesmerizing stillness as its antecedent, the sundial, which, precisely because it had no moving parts, conveyed all the more powerfully the same sense of death *in* time; as Shakespeare put it:

> Thou by thy dial's shady stealth mayst know
> Time's thievish progress to eternity.
>
> (Sonnet 77)

Regarded metaphysically, the clock with moving hands, and which ticks, is different only in that its stillness and silence are the louder, the more relentless. This image of stillness within movement, elsewhere of course a metaphor for eternity, is here, in the sundial and the clock, an image of death as immanent within life – almost the same thing, but not quite.

This immanence of death was what preoccupied Early Modern writers. Of the rose, so persistently cathected in the mutability tradition, Herbert says, with fine economy,

> Thy root is ever in its grave,
> And thou must die.
>
> ("Virtue")

The source of life is always already the place of death. "We kill ourselves, to propagate our kind," declares Donne ("An Anatomy of the World," l. 110), and we are all familiar with the Early Modern commonplace pun on "die" as both death and orgasm. Yet because the commonplace forecloses on what it recognizes – for us, if not for the Elizabethans – we can miss the fact that the death/desire connection was then experienced as a perverse dynamic. Understanding that, we think twice when, in the *Mutability Cantos*, Spenser warns: "thy decay thou seekest by thy desire," and Sidney proclaims: "Leave me, O Love, which reachest but to dust." Here "love" is both the beloved object, *and* the poet–lover's desire: the beloved turns to dust, even as she (or he) reaches for the poet, who in turn turns to dust. And desire itself turns to dust, nay "*reachest but to dust*": *the embrace of love is itself a dynamic of self-dissolution.* Desire is death, a "web of will, whose end is never wrought" and the lover who escapes it is left "Desiring nought but how to kill desire" (Sidney, "Thou blind man's mark").[11]

This is the recurring idea, variously represented: death is not simply the end of desire, nor simply its punishment; shockingly, perversely, death is itself the impossible dynamic of desire. And not just desire; life more generally is animated by the dynamic of death, as in another of Herbert's brilliant images:

> this heap of dust;
> To which the blast of death's incessant motion
> . . .
> Drives all at last.
>
> ("Church Monuments")

Here, energy and movement – ostensibly the essence of life – are more truly the dynamic of its dissolution, the "incessant motion" of death. Donne in his own perverse way theorized this in the first of his *Paradoxes*[12] which is entitled *That all things kill themselves* and which begins: "To ... effect their own deaths, all living [things] are importun'd." And if "the best things kill themselves soonest (for no perfection indures) and all things labor to this perfection, all travaile to ther owne Death ..." Perfection: from the Latin *perficere* – to accomplish, bring to an end; for Donne the perfection which living things aspire to is literally their end, death is even encoded in life's drive for perfection. So, for these writers, death does not merely end life but disorders and decays it from within, its force indistinguishable from the life force. Not merely an ending but an internal undoing. As such, the most cosmic, most culturally necessary of all binary oppositions, life versus death, is subjected to collapse; the absolutely different is inseparable from what it is not, cannot be. The absolutely other is found to inhere within the self-same as nothing less than the dynamic of its dissolution. *Media in vita in morte.*

As I indicated at the outset, the contradiction entailed by the death/desire dynamic is deeply undermining of human identity. If ever the subject was decentered, subverted or just rendered insignificant, it was here, in the apprehension of that contradiction. For William Drummond in "A Cypresse Grove" (1619),[13] as for Gregory before him, death not only destroys, but in the process, and long before death proper, transforms everything into its own opposite. Death, under the agency of mutability, inverts, perverts, contradicts. As a result Man is permanently unstable (Lacanians take note): "His Bodie is but a Masse of discording humours ... which though agreeing for a trace of tyme, yet can never be made uniforme." This very discord is at once natural and the agency of death – it is an *"inward cause of a necessarie dissolution"* (148, 151–2, 155) – a phrase which would not be out of place in Freud's *Beyond the Pleasure Principle*. If this intrinsic disharmony is the dynamic of life as death, it is also what makes for the impossibility of desire: "[Man] hath no sooner acquired what hee did desire, but hee beginneth to enter into new Cares, and desire what he shall never be able to acquire ... Hee is pressed with Care for what is present, with Griefe, for what is past, with Feare of what is to come, nay, for what will never come" (153). Compare this with Machiavelli's declaration in *The Discourses* that: "nature has created men so that they desire everything, but are unable to attain it; desire being thus always greater than the faculty of acquiring, discontent with what they have[,] *and* dissatisfaction with themselves[,] results from it."[14] Note how for Machiavelli a discontented desire for what one lacks is inseparable from a dissatisfaction with self. Drummond pushes this further; for him man is an entity so inherently and radically unstable, so contradictory, both psychically and physically, that "wee should rather wonder how so fragill a matter should so long endure, than how so soone dissolve, and decay" (152). Drummond also remarks, and wonderfully succinctly, our perpetual psychic vulnerability even, or especially, at the height of our power: "the glance of an Eye is sufficient to undoe [us]" (151). Death as eventual oblivion is devoutly to be wished; it is "the Thaw of all these vanities which the Frost of Life bindeth together" (156). A nice inversion: life is a frost which binds; death is the thaw. Here is the death-drive in Early Modern form, that desire for a state in which human kind, in Drummond's words, "nothing knowes, and is of all unknowne" (160).

In Castiglione's *The Courtier* mutability is internalized *as* sexual desire, something which is crucial in the history of the death/desire convergence. Those who seek sexual gratification are inevitably obsessive; they are like the fevered who "dreame they drinke of some cleare spring" but remain permanently unsatisfied.[15] They are doomed to repeat the experience of desire's impossibility. Eventually, says Castiglione, to covet the beauty of another is only to covet one's own death:

These kinde of lovers therefore love most unluckily, for either they never come by their covetings ... or els if they doe ... they come by their hurt, and ende their miseries with other greater miseries: for ... there is never other thing felt, but afflictions, torments, griefes, pining, travaile, so that to be wan, vexed with continuall teares and sighes, to live with a discontented minde, to be alwaies dumbe, or *to lament, to covet death* ... (305, my emphasis)

Following Plato, he finds that a rational apprehension of beauty can lead eventually to a heavenly release from desire. Yet this transcendent desire is indelibly marked by the death wish, namely the wish for the death of desire itself which is also, inevitably, a wish for the death of the self as currently known: "*there shall wee finde a most happie end for our desires*, true rest for our travels, certaine remedie for miseries"; there we shall "heare the heavenly harmony so tunable, that *no discorde of passion take place any more in us*" (321–2; my emphasis).

Compare Drummond, for whom death proper is also a release of the soul into a heaven where there shall be "an end without an end, Time shall finish ... Motion yeelding unto Rest," this being "the last of things wisheable, the tearme and center of all our Desires" (171, 165). In short this is a fantasy of desire as *absolutely* realized in relation to the metaphysical concept of the absolute: that is, a God who does not desire. Desire implies lack, hence imperfection. To be eternal and hence non-mutable is also to be free of desire. Conversely to be human is to be mutable and to desire. So the absolute object of desire is, experientially, a fantasy of the *absolute release from desire*, i.e., death of desire/death of self. Once again then, the fantasy of transcendent desire anticipates something like the Freudian death wish but with a difference I will explore shortly.

Shakespeare's *Sonnets*

The centrality of death, desire, and mutability to Shakespeare's *Sonnets* is obvious. I want to add a few remarks about how these things become crucial in the formation of the subject, of gender, and of fantasy – in effect, the gendered subject overdetermined by fantasy. Especially significant is the way that mutability becomes internalized as a condition of desire's impossibility. Hardly less significant, equally apparent, and obviously connected, is the way mutability is gendered and thereby displaced. Thus in Sonnet 20 mutability is displaced onto women – "shifting change ... is false women's fashion" – despite, or rather because of, the fact that it is so powerfully the internal dynamic of a male desire somehow decayed by its own abundance:

> [I] in mine own love's strength seem to decay,
> O'ercharged with burden of mine own love's might.
>
> (Sonnet 23)

Another instance of displacement, now in terms of the homosocial, occurs in *All's Well That Ends Well* in the form of a reproach to him who would prefer sexual congress to warfare,

> Spending his manly marrow in her arms,
> Which should sustain the bound and high curvet
> Of Mars's fiery steed.
>
> (II.iii.279–81)

To spend sexually: another commonplace. However, consider what is implied: manly marrow, an energy and an essence, defining of one's power and one's identity, is wasted, and wasted in a way which is debilitating. To avoid both waste and debilitation, it is identified with a higher power, military and homosocial, one which wreaks waste and debilitation on the world. The mutability of desire undergoes a sublimation which not only transfers mutability from a sexual to a social domain, but in the process reproduces it on a colossal scale. And not only externally: at the same time the mutability of desire is typically demonized and displaced internally within those societies at war or otherwise under threat. In Shakespeare's plays, we see how this process occurs in relation to deviants, and across gender.[16]

In Sonnet 147, from which my title derives, the desire of the poet is radically mutable and completely impossible; his is a longing whose object, far from giving satisfaction, only intensifies that impossibility:

> My love is as a fever, longing still
> For that which longer nurseth the disease.

It leaves the poet "frantic-mad with evermore unrest," possessed by thoughts "At random from the truth vainly express'd." Hence:

> I desperate now approve
> Desire is death.

The starkness of the statement should not obscure a lingering ambiguity and ambivalence revealing of the contradiction: it means most obviously "I experience, I demonstrate – reluctantly, in desperation – that desire is death"; less obviously, yet just as literally it means, I "approve" that desire is death; wracked with an impossible, contradictory, self-annihilating desire, I desire death.

For the poet, mutability informs desire, rendering it impossible. In the young man of the sonnets, however, we glimpse something very different: for him narcissistic self-regard is not, apparently, a reason for reproducing (that being the rational narrative offered by the poet) but, on the contrary, the basis of an erotic *complicity with* mutability, even, with death. The poet declares "Nor shall Death brag thou wand'rest in his shade" (18) but that is just what this youth would risk:

> Unthrifty loveliness, why dost thou spend
> Upon thyself thy beauty's legacy?
> . . .

For having traffic with thyself alone,
Thou of thyself thy sweet self dost deceive.

(Sonnet 4)

How interesting that the poet couches the reproach in onanistic terms:
what he chides he perhaps also desires; even as he reprimands the youth
for having sex with himself, the poet is attracted by the spectacle – or at
least the fantasy – of a sexuality which is narcissistic, perverse, and
reckless.

So, in the *Sonnets*, even as time, death, and mutability are deplored,
their indifferent power is strangely revered. The young man is much more
a foil, even a willing sacrifice, to this power than an object of desire to be
rescued from it. It is ironic that, despite the poet's alleged wish to
immortalize him, we do not know who he was and, in fact, hardly have
any vivid representation of him. What we do have is a young man as the
enabling condition for some of the most memorable descriptions of
mutability and loss ever written. We might go so far as to say that the
author of the *Sonnets* is more enamored of death than of the boy. Not so
much in the modern sense of wishing death, but more after Walter
Ralegh's remarkable encomium to death at the end of his *History*.[17] Here
death is deified and adulated, regarded indeed as a parodic, perverse
deity even more powerful than God. Death's aweful power is revered
almost ecstatically from a position of abjection; as he writes, Ralegh is
imprisoned, perhaps expecting death, and anyway in a sense is already
socially dead, as he declared in a letter to James after his conviction.

So because, and not in spite, of his impotence, Ralegh *identifies with* a
tyrannical omnipotence. Do we then detect here that paradoxical state of
mind which in our time has been called identification with the oppressor?
Possible, except that the terms remain misleadingly modern. Listen to
Ralegh:

[Death] puts into man all the wisdom of the world, without speaking a word,
which God, with all the words of his law, promises, or threats, doth not … Death
… is believed, God … is always deferred … "All is vanity and vexation of spirit"
but who believes it till Death tells it us? … It is therefore Death alone that can
suddenly make man to know himself. He tells the proud and insolent that they
are but abjects, and humbles them at the instant … He takes the account of the
rich, and proves him a beggar, a naked beggar, which hath interest in nothing but
the gravel that fills his mouth. He holds a glass before the eyes of the most
beautiful, and makes them see therein their deformity and rottenness, and they
acknowledge it.

O eloquent, just, and mighty Death! … whom all the world hath flattered, thou
only hath cast out of the world and despised; thou hast drawn together all the
far-stretched greatness, all the pride, cruelty, and ambition of man, and covered it
all over with these two narrow words: *Hic jacet!*

There is something at work here which recalls that interplay of power and desire in Sir Thomas Wyatt's penitential psalms. I find illuminating Stephen Greenblatt's account of the way that, in these psalms, desire – "hot affect" – is transferred from mistress to God by a characteristically Protestant submission to domination by a severe God who spurs the poet to righteousness:

> I, lo, from mine error
> Am plunged up, as horse out of mire
> With stroke of spur,.

Terror of God leads him to see that, in his flesh,

> Is not one point of firm stability
> Nor in my bones there is no steadfastness:
> Such is my dread of mutability.

> (Psalm 38)

Greenblatt finds here an "ascent through the acceptance of domination" with the corollary that while in its natural state sexuality for Wyatt is aggressive and predatory, in its redeemed state it is passive: "Sexual aggression ... is transferred entirely to the sphere of transcendent power."[18] An internalized, dreaded mutability, experienced as desire, leads to abject identification with an omnipotent vengeful God. So if the lack of "firm stability" and its corollary, a "dread of mutability," binds mutability into desire, it is also what provokes the quest for that stable self which seeks to overcome mutability and, in the process, typically *re*-identifies with a powerful coherence elsewhere and other. I've spoken briefly of three such kinds of coherence: death, the homosocial, and God. Sometimes, if only in fantasy, they come together.

Fantasy

In fact, everything I have described so far about the death/desire dynamic, and the internalization of mutability as desire, suggests the importance of fantasy. Though it is not my claim here, as this project developed it occurred to me that the origins of fantasy may also lie in the trauma of mutability. A supreme instance of how this might be so, is Shakespeare's *Romeo and Juliet*. The markers binding together desire and death are clear enough: in the play's Prologue the passion of the young lovers is described as a "death-marked love"; Capulet laments that "Life, living, all is Death's" (IV.v.40). It has been said that Romeo, when he dares "love-devouring death" (II.vi.7), desires death and that his belief that Juliet is dead in the tomb is less the cause of his own suicide, than the excuse for it: "unsubstantial Death is amorous, /... /

Thus with a kiss I die" (V.iii.103, 120). If so, once again death does not so much defeat desire as emerge from within it, as the dynamic of desire itself; as love, or rather death, at first sight.

The death/desire convergence in this play has been interestingly addressed by Denis de Rougemont and Julia Kristeva.[19] The first, in *Love in the Western World*, regards *Romeo* as a perpetuation of the *Tristan and Iseult* myth, itself a founding instance of the inherent perversity of romantic love, that archetype of our most complex feelings of unrest (18). According to de Rougemont, Tristan and Iseult are indeed in love but not with each other, or indeed anyone else. They are in love with death. From the twelfth century on, he argues, sex and religion had become fatally crossed, and the history of passionate love in all great literature from then to the present is the history of the secularization of this crossing, of the tragic and more and more desperate attempts of Eros to take the place of mystical transcendence by means of emotional intensity.

On this account, passionate love is a perversion and/or displacement of religion, even a hubristic surrogate religion seeking transcendence precisely where it cannot be found, in human sexual desire. This leads to an "impossible love ... a truly devouring ardour, a thirst which death alone [can] quench." For de Rougemont, *Romeo and Juliet* is "the most magnificent resuscitation of the myth that the world was to be given" until Wagner's *Tristan und Isolde* (*Love in the Western World*, 145, 178–9, 201, 243).

For Julia Kristeva too, this play shows how "erotic expenditure is a race towards death," but for an entirely different reason. The race toward death occurs not because of the fatal mixing of religion and sexuality, but because of the hatred which the lovers feel for each other. Quoting Juliet's "My only love, sprung from my only hate!" (I.v.140), Kristeva declares: "hatred consumes them in the purest moments of their passion" (*Tales of Love*, 61). This hatred is not to be confused with the social hostility between the two families; this last is the kind of hatred one can look in the eye, and its very existence obscures this other, deeper kind of hatred: "the familial, social curse is more respectable and bearable than the unconscious hatred of the lovers for each other. The fact remains that Juliet's jouissance is often stated through the anticipation – the desire? – of Romeo's death" (221). Kristeva also rejects the familiar and relatively comforting view that "love must die ... that eros and the law are incompatible ..." No: "More deeply, more passionately, we are dealing with the intrinsic presence of hatred in [desire] itself" (222).

Both accounts are fascinating, not least because of their perverse counter-intuitiveness, but both overlook the extent to which this play is, crucially, a *fantasy representation of* desire, one overdetermined by the trauma of mutability, and in which adolescent desire is therefore, thereby, cathected as well as depicted. More generally, as theatrical event, this play is not just about desire between two people, but about desire itself as a fantasy projection, a wish fulfillment complete with perverse complications. In short, *Romeo and Juliet* is an adult fantasy *about* adolescent desire in two, related senses. First, for the adult, adolescent sexuality is something idealized from the position of loss: idealized despite, and because of, the fact that it has been lost. Adults behold adolescent desire ambivalently: theirs is a gaze socially sanctioned in the name of hope, yet haunted by loss. If death is fantasized in this gaze it is not just to prevent illicit sex (the gaze of patriarchal surveillance), but to pre-empt the failure and loss which haunt adult desire. In such ways does the death/desire dynamic inform the adult gaze as it falls upon the adolescent. At its most intense the fantasy of *Romeo and Juliet* takes this form: a barely unconscious wish that death – that which mutability serves – be summoned in order to end mutability: to banish one kind of loss (mutability), another kind (death) is embraced. Absolute loss cancels loss across time. Second and more specifically, adolescent sexuality contains a powerful erotic charge for the adult regardless of sexual orientation. Gay people tend to be explicit about this. Yet the institutions of heterosexuality are invigorated by such eroticism, albeit in more sublimated and displaced forms – and sometimes in forms not sublimated, e.g. incest.

So I am reluctant to regard the death-wish in *Romeo* as immaturely "adolescent." For one thing the reckless excess of adolescent desire is too endearing and insightful for me to want to deny to it that wisdom which is antithetical to the sensible. More importantly, in this play it is much more the case that adolescent desire becomes itself the object of ambivalent desire, and that the erotics of death – death at first sight – far from being the intrinsic condition of adolescent desire, concern this adult fantasy about it. Hence that desiring gaze for Juliet dead:

> Death lies on her like an untimely frost
> Upon the sweetest flower of all the field.
>
> (IV.v.28–9)

At once unbearable yet desired. And desired because here death arrests beauty: transience, decay, decline, failure (including parental impotence) are averted in and through death. But then not quite, or rather not at all: at this stage she is drugged and only apparently dead. Here and in the tomb she is brought into the closest possible proximity to decay and decomposition, while being still very much alive. Beauty and death are fantasized as antithetically proximate. When Juliet finally succumbs to death proper (V.iii), it is again in a way whereby death momentarily enhances the beauty it has claimed: "And Juliet, bleeding, warm and newly dead." A fantasy redolent of that pathos which is synonymous with the tragic vision – a vision which is also obscene precisely because and not in spite of its wisdom.[20]

Romeo also kills himself. Not surprisingly perhaps: he is unhappy, having lost his other half. Here we could invoke Aristophanes' founding narrative of desire and death. Romeo might indeed be explained in these terms were it not for the fact that he has earlier switched his uncompromising desire from Rosaline to Juliet. Again it would be evasive to dismiss this as the fickleness of an immature, adolescent love. Let's say rather that Romeo's desire is already rather adult, at once fixated and mobile; on the one hand subject to compulsive repetition, on the other swept along by history. Which means that, for him, desire is a serious business, a state of lack which, if not exactly indifferent as to its objects, is prepared to substitute and replace them with that inconstancy which "true" love always disavows but never avoids. There is no distinction here between true and false, mature and adolescent, love: true love also, in its sexual forms, is inherently mutable. Lacan has said there is no such thing as the sexual relation. If only to avoid incurring the anger of those who are in love, I was tempted to settle for this proposition in its weaker form: there is no such thing as a sexual relationship which lasts. But that's not it; definitely not: for Romeo, Lacan's formulation is to the point.

In all this Romeo is the sublime adolescent – which is to say he is already old, already contracted to death, the object and creation of the desiring, ambivalent, adult gaze – as, in a different way, is the young man of the *Sonnets*.

In tracing the perverse dynamic linking death and desire in the Early Modern period I have considered the way desire experiences the fatality of *eventual* death in terms of an *ever-present* mutability: death is not merely the eventual termination of life, but an impossible mutability within life itself. The for-ever of eventual death becomes the ever-present process of mutability in life, Shakespeare's "evermore unrest," Herbert's "incessant motion," Drummond's "*inward cause of a necessarie dissolution*." Thus encoded in life, death of course reduces it to dust, but to apprehend this process is not only to experience physical dissolution, but also, and more desperately, the hollowing of life from within into desire as loss; a radical mutability lives internally *as* desire. Death is experienced as life's inner impossibility, and more specifically mutability is experienced as the inner impossibility of desire. Hence that paradoxical double-despair characteristic of the mutability tradition: first, to see death and mutability as not only thwarting desire, but rendering it impossible; second, to welcome death as total annihilation, and mutability as at once its truth, and what is cancelled by it. Thus is desire enclosed catastrophically, immediately, in that which would otherwise ruin it only eventually, *in time*. In the process this internalization of death as desire is both gendered and displaced, and generates a fantasy life which saturates social as well as psychic life, and cathects power in complex, fatal, and revealing ways. Thus the fantasy of Shakespeare's *Romeo and Juliet*, a night out for all the family.

Finally I turn to Freud, not in order to psychoanalyze the Renaissance, but rather to read the Modern via the Early Modern, to use history to read theory. The moment life flickered into being, in its earliest form, says Freud in *Beyond the Pleasure Principle* (1919), its most basic instinct was to die. This is the death drive, that which seeks to dissolve life back into its primeval inorganic state. Eventually though, death becomes less easy; the death instinct is resisted by the repressions which constitute social and psychic life. These repressions prevent that desired, regressive backward movement, instead driving the instinct forward, against its will, so to speak. Thus driven forward it becomes energized by lack, by the "difference in amount between the pleasure of satisfaction which is *demanded* and that which is actually *achieved*."[21] It is this difference, this gap, this energized lack, "which will permit of no halting at any position attained"· and now constitutes both the impossibility of desire and the hollowing out of desire by death. Socialized desire is a lack, impossible to appease because it is the lack of death itself, and life is merely an enforced substitute for death. Even so, the death instinct continues to strive for complete satisfaction, for, in other words, regression to non-being, since the most fundamental desire remains the desire to die. So, in Freud's own remarkable, unequivocal, words: "we shall be compelled to say that '*the aim of all life is death*'" (311, his emphasis).

Freud's theory was, on his own admission, a mythology, and not even a new one; he willingly acknowledged origins as diverse, and distant, as Empedocles and Schopenhauer. He was aware of the writers who preceded him, some of whom I have explored. Freud was never more provocative, crazier or truer than when, as here, he was being perversely speculative and derivative; when, as here, he was invoking, yet at the same time trying to avoid, an ancient, shocking vision – at different times a metaphysic, a theology, a mythology – whereby death is not simply the termination of life (that being the mystifying banality by which we are supposed to live) but its driving force: simply, *"the aim of all life is death"*.[22] The phrase is italicized in his own text. Its closest precedent is probably Schopenhauer, who concluded, in *The World as Will and Idea*, "Dying is certainly to be regarded as the real aim of life,"[23] but as I suggested earlier, it strikingly recalls Drummond's vision of death being to life "an inward cause of a necessarie dissolution." Yet it also echoes Montaigne: "the goal of our career is death. It is the necessary object of our aim."[24] Indeed, out of context it could almost be biblical.

What Freud adds or theorises – and I think it is crucial – is the theory of all instincts as essentially regressive: *"an instinct is an urge inherent in organic life to restore an earlier [inorganic] state of things"* (308, his emphasis). The earlier mutability tradition is shot through with world-weariness, nostalgia, loss, resignation, and regressive desire of the kind Freud describes, but in a way which remains reluctantly forward-looking and forward-driven: desire, savaged internally by death as a living mutability, is nevertheless driven forward by death to its own destruction, and death as future event is awaited as the end or transcendence of desire. Even though death and desire are lived as indistinguishable, they remain in contradiction; the subject is wrecked because positioned within, even defined as, that contradiction. By contrast Freud suggests an instinctual harmony between desire and death. Or rather he does and he doesn't. So far I have only given part of Freud's story. He also regards the death drive as countered by the life drive, or Eros.

Whereas the aim of Eros is "to establish ever greater unities and to preserve them thus – in short, to bind together; the aim of [the death drive] is, on the contrary, to undo connections and so to destroy things."[25] Yet Freud had to square this wish for a traditional, universal dualism between Eros and Thanatos with his recognition that these two opposing instincts can become indistinguishably fused together. More radically still, and on his own admission, one kind can actually turn into its opposite, and almost spontaneously as it were, via a transformation which is purely internal. If this does indeed occur, then on Freud's own account the Eros and Thanatos dualism becomes untenable (11.383). Footnotes added to later editions of *Beyond the Pleasure Principle* suggest that this dualism might not have been suggested by the death drive, but invoked to contain some of its more shocking implications – for example the footnote added in 1925 warning that the death drive theory "is the development of an extreme line of thought. Later on, when account is taken of the sexual instincts, it will be found that the necessary limitations and corrections are applied to it" (11.310). Whatever, I am struck by how radical the death drive is and how it is tamed in the context of the dualism. In the latter it becomes technically Satanic, destroying by undoing. Perhaps this is why it was a short step for some to rewrite the death drive as primarily an instinct of aggression. Yet, as Laplanche remarks, such a rewriting is in error since for Freud "the death drive is in the first instance turned, not toward the outside (as aggressivity), but toward the subject ... it·is radically not a drive *to murder*, but a drive *to suicide*, or *to kill oneself.*"[26] It emerges says Laplanche from Freud's attempt to "shatter life in its very foundations," from his "compulsion to abolish life."[27] And yet, and yet: does not Laplanche here echo precisely the terms of Satanic transgression; and isn't Freud's own definition of the death drive – the drive to unbind, to undo – also precisely Satanic?[28] Perhaps then what is new is only the introjection of all this: Freud's driving of death into the biological source of life entails a desire to die rather than murder, a desire which is sublimely guilt-less and utterly regressive.

NOTES

1   Michel Foucault, *The Order of Things: An Archeology of the Human Sciences* (1966; London, 1974), pp. 376, 387.
2   Michel Foucault, *Language, Counter-memory, Practice: Selected Essays and Interviews*, ed. with intro. by D. F. Bouchard, trans. by D. F. Bouchard and Sherry Simon (Oxford, 1977), p. 53.
3   Lucretius, *On the Nature of the Universe*, trans. and intro. by R. E. Latham (Harmondsworth, 1951), pp. 163–4.
4   William Shakespeare, *The Sonnets and A Lover's Complaint*, ed. with intro. by John Kerrigan (Harmondsworth, 1986).
5   William Shakespeare, *Romeo and Juliet*, in *Works*, ed. Peter Alexander (London and Glasgow, 1951).
6   Plato, *The Symposium*, trans. W. Hamilton (Harmondsworth, 1951).
7   Saint Gregory of Nyssa, "On Virginity," in *Ascetical Works*, trans. Virginia Woods Callahan (Washington, D.C., 1952), p. 13.
8   Peter Brown, *The Body and Society: Men, Women and Sexual Renunciation in Early Christianity* (New York, 1988), p. 286.
9   The title of a dissertation, related to me on a visit to Brown in Spring 1992.
10 "The invention and dissemination of mechanical time in the Renaissance brought about a complete reordering of sensibility." If I understand Kerrigan's claims correctly, he sees this invention of mechanical time as central to, if not the major cause of, that sixteenth-century "dislocation in man's sense of himself and the world so massive that arguably nothing like it has been seen again until, in this century, man discovered that he had the power to destroy not only himself 'but the great globe itself ...'" (Shakespeare, *Sonnets*, pp. 33–4); Kerrigan later discusses the importance of Protestantism, clockmaking, and the dissemination of mechanical time,

conceding that it is impossible to determine which preceded the other, religion or clock technology; pp. 35–7.

11 Sir Philip Sidney, *Selected Poetry and Prose*, ed. David Kalstone (New York, 1970).

12 John Donne, *Paradoxes and Problems*, ed. with intro. and commentary by Helen Peters (Oxford, 1980).

13 William Drummond of Hawthornden, "A Cypresse Grove," in *Poems and Prose*, ed. R. H. MacDonald (Edinburgh, 1976).

14 Cited from Stephen Greenblatt, *Sir Walter Ralegh: The Renaissance Man and his Roles* (New Haven and London, 1973), p. 40.

15 Baldassare Castiglione, *The Book of the Courtier*, trans. Sir Thomas Hoby (London, 1975), p. 305.

16 I have argued this elsewhere – see "Transgression and Surveillance in *Measure for Measure*," in J. Dollimore and A. Sinfield, eds., *Political Shakespeare: New Essays in Cultural Materialism* (Manchester, 1975), and Jonathan Dollimore, "*Othello*: Sexual Difference and Internal Deviation," in *Sexual Dissidence: Augustine to Wilde, Freud to Foucault* (Oxford, 1991), ch. 10.

17 Sir Walter Ralegh, *The History of the World*, in R. Lamson and H. Smith, eds., *Renaissance England* (New York, 1942), p. 517.

18 Stephen Greenblatt, *Renaissance Self-Fashioning from More to Shakespeare* (Chicago, 1980), p. 123.

19 Denis de Rougemont, *Love in the Western World* (1956), trans. Montgomery Belgion (revised and augmented edn., New York, 1966); Julia Kristeva, *Tales of Love*, trans. Leon S. Roudiez (New York, 1987).

20 This representation of Juliet finds confirmation in Elisabeth Bronfen's analysis of later works of literature and art in *Over Her Dead Body: Death, Femininity and the Aesthetic* (Manchester, 1992).

21 Sigmund Freud, *Beyond the Pleasure Principle*, in *On Metapsychology: The Theory of Psychoanalysis*, The Pelican Freud Library 11, ed. A. Richards, trans. J. Strachey (Harmondsworth, 1984), p. 315.

22 I have argued elsewhere that the older and largely lost histories of perversion – histories at once theological, political, and gendered – remain obscurely active inside modern psychoanalysis (*Sexual Dissidence*, Part 6). I am suggesting now that the same is true of ancient conceptions of death and desire.

23 Arthur Schopenhauer, *The World as Will and Representation*, 2 vols., trans. E. F. J. Payne (New York, 1966), II, p. 637.

24 "That to Philosophize is to Learn How to Die" (1572–4), in *Complete Essays*, trans. D. Frame [Stanford, 1958] p. 57. When Montaigne later repudiates this idea he does so in terms which could also be a rejection of the death drive: "death is indeed the end, but not therefore the goal, of life; it is its finish, its extremity, but not therefore its object. Life should be an aim unto itself" ("Of Physiognomy" [1585–8], p. 805).

25 *An Outline of Psychoanalysis*, The Pelican Freud Library 15, ed. A. Richards, trans. J. Strachey (Harmondsworth, 1986), p. 379.

26 Cited from Richard Boothby, *Death and Desire: Psychoanalytic Theory in Lacan's Return to Freud* (New York, 1991), p. 11.

27 Jean Laplanche, *Life and Death in Psychoanalysis*, trans. with intro. by Jeffrey Mehlman (Baltimore and London, 1976), p. 123.
28 Cf. Donne (*Anatomy of the World*, lines 156–8):

> We seem ambitious, God's whole work to undo;
> Of nothing he made us, and we strive too,
> To bring ourselves to nothing back.

INDEX